Marie Dressler

MARIE DRESSLER

THE UNLIKELIEST STAR

BETTY LEE

THE UNIVERSITY PRESS OF KENTUCKY

Frontispiece: Marie Dressler in her starring role as Carlotta Vance in the movie
Dinner at Eight. Metro-Goldwyn-Mayer Distribution Corporation, 1933

Publication of this volume was made possible in part by a grant
from the National Endowment for the Humanities.

Scholarly publisher for the Commonwealth,
serving Bellarmine College, Berea College, Centre
College of Kentucky, Eastern Kentucky University,
The Filson Club Historical Society, Georgetown College,
Kentucky Historical Society, Kentucky State University,
Morehead State University, Murray State University,
Northern Kentucky University, Transylvania University,
University of Kentucky, University of Louisville, and
Western Kentucky University.

Editorial and Sales Offices: The University Press of Kentucky
663 South Limestone Street, Lexington, Kentucky 40508-4008

01 00 99 98 97   5 4 3 2 1

Library of Congress Cataloging-in-Publication Data

Lee, Betty, 1921–
    Marie Dressler : the unlikeliest star / Betty Lee.
        p.   cm.
    Filmography: p.
    Includes bibliographical references and index.
    ISBN 0-8131-2036-5 (cloth : alk. paper)
    1. Dressler, Marie, 1869–1934. 2. Actors—United States
—Biography. I. Title
PN2287.D55L44   1997
791.43'0233'092—dc21
[B]   97-15244

This book is printed on acid-free recycled paper
meeting the requirements of the American National Standard
for Permanence of Paper for Printed Library Materials.

Manufactured in the United States of America

In Memory of Claire Dubrey
August 31, 1893–August 1, 1993

Contents

Illustrations follow page 158

PROLOGUE

She was homely, overweight, and decidedly over the hill, but in the early 1930s Marie Dressler easily outdrew such cinematic sex symbols as Garbo, Dietrich, and Harlow. To movie audiences suffering the hardships of the Great Depression, she was Everywoman. She was Bill's plain partner Min, Tugboat Annie, and Emma, the tough, no-nonsense broad who was more at home on the waterfront or in the kitchen than in the rarefied salons of Fifth Avenue. And, even if she happened to be invited to Dinner at Eight in one of those salons, Dressler was the actress who made it clear that she had not only bet her chips and collected her rewards in the great game of life, she had uncomplainingly paid her dues as well.

But then, Marie Dressler really had played the game as a winner and a loser, both as a performer and as a human being. Few actors working in Dressler's day—and certainly none now—could possibly have boasted her breadth of professional experience. She apprenticed as an eight-dollar-a-week chorus girl in touring stock and light opera companies and fought her way to stardom in Broadway musical comedy, vaudeville, and burlesque. Her knowledge of stagecraft was honed and perfected on the Great White Way, and she eventually managed her own theatrical companies. Her name was constantly in the New York headlines because of her work as a labor activist, an early feminist, a champion of the underdog, and an untiring salesperson on the First World War bond circuit. She was a born entrepreneur—not always successful but always eager to try her luck and test her skills, whether it was on the Coney Island boardwalk, in London's West End, or in Vermont as a dairy farmer.

Dressler was, in fact, actually a student of public mood and taste, anticipating its shift and change almost before the public itself realized what was happening. In the early years of the twentieth century, she starred in some of the first silent film comedies produced in the United States and even produced some of them herself. And when, after a long and disastrous decline in fortunes, the chance came for her to make her debut in the newly minted Hollywood talkies, she grabbed the brass ring with as much fierce enthusiasm as a woman a third of her age and refused to let it go until she became the most celebrated performer on the screen.

There was something about Marie Dressler personally that attracted both friends and enemies like a magnet. Despite her life-long identification with ordinary people, she sailed through life like a queen, even during the years when she was a penniless failure. There is some evidence that she truly believed she was a queen—or at least an aristocrat—and she infuriated her admirers when she relentlessly subjected them to her regal posturing. Off stage and screen she was loyal to her special friends and contemptuous of those who did not conform to her expectations. She was generous to a fault yet quixotically stingy, a professional who sometimes broke contracts as well as a trouper who would gladly invest every ounce of her energy on an assignment. She often exhibited extraordinary shortsightedness in personal relationships, even though those who loved her truly believed she was the wisest woman in the world.

As a *New York Herald Tribune* editorialist wrote the day after her death in 1934, "Marie Dressler's return from semi-obscurity to a dazzling success had a romantically spectacular quality about it that Hollywood could appreciate, just as it was nearly stupefied by the discovery that any woman of more than sixty could actually hold a great following merely because she was an able actress." But more than simply able, Marie Dressler was an actress for her time. She was a master of her craft who spoke honestly to her audiences, whether she was clowning through a vaudeville show in 1912, making 'em laugh in a 1916 silent comedy, or moving audiences to both guffaws and tears in a Depression-era photoplay. Troubled people out there in the comforting dark always recognized her as one of themselves.

1

BIRTHDAY WISHES

1933

It is Thursday, the ninth of November, 1933, and the evening is still and soft in Los Angeles. Eight hundred invited guests jam the entrances to the Metro-Goldwyn-Mayer lot in Culver City. Klieg lights spotlight comedian Will Rogers, wearing his familiar Stetson. Norma Shearer and her husband, MGM producer Irving Thalberg, emerge from their black limousine with the easy grace of royalty. Lionel Barrymore makes his way into the enormous sound stage that has been transformed for the festivities. Heads turn to note the arrival of Jean Harlow with her new husband, Hal Rosson. Clark Gable, Mary Pickford, Jimmy Durante, and Nelson Eddy arrive. Marion Davies enters on the arm of publisher William Randolph Hearst.

Political heavies flash their engraved invitations. United States Senators Henry Ashurst of Arizona and William Gibbs McAdoo of California, the mayor of Los Angeles, and a vast contingent of state and city bureaucrats are in attendance. Producer Cecil B. DeMille and Sid Grauman, owner of the celebrated Chinese Theatre on Hollywood Boulevard, are easy to spot. Loud applause breaks out as Louis B. Mayer, chief executive officer of MGM, makes his way to the head table with his daughter, Irene Selznick. This is, after all, the deep Depression, and the Boss has never been known to throw a wingding of this kind before, not even on his own birthday.

But, then, why not? Times are grim across the country, but the studio has done better than most, as moviegoers escape into the comforting dark of the theatres to enjoy MGM's top quality productions. And consider the roster of names now under contract:

not only Harlow, the Barrymores, Davies, and Gable, but Greta Garbo, Joan Crawford, Jackie Cooper, Jeanette MacDonald, and Wallace Beery. And, of course, this evening's guest of honor, Marie Dressler, the sixty-two-year-old actress with the two-hundred-pound figure and the face of a bulldog who is currently acknowledged as the top movie moneymaker in the world.

Everyone in Hollywood knows that Dressler was the first female movie actress ever to be immortalized with a cover story in *Time*. They know about her 1930-31 Academy Award for *Min and Bill* and the gold medal presented to her by British film exhibitors after fans voted her their favorite movie performer of the year. They also know that Dressler won the *Motion Picture Herald*'s poll as the top box-office attraction of 1932, and word is getting around that she will repeat the prestigious win for 1933 as well. No wonder, after her recent successes in such back-to-back blockbusters as *Dinner at Eight* and *Tugboat Annie*. And her soon-to-be released "birthday" film, *Christopher Bean,* is predicted to be a smash hit, too.

The guests rise to their feet as Dressler appears on the arm of Governor James Rolph of California. The applause is thunderous, accompanied by loud shouts of "Marie . . . Marie!" Dressler wears a black sleeveless evening gown, on her left shoulder a spray of white orchids—given to her, it has been widely reported, by an adoring Will Rogers. She smiles that familiar Dressler smile, a beguiling mix of defiance and vulnerability. She seats herself at the head table between Governor Rolph and L.B. Mayer after raising her arms in mock astonishment to acknowledge the lavish display of red roses behind her chair, spelling out the message "Happy Birthday Marie."

Mayer stands to welcome the guests and brief them on the evening's agenda. First, a gala dinner offering, among other delicacies, three of Marie's favorite foods—East Coast oysters, whitefish, and roast duckling. Then, songs by Jeanette MacDonald, Nelson Eddy, and John McCormack. Tributes from Marie's friends and colleagues will be broadcast over an international radio hookup. Broadcast also, he adds with a typical Mayer grin, to Cobourg, Ontario, the town where Dressler was born. He calls attention to mountains of telegrams and cards and a scroll signed by twelve thousand fans, headed by Franklin D. Roosevelt. The president, smiles L.B., asked him to tell Marie how much he and Eleanor had enjoyed her latest visit to the White House just two weeks before and to remind her to come again soon.

The guests applaud in delighted response, and platoons of waiters busy themselves serving the first course. Henry Jackson's NBC orchestra plays soft background music. Dancing till dawn is promised after the tributes. The room fills with a buzz of excited conversation. So wonderful that L.B. is doing this for Marie. Isn't she a fine old trouper? The rumor all over Hollywood is that she is not sixty-two, but sixty-five! And how the hell did she catch on so fast in movies? Of course, she was a headliner in vaudeville back in the early years of the century, but it has only been four years since she stole the show from Garbo in *Anna Christie*. And not long before that, the word is that she was practically on the breadline in New York.

The dinner is over, and the tributes are under way. Marie eventually responds by telling the oft-told tale about how she got into show business at the age of five by playing a clumsy Cupid in a Lindsay, Ontario, church pageant. She ends her speech by insisting that the party is really for everyone in the movie business, not just for her. The guests applaud as L.B. congratulates Lindsay, Ontario, for its perspicacity in first recognizing the world's best-loved actress and expresses the hope that Cobourg, Ontario, is enjoying the broadcast.

Mayer signals to someone in the wings, and the lights go out. After some mysterious scuffling, the studio arc lights spotlight a monster cake mounted on a truck. The confection must weigh at least five hundred pounds, and it stands eight feet tall. L.B. is on his feet, waving his arms and shouting, "Happy birthday, Marie!" He and Governor Rolph escort the guest of honor to the floor, and the three of them look up at the cake with something like awe. Marie smiles and nods and weeps a little, and she is heard to remark in that well known growl of hers that after everyone enjoys a piece of the cake, she hopes they will send the rest to the children's hospital.

Her face is caught briefly in the harsh lights, and those close to her are shocked to see that she looks tired and ill. There are those in the audience who know that she is indeed tired and ill. The tragedy is that the top movie actress in the world has made her last film for MGM and the Boss. She will die before she can celebrate her next birthday.

2

FIRST TASTE OF DRAMA

1868-1882

In the mid-nineteenth century, Cobourg, Ontario, was a muddy little community of six thousand residents with a good harbor but fading dreams of competing with the Southern Ontario cities of Hamilton and Toronto as a center of industry. Back in the 1850s, the city fathers believed that the building of the east-west Grand Trunk Railway from Toronto to Montreal and the construction of the north-south Cobourg and Peterborough Railway would bring prosperity to the region. But by 1860, the Cobourg and Peterborough line had almost ceased operation because of a successful challenge from the rival Port Hope to Lindsay line plus trestle problems at Rice Lake to the north, and the community was in deep debt because of the million dollars spent to design—by prestigious Toronto architect Kivas Tully—and construct the extravagant town hall, which was opened in 1860 by Edward, Prince of Wales. "It seems to be a generally admitted fact that Cobourg, as a business and commercial town, is gone down or gone up, it matters very little which," wrote Henry Hough in the *Cobourg World* on May 13, 1864. "Now it appears to be a well-understood thing that men in business must scratch along just so long as their capital will hold out." "It is a rather melancholy spectacle to walk down to the wharf and see that magnificent harbor . . . a complete waste. Not a sail flutters in the breeze, not a single vessel raises her cheerful masts above the noiseless scene. Cobourg, we fear, has seen the summit of her glory," agreed an editorialist in the local *Sentinel*. No wonder one shrewd Yankee observed in print after visiting the new town hall, "That is indeed a splendid building, but where is the town for whose use it was built?"

Over the years, Marie Dressler claimed to have been born in 1869 and 1870; her death certificate listed 1871. But the records of St. Peter's Anglican Church in Cobourg show that she was born in the small lakeside community on November 9, 1868, and baptized on June 27 the following year. The records also show that her original name was Leila Maria Koerber and that her parents were Anna Henderson and Alexander Rudolph Koerber, a "professor of music."

Leila's father was an Austrian student of the piano who, his daughter always insisted, moved with his parents to Prussia at an early age. As an adult, Dressler frequently embroidered the story, but she generally stuck to one basic scenario: that her father joined the German cavalry, then at the outbreak of the Crimean War deserted to the British army. Because of this defection, the reason for which Dressler never explained, Koerber found he could not return to Germany and decided to emigrate to North America sometime after the conflict ended in 1856.

Dressler offers no clues as to when her father met and married Anna Henderson. It seems likely, however, that Anna was a native of Port Hope, a town situated just west of Cobourg on Lake Ontario, and that her parents were Jane Ann Marsh and George Henderson Jr. The marriage almost certainly must have been celebrated before 1863, because Leila's older sister, Bonita, was born that year. Dressler also gives no clue as to when the Koerbers arrived in Cobourg, but church records show that the professor of music landed a job as organist at St. Peter's in 1868 at an annual stipend of $172. The Koerbers apparently lived in at least three rented Cobourg homes, and Leila was most likely born in a one-story house at 212 King Street West, not far from the fine new town hall.

There is no firm evidence as to why Alexander Koerber brought his wife and child to a depressed Cobourg in the 1860s; perhaps he was forced to quit whatever town in which he had previously worked. One fact that everyone who knew Koerber agreed upon is that the heavy-set Austrian had a vile temper. One Cobourg resident, Mrs. Floyd Smith, who as a child took music lessons from Koerber, remembered that he had "a very quick temper." Dressler herself recalls the parlor door of whatever house they happened to occupy flying open and her father stalking out, "his great body quivering, his very mustache electric with rage. 'I can't teach that brat!' he would shout. 'Dolt! Idiot!'" Inevitably, his roster of pianoforte pupils would dwindle, and, just as inevitably, there would be a falling-out with the church's rector.

Dressler never mentioned how long the family lived in Cobourg, though she does say, "Never shall I forget those naked, clean-swept little Canadian towns one just like the other. Before I was twelve years old, I must have lived in fifty of them. The only thing Mother required of a new one was that it should have an Episcopal church and that the church should have an organ." Dressler's "fifty of them" statement is probably a gross exaggeration, much like many of her other well publicized pronouncements over the years. A February 1869 report (the year Dressler was baptized) in the *Cobourg Sentinel* states that "Professor Koerber held a concert of vocal and instrumental music and tableaux, one of which portrayed Mary Queen of Scots." This clearly indicates that the family was living in the town for at least four months after Leila's birth. Cobourg historians Murray B. Smith and Andrew Hewson mention a five- and even a ten-year Cobourg residency by the Koerbers, but Dressler insists that she "seldom lived more than a few months in any one place" as a child. "Sometimes the months stretched into a year, but not often."

One of Dressler's most famous childhood stories involves a tableau staged by her mother in Lindsay, a rural town north of Cobourg, when the actress was five years old. Her mother had cast her as Cupid, posed on a pedestal. "I didn't move, but the pedestal did," Dressler remembers. "Grimly I stuck to my post. Whereupon, clothed in only my pink birthday suit and clinging desperately to my little bow and arrow, I landed squarely on the lap of the town's greatest ladies' man." Because the Koerbers would have had little reason to stage tableaux in communities other than their own, it is highly probable that they had settled in Lindsay by the year 1873.

Although Dressler's devotion to chronological details was almost nonexistent, she made sure that her autobiographical ramblings stressed at least three points: she disliked her father, she adored her mother, and she came from a family of class, money, and even a touch of the aristocracy. In both of her autobiographies she takes pains to emphasize that her mother's family, the Hendersons of Port

Hope, were practically landed gentry. Grandfather Henderson—she never provides the gentleman with a Christian name—was an Irish Canadian who owned a string of trading stores, a fleet of sailing ships, and the finest racing stables in the Province of Ontario. She once informed a reporter that her uncles were members of parliament. The truth is, however, that no Henderson relative ever served as an MP, and no evidence exists that her maternal grandfather ever owned stores, sailing ships, or racehorses. According to Dressler's second cousin Irene Marsh Powell, George Jr. was a relatively poor man who worked as a harbormaster in Port Hope. (George did have a brother named Thomas, however, who not only made a pile of cash in Australia but had the distinction of being murdered in 1856.) Perhaps Dressler invented the story of a wealthy grandfather to endow her mother with a distinctive background and to set up the equally distinctive story of a father who withdrew financial support because he disapproved of his daughter's marriage to a testy Austrian. "Although grandfather's door remained open to her and her children, he refused to help out with money as long as mother stubbornly remained with father," Dressler said.

She recalls one highly dramatic incident concerning the Henderson family. As she tells it, her grandfather had returned from a trip to Montreal with a handsome pair of chestnut horses and invited his somewhat reluctant wife to take a drive with him. "Grandmother did not return alive from the outing," wrote Dressler. "Just as they started to cross a bridge, the horses shied at the sudden downward swoop of a bird. Grandmother was thrown out of the cart and instantly killed." Dressler says she was seven at the time, which would make the date of the accident 1875. According Bruce C. Stinson, Marsh family historian, however, Jane Ann Marsh died in 1881, and her husband had already expired ten years earlier, when Dressler was three years of age. The actress never provides any firm evidence to the contrary.

But there is no doubt that Anna Henderson was a heroine to young Leila. "If ever there was an angel on earth, it was my little mother," she wrote. "Slight, never too well, she had the strength of ten lions when it came to fighting for her two children." Grandfather Henderson, recounts Dressler, married his housekeeper after Jane Ann's untimely death. The woman, according to the story, loathed Anna Henderson and "fanned the flame" of her husband's hatred for Koerber. When Henderson died, Dressler says, he left her mother a small fleet of merchant ships; somewhat inconveniently for the sake of documented follow-up, the vessels caught fire and burned during a storm. And, of course, there was no insurance.

Whatever one believes about Dressler's stirring saga of the Henderson clan, it is clear that her dislike, even hatred, of her father was real. "My father was the cause of our frequent movings," she said. "I never liked him and I shan't pretend that I did. . . . He was his own worst enemy. I am sure that he was bitterly frustrated and unhappy. No doubt he dreamed of a great career in the New World. And instead of brilliant triumphs on the concert stage, fate decreed that he should guide clumsy fingers through stupid scales. . . . He hated Canada, he hated privations and he hated his life as a music teacher. Sometimes I think he hated his children." Despite her feelings about her father, Dressler took considerable pains to provide him with a colorful background as well. She sometimes claimed that his name was "von Koerber" and recounts that during a visit in the 1920s to the tomb of Emperor William I of Prussia, she studied the ruler's effigy and felt it resembled the face of her father. "What it all meant I shall never know," she wrote, "for I did not try to trace the connection."

Resentment of her father's "erratic decisions," neglect of his family, and frequent outbursts of temper shows clearly through the early chapters of Dressler's autobiographical reminiscences. She tells of a "succession of clashes" between father and daughter, and she conjectures that her homeliness—which became more pronounced as she grew older—"was an offense to his fastidious love of the beautiful." Dressler confesses that as a child she preferred playing with boys rather than with her ladylike sister, and she was allowed to crop her red hair and dress in a pair of her father's old pants cut down to fit her ample body. Later in life she liked to look back on her pre-adolescent years and conjecture that it was her distinct plainness combined with the fact that she was forced to make new friends in each new town that steered her toward a career as a theatrical clown. When the audience laughed at her during the celebrated Lindsay pratfall as Cupid, Dressler told interviewers, it was the first time she had been favored with so much upbeat attention. "No act of mine, before or since, has ever scored such tumultuous applause," she remembered. "This I might add, marked the beginning of my long career as a past mistress of the gentle art of falling. . . . I soon learned to be just as happy when folks said, 'Isn't she funny!' as if they had ah-ed and oh-ed and exclaimed, 'Isn't she beautiful!'"

Dressler never discussed her schooling. Cobourg historian Andrew Hewson suggests that young Leila attended a private school in the community, but that is doubtful; if Dressler's recollection of family poverty is correct, the Koerbers could not have afforded expensive instruction for their children, and if Dressler was only five years of age when she played Cupid in Lindsay, she might not have attended a Cobourg school at all. Constant movement from community to community may have forced the Koerbers to forgo any formal classroom registration for their two daughters. Anna Koerber may have taught Leila and Bonita to read and write—Dressler often recounted her mother's advice to "read a good newspaper every day, wherever you are." Those who knew the actress in adulthood never saw her actually write a word, except for a few brief letters; significantly, only two or three handwritten notes of thanks from her pen survive in library collections. She did not write either of her autobiographies; the first (*Life Story of An Ugly Duckling*) was ghost-written by well known authors, and information for the second (*My Own Story*) was dictated to a secretary. Her father most likely gave her piano lessons—she once said she gave a concert in a barn at the age of four—but the tensions during these sessions must have been palpable.

Continuing problems at home persuaded young Leila to find a job. She does not tell us where the family was living when she did so; it could have been Saginaw or even Findlay, where Koerber is known to have worked in the late 1870s or early 1880s. Dressler says she was barely thirteen when she "openly rebelled at the sight of mother slaving her life away in an effort to keep a roof over our heads." Her mother, she recalled, "was little and frail; I was so big and strong." Apparently she applied for a position in a local dry goods store and was immediately assigned to the underwear counter. A day and a half later, however, she was unceremoniously fired. Typically for Dressler the raconteur, the reason has its dramatic overtones. The actress says she had mistakenly wrapped a pair of men's red flannel drawers in a package "destined for the primmest old maid in town." She asks us to picture the "thin, gaunt old woman, shaking an umbrella" in Dressler's face "as she explained she found the enclosed lingerie not quite to her taste."

Dressler confesses that she had no interest in clerking and that she really longed to be a chariot driver in a circus. She recalls that she paid a visit to some unnamed relatives in an unnamed village where a small unnamed wagon show was wintering. After "hanging about the black cook wagon and the performers" for an unspecified period of time, she confided to a group of circus folk that she wanted to join the show. Her newfound friends were understandably skeptical of her professional abilities, but she told them she had been riding bareback on her grandfather Henderson's farm and felt equipped to begin training in earnest. Dressler follows this up with a sketchy description of how some good-natured equestrienne taught her to stand on the back of a "galloping steed" in just three days.

During these adolescent years, Leila was also dabbling in amateur theatricals. Dates are typically fuzzy, but after she became well known as an actress, residents of Bay City, Findlay, and Saginaw wrote to their local papers with reminiscences of the girl. A Mrs. Shirmer remembered in the *Bay City Times* after Dressler's death: "Leila was always the ringleader. She usually wrote, directed and starred in the productions and because she was so much fun, we were always glad to let her. However, her mischievous nature sometimes led our parents to question the desirability of her influence." A Mrs. McCron, a neighbor of the family when they lived in Saginaw, gives us a glimpse of Alexander Koerber's attitude toward young Leila at this time. In a news clipping headed "Famous Persons Who Lived in Saginaw," she wrote: "When Marie was in Saginaw she took part in numerous theatrical ventures . . . and used to aggravate her father and mother at times with the declaration, 'All right, if you don't like it, I'll go over to Boardwell's Opera House and dance on a barrel.' Boardwell's in those days was in the 200 block, South Washington Ave. Its reputation left something to be desired." It is clear that few neighbors believed Leila had any chance of becoming a glamorous stage star. In a 1905 news story, a Findlay resident remembered: "She was about the dowdiest looking creature that ever walked our streets, so she was generally commented upon. She never seemed to mind how her clothes looked, but she had a genial whole-hearted way that made you forget her appearance when you knew her."

Tensions between Leila and her father continued to build. Her cousin Irene Powell recalled that "one night when Marie was fourteen, and at the command of her father who was rather a tyrant, she was washing the dinner dishes and she rebelled, dried her hands and told him, she 'did not intend to be a slave to any man as her mother had been to him.' The next morning she made plans to join a theatrical company. Dressler's own description of her early exodus from home is so coolly matter-of-fact, it is tempting to wonder whether the actress is deliberately sidestepping a highly sensitive issue. The fact that her nineteen-year-old sister Bonita left home at the same time could mean that there was some serious physical and/or sexual abuse in the home. Of course, it could simply mean that Leila's parents accepted her headstrong decision to leave and perhaps encouraged their eldest daughter to accompany her as a chaperon. In any case, it does seem somewhat unusual for an apparently gently bred, fourteen-year-old female—even with an older sister in tow—to launch out on her own in the early 1880s.

Whatever the details, Dressler recollects that she read a newspaper ad (possibly in Bay City or Findlay, but never actually specified) placed by a cheap dramatic stock company in the hope of recruiting actors. The company was managed by Robert Wallace, brother of well known actress and prima donna Emma Nevada, and it traveled from town to town giving theatrical performances. "In those days there were hundreds of companies, composed of broken old professionals who had come down the ladder and eager amateurs on the way up. Nevada's collection ran the scale from has-beens to would-bes," Dressler remembered. As an enthusiastic would-be, and apparently without her father's knowledge, Leila wrote a twenty-page letter—a claim difficult to believe based on the fourteen year-old girl's standard of education—insisting that she had played various roles in amateur entertainments and that she felt she would be a suitable addition to the Nevada company. She wrote that she was eighteen years of age and that she had a sister who might be persuaded to join the troupe as well. To Leila's pleased astonishment, she received a prompt offer of employment, both for herself and Bonita. Her only problem now was how to break the news at home.

Dressler has given us somewhat different versions of the event, but it seems that she quarreled bitterly with her father when she told him about the Nevada job and that this was the historic moment when she decided to change her name from Koerber to Dressler. "Even then I was struck by the unfairness of his attitude. He was ready and eager to take advantage of his authority as a parent, although he had long overlooked the responsibilities attached to parenthood. 'You'll never drag the name of *von* [author's italics] Koerber through the mud by showing off behind the footlights!'" the actress says he bellowed at her. "'I'll take another name!' I thundered back at him. . . . It was my temper against his. Eventually he must have recognized in me his own stubbornness for he gave in and I became Marie Dressler, after an aunt whose name the family did not seem to feel was as sacred as that of von Koerber." Dressler never explained the identity of the aunt whose name she adopted. There is no evidence that she was a member of the Henderson or Marsh clans, so it can only be assumed that the now-forgotten woman was a relative on her father's side of the family. To muddy the story still further, a New York newspaper reported in 1915 that Dressler took her name from an awning on a pie shop she encountered in some Midwestern town during a stopover. Several months later, though, the actress swore publicly that this was not true.

Despite her father's dramatically documented wrath when told of his daughters' imminent defection, Dressler remembers that Koerber took a supply of lumber that had been sent to the house and began fashioning it into a "nightmare of a trunk." The actress leaves us to conjecture whether this was a genial gesture or a vindictive way of saddling the two young travelers with an unwanted millstone. "It looked more like a dog house than a piece of luggage," remembers Dressler. "By the time we reached our first stop, we had become so worldly minded that we gave our white elephant to a boarding-house keeper who said she had always yearned for a summer house. We left her trying to train ivy up its rugged sides." But the gay abandonment of Koerber's farewell gift marked an important turning point in Dressler's life—it was her first indication that the burdensome ties that had bound her to her father had at last been broken.

3

ON THE ROAD

1882-1892

Marie Dressler gives us no information as to where she and Bonita began working with the Nevada Stock Company, but she does tell us in her autobiographies that she made her professional debut as Cigarette in *Under Two Flags*. Dressler writes that she was almost paralyzed with stage fright before her first appearance, and no wonder. *Under Two Flags* was a dramatization of British novelist Ouida's somewhat naughty novel of life in the Foreign Legion. The stage treatment had been written by Richard Ganthony, a young playwright who traveled with the Nevada company. Ouida's description of the dancing girl Cigarette reads: "She was dancing now like a little Bacchante, as fresh as if she had just sprung up from a long summer day's rest . . . soft short curls all fluttering, her cheeks all bright with a scarlet flush, her eyes as black as night and full of fire. All the warmth of Africa, all the wit of France, all the bohemianism of the Flag, all the caprices of her sex were in that bewitching dancing."

No photographs survive of Dressler at age fourteen, but she herself admitted that she was always "too homely for a prima donna and too big for a soubrette." She was five feet, seven inches tall, with red hair and green eyes. It was once reported that she had "the loveliest hands in the world, small, firm taper-fingered and delicate." Perhaps it is a comment on the paucity of talent in the Nevada company that manager Robert Wallace decided to cast the untried newcomer as the sexy young star of the As de Pique cabaret in Algeria. No review has ever been found that would tell us more about how she fared that night, but she did play the same role in Findlay, Ohio, three years later, and a local resident named Mrs. Hurin remembered in a newspaper article, "She appeared in extra short skirts in a day when women were not supposed to have ankles, let alone legs. Although the costume caused comment, the performance was above average." All her life, Dressler would recall that first appearance with the Nevada Stock Company because "there began a battle that has raged throughout my career," she wrote. "My dogged, never-ending fight against stage fright so dreadful, so devastating, that it often leaves me limp and nauseated. To this day, I can't walk on a set for a two-minute shot that my palms aren't cold and wet and my back crawling with terror. But once actually on the stage, I become a different person. I burn with a strange zest which the audience gives me, and which I want to give back to them, full measure and heaping over."

Actually, the young Dressler could not have chosen a more fortunate time to try her luck in show business, even though she was paid only six dollars a week. (She lived on half of this amount and sent the other three dollars home to her mother.) In the last decades of the nineteenth century, the Road, as touring entertainment was affectionately called, was booming in North America. Traveling circuses, minstrel shows, and Wild West spectaculars (Buffalo Bill Cody sold out wherever he appeared) were setting up their tents throughout Canada and the United States.

The burgeoning railroad system made small theatrical touring companies financially feasible, even if they decided to peddle their tickets in towns boasting as few as fifteen hundred or two thousand residents. Important cities such as New York and Boston were attracting foreign companies, and world-famous stars such as Sarah Bernhardt, Maude Adams, and Sir John Martin-Harvey were appearing regularly in the theatres. In 1883, the year Dressler joined the Nevada company, Sir Henry Irving, accompanied by Ellen Terry, decided that business had been so successful in the United States that they would venture into the wilds of Canada. The thespians were so impressed with their reception, they returned for five more tours. But there were many home-grown favorites as well, showcased by regional and national groups such as the Boston Ideal Opera Company, the Alice Oates Opera Company, and the Castle Square Light Opera Company of Boston.

Audiences, in fact, were hooked on live entertainment. Tastes in the 1870s, '80s, and '90s evolved from a fascination with the Uncle Tom's Cabin type of melodrama to a love affair with French opera bouffe—Jacques Offenbach's *La Grande Duchesse de Gerolstein* was an enduring hit—and a passion for the comic opera genius of Gilbert and Sullivan. Dressler must have been well aware of the names currently making the headlines in the theatrical columns: Lilly Post, Berthe Ricci, Pauline Hall, and the great clown Francis Wilson. While she was working with the Nevada group, though, these luminaries were as remote to her as the far-off stages of New York City. Instead, she hobnobbed with third-class actors she knew as Jake and Mary and Henry and only half-noticed that the town in which she was playing was called Sheboygan or Traverse City. "How grand it was for audiences to have September leading into the whole winter filled with wonder down at the theatre. It made life brighter in Calumet, Michigan, and Opelika, Alabama—for three hours each evening you could forget your rut, your town, just as people attending the theatre could forget the city turmoil in New York, Boston, Philadelphia," writes author Philip Lewis. Theatre buffs in these communities thought that to be an actor and please so many so much must be a wonderful thing. And usually, Lewis says, the actors agreed, "although after a few seasons, there wasn't an actor who didn't marvel at his survival. They endured because they were troupers."

Dressler is more restrained in her memories of life with the Nevada company. Her autobiographies mention dingy hotel rooms, landlords who followed her to her room in the hope of sexual favors, times when there was little to eat. And memoirs of contemporaries tell of train carriages dimly lighted with kerosene lamps and underheated with coal stoves. Theatres were likely to be barns, tents, or converted warehouses. Dressing rooms were crowded, unheated in winter, and stifling in the heat of summer. Personal hygiene was often a difficult problem: baths were a luxury and laundry was a constant headache. Dressler did seem to recognize the value of her experience with the Nevada, however. "The company proved a wonderful school in many ways," she wrote. "Often a bill was changed on an hour's notice or less. Every member of the cast had to be a quick study. I have gone on in a part which I had only read over hastily while dressing, more intensive study being pursued while I waited in the wings for my cue. . . . An actor was judged largely by his skill of ad-libbing. If they had a sketchy outline of the plot and a rough idea of the characterization, a troupe of old hands could almost create a play as they went along."

The Nevada company played mostly in the American Midwest, but Dressler remembers landing in a little sagebrush town in Texas, "half starved, not because we hadn't money enough to buy food—though, heaven knows, we had precious little cash at any time—but because there had been no food to buy along the way. No sooner had the engine jerked to a standstill than the younger members of the company piled out like a lot of calves suddenly let out of the corral. . . . Just back of the station was a lunch wagon. I discovered it first." The hungry thespians invaded the wagon, to the fright of the attendant who promptly quit the scene. Dressler took her stand by the cash register and carefully collected for each item eaten. "We cleaned out his larder but we certainly left him with a swollen till."

Despite the rigors of the touring life, Dressler always remembered that the Road was a fascinating new experience. She insists she was too excited to be homesick. References to Bonita are scarce in her two books, although she says her sister was a help in the continuing effort to conceal her real age and lack of theatrical experience. "I was constantly appealing to Bonita, 'My dear, where did I play Lady Macbeth first? Was it Cobourg or that nice town just beyond Ottawa?'" She writes that her knowledge of Canadian geography was convincing. Because of the Koerbers' continual changes of residence, it was easy for her to rattle off impressive statistics about the population of this or that provincial center. In the meantime, of course, she was learning the tricks of the trade and quickly absorbing the special thrill of being a showbusiness personality. "I also found countless opportunities for observing life in the raw," she writes. "From boarding-house and hotel keepers, from waitresses, train conductors and my fellow passengers and boarders, I learned to read human nature. And I taught myself to turn my observations to my own uses. Many a woman who shared my boarding-house prunes and corned beef in one town would have been surprised to see herself on the stage in the next." There's no doubt that this experience laid the foundations of Dressler's future preeminence as an impersonator.

The actress's apprenticeship with the Nevada Stock Company lasted for almost three years, during which time Bonita left the company to marry the young playwright Richard Ganthony. Eventually the group found itself stranded without money or a booking in a small Michigan town, and Dressler thought for a time that her stage career was over. Luckily, she heard that another small group, the Robert Grau Opera Company, was touring the Middle West, and she applied for work. She was accepted as a member of the chorus for eight dollars a week, a munificent raise from her six-dollar Nevada job. Dressler is not too specific about how long she stayed with the Grau company, but she does tell us that she was never paid a cent of her promised wages. Grau was apparently a bad manager, although he considered himself a talented businessman, and felt that a "drinking allowance" of twenty-five cents a week was enough to keep his performers happy. When Dressler told him that she didn't drink and preferred to collect the money he legitimately owed her, Grau decided to get rid of the dissident. According to Dressler, he arranged with his brother to send a telegram: "Send Dressler to Philadelphia. Want to get her clothes for opening here."

Years later, Dressler admitted that she was thrilled to be dispatched on such a glamorous assignment. But when nobody met her at the station in Philadelphia, she was naturally suspicious and frightened. She had just fifty cents over and above the railway fare Grau had given her, so she decided to ask a policeman for help. His advice was to go to the Continental Hotel, a hostelry that was considered the best in town, and, incredibly, her impassioned pitch to the clerk earned her a room for the night. The next morning she found an envelope under her door containing two dollars and the note: "I got a kid of my own."

That day, Dressler spent a few cents on a cup of coffee and a copy of the morning paper and found that the Starr Opera Company, managed by Frank Deshon, was enjoying a long run in town. She knew that two of her old comrades from the Road, May Duryea and May Montford, were members of the company, so she decided to hike uptown and catch them at rehearsal. The two Mays, who would remain Dressler's lifelong friends, were indignant at the way she had been treated by Robert Grau and immediately implored Deshon to give the young woman a job. "I landed it for $8 a week," she remembers. "Just what Grau had promised but never paid me." Dressler was back in the chorus, but because the Starr company was professional enough to be booked into larger cities such as Philadelphia and Detroit, the actress found she was being challenged to turn in a more polished performance. She also found that she enjoyed singing rather than dancing and dreamed of performing such Wagnerian roles as Brunnehilde. Deep down, however, she realized that although she might have the physique and stamina for grand opera, her naturally pleasant voice was scarcely trained for the work.

Then the actress fell in love with the role of the portly Katisha in the Starr company's production of Gilbert and Sullivan's *The Mikado*. "The part was conceived in heaven especially for me," she remembers. "I bought the score and in three days I could have sung Katisha backward or upside down." The actress admits that she never really believed she would ever play the comical role on stage. After all, the part had been assigned to an actress named Agnes Hallock, who was apparently an exceptionally robust young woman. Then, if we are to believe Dressler's story, the fickle finger of fate put Agnes on the sidelines with a sprained ankle, and the young Marie promptly presented herself to Deshon as a qualified understudy. The manager gave her the role, mainly because the costumes fit her. Years later, she grandly insisted, "I was a riot in the part."

The Katisha break did not make her an instant star, but even though she was eventually returned to the chorus, she gained invaluable stage experience with Deshon. Typically, her threadbare autobiographies give us little hard information about her early roles, but later in her career, she remembered some of them when interviewers begged for some details. She was sometimes called on to play Katisha, and she worked as a chorus member in Robert Pauquette's cliché-ridden, sentimental opera, *The Chimes of Normandy*. She admitted she had a secret yearning to play Serpolette, the lively country wench, but was never given the chance. An Ann Arbor theatre history records that she played the reasonably substantial role of Princess Flametta in an 1887 production of Edmond Audron's *La Mascotte*, a romantic opera bouffe that immortalized Bettina, a turkey-girl, and Pippo, a shepherd. It featured, among other songs, an animal duet, complete with yodeled farmyard noises in praise of turkeys and sheep.

Dressler remembers trying to find her niche at this time and wishing she "had a voice good enough for grand opera." It seems clear that her outgoing, even dynamic, personality set her apart as a theatrical natural. Certainly her expressive, highly mobile face, hourglass figure, and strong contralto voice guaranteed that she would be noticed on stage. Though Katisha was her dream role, in those days, she was forced to accept any assignment handed to her by the companies that hired her—mainly the somewhat syrupy opera comique shows rather than the more expressive Gilbert and Sullivan musical plays. But, she began to wonder, was she really getting anywhere with the Starr Company? Besides, she finally admitted to herself, "now the first glamour of independence had worn off, I allowed myself the luxury of homesickness. . . . In fact, I had come to the place where I couldn't wait any longer to see mother. Therefore, at the end of my run with Deshon, I did not look for another engagement. I joyfully prepared to go home." By the time she decided to leave the Starr Company, her salary had been boosted to eighteen dollars a week.

Home for Anna and Alexander Koerber at that time was Saginaw, Michigan, but, as Dressler remembered, "as always, home was simply where my mother was . . . and I couldn't get to her fast enough. Alas for the stability of human emotions, I had no sooner unpacked my trunks than I realized I should never be content to live at home again." In a few days, in fact, "father's tyranny became unbearable. I saw that I could no longer pretend to submit to it. Now that I had seen the great outside world, I realized afresh how shabby, how pathetically threadbare was my mother's existence. I dreamed of hanging pearls about her throat, of draping sables about her slender shoulders. I would go back and find a better job."

During the time she spent with her parents in Saginaw, the Bennett and Moulton Opera Company, managed by George A. Baker, came to town. The company had earned a solid reputation in the small cities of the Middle West and New England, playing week-long stands and daily matinees. The company was a pioneer of the ten-, twenty-, and thirty-cent staggered seat-price policy. For a thin dime, small-town theatre addicts could enjoy a well-produced comic opera from a vantage point in the gallery. George Baker had the professional reputation of being a successful "choir snatcher." Like many other theatrical managers of the day, he would make a point of scouting local churches in search of vocal talent. "More than one musical-comedy star who a generation ago thrilled Broadway with her pink tights and naughty songs owed her fame to the fact that she sat in a village choir on a Sunday morning when a wandering impresario was worshipping in their midst," Dressler explained. She was not in the choir the day that Baker spotted her, but in the congregation with her mother (there is no indication that her father was playing the organ). "If I hadn't gone," she once wrote, "I probably would have missed a job that was to prove one of the most important of my life."

The actress has never offered any information as to why Baker picked her out of the congregation, so we can only assume that her past experience on the Road endowed her with a certain panache as she belted out the morning's hymns. We can also only assume that her mother offered little if any objection to her daughter's taking off with Baker. Dressler tells us nothing about her father's reaction to the new turn of events. But the actress was correct in remembering that the stint with Bennett and Moulton was important to her early career. She was with the company for almost three years, during which time she learned everything about the theatre from the making of costumes and the refurbishing of scenery to the playing of every kind of role from a child to an octogenarian. Discipline was "severe, but fair." She thought nothing of mastering a new light opera every week, even while she was playing in one and rehearsing a second or third. In fact, at the end of her first year with the company, Dressler says she already boasted a repertoire of forty or so light opera parts.

Many of these were roles of royalty, probably because of her undeniably imposing figure. "In *Three Black Cloaks,* I played the Queen, except when the King was drunk and I played the King," she remembered. "I was the Queen in *Bohemian Girl.* When occasion arose, however, I could play almost every role in the repertoire." When she was given the comic role of Barbara in a Sydney Rosenfeld adaptation of Carl Millocker's *The Black Hussars,* she remembered: "the lines and especially the business of Barbara were meat, drink and custard pie to me and I went at them like a famine sufferer. This was my first opportunity really to get an audience and I realized then that I was portraying a type more human than a Grand Duchesse or a Queen. And that this would get one over the footlights and into the hearts of those on the other side." In this particular role, Dressler would whack a baseball right into the ten-cent gallery seats, which, besides being fun, also showed her the value of allowing those out front to participate in the performance. The youngsters in the upper seats would toss the ball back to Dressler and, she noted, she "had to watch like the Dickens to get it when it came." Most important, she realized, she acquired "that desirable box office commodity, a following."

Life on the Road, however, was still as Spartan as it had been during her previous theatrical stints. Salaries were so minuscule that the run-of-the-mill players could not afford to stay in hotels. The names of decent boardinghouses were exchanged among the Bennett and Moulton actors and with colleagues packing their bags on their way out of town. Dressler always remembered that she loved playing in Cleveland because of particularly enthusiastic audiences and that she dreaded engagements in New England. Doors of the better boardinghouses in that part of the country were invariably slammed in the actors' faces. "Nobody wanted troupers," she remembered. "We usually wound up by going to rooming houses and eating in drab restaurants."

When Dressler's contract with George Baker came to an end in 1891, she decided to accept an engagement in Chicago with a Harry B. Smith musical piece called *Little Robinson Crusoe*. One of the cast had fallen ill and, although the part offered was small, Dressler jumped at the chance of working with Eddie Foy, a puckish comedian and acrobat who was making a big name for himself in the theatre. The association made a lasting impression on the young actress. "I have always called Eddie 'the prop comedian' because he was invariably hunting funny accessories for business," she recalled. "Perhaps it was because of his continual trouble in locating and keeping them at hand, always getting fussed if one were missing, that I unconsciously developed my own aversion to their use. At any rate, I have never used a prop of any sort. This has inconvenienced me at times, since this eccentricity excludes even a handkerchief, that delightful piece de resistance of most actresses." After the closing of *Little Robinson Crusoe*, Dressler was cast in the road production of yet another Harry B. Smith musical called *The Tar and the Tartar* (she played the vixenish Tartar), a piece about the disappearance of a ruler and the substitution of a commoner who resembles him. Smith himself was later accused of stealing the plot from the well known play *The Prisoner of Zenda,* but he always reminded critics that *The Tar and the Tartar* had been written at least three years before *The Prisoner* appeared. *The Tar and the Tartar* finally folded on the road. Dressler reviewed her options, then decided to buy a ticket to New York. After all, she reasoned, New York was where the theatre was booming—everything from comic opera and drama to burlesque.

In 1892, in fact, New York boasted forty-one theatres, more even than London's thirty-nine. Actresses such as Lillian Russell, Pauline Hall, and Christie MacDonald had become the darlings of the town. Surely, Dressler told herself, something would turn up that would finally set her on the path to theatrical success. It was about time, she thought. She was already twenty-four years of age.

4

CHAMPION OF THE UNDERDOG

1892-1900

The boom on Broadway in the early years of the 1890s was an extension of the economic euphoria that gilded the 1880s. In the United States, industry had expanded rapidly since the Civil War. Trusts had developed to limit competition and to fix prices for oil, sugar, and other commodities, and there was even talk of a syndicate or trust being planned to control theatrical booking activity. Overproduction was rife: too many stoves and not enough people to buy them, railroads overbuilt for the number of passengers buying tickets, and banks staggering from high-risk loans. The American economy was ripe for a crash, and when it happened in 1893, economy-watchers were not surprised. The fallout from the Panic, as it was soon called, would plague the nation for nearly five years. But in 1892, New York City's affluent upper middle classes were still spending lavishly to enjoy the delights of the legitimate theatre and to patronize the rapidly growing number of houses offering vaudeville. Tony Pastor's Music Hall on Fourteenth Street was packing in big audiences, and Rudolph Aronson's new roof-garden Casino at Thirty-Ninth Street and Broadway with its distinctive Moorish design was reporting standing-room-only business for its lavish productions of European operettas.

When Dressler arrived in the big city, she took the advice of her chorus colleagues in Chicago and sought out a decent boardinghouse in Brooklyn. Her wallet was dangerously thin, so she decided to walk across the still-new Brooklyn Bridge to the theatrical district each morning, then back again after she had spent the day inquiring after jobs in the depressingly furnished offices of the New York agents. "Usually, you walked up two or three flights of musty stairs to a dim, airless anteroom, as changeless as time itself," she remembered. "The curls of dust in the corners, the hard shabby chairs against the dingy wall, the very faces of the occupants of the chairs made a sort of horrid, recurrent dream from which there was no waking. For days on end, week in and week out, the fantastic pattern of those faces rarely changed. . . . There was the dapper young man with the nervous hands, whose courage ebbed visibly each afternoon but was mysteriously renewed each morning. On the sagging sofa under the picture of [the great Irish-born actress] Ada Rehan a group of ingenues huddled together, chattering excitedly of the part they almost got. Oh, it was all dreadful beyond any power of mine to describe: sitting there, the endless waiting for the rabbit-faced office boy or the haughty ex-chorus girl secretary to pop through the door with the same old refrain: 'Nothing today.'"

Eventually, in May 1892, an excited Dressler landed a part in a musical play called *Waldemar, the Robber of the Rhine*, a somewhat clumsy variation of the Robin Hood legend. She had heard about the opening from "a friend of a friend" of the man who had put up the money for the production. The music for the show had been written by Charles Puerner and the book by Maurice Barrymore, father of Lionel, John, and Ethel. Dressler reported optimistically for rehearsals at the Fifth Avenue Theatre, but her enthusiasm quickly disappeared. The show ran for just five weeks, most of them painful for the young actress. "Nobody wanted me in the cast and everybody did everything they could to get rid of me. I pretended that I was a rhinoceros and laughed gaily at the barbed darts." Fortunately for the actress's professional pride, both the director, Richard Barker, and Barrymore himself congratulated her on a spirited portrayal of Cunigonde, a comical brigand. She remembered years later that she hated the part because at that time she was still harboring the hope that she might develop into an operatic diva or at least a tragedienne. But "it was Maurice Barrymore who first fathomed my secret ambition and warned me against it. 'You were born to make people laugh, Marie,' he told me gently. 'Don't try to fly in the face of fate!'" In hindsight, about the only reason for remembering *Waldemar* today was that it introduced both Dressler and a soon-to-be-famous actor named Haydin Coffin to Broadway.

After *The Robber of the Rhine* folded, Dressler found herself in a desperate financial situation. Not only was she still supporting her parents in Saginaw, she was now expected to shoulder some responsibility for Bonita and her husband Richard, who had both returned home after losing their jobs. Dressler also mentions the presence of "two elderly aunts" at this time, but nowhere does she identify them by name or explain whether they were relatives of her mother or her father. Faced with the frightening realization that she had become the sole breadwinner for her family, the young woman resumed her vigil at the agents' offices, quickly grabbing the opportunity to sing two songs a night at the Atlantic Garden on the Bowery for ten dollars an engagement. No New York critic felt the necessity to comment on her performance. On Sundays she sang at Koster and Bial's vaudeville house on Twenty-Third Street for fifteen dollars a night, most of which she sent home to Saginaw.

Early in 1893, Dressler managed to land the role of Queen Isabella in a revival of *1492*, a curious play by writers Ed Rice and Robert Barnet. The production had originated in Boston and turned out to be the surprise hit of the season because of its frequent and unannounced revisions. Audiences were always delighted when the producers would suddenly insert a fashion show cum ballet entitled "Six Daily Hints from Paris" or a creative "dance of the store window mannequins." Dressler herself enjoyed her association with *1492* and unhappily resisted when, for some reason, Rice attempted to and eventually succeeded in steering her into another show. The new production immediately flopped.

In October of that year, the actress landed her first big-time chance in a lightweight Charles Alfred Byrne and Louis Harrison play with music by William Furst called *Princess Nicotine*, starring the popular Lillian Russell. The story revolved around a pretty cigarette maker by the name of Rosa (Russell) and her marriage to a rich tobacco planter (Perry Averill), who mistakenly believed his wife was dallying with the local governor. Explanations followed in time for a happy ending. Dressler was cast in yet another "royal" role, this time as the Duchess, wife of the governor, played by Digby Bell. The show was produced at the Casino by George W. Lederer for the Canary and Lederer/Opera Comique Organization. It is clear from Dressler's own recollections that she was flattered, even over-whelmed, to be working with Russell. By then, the Iowa-born light opera star was thirty-two years of age, but she was without doubt the reigning stage beauty of the day. And as a personality she appealed enormously to Dressler. For one thing, Russell admitted that she had known she was destined for the theatre at an age even earlier than when Dressler had first begun dreaming about her future. Her mother, Cynthia, Dressler discovered with awe, was a prominent women's rights activist who had once run for mayor of New York on a feminist ticket. And Russell herself was widely known as "airy, fairy Lillian" because of her beguilingly independent penchant for switching from company to company rather than settling down safely with one established troupe. Even more intriguing for the still somewhat naive twenty-five-year-old Dressler, Lillian Russell not only had every man on the Great White Way at her feet, she had already been married and separated (one divorce, one annulment) twice and was now eyeing another possible liaison.

Dressler and Russell bought bicycles in an effort to keep them-selves trim, and the two actresses would pedal from Russell's house on Seventy-Sixth Street into Central Park for a turn around the reservoir. "People used to call us 'Beauty and the Beastie,'" Dressler remembered. "But I didn't care." The actress once recalled with obvious relish that during these bicycling excursions Russell would wheel into the driveway of a house occupied by a New York rake named Judge Smith. The judge (of horseflesh, not the law) would act like a gentleman at all times, although he insisted on plying the women with scented cigarettes.

Dressler was earning a respectable fifty dollars a week—versus Russell's seven hundred dollars—by the time *Princess Nicotine* completed its three-month Broadway run, followed by a success-ful swing on the Road. Lederer, in fact, was so pleased with "the big gal" and her growing box-office appeal, that he cast her as Russell's mother, Aurora, in a revival of Charles Lecocq's some-what creaky opera bouffe, *Girofle-Girofla*. The play opened in March 1894 at the Casino, but even with Russell heading the cast, it enjoyed limited success. At the time, theatre enthusiasts were stampeding to buy tickets for the D'Oyly Carte Company's pro-duction of the latest Gilbert and Sullivan hit, *Utopia Ltd.*, at a com-peting theatre on Broadway.

Dressler's private and emotional life is difficult to track in the early 1890s. She seemed to be more interested in Lillian Russell's unfortunate love affair and marriage to a tenor named Signor Perugini—whose real name was John Chatterton—than in her own personal state of mind. There remain no hints that she formed any romantic attachments during the last years of the nineteenth century, though she once almost shamefacedly admitted she had an unrequited crush on an actor named Terry during her days with the Nevada Stock Company. Certainly Russell revealed no details of her young Canadian friend's private life at the time. But Dressler had more practical matters to think about. Alexander and Anna Koerber were still living in Saginaw in 1894 and 1895, and the actress herself was resigned to existing like a gypsy in New York and Brooklyn boardinghouses. It wasn't until 1896, in fact, almost three years after her appearances with Russell at the Casino, that she thought seriously of renting a small house on Long Island and inviting her parents to join her.

In the meantime, her theatrical career drifted on somewhat of a sideways course. She was still searching for a personal style, but her work with Russell had helped her find a new freedom on stage. George Lederer allowed her an unusual flexibility of role interpretation, and at the Casino she developed her trademark knack for inspired ad-libbing and the use of creative comic business. Dressler once recalled that a stage director at the Casino had tried to give her some difficult directions and that she felt so awkward she broke down and wept. Lederer, who was watching the rehearsal, shouted from the back of the house, "Oh, let her do it her own way, she's funny!" After that the actress was allowed to play a part as she wished, inventing new business and introducing amusing ideas "which the stage manager would never have thought of." Her unique professional rapport with Lederer soon became common knowledge around the theatrical community. "And it became an unwritten law with all stage producers that Marie Dressler was to have the privilege of interpreting her own part as she saw fit, and putting in any new business that she wished to create," she once proudly remembered. "This gave me such a wide latitude for fun and original ideas that I really did a lot of absurd things. But the public laughed at me and my salary grew bigger and bigger." Drama specialist Dr. Roberta Raider Sloan of the University of Central Oklahoma has analyzed the actress's early persona and believes her ability and opportunity to ad-lib was highly important in her creative development. "Besides being an attractive feature of the show, these ad-libbed scenes probably resulted in affecting Miss Dressler's style," Sloan concludes. A result of improvisation, according to Sloan, is excitement and energy. "Having to invent responses to an unknown situation keeps an actor's mental processes at a high pitch of creativity," and, of course, "these qualities were to become vital elements of her style."

In 1895, Dressler was cast in the A.M. Palmer production of *A Stag Party,* or *A Hero in Spite of Himself.* The musical play, which laboriously told the story of a gun club preparing to hunt a stag, starred Louis Harrison and Leo Ditrichstein and occupied the Garden Theatre at Madison Avenue and Twenty-Seventh Street for only two weeks. Most critics panned the production, which was generally considered to be a "dreadful fiasco." Dressler, though, received good notices and was rewarded with an increase in salary, bringing her wages to one hundred fifty dollars a week. "Marie Dressler makes an acting hit . . . although she is only a feeder to Mr. Harrison, who plays himself as usual and deserves praise for speaking the words of his songs distinctly," wrote the *New York Spirit of the Times.* The play folded, and the actress quickly accepted the opportunity to join the Camille D'Arville Company for a tour of the Midwest—a favorite stumping ground during her apprenticeship with the stock companies. The play was *Madeleine,* or *The Magic Kiss,* and Dressler was cast as Mary Doodle, a comical widow. The part gave her ample room to clown and mug her way through the engagement

Early in 1896, Dressler struck gold. Broadway had been buzzing with rumors that a smash-hit English operatic comedy called *The Lady Slavey,* with the book by George Dance and new music by Gustave Kerker, was on its way into New York and that George Lederer would be casting it for a run at the Casino. And there were other rumors circulating on the footlights grapevine. The great British eccentric dancer Dan Daly was said to be already signed to play William Endymion Sykes, the lackadaisical sheriff. As for the pivotal role of Flo Honeydew of the Music Halls, the gossip was that Lederer had auditioned five actresses, all of whom had failed to make the grade. To Dressler's astonishment, Lederer sent for her on a chilly January morning and asked if she would play Flo. She almost swooned with delight as she sat sipping tea in the producer's office, but she clenched her fist, bit her lip, and decided to take an enormous gamble. Yes, she said, she would accept the role, provided she could dance with the tall, thin, and graceful Daly. The producer grinned a little, then agreed, provided the British star would go along with the idea. Dressler remembered later that Daly almost turned it down. "'Dance with that elephant of a Dressler?' he snorted. 'Not if I know it.' But Lederer persuaded him to humor me," the actress recalled. "'We'll probably drop the number before the opening,' he promised."

Years after Dressler became a genuine celebrity on the Great White Way, she still savored her success in *The Lady Slavey*. Not only did she dance with the legendary Dan Daly, the "thick and thin" couple eventually stopped the show nightly with an acrobatic waltz called "the Human Fly." Dressler also frequently enhanced the proceedings with inventive bits of stage business, made somewhat easier because of her naturally strong, acrobatic body. "As we started off stage on opening night in Washington," she recalled, "I whispered, 'Jump on my hip and I'll carry you off.' Daly hesitated a second, then did as I told him and we went off in a whirlwind of applause. As we stood panting in the wings, listening to the deafening clap-clap of the many hands . . . he said worriedly, 'My God, what'll we do for an encore?'"

At that same opening performance—at which the great Buffalo Bill Cody was in the audience—Dressler almost choked with stage fright, then accidentally hit her huge hat in an agony of nervousness. "It twirled clear around my head. A shout of laughter went up. I tried the twirl again and to my surprise it worked. The more they laughed, the more I twirled the hat and knew that I had gone over, which is the sweetest thing in the world for an actor." *The Lady Slavey* was the show in which Dressler became well known for her hilarious facial expressions, including her seriocomic reactions and double takes whenever disaster befell her on stage. The critics almost unanimously agreed that the young and highly energetic Dressler seemed to be on her way to stardom. "Marie Dressler as Flo, captures the whole play and the audience," announced the *New York Spirit of the Times*. "We predicted when Marie appeared in the *Stag Party* that she would show herself a great burlesque actress if she ever found a part to suit her."

The Lady Slavey played the Casino for two sold-out years, and Dressler began to enjoy the life of a Broadway celebrity. In the 1890s, the theatre district, or Rialto as it was commonly called, stretched from Twenty-Third Street to Herald Square, and despite the 1893-98 depression, it was beginning to stretch north to Longacre Square—later to become Times Square—and Forty-Second Street. The area was crowded with as many streetwalkers as there were sightseers (the well known sales pitch: "It costs a dollar and I've got the room"). As editor Henry Collins Brown once wrote, "All the world came to Broadway, to shop, to flirt, to dine, to gamble, to find amusement and to meet acquaintances." The legend was that "one standing in the portico of the Fifth Avenue Hotel would one day meet any long sought acquaintance whence-ever he might come." As a currently popular performer with her name in lights at the Casino, the effervescent Dressler was welcomed at George Considine's famous bar and restaurant at the Metropole on Forty-Second Street. After the theatre she enjoyed "bird and bottle" suppers with her friends at Rector's, Delmonico's, or Sherry's and was beginning to be recognized on the Great White Way by such celebrated colleagues as John Drew, Maude Adams, and Eva Tanguay. The great star-maker Charles Frohman would tip his hat to the young Dressler, as would architect Stanford White and impresario Oscar Hammerstein. Dressler could now afford a maid, and she hired a black woman named Jenny, who began working for her backstage during a run in Washington.

In the first few months of The Lady Slavey stint at the Casino, she roomed with her old stock-company friend May Duryea, who would soon take over the role of Lady Slavey from Virginia Earle, but after counting her money, she purchased a cheap frame house on the outskirts of Long Island City and asked her mother and father to join her from Saginaw. "Of course father knew he was included in the invitation," Dressler remembered somewhat tersely in My Own Story. "But we both adored mother and we were glad to put up with each other for her sake." For Dressler herself, though, the relocation of her parents represented a huge investment in energy and patience. Every night after the performance she would take the ferry home, a trip of approximately ninety minutes, with another inevitable ninety-minute trip back to

Manhattan the next morning. At one point, she rented an apartment at 1566 Broadway, then later moved into the Metropole Hotel. She even sold the Long Island property and brought her parents to live with her at the Metropole, but her mother soon complained that she missed Long Island. Without further comment, Dressler bought a small farm at Bayside on the shore of Little Neck Bay. She commuted from the farm to New York, as she had done from the previous house, this time every working day for three years. "But Sundays in the summer were heavenly after the heat of the city," she recalled. "I can still remember the sigh of satisfaction I used to have when I unhooked my Mauve Decade stays and plumped down in a porch rocker."

The theatre world was changing in the United States, and the revolution was beginning to impact life on Broadway. Show biz had become Big Biz, and in 1896, a group of six entrepreneurs dominated by self-styled theatrical czar Abraham Lincoln Erlanger had formed a syndicate with the Frohman Brothers, Marc Klaw, Sam Nixon, Alf Hayman, and J.F. Zimmerman, which had developed into a virtual monopoly. Because bookings were made somewhat haphazardly, the syndicate could streamline the process, but by 1889, it became abundantly clear that if a sought-after actor or producer did not sign an exclusive contract, the syndicate could block the booking of any theatre in New York. The monopoly could even make it impossible for a producer to mount a worthwhile national tour.

Dressler was apprehensive but not unduly worried when she heard that Erlanger and Klaw had bought the rights to *The Lady Slavey* and were booking the show on a cross-country swing. The actress, in fact, was beginning to feel increasingly confident and comfortable with her new professional status. She was commanding a good salary from George Lederer, and there was no reason to think that she would not be a valuable drawing card for the Erlanger-Klaw interests. For several months, indeed, she pulled in big houses on the tour. But when the company played Denver, Dressler suddenly became ill and quit the show to return to New York. The actress never revealed the nature of her indisposition in Colorado, but Erlanger was convinced that she was bluffing and that she really wanted to get back to the bright lights of Broadway. In any case, Dressler was fired from *The Lady Slavey* company and blacklisted by the syndicate in New York.

Once recovered from her illness, Dressler shrugged her ample shoulders and cheerfully joined the Rich and Harris touring company of a play called *Courted into Court* in the role of Dottie Dimple—replacing the equally amply built actress, May Irwin. The *Courted into Court* tour began in Cleveland, then traveled extensively, mainly in the West. Typically for Dressler's career at that time, the engagement added to her reputation as a highly versatile artist. This was the show in which she began dancing her individualistic version of the cakewalk, performing impromptu cartwheels across the stage, and singing "coon" songs. One journalist, Peter Robertson of the *San Francisco Chronicle,* wrote after seeing *Courted into Court:* "Dressler is a genuine woman comedian, as distinguished from a soubrette. She acts with intelligence and with a clear insight into the comic propositions. She contorts her face until it looks like the wattles of a turkey gobbler in a rage and she sways her huge frame about until she falls into all sorts of awkwardness; but she has magnetism and she is a comedienne."

Apparently, however, there was someone in Dressler's life who believed she was attractive enough to woo. It is difficult to pin down the date, or even confirm that there was a date, when she met and married a theatre ticket-seller named George Hoeppert. But years later, in 1934, when the House Committee on Immigration and Naturalization was investigating a new measure that would require foreign thespians to obtain permission to enter the United States, Dressler insisted that she had married some time around 1899. "I've been in the United States ever since I came here from Canada fifty years ago," she told the Associated Press. "Thirty-five years ago I married an American. His name was George Hoeppert and we were married at Elizabeth, N.J. These are matters of record. My marriage made me an American citizen and I've been one ever since. I'm sick and tired of all these little digs at my citizenship. It has been one of my life's ambitions to be a good American citizen, and I believe I have accomplished it." Dressler always actively discouraged questions about her marriage to Hoeppert, although she does confess in her autobiographies (without any further elaboration) that she married "for thrills," which quickly evaporated.

In 1933 some journalists would hint that the actress also bore a child that died in infancy, but because her roster of engagements were fairly consistent in the 1890s—except, perhaps, for the brief time after she quit *The Lady Slavey* company and before she joined up with *Courted into Court*—it seems highly unlikely that she would have found the time or the opportunity to disguise a pregnancy and a tragic birth. Interestingly, there was widespread speculation in 1899 that Dressler was engaged to a British musician named Jack Stavordale. But when confronted with the rumor, Dressler exclaimed in mock horror: "But he's an Englishman! In any case, no man can ever have the great privilege of supporting me."

Dressler enjoyed telling the story about how the villainous Abe Erlanger blacklisted her from the Great White Way for four years. But news clippings and theatre records show that she was back at the Herald Square Theatre in New York as early as October 1898. She was engaged to play the rollicking role of Flora the Circus Queen in an Americanized version of the French vaudeville operetta *Hotel Topsy Turvey*. The show played to full houses for twelve weeks, during which time Dressler suffered a painful accident during an athletic routine with her costar, Aubrey Boucicault. The actress was apparently thrown to the stage with such force that she injured her head and neck. Her understudy, Beatrice McKenzie, took over for a few performances, but true to her show-must-go-on image, Dressler insisted on returning to the play as soon as she could perform her athletic stunts without visibly wincing.

At thirty years of age, Dressler was in exuberant physical shape. She had learned to move with extraordinary grace and authority, with a gliding, effortless step that grabbed attention. She still had trouble keeping her two-hundred-odd pounds under control. The bicycle treks with Lillian Russell were now a thing of the past, but she made an effort to exercise in other ways, if only to facilitate her energetic routines on stage. In the fall of 1898, the *New York Telegraph* reported that she was thinking of organizing an athletic club for professional women in New York. Dressler had been attending a fashionable swimming school on Forty-Fifth Street with other female members of the *Topsy Turvey* company. Soon, however, the small Dressler group became a crowd. "Ladies from the Casino, from Weber & Fields, from Koster & Bial's and from other theatrical companies, joined in the push," reported the *Tele-*

graph. "Some of the society ladies who patronize the institution were shocked when they learned that the crowd headed by Miss Dressler was made up entirely of women who were identified with the stage and that some of them belonged to the chorus. . . . What practically amounted to a boycott was declared against them." Nothing ever came of the professional athletic club, though Dressler and the *Topsy Turvey* cast attracted considerable amounts of ink in the New York press for several days as officers, all of them drawn from the actress's closest group of friends, were ceremoniously chosen.

The swimming club incident highlighted the fact that Dressler was forging a love/hate relationship with the press. In the years to come, she would seldom refuse an interview, even though a study of these articles reveals that she often gave the same basic interview. And during her stage career she actively encouraged stories that smacked suspiciously of publicity stunts. Her friendly rapport with the journalistic establishment did backfire disastrously at times, but if there was any possibility of getting her name—and the name of her current show—into the newspapers, Dressler did her best to oblige. The swimming club story also signaled two important turning points in Dressler's relationship with the world around her. From then on, she lost no opportunity to publicize the fact that she yearned for a day when actors—particularly female members of her profession—would be accepted as respected members of society. And she herself began to fancy herself as a somewhat militant social arbiter—a fancy that eventually evolved into a full-blown yearning for personal recognition as a pillar of the social establishment.

Incidents from the late 1890s illustrate the twin persona of Dressler—the often vulgar clown and the would-be leader of social taste and behavior. An April 1899 report smacks of an outrageously contrived publicity plant and was prefaced by a short paragraph: "To whom it may concern: This is not a Marie Dressler press notice. To prove this contention, it is only necessary to add that the story is true." The report goes on to say that Dressler was eating a "light" lunch—porterhouse steak, broiled lobster, English chops, green peas, succotash, lyonnaise and french fried potatoes, mushrooms, sauerkraut, boiled onions, lettuce salad, brussels sprouts, charlotte russe, ladyfingers, macaroons, Roquefort cheese, crackers, café noir, nuts and raisins—at the Forty-Second Street dining room of the Hotel Metropole when her friend May Duryea entered in the company of actress Beula Coolidge. "What a great, coarse creature she is," remarked Miss Coolidge, well within Dressler's hearing. Duryea tried to quiet Coolidge by warning that her large friend was well versed in the art of self-defense, but the actress continued with the loud taunt. "She can't lick me, May, and I want her to know it." The report goes on: "Then, to the best of testimony, Miss Dressler swallowed a pound of rare steak, hastily gulped down a schoppen of best California claret, kicked aside her chair and approached the Coolidge table. 'Can't lick you, eh?' she is reported to have said, great firmness marking her utterance. 'Why, you little ill-mannered whippersnapper. Take that!' But Miss Coolidge was expecting the blow. Her guard was superb. She dodged the lunge and with a swift counter, caught Miss Dressler just above the solar plexus. This advantage she followed up with a neat swing on the jaw that left her larger opponent half dazed on the ropes. But Miss Dressler quickly recovered and rushing at Miss Coolidge, landed a stiff left hand punch on the point of the jaw. Then, still feeling somewhat groggy, she clinched." The rest of the piece informs us that May Duryea rushed to pull the opponents apart and that Dressler cried foul because she claimed Coolidge had fractured a rib of her corset. Apparently the head waiter also joined the act, and the two actresses were persuaded to leave the premises. So did it really happen? Neither Coolidge nor Dressler confirmed or denied the incident, but Duryea informed the breathless press that the boxing match did indeed take place and that she felt it ended in a draw. Nevertheless, the headline on the newspaper story read "Heavyweight Was Vanquished." Broadway buzzed over the tale for days.

Later that year Dressler drew more excited press comment when she and May Duryea appeared in a box at the New York Aerial Grove theatre accompanied by the actress's black maid, Jenny. "And they attracted nearly as much attention as the stage performance," one newspaper reported. "The sight of two women in a box accompanied by a maid is a novel one, even in New York. But when the maid has a heightened color and is invisible in a dark room and is also permitted to sip beverages, the sight becomes not only novel but unprecedented even in a community where the fifteenth amendment is highly regarded." The reporter seemed shocked that the maid was not only permitted refreshment but a part in the conversation as well. "Miss Dressler and Miss Duryea sat on each side of the box while the maid sat between them, well toward the front of the box. When the champagne, which Miss Dressler ordered, was passed around, the maid was also allowed to quench her thirst. When Miss Dressler made bright remarks, the maid laughed and when the conversation lagged the maid did all she could to keep it from dying out entirely by becoming enthusiastic over the stage performance." The story concluded with the sharp warning that, although New Yorkers were pretty liberal in their way of thinking, the actress had better not push her "love for the household picture of Abraham Lincoln striking the fetters from the wrists and ankles of the negro race" too far. One remark by the reporter seems to accurately depict much more than the theatre incident he was describing: "Miss Dressler did not seem in the least disconcerted over the attention she attracted."

5

ENTREPRENEURIAL SPIRIT

1900-1904

The turn of the century was a magical time on Broadway. The 1899-1900 season had offered eighty-seven theatrical productions, with no less than five openings on New Year's Eve alone. The new century's theatrical celebrities were such legendary thespians as Ada Rehan, John Drew, and the popular Maude Adams. Minnie Maddern Fiske was playing in Langdon Mitchell's *Becky Sharp* at the Fifth Avenue Theatre, and Lionel Barrymore was the star—and also the victim of atrocious reviews—of James A. Herne's *Sag Harbour.* The Spanish-American War had helped vitalize the national economy, and Americans were flush with cash again after the downturn of the mid-1990s. They gladly paid top prices to watch Julia Marlowe not only act marvelously but fire a rifle as well in Clyde Fitch's *Barbara Frietchie.* And over at the Metropolitan on Thirty-Ninth Street, opera enthusiasts were paying an astronomical five dollars a seat to hear such internationally acclaimed divas as Nellie Melba, Lillian Nordica, and Emma Calvé.

With lighter shows drawing sold-out audiences at New York's seven vaudeville and six burlesque houses that year, Dressler had little trouble finding good roles. In 1899 she scored a major success as Viola Alum in *The Man in the Moon,* a "spectacular fantasy in three acts and seven scenes" produced by the ever-supportive George Lederer at the New York Theatre. The critics were clearly impressed with the lavish show, which, according to reviewer Alan Dale, presented "masses of gorgeous scenery, large bands of variously-clad dancing girls and a group of clever players, including such established favorites as Miss Marie Dressler, Walter Jones and John E. Henshaw." Celebrity writer Ella Wheeler Wilcox was delighted to tell interviewers that she found the new play "gorgeous beyond description." But some caveats appeared in print, a few of them personally involving Dressler. "Miss Marie Dressler worked very hard in a number of parts that were devised to show her versatility," wrote Dale. "Among other feats was her ascent in the basket of a balloon from the stage to the flies, followed soon afterward by her descent. That must have taken some nerve, but otherwise it was not amusing. Miss Dressler, by the way, is always least amusing when she tries hardest."

There were some hints during the 192-performance run of *The Man in the Moon* that Dressler was growing uneasy. Clues to her professional restlessness had already surfaced during the first few months of the current run, when the actress had almost "escaped" the musical stage to become a dramatic actress. Her liberator was to have been legendary producer Augustin Daly, who managed John Drew, James Lewis, Mrs. G.H. Gilbert, and Ada Rehan. According to the story, which Dressler would never tire of telling in the years to come, Daly had approached her with the surprising suggestion that she become a regular alternate with Rehan, the reigning queen of drama. In other words, the producer was asking her to desert the comedy stage and become a tragedienne. Dressler later insisted that a contract was ready to be signed when fate intervened: Daly died in late 1899. "I still wonder what I would have been like if I played Ophelia in my younger days," Dressler said in a 1914 interview. "I might have been the greatest tragedienne the world has ever known. And then again, I might not have been."

Still apparently itching with restlessness, Dressler acquired a manager named Joseph Immerman in mid-1900. Then, in a somewhat reckless orgy of entrepreneurial activity, the two put together an independent company. This venture produced the need for cash, of course, and Dressler gaily borrowed a good deal of it from friends and business acquaintances. Her choice of plays was something called *Miss Prinnt,* a musical farce written by George V. Hobart with music composed by her friend John L. Golden. The story involved a woman newspaper publisher (played by Dressler) who got herself into comical difficulties with an entire town. The show previewed in Albany and Boston and opened at the Columbia Theatre in New York City in late 1900. Alan Dale's review sums up the general critical reaction to the venture: "Whoever dished up for her such a ghastly collection of decayed jokes, taphouse slang, meaningless music and direly trashy story must have owed a deadly grudge." He did concede, however, "I should say that *Miss Prinnt* might be a good thing with everything eliminated except Miss Dressler."

This failed exercise in independence hurt Dressler. So badly, in fact, that she ignored specific details of the show in her autobiographies and never alluded to it in any future interviews. Not long after *Miss Prinnt* folded on tour in Philadelphia, Dressler filed for voluntary bankruptcy to escape her string of creditors, admitting that she owed twelve thousand dollars and, according to a press report at the time, "has for assets only a few of last summer's hats and some of an even earlier vintage." Among her creditors were such individuals as Leander Sire the producer, for the borrowed sum of nine hundred dollars; her lawyer Emanuel Friend, for one thousand dollars; and her longtime colleague from the Road, May Montford (by then married to producer John Golden), who had sympathetically loaned Dressler five hundred dollars. A Broadway tailor, E.F. Morrison, was owed three hundred dollars and had the distinction of being the only creditor to object when a United States District Court commissioner in bankruptcy discharged the actress from her obligations in July 1901.

It is difficult to know whether Dressler's unflattering joust with insolvency affected her relationship with the top Broadway producers. In any case, there was some tut-tutting along the Great White Way when it was announced that the actress was joining the Sire Brothers management team. Leander Sire had already ingratiated himself with Dressler by forking over the nine hundred dollars to help launch the ill-fated *Miss Prinnt* venture. But as everyone in New York's theatrical community knew, the Sires were an impetuous pair of speculators who would bet on any dark horse yet actively resist the realities of meeting a legitimate payroll.

The Sires came to an agreement with Dressler to stage a musical play called *The King's Carnival*. Dressler would play the lead role of Queen Anne, and the brothers agreed the pay the comedienne the large sum of twenty-five thousand dollars for a season at the New York Theatre. They sweetened their offer by putting to-

gether a first-class supporting cast, including well-known thespians Dan McAvoy, Amelia Summerville (who played the Infanta and
was rocked by Dressler in a huge cradle), and Maybelle Gilman.
The show itself drew good houses during the blisteringly hot summer of 1901, but theatrical historians remember it chiefly for
Dressler's lusty rendition of "Ragtime Will Be My Finish," written
by her friend George Hobart, and a spectacularly daring fall by
the actress, Louis Harrison, and Dan McAvoy. "I suggested that
we dance backward to three throne chairs, sit in them and then
disappear, heels over head," Dressler recalled years later. "Both men
objected. 'All right, I'll fall,' I said, and of course they would not
let me get away with this alone, so they had to fall too. Not knowing the technique of stage falls, they hurt themselves every night
and only the roars of laughter we evoked kept them at the task."

Dressler never revealed whether the Sire Brothers actually paid
her the promised twenty-five thousand dollars, but it was reported
in late 1901 that she was negotiating for the purchase of a hotel in
Saratoga, New York, owned by a local personality called "Kid"
McCoy. This was to be Dressler's first of many nibbles at the possibilities of hotel management. "But," reported a *Billboard* story,
"after reviewing the situation, Miss Dressler found the property
so badly involved that she instructed her attorney not to touch it.
However, she has her own ideas about running a hotel and says
she will yet conduct one."

An incident during that summer of 1901 seems to confirm
Dressler's growing militancy as a champion of the underdog and
people of color. During the run of *The King's Carnival,* the actress
had a heated confrontation with Florence Crosby, who played the
Duchess of Jaloa. Crosby apparently insulted a black laundress
named Josephine who had come to the theatre asking for payment
of a bill. Dressler overheard the exchange and threatened to leave
the cast if the Sires did not dismiss Crosby immediately. Not only
that, Dressler summoned a policeman and asked him to take Crosby
into custody upon the complaint of the colored woman in the case.
The policeman declined, but Henry and Leander Sire did dismiss
Florence Crosby. "Miss Crosby has left her apartment at the Parker
House," reported a New York newspaper, "and it is not known
whither she has gone. Miss Dressler was seeking cool breezes last
night at her home in Bayside, Long Island."

Bayside was still Dressler's refuge from the often-frustrating job of maintaining a high profile on Broadway. Sister Bonita and her husband, Richard Ganthony, had sailed for greener pastures in London in late 1899, and Dressler had taken over their fully furnished flat at the Louella Apartments on Forty-Fifth Street. The apartment was just around the corner from the New York Theatre, an arrangement that the actress found highly convenient. But as soon as possible on Sundays, Dressler hightailed it to Long Island to visit her "darlings," as she insisted on calling her parents. Requests by reporters for any information about her father invariably resulted in the production of a portrait and the smiling comment that, yes, he did look a lot like the late Emperor William I, didn't he? One article written by a local reporter contained the curious and obviously manufactured story that her father was aware that as a child she was fascinated with individuals who owned glass eyes or "other jewelry in the face." But, she told the writer, apparently with a straight face, her father's only thought was to make her happy, so he found a California-based relative who sported a wooden leg and invited him to visit. "When Uncle Reginald arrived and our haughty neighbors saw his wooden leg, they were stumped," she said.

But Dressler preferred chatting about her mother's horse, a big bay called Teddy Roosevelt, which she insisted she rode every weekend at Bayside. And her dogs, a prize bull terrier, a Russian poodle, a pet fox terrier, and a collie, attracted gallons of ink. In 1901, she admitted to spending as much time as possible at the Sheepshead Bay races. When asked about her favorite pastimes, she told a reporter that "I like to eat meals and wear clothes and listen to papa play the piano." She also confessed that she enjoyed sewing, and, in fact, Dressler's penchant for making her own clothes would become famous over the years—particularly as her self-made creations became progressively more bizarre.

Observers along the Great White Way were mildly astonished during the winter of 1901-2 that Dressler was sticking with the often unpredictable Sire Brothers. But because of the actress's increasing confidence in herself as a leading lady, it is possible that she cowed the pair into meeting her demands, even to providing better conditions for the show's chorus girls—a cause she would take up in earnest sixteen years later during the Actor's Equity

Strike. Wrote one Broadway reporter of Dressler's complaints about the treatment of minor female cast members: "Miss Dressler depreciates the miscellaneous pulling and hauling and kissing, fondling, cuddling and slobbering over which the average stage manager of comic opera and extravaganza regards as among his rightful perquisites."

In any case, the actress was sufficiently comfortable with the Sires to sign up for a February 1902 production of *The Hall of Fame,* written by George Hobart, Sydney Rosenfeld, and A. Baldwin Sloane. Dressler played the leading role of Lady Oblivion, and Amelia Summerville was cast as the Goddess Fame. Louis Harrison played a fame-starved actor who was told there would be no real glory for him until after his death, after which he announces he will go over Niagara Falls in a barrel; when the barrel is eventually found to be empty, he is taken for dead and immediately achieves the fame that had eluded him. Dressler performed her usual on-stage pratfalls, cartwheels, and other bits of athletic business and also sang the hit tunes "When Charlie Plays the Slide Trombone" and "My Pajama Beauty." She and well known actor-comedian Sam Bernard stopped the show every night with a hilarious, ad-libbed sketch that soon stretched from a scheduled two minutes to more than twenty. *The Hall of Fame* earned mixed reviews. One critic complained, "The Sire Brothers have spent money, in short, and have secured in return almost everything except genuine fun. If Marie Dressler hadn't been on hand last night to unbosom herself to her audience in a heart-to-heart talk now and then, the proceedings would have frequently proved funereal."

The show lingered at the New York Theatre for a month or so, then the producers began rehearsing *King Highball,* a play about an astronomer who communicates with Mars and finally manages to visit the planet. Here again, the critics were underwhelmed. "Frederick Bowers' score was as undistinguished as Charles Horwitz's dialogue," wrote one reviewer. "The most rewarding moments of the evening probably came when the star, Marie Dressler, displayed her rambunctious brand of clowning." *King Highball* opened at the New York Theatre in June of 1902 and enjoyed only a brief stay.

By this time, however, the Sires had clearly run out of both money and patience with the fickle audiences of Broadway. No new production was announced, so Dressler, with typical good humor, asked her manager Joe Immerman to find her some work. He immediately signed her with producer/author Elmer Rice to appear at his Sunday concerts at the New York Theatre, and she also began accepting out-of-town dates on the burlesque circuit.

After an appearance in Detroit during the fall of 1902, Dressler complained of fatigue and canceled engagements so she could rest at the Long Island farm. She seemed to be recovering her strength and was about to summon her manager for a strategy session when she became violently ill. She was diagnosed with typhoid fever, probably a hangover from a serious epidemic that had killed seven individuals in Bayside that summer. Dressler rallied after a week or so, however, and despite the warnings of her local physician, decided to honor a commitment to perform at the Metropolitan Opera House at a benefit for the State Railway Association. According to an October 5 report, she sang two songs, delivered a recitation, then fainted in the wings. Two evenings later, she turned up in the audience at the New York Theatre "looking very much like herself." Broadway colleagues crowded around her during the intermission to hear her declare with familiar Dressler bravado, "So they have me down with typhoid, eh? Well, I'm just about the sauciest, liveliest case of typhoid fever you ever saw. . . . I don't remember ever having felt spryer in my life." But a few days later, after a typically vigorous performance at the Orpheum Theatre in Brooklyn, Dressler fainted again. This time, an alarmed Joe Immerman engaged a nurse to accompany the actress during her trips between the theatre and her flat on Forty-Fifth Street. On the way across the Brooklyn Bridge, she became delirious and tried to leave the vehicle and leap into the river. Immerman and the nurse struggled to restrain her, and she seemed to be calmer by the time she reached home. But she insisted on returning to the Orpheum the next evening, after which she once more became delirious on her way back to Manhattan. That Sunday, Dressler finally collapsed with a dangerous temperature of 105 degrees.

The actress was close to death in October and November 1902. Immerman kept the newspapers informed of her condition, which progressively grew from serious to extremely grave. Even if Dressler recovered from the illness, Immerman told reporters, it would probably be weeks or even months before she could reappear on stage. Her physician, Dr. Henry Frauenthal, was so certain that Dressler's condition was terminal that he sent messages to Bayside urging her parents to come to Forty-Fifth Street as soon as possible. Her father made the trip, but her mother, whom Dressler repeatedly asked for during her illness, was unable to travel because of a recurring heart problem. On November 19, Dr. Frauenthal issued a bulletin to the effect that Marie Dressler had only a few days to live. Of course, Dressler miraculously survived, although it was well into 1903 before she was well enough to return to the stage. The real tragedy of the episode was that Anna Koerber died in Bayside on December 7 at the age of seventy-four while her daughter was still struggling for her own life. Dressler was not told of her mother's death until weeks later, although she always insisted that she had hallucinated about "the boarded-up house in Bayside" and her mother "lying under a sheet."

Dressler's weight dropped from 210 to 130 pounds during her illness, and she lost her luxuriant, reddish-brown hair—shaved on orders from her doctor. When Immerman released the news of the shearing, a number of New York wigmakers asked to buy the tresses. Dressler finally sold them for $125. She was aware, though, that her hair would need to grow back as healthy as ever if she was to regain and retain her stage image, so she engaged an expert to call at the Louella each morning and work on her scalp. As one Broadway gossip columnist put it: "Under this careful attention, the mass of wavy locks are gradually reappearing and by the time Miss Dressler is able to leave her bed, there is little doubt that she will have enough to make a very respectable switch on the top of her head." In the meantime, Dressler's friends on Broadway were showing their shock and concern for the actress. The story of her mother's death combined with her own close encounter with the grim reaper made the front pages in all of the New York dailies, and Jenny, Dressler's maid, was kept busy at the apartment door, accepting gifts of flowers and food. Joe Immerman was besieged with a wide variety of kind offers from people willing to act as couriers, sitters, and delivery personnel.

In December a sympathetic theatrical community decided to stage a testimonial benefit for their favorite clown. The idea was announced at the Metropole Hotel by producer Charles J. Ross, who immediately subscribed one hundred dollars for two seats "to help fill the biggest theatre in town." The testimonial itself was held later that month at the Victoria Theatre—scarcely the most spacious house in town—and netted the handsome sum of eight thousand dollars. The response from Dressler's theatrical colleagues was overwhelming; comedian Sam Bernard acted as stage manager, and such headliners as Eddie Foy, Dan McAvoy, George Fuller Golden, and Bernard himself appeared in the show. Actress Edna Wallace Hopper presented her hit song, "Four and Twenty Little Men," in which she was assisted by two dozen chorus "boys and girls." Fay Templeton appeared with members of her own chorus and, according to one report, sang "some of the coon songs she has helped to make famous" and presented some of her imitations. The legendary Dan Daly telegraphed Bernard that, as his show *The New Clown* would be in New York during the week of the benefit, he and his entire company could be depended upon for anything the stage manager might ask. The theatre was packed for the performance.

Dressler was moved and flattered by the magnanimous gesture; perhaps Joe Immerman did not show her a sour *New York Telegraph* editorial that ran early in January. "Now that it is all over and that poor decimated Marie Dressler is richer by some eight thousand dollars than she was the day before yesterday, it is not impertinent to wonder why she should be in need, anyway," wrote the editorialist. "To be sure she has had a long, painful and expensive illness. Yet this actress has been enjoying for years very lucrative engagements. She was with the Sires all last season at a very high salary—something between five and seven hundred a week. She got seven hundred from Rice this season and one thousand a week in vaudeville after *King Highball* broke up and just before her illness. With such an income as this it seems strange that all at once she should be discovered to be destitute and need the balm of a benefit. Nobody begrudges her the money. Heaven knows she is welcome to it, but the thought simply suggests itself, how is it these children of the stage get away with such a plenty?"

Dressler continued with her recuperation during the first few months of 1903, then Joe Immerman booked her into a few limited vaudeville engagements in May and June. Her hair was growing in well, and she even decided to use the well publicized shearing as part of her act. Dressler's cousin, Moss MacWhirter, recalled that "on her return to Broadway, her public were so delighted to have her back that they applauded and applauded until she could do no more, so she took off her wig and stood there. From all accounts, the women cried and men threw their hats in the air."

Joe Immerman was spreading the word among producers that Dressler would take a vacation during the summer, then be available for vaudeville engagements in the fall. During the summer, she made a brief trip to Canada, most likely in the company of her father, and she also pondered the disposition of the Bayside property. The farm had painful memories for her, and she eventually decided to sell it and buy a small house in the relatively rural environs of Elmhurst, Long Island, where Irish comedian John T. Kelly had established an actors' colony. Apparently she was getting along much better with her father, for once the new property was habitable, she invited him to live there as housekeeper/sitter while she was working in Manhattan.

By fall, Elmhurst had been discovered by many other Broadway luminaries, and Sundays became a slightly lunatic salon of actors, producers, songwriters, and dancers. Tony Pastor became a resident, and so did Dressler's longtime colleague, Georgie Caine. Librettist Edgar Smith, comedians John and James Russell, and vaudevillian Lew Dockstader also bought properties in the colony. On weekends the place was overrun with a large assortment of dogs and children. A feature writer from the *World* interviewed Dressler at one Elmhurst gathering, asking, "What do you do out here to pass the time?" Dressler replied: "Oh, we don't. The time just passes us. We lead the simple, unwholesome lives of vaudeville farmers. Up at 11 o'clock in the morning, watering the milk and cutting jokes out of the Sunday newspapers. Then we have to feed the dogs and watch out that our own individual pet pups don't get the worst of the fighting. Bowling, poker, parties, conversations . . ." And, the writer added, "that kindly old gentleman, Mr. Koerber, Marie's father, is very handy with the highball ingredients and impromptu wiener-schnitzel feasts."

Odds and ends of vaudeville appearances kept Dressler busy during the remainder of 1903, and in March of 1904 she played the Belasco Theatre in *Sweet Kittie Swellairs,* a weak "travesty" of a current comedy called *Sweet Kitty Bellairs* starring Henrietta Crosman and produced by J. Cheever Goodwin. "Why is Marie

Dressler wasting her ability in such an offering?" mourned Robert Spleare in a *New York Telegraph* review. "*Sweet Kittie Swellairs* misses its aim in every particular."

Despite this unpromising return to the stage, Dressler was exulting in the fact that her health had improved, she was putting on weight, and she was beginning to feel herself again. A few producers, in and out of New York, were feeding Joe Immerman with ideas for possible shows, but the actress felt she needed a radical change to celebrate her escape from certain oblivion. And, although she had been earning fair-enough paychecks on the vaudeville circuit, she wondered if she could pull off some entrepreneurial trick to inject more cash into her bank account. In April, even her best friends were surprised to learn that Dressler had bought a Coney Island "Dreamland" concession that included a peanut stand. "When this amazing bit of news trickled along Broadway yesterday," read one New York report, "its effect was like that of an absinthe frappe. Four theatrical managers eagerly sought interviews with Miss Dressler, three composers simultaneously began to ponder the peanut motive for a new musical comedy, 400 actresses out of work started to negotiate with dealers in confectionery, lead pencils and bananas and most important of all, a slight rise in the price of peanuts per hundred pounds was reported in the wholesale district." Dressler's "peanut adventure" has been written about and chewed over by many writers, including Adela Rogers St. John who even suggested that the actress sold peanuts on the Coney Island boardwalk just to make ends meet. The truth is, however, that Dressler poured a respectable amount of capital into the Dreamland concession and might well have retired from the stage if she had managed to make her fortune from the enterprise. In one interview that April, in fact, Dressler is quoted as saying, somewhat sourly, "I haven't been happy in my professional work since I stopped carrying my grip from town to town as a chorus girl."

Curious thespians as well as reporters with cameras at the ready descended on Coney Island that summer to see for themselves what Dressler was doing on the boardwalk. Peanuts, yes—presented in fetching, pink-striped bags with "Marie Dressler Peanuts" printed on them in bright red, sold by forty boys in smart uniforms with "Marie Dressler" inscribed on their caps. Dressler herself appeared at various times as "sort of high priestess of

Arachia Hypogaen, in robes of state and dignity, collecting the tribute of the goober devotees with a benevolent smile and fine dulcet manner of Lady Bountiful," as Mlle. Manhattan of *New York Sunday* wrote with overwrought relish. But, as the trusty fifth estate gleefully reported, there were more than peanut vendors at Dressler's concession. She served tea in a Chinese eating emporium. She offered glasses of "pure water" at a special booth. And patrons could win a prize at her "Rough House" if they broke three panes of glass with a wooden ball. There was also a popcorn stand, the occasional appearance of a large parrot owned by Dressler, and—incredibly—a tiny baby that Dressler implacably advertised as weighing only sixteen ounces, even though pictures of the child seem to show that it was of normal size. The infant was the occasional tenant of a newfangled technological contraption called an incubator.

Dressler did not make a fortune at Coney Island. As a matter of fact, she was sued by the Puritan Company for a balance of one hundred dollars, alleged to be due on a bill for more than a thousand gallons of pure mineral water that had been delivered to the booth at Dreamland. "Miss Dressler's perennial vivacity has long been the admiration of her friends and now they are asking if she has discovered a secret in mineral water," joked one New York writer. "The Coney Island season is less than 150 days in length and it seems incredible that the actress could drink a thousand gallons in that time."

And, then, by the end of the hot New York summer, Dressler had moved on again—this time to a new stage of her career at the Weber Music Hall.

6

THEATRICAL ARISTOCRAT

1904-1907

If you wanted to enjoy an evening of light entertainment on Broadway in 1904, you had a multiplicity of choices. But the best bets were Proctor's Palace at Twenty-Third Street, Tony Pastor's Music Hall on Fourteenth Street, Keith's at Thirty-Fourth Street, and the Weber and Fields Music Hall on Twenty-Ninth. At these theatrical emporia, you could hear the top popular vocalists and comedians of the day. And there were also the choruses—squads of attractive young men and gorgeous young women who danced their way through lavishly produced musical extravaganzas. The eight-hundred-seat Weber and Fields Music Hall was very much in the news that year. Joe Weber and Lew Fields had been comedy/management partners since 1896, but after the successful run of *Whoop-Dee-Do,* their 1903-4 offering, the team had decided to split. Weber opted to spend money on renovations, mainly to satisfy new fire regulations, and to keep the music hall open. After all, his audience was assured: Weber and Fields was where the rakes went to ogle female legs (known as Frankie Baileys in those days, in honor of the actress with the most stunning extremities in town) and to enjoy such entertainers as Lillian Russell, Sam Bernard, and Peter F. Dailey—not to mention Joe (the short, fat one) and Lew (the tall, skinny one) themselves, easily the funniest men in show business. Joe Weber also reasoned that the Music Hall had become a favorite meeting place for society's glittering "Four Hundred" upper-crust notables: at intermission on any performance night, you could glimpse the Vanderbilts, the Astors, the Goulds, the

Stuyvesant Fishes, the Belmonts, and the Roosevelts strolling the broad promenade behind the mezzanine boxes.

Marie Dressler was an ideal candidate for Weber's new company. At thirty-six—in spite of some recent lackluster years—she had established herself as one of the most accomplished comics on Broadway, an unabashed ham in her broad approach to humor, and unfailingly determined to coax—even command—an audience to respond. The way the oversized, bulldog-faced Dressler stole the show from other headliners was legendary: A mere grimace, even when another performer was emoting, would send an audience into obedient hysterics. Her acrobatic comedy technique—"bumping into scenery, knocking over things, crashing about like a bull in a china shop," as she herself described it—raised an excited expectancy every time she appeared on stage. And audiences also expected Dressler to improvise and communicate. She was as likely to engage in informal conversation with patrons in the front rows as she was to deliver her written lines. And Weber also knew that Dressler had become a personal favorite of the social establishment—principally the acknowledged leader of the Four Hundred, Mrs. Mamie Stuyvesant Fish, who had "adopted" Marie after the actress had cheekily chucked a basket of onions—or was it actually fish as some gossips insisted?—at the socialite's head during a performance at Proctor's.

Weber offered Dressler a leading role in his 1904-5 Broadway show, *Higgeldy Piggeldy,* a production with book and lyrics by Edgar Smith and music by Maurice Levi. The actress and the manager agreed to a fifty-thousand-dollar, three-year contract. The now solo entrepreneur also decided to bring a young Florenz Ziegfeld Jr. in on the action, partly because he felt in need of some professional support and partly because he could sign up Ziegfeld's stunning common-law wife, Anna Held, as a member of the company. He also signed Charles Bigelow, the handsome Aubrey Boucicault, and romantic actress Bonnie Magin. Well known comedian Barry Morris was picked to play opposite Weber in the "Dutch" or German-Jewish duo act that had once included Lew Fields.

Dressler immediately dominated the stage as Philopoena Schnitz, daughter of Adolph Schnitz (played by Weber), a wealthy mustard manufacturer. She proudly wore a monstrous diamond pickle on her breast to prove she was indeed an heiress and regularly brought down the house with her uproarious rendition of "A Great Big Girl Like Me," a song that would become a lasting favorite in her repertoire. Reviews of *Higgeldy Piggeldy* were unanimous in announcing that Marie Dressler walked away with the show, even though Weber had played politics with Ziegfeld by placing Anna Held's name above Dressler's on the billboards. The *New York Mail*'s critic complained: "Miss Anna Held was announced as the star of this performance. In all her theatrical career she never was more tiresome than she was last night. Her whole theatrical equipment appears to be a libidinous smirk and the tedious refrain 'Won't you come and play with me?' Actually, at this day, Miss Anna Held could find nothing newer than that!" Anna Held would stay with the play for several months before deciding to leave the company; Ziegfeld left Weber in February 1905.

Despite the somewhat vapid presence of Anna Held, however, *Higgeldy Piggeldy* played the Music Hall for 185 performances, including a matinee that Dressler would never forget. At one point in the show, Joe Weber and a friend are about to be pushed over a rocky precipice in Switzerland by some angry mountaineers when the Dressler voice pounds out:

> I pray you spare my father
> Ye hardy mountaineers
> Ah! Let your hearts be tender;
> and heed a daughter's tears
> I know you will not send them
> to meet a fate so sad
> When I have told you he's the only
> Pa I ever had!

At this point, where the audience usually exploded with laughter, "a little white-haired man with good-natured whiskers and an expression of amusement . . . arose from his seat in the third row," as one reporter told it. "Trembling with emotion he said quietly, but distinctly enough for the audience to hear: 'How about me, Marie? Where do I come in?' 'Father,' whispered Miss Dressler. 'Your own?' asked Weber quickly. 'Yes,' said Miss Dressler." All action was suspended for a moment. "The orchestra had stopped playing, for the chorus did nothing but look aghast at Miss Dressler.

Then did the instinct of the manager and seasoned actor enable Weber to save the day. He waddled down to the footlights and leaning over the head of Maurice Levi, the conductor, shook his finger at the earnest old man in the audience and said: 'I giff her to you, olt man, right after der performance. She's more den I can menach.'"

Higgledy Piggledy toured Philadelphia, Chicago, and Cleveland during the first few months of 1905, earning rave reviews for Dressler and for a new burlesque called "The College Widower" that Weber shoehorned into the show. This bit of inspired nonsense introduced a football match between a male and a female team, with Dressler strutting the stage as a gigantic football heroine. And Maurice Levi's songs for the show were becoming the hits of the day. "*Higgledy Piggledy* with such big hits as 'Game of Love,' 'Nancy Clancy,' 'Big Indian and His Little Maid,' etc. created a sensation in Philadelphia the past week," reported a local paper in April 1905. "Between the first and second acts of the production at the Garrick Theatre, Maurice Levi, composer of the music and musical director of the company, was compelled to wave his baton with the audience whistling 'The Game of Love' without orchestra accompaniment."

Despite her current success, however, Dressler was again experiencing familiar hot flashes of entrepreneurial fever. In Cleveland that spring, she and Joe Immerman toured a new local amusement park called White City on the Lake. She soon announced that she had signed a contract to bring her Coney Island attractions to Ohio in the summer. Not only that, she had decided to lease the bump-the-bumps concession at White City. "Because," she explained, apparently with a straight face, "it appeals to me. It is a comedy hit of the most ludicrous sort. It is a series of gradually rounded bumps on an inclined plane, down which men and women slide to their own great exhilaration and the intense amusement of the spectators. Grave and dignified statesmen and men eminent in professional and commercial life mingle in the most democratic manner with snub-nosed urchins and ladies of the social set." When reporters snickered, Dressler retorted that she had seen Governor Odell of New York, accompanied by the secretary of the United States Senate, two judges of the federal bench, and a couple of congressmen sliding merrily down the bumps at Coney Island's

Dreamland. The story was printed in Cleveland without comment. The Dressler concession at White City opened in May 1905. Joe Immerman had been co-opted to work as manager of the enterprise, but Dressler turned up as often as she could—minus the peanuts and the popcorn that had made headlines at Coney Island, but still exhibiting a small and suspiciously anonymous baby in an incubator. In mid-summer, though, when the Broadway theatre was snoozing through its summer siesta, there was a report that the actress had been spotted in London. This was coupled with gossip that the well known British theatrical manager, George Edwardes—the Guv'nor himself—had seen *Higgeldy Piggeldy* on a visit to New York and had pronounced Dressler one of the finest performers currently gracing the stage. This snippet of news may or may not have been a surprise to Joe Weber, but he quickly announced that the fall season opening date of Weber's Music Hall, with a re-run of *Higgeldy Piggeldy* and "The College Widower," would be postponed for a few days—at least until Dressler arrived back in New York on the steamship *Minnesota* on August 28. Dressler made this first trip abroad with her longtime friend, May Montford. The women booked a modest double cabin on the *Minnesota,* but Dressler always enjoyed telling the story that after her identity became known to the purser, she and May were moved to the bridal suite, courtesy of the White Star Line.

It seems a reasonable assumption that Dressler's visit to London had rattled Weber considerably. In an effort to ingratiate himself with his star, the comedian/manager commissioned an ocean-going tug, draped it with bunting, hired a brass band, and invited as many of Dressler's friends as possible to sail out to meet the *Minnesota* in New York harbor. "The reception committee acted with proper decorum when the tug came near the big steamship," reported the *New York Mail.* "The band that accompanied the Weberites played the *Higgledy Piggledy* overture and 'We Cert'nly Have Missed You, Honey'. . . . Maurice Levi played a cornet solo and the soldiers stationed at Governor's Island mistook the popping of corks for a bombardment and manned the guns." Dressler was apparently hustled to Weber's Music Hall in a cab and immediately went through a rehearsal of the show. She was found to be, according to the *Mail,* "letter perfect."

For a time, Dressler seemed content to bask in the glow of

her growing celebrity on Broadway. She had even made some money with her bump-the-bumps concession at White City that year. When Joe Weber asked her to headline his newest musical offering, *Twiddle Twaddle,* scheduled to open on New Year's night, 1906, after a tryout in Rochester, she cheerfully accepted. The show, Weber assured her, would be lavishly produced: book again by the successful Edgar Smith, score by Maurice Levi, and legions of expensively outfitted chorus girls, flower girls, Vienna coquettes, "and every other kind of pretty young woman who could sing, dance and wear good-looking clothes." Charles Bigelow and Bonnie Magin were rehired, and Weber also signed the up-and-coming actress Trixie Friganza and Dressler's friend May Montford. Reported the *New York Post* after opening night: "It was a great, gay and gorgeous affair. . . . the same glut of cabs interfered with street cars out on Broadway, the little lobby was full of orchids, roses, hyacinth horseshoes and gaily decorated young orange trees—it was a Weber and Fields opening, with Fields alone absent. In the boxes and orchestra chairs and in the corridors to the right and rear, the same old crowd was packed. Somehow it has become a sort of event in the New York theatre season—this opening of our littlest theatre—and the same faces are always there." Some of the faces at the big opening included many of Dressler's society friends, who adoringly showered the actress with flowers from their stage boxes. Dressler was clearly flattered by the upscale attention. The Weber Music Hall years, in fact, marked the emergence of Dressler's somewhat schizophrenic "grand dame" persona, which had probably been germinating since 1897 when she vacationed on Lake George, New York, after a season with *The Lady Slavey.* According to the story, the guests at the Marion House where she stayed that year would have nothing to do with a "common" actress until she accidentally struck up a friendship with another vacationer, Mrs. Ulysses S. Grant, widow of the eighteenth president of the United States. The dramatic change in attitude because of her new aura of upper-crust respectability made such an impression on Dressler that she never hesitated to tell the story whenever an interviewer asked for some details of her early life. Dressler not only retained her friendship with Mrs. Grant, she suggested that she build a summer home in her birthplace, Cobourg, Ontario, and the former first lady took her advice and built The Hill, an estate that was eventually inherited by her daughter, Mrs. Nellie Grant Sartoris.

Mrs. Stuyvesant Fish, however, really opened the doors of the social establishment to Dressler. In the first months of the friendship, New York's arrogant, fabulously wealthy leader of the Four Hundred—who openly adored Music Hall fare because of her aversion to operas and classical musicales—showed her affection for the actress by inviting her to champagne parties in her box at the theatre. Soon she was asking Dressler if she would come to her home, initially to entertain her guests after dinner, but then to sit at her table as well. Dressler had made a point of learning about Mrs. Fish's likes and dislikes and soon knew that the hostess abhorred the stuffy and the dull. Deciding to take a chance at an early point in the relationship, the actress once borrowed a tray from a waiter and coasted down the Fish staircase on her ample stomach. The hostess was delighted with the outrageous stunt, and after Dressler's postprandial performance, gave her a gold mesh bag containing a one hundred dollar bill. On another occasion, Mrs. Fish presented the actress with a jeweled bracelet. "Here, Marie," Dressler remembered the socialite saying as she took the expensive bauble from her wrist, "I'm tired of this thing. You wear it."

Dressler's acceptance by Mrs. Stuyvesant Fish led to recognition by hostesses such as Mrs. William R. Travers and Mrs. George Gay Griswold. She received invitations to drive in Central Park with such famous "whips" as Alfred Vanderbilt, "Fatty" Bates, and James Hazen Hyde. For years, she dined out on the story that Mrs. Fish once called for her in one of the first luxury automobiles to be seen in New York and encouraged her to wave regally to her fans along Fifth Avenue.

It is possible, in fact, that this beguiling attention gave Dressler the idea that a theatrical aristocrat such as herself might do very well in the truly gilt-edged environs of London's West End. She was still corresponding with George Edwardes, who continued to be encouraging about the possibility of the actress joining one of his theatrical companies. Then, discounting the incredible success of *Twiddle Twaddle,* and its accompanying burlesque "The Squaw Man's Girl of the Golden West," as well as the flattering adulation of New York's social elite, she dispatched Joe Immerman to England in March 1906 to test the managerial pulse. When reporters asked for a statement, Dressler smiled vaguely and replied: "Maybe I can stay in London forever and live on Easy Street. I mean to stay in London, anyway, with little flyers to Paris and Berlin rather than Broadway and tours on the road."

Naturally, all of this came as somewhat of a shock to Joe Weber, who reminded Dressler that his contract with her was good until May 1, 1907. The actress shrugged when the manager read her the riot act. She also shrugged when, in May that year, White City in Cleveland burned to the ground, taking the bump-the-bumps concession with it. Joe Immerman, who had recently returned from England, was slightly hurt when he jumped to escape the flames. "Yes, I've just heard about it," Dressler said when a reporter brought her the news. "I received a telegram from Mr. Immerman, my manager, and he said we were losers. We had $67,000 worth of stock in White City and I don't know whether there was any insurance. He attended to that." According to the journalist, "Miss Dressler did not seem to be worrying much." Still smiling vaguely, she said: "My dear, I have been getting it in the neck so much lately, that I am used to it. There's no use crying over spilled milk."

Dressler was certainly getting it in the neck that spring of 1906—both from Joe Weber, who continued to remonstrate with her, and from the theatrical press. When the threatened defection to London reached the ears of Rennold Wolf, a writer with the *New York Telegraph,* he immediately complained: "Why is it that playerfolk the moment they attain success, lose their equilibrium and topple over under the weight of an exaggerated cranial development? Marie Dressler, beyond doubt the most amusing woman on the American stage is, according to her own declarations, about to surrender a large share of her popularity by leaving Joe Weber in the lurch and pinning her pulsating young being to the cohorts of George Edwardes in London. She mentions May 26 as the date of her positively last appearance with the stock company." Wolf was even tougher—and perhaps unfair—in his assessment of Dressler's career prior to the Weber Music Hall contract: "Two years ago when Mr. Weber did her the honor of offering her the position she now holds, he was the only prominent manager in New York who believed her deserving of the hire she demanded. After the burlesques at the New York Theatre were abandoned,

Miss Dressler was a rudderless canal boat adrift on the placid waters of inaction." The writer predicted that once Dressler was in London, George Edwardes would probably review her obligations to Weber and be "guided by the rules of ethics." Dressler ignored the public and professional scoldings, gave some expensive farewell parties, then sailed for England. Weber threw up his hands, hired actress Stella Mayhew to take Dressler's place, then instructed his lawyers to prepare a packet of information for George Edwardes's perusal, to be sent posthaste to London. The documents proved, in effect, that Dressler was breaking a bona fide contract and that Weber expected the British manager to respond as a gentleman should.

Once in England, Dressler made an appointment to see Edwardes at his Daly's Theatre headquarters in Leicester Square. It was a week or so before the Guv'nor could accommodate her, but the actress spent the time in an orgy of excited sightseeing in London—shopping for perfume at Rimmel's ("The Scenter of the Strand"), lunching on steak pudding and oysters at Gow's, and perusing the theatrical press for the latest news of such West End idols as her old *Waldemar* friend Haydin Coffin, Matheson Lang, and Maude Adams, and possible productions in the works by legendary managers such as Edwardes, Charles Frohman, and Sir Oswald Stoll. By the time Dressler was finally ushered into Edwardes's office, she was on an exhilarated high, imagining the Great Man offering her leads at the Gaiety, the Prince of Wales's, or one of the other theatres he controlled. In fact, the walrus-mustached Edwardes was kindly, courteous, even flattering, but he lost no time in confronting Dressler with Weber's complaint of contract violations. The actress almost choked with shock and surprise. At one point, she countered that the New York manager had actually broken the agreement himself "in some other particulars," but her countercharges were so insubstantial that she knew she was beginning to sound ridiculous. Edwardes tried to keep the proceedings as friendly as possible, but he was adamant in telling the disappointed actress that there was no work for her in his organization. He gallantly hoped she would have a pleasant stay in England.

Dressler brooded over the depressing turn of events for several days, then sensibly recovered enough to take in some plays and to visit her sister and her husband in Surrey. In a somewhat rebellious gesture, however, she took time to look into suitable sites for a future home in England, settling on Maidenhead on the Thames as a perfect spot. Then, gritting her teeth, she wrote a contrite letter to Joe Weber, offering to sail for New York in August. Weber himself swallowed his anger and promptly wrote back, suggesting she join the company in Chicago for a tour with *Twiddle Twaddle*. (At that time, he decided not tell the absconder that the Mayhew switch had been a disaster and that he had been forced to close the show a week after Dressler had sailed.)

If there were any hard feelings between Dressler and Weber after her return from England, they were not evident on stage. The actress set about reinventing and sharpening the role of Matilda Grabfelder, the daughter of the fat and ill-bred German sausage tycoon played by Weber. One critic who saw her in the show reported that she "plunged through her scenes like a wild-cat locomotive or a star fullback." She was still being accused of excessive coarseness, and one disapproving reviewer scolded that "there are those that won't let her fun excuse her vulgarity." But Dressler's growing mastery of stage business, her use of outrageous costumes, and her impromptu speeches invariably brought the house down. *Twiddle Twaddle* will always be remembered by theatre historians for Dressler's "Hats" number in which she trundled out twelve hatboxes and tried on the headgear one by one until she finally donned a little monkey cap and hooked the elastic under her nose. And for a hilarious Spanish dance.

But it was clear by late fall 1906 that Dressler's love affair with the Weber company had faded. When she told Joe Weber that she wanted to move on, the rotund manager decided not to argue the point. *Twiddle Twaddle* was closing in December, and the manager had not yet begun to cast his next (and still uncompleted) offering, *Hip! Hip! Hooray*. Marie announced that she had signed with manager Percy Williams—at two thousand dollars a week—to appear in vaudeville. Her old nemesis Rennold Wolf commented in the *New York Telegraph*: "No one knows—and this includes Miss Dressler—what the comedienne will offer in vaudeville. Whatever it may be, it will be in the nature of a monologue with extemporaneous patter, several songs and some of Miss Dressler's elephantine jig steps. Mr. Williams has displayed great energy in beating his competitors to this prize."

Dressler made her first vaudeville appearance for Percy Williams on New Year's Eve, 1906. The show was staged at the Colonial Theatre and featured a skit by her friend, John Golden, entitled "Oh, Mr. Belasco." In it, Dressler burlesqued some of the roles made famous by Mrs. Leslie Carter, David Belasco's durable star: Madame Du Barry, Yo San from *The Darling of the Gods,* and *The Girl of the Golden West,* all of which set Broadway buzzing yet again, this time with rumors that Dressler could be thinking of signing with Belasco some time in the future. The gossip machine also reported that Dressler had already appeared at two semiprivate entertainments given at the Belasco Theatre during the Christmas season.

Even though she was enjoying huge successes at Williams's theatres in New York and Boston, Dressler was again exhibiting some of her famous symptoms of restlessness, combined with intermittent and well-publicized bouts of tonsillitis and grippe. Twice in February 1907 she bowed out of performances because of reported illness and took another brief hiatus during an engagement at Keith's Chestnut Street Theatre in Philadelphia. Then, in late April, she disappeared from the circuit altogether and turned up again in Maidenhead on the Thames. Not only had she found a house in England for the summer, she announced to curious British reporters, her physician had ordered her to retire from the stage. Retire? "Well, at least for the present," she added, without inviting further inquiry. After all, in Maidenhead, the sun was shining, the flowers were blooming, and there are indications that James H. Dalton had then become an important part of her life.

7

Sunny Jim

1907-1910

Details of James Henry Dalton's installation as a thirteen-year-long presence in Marie Dressler's life is still somewhat of a mystery, partly because of the actress's lifelong unwillingness to discuss the relationship and partly because stories that have managed to surface are often skewed. Dressler did make a statement when Dalton died in 1921 that she had met him in 1907 and that he had been in financial distress at the time. Other snippets of information about Sunny Jim, as he was widely known despite his ugly temper, show he was amply built—at least as large as Dressler. He had sandy hair and a neat mustache, and he liked to wear snappy clothes and gold chains. Rare newspaper clippings show only that he was tall, corpulent, and wore a bowler hat with flair. He was probably in his mid-forties at the time he met the actress. Reporters who occasionally tried, unsuccessfully, to profile Dalton, found that he hailed from Boston, that he claimed to own some mining interests, and that he had once controlled a small chain of grocery stores. There were rumors of a previous (or even current) marriage to one Lizzie A. Dalton, but the press largely ignored this lead for years. Dalton had little or no experience in the theatre, yet he eventually shouldered the responsibility and title of Dressler's business manager and may even have influenced the actress's truculent behavior during the untidy Weber/Edwardes episode. By 1910, he had quietly assumed the title of husband as well.

At the beginning of the relationship, it is possible that Dressler told no one—including her cronies in New York—about Dalton.

He probably sailed with the actress to England in the summer of 1907, but Dressler herself made no mention of this in her two books. Instead, she insists that she was accompanied by her father, who had expressed a wish to visit Bonita and Richard Ganthony. But if her story of a 1907 meeting is correct, Dalton was likely on board the transatlantic liner as well, since Dressler did not return to New York until the spring of 1908.

Dressler luxuriated in her summer at Maidenhead. For the privileged upper classes, Edwardian England was a lotus land of titled ladies and gentlemen, handsome rakes in white flannels, and perfectly served dinners at the Savoy. The theatrical world was dominated by Gerald du Maurier, Edwardes, and the American manager Charles S. Frohman, who had extended the influence of the Klaw and Erlanger Syndicate to the West End. The reigning national playwright of the time was James M. Barrie, creator of the smash hit *Peter Pan,* a show then starring Pauline Chase that was in its fifth year at Frohman's Duke of York's Theatre. The Barry-mores had already tested the London waters, and the gossip was that up-and-coming politician Winston Churchill was simply mad about young Ethel. Dressler felt perfectly at home at Maidenhead cricket matches, swishing across the lawns in her long white skirts, chatting with the gentry, and eating dishes of strawberries and cream.

But despite the distractions, the actress was also busily lobbying George Edwardes to reconsider her candidacy for a theatrical assignment, now that her controversial Weber connection had been satisfactorily voided. Early in the fall of 1907, Edwardes did indicate that he might tap Dressler to play Mrs. Pipp in a production of the Augustus Thomas comedy *The Education of Mr. Pipp.* The plan was to transform the script into a musical comedy, with Leslie Stuart, composer of the hits "Floradora" and "The Belle of Mayfair," handling the score. But somehow the project never did get off the ground; perhaps Edwardes was still wary of Dressler's professional reliability and perhaps he was cautious about investing new money at a time when his organization was in some financial trouble. Dressler waited impatiently for the call, but when it was obvious that Edwardes would not sign her for the role, she let it be known in the West End that she was available for work. To her delight, there was an immediate response—an offer from manager Alfred Butt to appear at the Palace Music Hall, which had achieved theatrical respectability as A Theatre of Varieties, for fifteen hundred dollars a week, starting in October. As it turned out, the run at the Palace would last—except for a brief hiatus in January—until the following March.

Dressler's debut in London was not only a personal triumph, it undoubtedly convinced her, and naturally Dalton as well, that she was at the top of her class as a comedienne. "Miss Dressler had not been a couple of minutes on the stage before she had justified the great popularity she enjoys on the other side of the Atlantic," wrote a London reviewer. "Her success, indeed, was instantaneous and the favorable impression she made by her very first song seemed to be intensified by each succeeding essay." A *New York Herald* reporter caught up with Dressler in her dressing room on opening night and gleaned some information that is particularly revealing of her state of mind at this time, while possibly pinpointing the elusive Dalton's whereabouts as well. "Miss Dressler is accompanied here by a companion and her aged father, who is a veteran of the Crimean War. She has taken a house at No. 18 Thurlow Place and will make London her permanent home. She is under a three-year contract with her London managers."

Confident that Londoners would appreciate her Weber Music Hall songs just as much as New Yorkers unfailingly did, Dressler belted out "A Great Big Girl Like Me" and "Hard to Be a Lady in a Case Like That." She even sat down at the piano and reeled off a very American coon song (probably one of the current favorites such as George M. Cohan's "Hot Tamale Alley") with, as one observer remarked, "a strong touch of pathos in it." A *New York Herald* correspondent who was at the opening night confirmed that Dressler was a smash hit. "She toned down some of the strenuous horse play she was wont to indulge in at Weber's, but didn't omit to sit down on the stage when she tried to make a bow." Possibly, Dressler's toning down of her more outrageous antics was a respectful incline of her head to the Palace itself. The West End's Theatre of Varieties did not offer scantily clad choruses or off-color jokes as did some of the other music halls in town. Patrons actually *dressed* in the dress circle, and although the air was always blue with smoke, it emerged from expensive cigars. People drank champagne rather than ale at the bar, and if a gentleman happened to imbibe a tot too many, he was gently escorted to the discreetly curtained drunks' door and never admitted to the Palace bar again.

Because she was a consummate professional, Dressler also knew she was treading historic boards at the House of Varieties. An uninhibited lady named Maud Allan had once danced barefoot and barelegged to classical music at the Palace and immediately became the rage of London. Alfred Butt had followed this up by introducing the even barer extremities of Lady Constance Stewart Richardson, who actually drew annoyed remonstrances from King Edward VII, who felt the dancer was letting down the aristocratic side. And there was Margaret Cooper, a distinguished-looking singer who—as Gypsy Rose Lee would many decades in the future—took endless and erotic minutes to remove her furs, jewelry, and long white gloves before sitting down at the piano. Dressler, in fact, pulled out all of the stops at the Palace while prudently subduing her most vulgar on-stage antics. She often told friends she particularly prized the review of her show published in London's *Morning Post:* "It is not easy to describe Miss Dressler. The obvious and perhaps the truest thing to say about her is that she is characteristically American. To compare her with Madame Yvette Guilbert is bound to mislead; yet to compare her with any inferior artist would mislead still more. She is a Madame Guilbert raised to some unknown power, a Madame Guilbert magnified a thousand times and using a megaphone."

The Palace engagement attracted huge business, with Dressler inventing a burlesque of Fluffy Ruffles, a popular London cartoon character. She also revived her "Hats" sketch, calling it "The Bonnet Store-y," plus a burlesque on *The Merry Widow* waltz that was surely a friendly jab at George Edwardes, who had bet his failing fortunes (and was winning) on an extravagant production of Franz Lehar's operetta at Daly's. But it was clear that Dressler was not taking the much-publicized three-year contract with Alfred Butt too seriously. "Oh," she told a reporter offhandedly, "I signed it hurriedly on the stage without even taking time to read it. Now, I feel it's not really to my liking." Another report in January 1908 stated, in fact, that the actress was actually planning to study grand opera in Milan. And there was also a story that she wanted to stage a new musical comedy under her own management, "the work," it was said, "of a famous Continental composer."

That January Dressler suddenly dropped out of the Palace program and went into unexplained seclusion. The defection was short, but it was a harbinger of the following March when the actress decided to quit the Palace altogether and take off for Monte Carlo. Dressler never explained why, but it is significant that in 1914 Dalton stated publicly that he and Dressler were married "on the Continent, six years ago." Also significant—and never explained by Dressler—is a report in the *New York Telegraph* on April 19, 1908, when the actress arrived back in the city from Europe. "Since reaching New York, Miss Dressler has enveloped her movements in the darkest mystery. Indeed, her mysterious fit began when she sailed for Broadway under the nom de plume of 'Mrs. _____' [no name was actually given by the newspaper]. No one seems quite sure whether this was comedy or a clerical error on the part of the purser, for no one saw any stranger likely to be Mr. _____ on board the boat. Since reaching New York, Miss Dressler's whereabouts have been as carefully concealed as possible." Interesting also, after a few London-based glimpses of Alexander Koerber in 1907, nothing more was reported on Dressler's father. She did not include his name in subsequent pages of her books, he was not mentioned in clippings after that date (except for a weird 1914 story), and there is no known record of his death.

If it can be assumed that Dressler had entered into a serious relationship with Dalton by this time, it can also be assumed that it was a major, even unprecedented event in the thirty-nine-year-old actress's life. Apart from the strange, almost unbelievable story of her 1899 liaison with the invisible George Hoeppert, Dressler's name had not been linked romantically with any man in New York or on the Road. Indeed, she enjoyed scoffing at the possibility of marriage and openly reveled in her public image as a "man-repellent" ugly duckling—a display of bravado, perhaps, that might well have concealed a growing loneliness and a need to forge a close and exclusive alliance. Reports of the actress's unusual "reticence and reserve" in the spring of 1908 seem to reflect the likelihood of a New York honeymoon with Dalton, discreetly shielded from the public eye. "To a few of her close intimates, Miss Dressler has been now and then visible," reported the *New York Telegraph*. "But as a rule, all inquiries at Zella Frank's flat [where Dressler was apparently staying] whether at 11 o'clock in the morning or at 11 o'clock at night, have been met by the amazing information that Auntie Marie has just gone out to luncheon."

The question, of course, is why Dressler went to such lengths to hide her affair with Jim Dalton. Considering her fascination with favorable publicity, it is clear that there must have been far more aspects to the liaison than met the eye. Even today, no clear story has ever been revealed, and most of what has been written by such intimates as journalist Adela Rogers St. Johns and Hollywood scenarist Frances Marion are either out of context or wildly inaccurate. But a careful study of what is known for sure and what was eventually confessed by Dalton, his wife Lizzie, and (reluctantly) by Dressler herself produces a likely scenario: After Jim Dalton wooed and won Dressler in 1907, he told her that his wife had sued for divorce but that she was demanding periodic payments of money in return for her silence about his involvement with the actress. By January 1908, when Dressler was appearing at the Palace Music Hall, Dalton was telling her that he was a free man. Then he and Dressler left London for Monte Carlo, where they went through a marriage ceremony. Much later, it was discovered by the actress that the "minister" was actually a local man paid by Dalton to stage a fake wedding. Dressler also eventually discovered that Dalton's wife never sued for divorce, and this was confirmed by Lizzie Dalton herself in 1914 and at Dalton's death in 1921. Early in the relationship, Dressler was clearly worried about any public scrutiny of her "marriage" to Dalton and obviously decided to keep Sunny Jim discreetly in the shadows. This low profile stance persisted until at least 1910, even though Dalton became an active participant (and often a loose cannon) in her theatrical ventures. Years later, Dressler actually told reporters that she had faced Lizzie in company with Dalton's brother to beg her to divorce her husband, but this story was denied by Lizzie herself.

In any case, Dalton was kept strictly under wraps when the couple returned from London in 1908. But when manager Percy Williams finally ran Dressler to ground and asked her to join the bill at the Colonial Theatre, she accepted, albeit with a touch of reluctance. The engagement opened on April 20, and the audience "greeted her return from England with shrieks of applause," according to the New York critics. Dressler clearly figured that her fans were expecting more of the same—or perhaps she was not interested in creating new numbers—so her performance included the somewhat shopworn "Great Big Girl," a coon song, and a recitation. She may have confided to Williams that her current stay on Broadway would be brief, but the most specific news of things to come arrived via a *Chicago Journal* writer who filed a revealing story in May: "Marie Dressler is doing a turn in vaudeville down east and hoping to get back to England, which has won her heart and soul. She declared she's going to keep away from the theatre after another year and quit the thrilling life. 'I'm going to settle down and lead a decent life,' said the big comedienne to an anxious friend a few days ago. 'No more yelling and shouting, no more playing the fool on all fours all over the stage; no more whacking German comedians over the head with a slapstick. If I stay on the stage I'd have to play fool parts all my life. The public won't have me in anything else. I'd like to be quiet and artistic but they won't let me. I can make 'em laugh by running fifteen miles round the stage and that's what I have to do. I do my very best to get at my audience, to rouse it and interest it, and I love the way it treats me. But I'm dead tired of it all.'" The story went on to report that she was planning to produce a show of her own in London the following fall and that she was already getting a company together. "Of course, I hope to make a big success, but whether I do or not, I shan't remain on the stage for more than another year. After that it will be the simple life for me. I have my winter home already picked out—a little place near Monte Carlo, right on the Mediterranean, with a garden full of roses and sunsets and silver moons that no scenic artist ever dreamed of. In summer, perhaps, I shall travel, but no more stage for little Marie. I won't even go to the theatre. I'd rather stay at home and play cards." Within a week or two, Dressler made it all official by ending her engagement with Percy Williams and announcing she would sail for England by the end of the month. She was planning, it was reported, to produce a musical comedy with the help of her Weber Music Hall colleagues Edgar Smith and Maurice Levi.

There's no doubt that Dressler believed she had enough capital to mount a show in London. She had been drawing fat checks in England, and Percy Williams was always known as a generous American employer. Dalton persuaded the actress to sell her property in Elmhurst to help sweeten the London pot. This must have been a difficult decision for Dressler, but the evidence is that she was already under Dalton's spell, even though details of his betrayal in Monte Carlo were then beginning to surface. The couple sailed for Europe once Dressler settled her financial affairs in New York. By late fall, she was negotiating with theatrical manager Charles Frohman to take over the lease of the Aldwych Theatre in the Strand. Her planned production, it was reported in the show business press, was a musical comedy entitled *Little Minna*.

The West End Adventure, as Dressler's foray into European theatrical management came to be known, began on a high, even euphoric note. As a kind of warm-up, she signed a short contract with manager Sir Oswald Stoll to make some appearance at the London Coliseum, a theatre that, unlike Alfred Butt's high-toned Palace, catered to family audiences. The delighted Sir Oswald agreed to pay the actress twenty-five hundred dollars a week and, after reading both the reviews and the resulting box-office receipts, he must have decided he had lucked into a bargain. "Again, Miss Marie Dressler has captured London," gushed a correspondent for the *Chicago Record-Herald* on December 8, 1908. "She appeared last night at the Coliseum before an audience which filled every seat and all available standing room. The ovation she received was more spontaneous and more enthusiastic than any I have ever seen in London." The British newspapers were equally as starstruck. Dressler was clearly impressed and encouraged by the warmth of her return to London. She remembered her appearance at the Coliseum as "a great personal triumph." But she muddied the historical record by also remembering that "the triumph was so great in fact, that three influential theatre men promptly suggested that I put on *Higgledy Piggledy*, which had been such a tremendous success in America."

A more accurate version of the story is that, although some "influential theatre men" might have nodded encouragingly when Dressler confided her management plans, the decisions were all hers—aided and abetted, no doubt, by the shadowy Jim Dalton. The successful *Higgledy Piggledy* had clearly been in her mind when she announced earlier in 1908 that Smith and Levi, the authors of the Weber Music Hall show, would be helping her stage a musical comedy. "And," as a *New York Telegraph* writer reported somewhat cynically in early 1909, "Joe Weber thinks he knows the foundation of that musical play is *Higgledy Piggledy*, which once did service at Weber's Music Hall and to which Weber holds the rights." Interestingly, Joe Weber did not, at least publicly, confront Dressler concerning the ownership of *Higgledy Piggledy*, and there seems to have been no attempt to dissuade Smith and Levi—who apparently went along with the plan without question—from booking passage for England.

When they arrived in London, however, the authors found that Dressler's widely publicized preparations for the show were very sparse indeed. Letters and cables from the actress had led them to believe that literally dozens of British comedians, prima donnas, character actors, and leading men had been placed under contract. But once at the Aldwych, the New York duo discovered that, apart from an option on the services of one actor and a vocal quartet, Dressler had made little progress at all. The actress listened dutifully to a sharp lecture from her Broadway colleagues, then began hunting for local talent. The name of the show was changed—perhaps under pressure from a cautiously concerned Smith and Levi—to *Philopoena*, the name of *Higgledy Piggledy*'s leading character. Eventually, rehearsals began. More than likely, Dalton was very much in evidence at the Aldwych, but his name never appeared in connection with the show. *Philopoena* opened on February 27, 1909, at what was advertised as "Marie Dressler's Aldwych" and closed just over a week later. The sixty members of the company assembled glumly in early March to read a letter posted by Dressler on the stage-door bulletin board: "I am unable to continue the fight. Fate is against me. I am too ill to explain as I would like to, but I want you, my company to know that I mortgaged everything I had in the world to pay you your last week's salary."

Back in New York, after an Atlantic crossing on the *Mauretania*, Edgar Smith and Maurice Levi met an army of reporters, demanding some explanation for the *Philopoena* fiasco. Said Levi: "They had a good orchestra and good scenery. But Miss Dressler couldn't carry the whole thing herself. It was about the poorest company that I have ever seen. The play went all right when it had a chance. But that company—well, they wouldn't have stood for it in one night stands out West. Nobody could do anything with such help. They were all English and not a well-known person among them."

Dressler herself had a great deal to say about the West End Adventure at the time. After admitting that she had dropped a cool forty thousand dollars on *Philopoena,* she placed the blame on everything from fate to the London booking agencies and newspaper critics, who "wrote their reviews after staying for one act." There's no doubt that the actress was devastated by the failure of her ambitious enterprise. In her 1934 autobiography, she says that she pawned her jewelry and borrowed money from Sir Oswald Stoll in order to pay the company two weeks' salary. Then, according to her book, she was taken ill with an ulcerated throat and hurried back to New York for an operation. "When I recovered," she remembers in *My Own Story,* "I found that none of my bills had been paid, and that the money had apparently done a disappearing act." Nowhere is there any real evidence as to whether Sunny Jim returned to New York with the actress or was left in London to manage—or mismanage—the financial mess. All that Dressler tells us is that she regarded the shortfall as a "debt of honor" and eventually paid it in full in 1930.

Back home, the theatrical writers and critics pulled no punches in their comments concerning the woeful event in London. Ormesby Burton of the *Morning Telegraph* ran an editorial gleaned from London's *Evening Standard* in his influential column: "The mistake Miss Dressler made is that which many American managers and actors have made before her. They bring to London a very American play and expect London to welcome it by laughing at jokes which require special knowledge for their appreciation." Respected theatre critic Alan Dale wrote: "If the Marie Dressler London show was of the Weber and Fields brand, it was foredoomed. There was not a fighting chance for it. The London musical show must be pretty, dainty, refined and filled with very tame, and what we consider, very fruitless humor. Our mania for dialect-broken English is not tolerated over there. It is not considered sport to make merry over imperfections of language. . . . It is dangerous enough to be funny at home, but to try to be funny abroad is the limit of audacity and foolhardiness." *The New York Telegraph* ran a letter to the editor written by a reader who had seen *Philopoena* at the Aldwych: "We went to see a musical comedy and we saw a hotch-potch thrown together anyhow; for instance, one girl apropos of nothing came on and sang the *Jewel Song* from Faust; she sang it well, too; but surely we had not gone there to hear that. The real facts are that Miss Dressler was a success [in London] because she was a real and original artiste, and the show was a failure because it was a very bad one, or at least very unsuited to a British audience."

In England, the Westminster County Court ordered Dressler to pay the Comedy Quartet five hundred dollars for breach of contract, and other suits were launched in an attempt to recover some of the salaries never paid. Dressler suffered through the financial storm stoically, but on September 3, she filed a voluntary petition in bankruptcy in the United States District Court. Her liabilities were set down at $24,886.32, and her only assets were said to consist of necessary wearing apparel, worth one hundred dollars. Commented Dressler on a stopover in Chicago: "As an individual, an American may make as much of a hit as one wishes in London. But an American star in an American play has no chance there. They hate Americans and I do not believe I ever will be foolish enough to play in England again." Interestingly, Dressler also told the Chicago reporter that she was on her way to inspect her copper mine in California. Just as interestingly, mention of this mine then evaporates from Dressler press clippings and records. It is tempting to conjecture that the actress was as unimpressed with Jim Dalton's holdings in California as she was with her box-office receipts in London. Clearly, the spring of 1909 was a spectacular disappointment for the actress, who had believed just a few months before that she was launching a brilliant new professional and personal career. "England needed a funny show," she blurted out bitterly to one Western reporter. "Heaven knows they haven't got three funny people in all England, outside of Parliament, and that is a continuous laugh. Any people that are so narrow, so prejudiced, jealous and vain, must cease to be a nation."

Despite her obvious hurt and distress, however, Dressler managed to rally well enough to sign with manager and writer Richard Carle to star in a summer show called *The Boy and the Girl*. The musical play opened in May 1909 to mixed reviews in Philadelphia, then moved on to the New Amsterdam Aerial Gardens in New York at the end of the month. Here, the critics were even more scathing: "Summer shows are not supposed to have either continuity or sense, being intended solely for amusement in the silly season," wrote the *New York Post,* "But they should at least be bright and lively, with catchy music and good dances. *The Boy and the Girl* has practically none of these attributes and consequently a large audience was badly bored at the Aerial Gardens on the roof of the New Amsterdam Theatre last night. The applause was infrequent and from the temper of the spectators, the chances of long survival are slight. Miss Marie Dressler worked hard over a hopeless case and Miss Harriet Standon and Mr. Burrell Barbetto sang agreeably. For the rest, the silence is merciful." *The Boy and the Girl* tottered on for a few weeks.

Dressler was flat broke after her London experience, so she quickly accepted a mid-summer vaudeville engagement at Young's Pier in Atlantic City. There seems little doubt that her morale was at a low ebb when she took the train to the seaside community. The mauling she had suffered because of her contribution to the Richard Carle venture had been vicious. "Miss Dressler scored best with 'I'm a Poor Working Girl,' chiefly on account of its accompanying grotesque dance," wrote a Philadelphia critic. "She retains her usual direct and forceful methods of securing comedy and at times her actions are less funny than coarse." She badly needed an upbeat theatrical booking to restore her bruised self-confidence. Fortunately, the audiences at Young's Pier, and later at Brighton Beach, were loudly responsive. "Miss Dressler drew the banner crowd last night," reported the *New York Star* on July 13. "Seats were at a premium before the curtain went up, although the house last night was not full. Before the time announced for Miss Dressler's appearance, however, every seat had been taken and when she came before the footlights she was met by so many smiling, welcoming faces that she must have felt very much at home." Probably crossing her fingers for luck, Dressler coolly demanded two thousand dollars a week for her Young's Pier engagement and, it was reported, "the local management seems to think she is cheap at the price, for already she has been booked here for another week." The *Star* reported: "Miss Dressler will be seen later at Brighton Beach and at other important points and, judging by her opening success, she probably will be a big feature in vaudeville as long as she cares to remain in that line of stage endeavor. She must, however, later report to Lew Fields to whom she is under contract to star in a new musical comedy in the fall."

Negotiations with Fields had been quietly going on for several weeks, though Dressler had not been optimistic about the eventual outcome. The prospect of returning to the stage was intriguing, but her humiliating experience with *Philopoena* and *The Boy and the Girl* still rankled. And she had another worry: the very real possibility that she would be abandoning her current upswing of fortunes on the vaudeville circuit for nothing more than a short-term theatrical bust.

8

THE WORKING GIRL

1910-1912

The Klaw-Erlanger-Frohman theatre syndicate was still very much in evidence in 1909, but the powerful trust had been challenged by another show business group. The Shubert Theatrical Corporation, controlled by brothers Jacob (Jake) and Lee Shubert, scored a major victory over the long-entrenched combine. In 1906, the brothers had thumbed their noses at Abe Erlanger's edict that if sixty-one-year-old Sarah Bernhardt appeared in America under the Shubert banner, all Klaw and Erlanger houses daring to accept a Bernhardt booking would be shut out of the trust. In defiant response, the Shuberts presented the great Parisian actress in such nontheatrical settings as circus tents and city halls. Not only did Jake and Lee make money, they also scored a major public relations victory over an infuriated and embarrassed Abe Erlanger. The Shuberts were also gaining other friends and colleagues. The great Shakespearean actor E.H. Sothern left Erlanger to sign with the Shuberts as did his good friend, actress Julia Marlowe. Then, in 1906, Lew Fields—already gaining a strong reputation as an actor-manager—decided to join the Shubert group in return for a promise of financial backing. Fields was still enjoying a close relationship with Lee and Jake Shubert in 1909. By then, too, the Shuberts and Abe Erlanger had agreed to cooperate in at least one area of show business: vaudeville. The United States Amusement Company was incorporated with a capital of one hundred million dollars to produce vaudeville shows, with Erlanger as president and Lee Shubert as vice-president. William Morris was the company's chief booker.

With such powerful backing in the wings, Fields approached Dressler in the fall of 1909 with the script of a musical play called *Tillie's Nightmare*. The book and lyrics were by Dressler's old friend Edgar Smith, with music by A. Baldwin Sloane. Well known dancer and director Ned Wayburn was signed to stage the production. The story was fairly simple (typically for a Fields project, which could only be described as extended vaudeville) and smacked somewhat of the age-old Cinderella legend. A homely boardinghouse drudge named Tillie Blobbs lives in an upstate New York town called Skaneateles. The establishment is owned by Tillie's mother, who favors her beautiful daughter, Maude, and puts the ugly duckling in charge of the kitchen work. One night, Tillie is promised an evening out, but the plan goes awry and she is left alone in the house, reading the Sunday supplements. She sits wistfully at the piano and sings "Heaven Will Protect the Working Girl." Then she falls asleep and dreams "a musical comedy dream that lasts two hours and is duly visualized"—she marries a millionaire, travels on a steam yacht, goes to Paris, and flies in an airship.

After reading the script, Dressler became enthusiastic about the *Tillie* idea and agreed to sign with Lew Fields for fifteen hundred dollars a week. The actress was still luxuriating in the warm notices she had received during her summer appearances at Brighton Beach and Atlantic City, and now it seemed as though Fields's offer actually involved a major production. As a Joe Weber alumnus, she was still somewhat cautious of an alliance with Fields, but the vision of the increasingly powerful Shuberts hovering in the background was too attractive to ignore. Besides, Fields assured her that she would be free to develop the Tillie role as she felt best.

Rehearsals for *Tillie's Nightmare*—involving a large company of sixty principals and chorus—began in October 1909 at the Broadway Theatre, then ground to a halt a month later. The problem seems to have been that no one in real authority deigned to turn up regularly to monitor work in progress, and although Dressler nagged stage manager Wayburn to name dates for the show, none were confirmed. Finally, an alarmed Dressler delivered an ultimatum to the director: she wanted a firm list of bookings or she would quit. Wayburn replied somewhat reluctantly that he had been told the premiere might actually be deferred for at least another month. Dressler gave one of her famous sniff-and-shrugs, informed the director that she was not inclined to wait for more than another two weeks for an opening, then walked out of the theatre. "Temporarily, at least, rehearsals have been suspended," wrote Rennold Wolf of the *Tillie* affair. "There was none yesterday. Miss Dressler sent to the Broadway Theatre for a trunk containing her wardrobe and had it moved away, which is assumed to be an act representing her swan song." Lew Fields's apparent lack of interest in *Tillie's Nightmare* could have been because he was having his own share of bad dreams at the time. *The Jolly Bachelors,* one of his joint productions with the Shuberts, had been awarded the unofficial prize as the most complete fiasco of the Broadway season, and reports of another show, *Old Dutch* (with music by Victor Herbert and with newcomers Helen Hayes and dancer Vernon Castle in minor roles), in which he was personally appearing, were dismal indeed. Dressler's dramatic exit galvanized the manager into action, however, and he settled down to slot *Tillie's Nightmare* into several theatre dates, beginning in Albany, moving on to Chicago, Kansas City, and Philadelphia.

Tillie's Nightmare proved to be a monumental flop in Albany and at other early outings as well. A displeased Chicago critic wrote after a January 2, 1910, opening at the Great Northern Theatre: "Nobody with ordinary dog intelligence could think of *Tillie's Nightmare* without shuddering. It is a noisy dicker between the ugly sights and tabulated humor of the grimy past. The show is dominated by an actress whose main aim is to make herself a monstrosity so she may use ugliness as a bludgeon to wallop the ignorant into blithering and painful laughter. Miss Dressler is so offensive in a simulation of drunkenness and another of seasickness that few people not hired for that purpose could be requested to sit through these irksome exhibitions." Dressler was devastated as she digested the storm of adverse criticism that greeted the *Tillie's* debut. She went into a series of huddles with Edgar Smith and Baldwin Sloane, suggesting changes including a severe toning-down of the overdone horseplay that held up plot advancement. She also pushed for a revision of the seasickness and drunkenness scenes that were already beginning to draw boos and hisses from the audience. The authors responded by firing some of the weakest members of the cast, but they were not overly impressed with Dressler's other ideas, particularly when she told Smith in a typically aggressive tone that the story itself needed to make some understandable point.

Before the play opened in Kansas City, Smith and Sloane were temporarily absent, and Dressler took full advantage of this by making the revisions she had suggested. The offensive choking and puking in the seasickness scene were judiciously trimmed as was the intoxication segment. Dressler introduced some new lines that helped with previously muddled transition and threw out much of the pointless slapstick that had scrambled the earlier script. She expanded the seven scenes that highlighted her talents as a comedienne, singer, and dancer. She honed in on a believable, hilarious, and occasionally tear-jerking characterization of Tillie the drudge and how she found unexpected Nirvana in her dreams.

Smith and Sloane returned to the show after its opening in Kansas City and stormed backstage after witnessing Dressler's changes. They were, they argued, the authors of the show, and Dressler had no right to tinker with the script without their permission. Dressler herself was adamant and there's no doubt that Jim Dalton—whose name was cropping up more frequently in news reports of the show—played some part in the argument as well. Finally, the authors took a train back to New York, confronted Lee Shubert, and demanded that he close *Tillie's Nightmare*. Shubert shrugged and referred them to Lew Fields, who also shrugged and informed the two angry men that he could not close without running the risk of being sued by the entire company, including Dressler, who was commanding fifteen hundred dollars a week. But Fields made a point of turning up at *Tillie's* next date in Pittsburgh to check the changes for himself. What he saw was a tight, uproariously funny play that showcased what everyone in the audience had come to enjoy: Marie Dressler being Marie Dressler. The manager was so impressed, he wired the Shuberts that as far as he was concerned, Dressler had done wonders with the show. But the Shuberts were not completely convinced. Ned Wayburn—who had by then returned to Ziegfeld as principal dancer—was told to travel posthaste to Pittsburgh to fix the show for a New York opening. Dressler rolled her eyes. Fix? But Lee Shubert had made his decision, and Wayburn moved in as ordered. Some of the offensive bits of stage business were resurrected, more knock-about horseplay was introduced, and Dressler's time on stage was trimmed. The audience was definitely not amused.

Frustrated and furious, Dressler again threw down the gauntlet. Unless the show was returned to the way she had redesigned it, she would not stick around long enough to open on the Great White Way. The Shuberts retreated into a brief conference with Lew Fields, then capitulated without a whimper. *Tillie's Nightmare* opened at the Herald Square Theatre on May 5, 1910, with Dressler as the star, supported by Horace Newman, Octavia Broske, May Montford, and J. Clarence Harvey.

It was a Broadway opening to remember. Crowds of Dressler's admirers from the social register reserved boxes at the theatre, bringing sheaves of flowers to toss as tributes. Longtime Dressler fan Mrs. Stuyvesant Fish was there, of course, together with a retinue of bejeweled women, escorted by distinguished gentlemen in full evening dress. Alfred Vanderbilt arrived with members of his family, and so did the former Bessie Stokes, now Mrs. Jules Vatable, and society hostess Mrs. James Speyer. The balcony was packed with the belles and beaux of the Bronx and Brooklyn. After the first act, the applause was so noisy and demands for a speech so insistent that Dressler had to come forward and thank the audience before changing for the rest of the show. The *New York Times* was enthusiastic. "Marie Dressler, whom a very clever woman described last night as the human steam roller—only there never was one that could keep it up so long without assistance—came into the Herald Square Theatre last night, sent an audience into hysterics, almost put the furniture out of commission and generally raised such a ruction as only a very large and very noisy and very clever person can raise without being arrested." The *Evening Sun* agreed. "*Tillie's Nightmare* made another of manager Lew Fields's day dreams come true at the Herald Square last night. If you want to laugh your head off, go to that theatre and see Marie Dressler as the elephantine Cinderella, the boardinghouse drudge, Tillie Blobbs of Skaneateles, N.Y. Miss Dressler has won many triumphs in her career, but never in any role has she been one half so funny as she has in this production." Inevitably, there were a few caveats. The *New York Telegraph* reported, "Tillie was a fat Cinderella—Miss Marie Dressler, as you imagine—and she had her usual ebullient self much in evidence. Miss Dressler has a repertoire of laughs up her sleeve and she delivers them with promptness as soon as she gets on the stage. Shooting forward, then waving the arms, striking the falsetto and parodying the pathetic 'home and mother' stuff—all this is Miss Dressler's stock in trade and you can always be sure of getting it and enjoying it for about half an hour." The critic conceded, however, that "the programme is well gotten up." The success of *Tillie* made news across the country in May 1910. The *Chicago Journal* gave Dressler credit. "After discovering in Chicago several months ago what was the matter with *Tillie's Nightmare*, Marie Dressler dragged it about the country until she could make it over. She has now taken it into New York and the Manhattanese love it."

Tillie's Nightmare received ample space in both of Dressler's autobiographies. "The part of Tillie which I enjoyed most—and I hope I may be forgiven for saying it was a favorite with the audiences too—was my song 'Heaven Will Protect the Working Girl,'" wrote Dressler. "From Bangor to Spokane and from Boston to Miami, it was on every lip. If ever a song had an immortal soul, this one did." Actually, the melody of Baldwin Sloane's song, which the composer adapted from a nineteenth century music hall tune, is easily forgettable, but Dressler endowed Edgar Smith's words with such a beguiling mix of pathos, vivacity, and humor that audiences invariably emerged from the theatre chanting the punch line, "but heaven will protect the working girl." The sheet music, published by Chas. K. Harris of New York, sold thousands of copies, and nearly every theatre buff could eventually recite at least one of the verses:

A village maid was leaving home,
her eyes with tears was set
her mother dear was standing near the spot
She says to her—Neuralgia, dear, I hope you won't forget
That I'm the only mother you have got
The city is a wicked place, as any one can see
and cruel danger round your path may swirl
So every week you'd better send your wages home to me
For Heaven will protect the working girl.

In many ways, *Tillie* could be called the high point of Dressler's career in the legitimate theatre. She had mastered her timing techniques and knew instinctively how to gain firm control of her audience. She had come to terms with the fact that her comedy style was, as one critic put it, "about as subtle as a billboard," even as "coarse and as rasping as XXX sandpaper." But she did manage to keep herself from descending the slippery slope of good taste. She made all of the costumes for the role herself—actors and actresses were expected to provide their own wardrobes in the early years of the century—and all of them were hits in themselves. "It sends the women in the audience at the Herald Square into peals of laughter," wrote one journalist of Dressler's first-act costume. "It is a one-piece suit, made with the extremely narrow skirt now in vogue. This is pulled in at the knees by a ribbon and decorated with a limp bow at the back." In another segment of her stage dream, she played the part of Little Bo Peep in a dress patterned after that of a small girl with lacing across a tiny bolero jacket. Dressler's designs ran the gamut from the rags of the pathetic kitchen slave to the eye-catching but still satirical creations that clothed her in her fantasies. Most important, Dressler's hilarious portrayal of Tillie was thoroughly human, even poignant, an awesome theatrical balancing act that would eventually stand her in good stead in front of the motion picture cameras.

Dressler herself was clearly enjoying her return to the top of the theatrical heap, though she had suffered some personal tragedies and disappointments. Her maid, Jenny, died not long after *Tillie's Nightmare* opened; Dressler took her friend's body home to Washington in a private railway car and paid for a first-class funeral. And there is no doubt that her relationship with Jim Dalton—who had revealed an insatiable thirst for strong drink as well as an inordinate taste for chorus girls—was a continuing worry. But, as she never tired of telling interviewers, she had always hankered after the domestic life; her partnership with Sunny Jim was clearly the nearest she had ever come to achieving it.

Her private dream seemed to be taking a more realistic turn when she decided that her finances were in such good shape that she could buy the special house she had always wanted. As she remembered in her autobiography, on a Sunday morning as she drove through the Berkshires, she "saw and fell in love with a white Vermont farmhouse." She recalled that "it was the sort of home I had never had and consequently yearned for. When I found it was for sale, I threw discretion to the winds, waved an airy hand and said, 'Wrap it up, please. I'll take it home!'" Dressler often told differing stories about the beginnings of what was eventually known as Loafhaven in Vermont. In the fall of 1910 she informed a reporter that she had made a down payment on the 125-acre estate during her 1909 engagement in Brighton. She claimed that she had consulted a palmist and psychic reader who had set up shop next door to the theatre, and he had predicted that she would become the owner of a farm not far from New York. Within two months, according to the story, she had located the Vermont property. In another interview, she told the writer that she bought the farm for a bargain price after negotiating with a Vermont resident who had fallen on hard times. In any case, newspaper reports show that Dressler and Dalton had taken possession of the rambling house near Windsor, Vermont, by the summer of 1910.

Dressler's interest in entrepreneurial activity outside of the theatre surfaced again in Vermont. No sooner had she unpacked than she set up a new company called Windsor Farms Incorporated and spread the word that she intended to make money raising and selling hogs and cattle and marketing dairy products, eggs, and chickens. There is no evidence that she ever made a penny. On the contrary, the cost of feed for her cows and the bill for electric light in the barns far exceeded the amount she received for her produce. Not only that, Dressler, who was probably the first automobile owner in New York to employ a female driver, made a practice of having pounds of farm butter delivered by her chauffeur to her society, media, and theatrical cronies. The acquaintances themselves also soon discovered that if they headed for Vermont when they knew the actress would be "at home," Dressler and Dalton, who had become known as Mr. "What'll you have?", would cheerfully invite them to stay for as long as they pleased. Loafhaven, in fact, soon became an extravagance, particularly after Dressler decided to install a swimming pool and build a small casino to amuse her guests when they tired of relaxing, eating, and quaffing vintages from her well-stocked cellar.

Despite the heavy drain on her finances, the actress continued to float on a professional high. There was an unpleasant scene in July 1910 when Dressler airily notified Lew Fields and the Shuberts that she intended to take off for a few weeks during the heat of the summer. But after some blustering and angry pronouncements that they would ask popular actress Trixie Friganza to take over for Dressler, including a veiled threat that the change might become permanent, the management finally gave in and temporarily closed the show. *Tillie's Nightmare* marked its 250th performance when it reopened at the Herald Square Theatre on August 11. When the 300th performance was celebrated on September 24, Fields announced the beginning of $1.50-a-seat Wednesday and Saturday matinees. To compensate for the extra work, Dressler's salary was raised to two thousand dollars a week. Fall and winter of 1910-11 were undoubtedly among the busiest seasons of Dressler's theatrical career. After a sold-out, six-month run in Manhattan, *Tillie* took to the road, playing dates at the Brooklyn Majestic and in Albany—where the play had flopped only a year before—Cleveland, Syracuse, and Philadelphia. In January 1911, the company traveled north to Toronto, where *Tillie* spent a week at the prestigious Royal Alexandra Theatre. And, of course, the local press not only emphasized the fact that Dressler had been born in nearby Cobourg, the actress took full advantage of the Canadian connection by making an appropriate curtain speech after each performance.

That January, Dressler and Dalton, who by now was unquestionably accepted as her husband, paid a well-publicized visit to Skaneateles, the town immortalized in *Tillie's Nightmare*. Dressler protested that she had always believed the place was fictional, but when she began receiving fan mail from residents, she found Skaneateles was indeed a real community, situated just south of Syracuse, New York. Initially, the visit was to include a special performance of *Tillie* to be staged in nearby Auburn, but instead Dressler and Dalton met with town VIPs and dutifully toured the local sights. Dressler then made headlines by announcing she would henceforth feature the *Skaneateles Democrat* in the first act of *Tillie*. A special edition of the newspaper with the name printed in "heroic" letters was hastily produced for her to use that very night.

In 1911, the longevity of *Tillie* and the inevitable one-night stands were beginning to pall, even though the famous drudge of Skaneateles was continuing to do wonders for the Dressler bank account. During the dog days of July, Dressler crankily announced that she had decided to honor an often-postponed contract originally signed with the Oswald Stoll Circuit in 1909 for a ten-week engagement at the London Coliseum. She insisted she would begin the English stint in early September. The stated reason: a "mis-understanding" with Lew Fields and the Shuberts. The only public explanation of this misunderstanding was that Dressler had requested "repairs to the production" before *Tillie* moved back into the Herald Square Theatre for the following season. But there were other conflicts as well. Jim Dalton had apparently managed to extract a sizable sum of money from the *Tillie* company treasurer after convincing him that he should be paid for management services. As Lee Shubert angrily complained to his lawyer, William Klein, in mid-June, "Note the attached letter from Mr. Dalton. Let me know how to reply to same in such a way that I can call him a blackmailer and a liar. He was Miss Dressler's representative at all times and had nothing to do with the management of the company. We had our own manager and treasurer. I called him down in the office and told him he was a crook and was dishonest in trying to obtain money under false pretenses from Coombs. Something must be done about getting this money back." The row raged on until August, when Dalton was sued by Lew Fields (with Lee Shubert, Edgar Smith and A. Baldwin Sloane signing affidavits) for recovery of the money.

In the meantime, the Shubert organization was also considering litigation to prevent Dressler from leaving the *Tillie* cast and sailing off to England. William Klein wrote Shubert on August 14, 1911, "As I told you the other day, Guggenheimer, Untermyer and Marshall are the attorneys for Marie Dressler. It ought to be a simple matter for you to convince them that she is taking an arbitrary step under her contract with you, and I think if you had a good talk with Mr. Alvin Untermyer, either over the telephone or otherwise, it would result in her coming back and playing the part. . . . In all probability he will be able to swing this thing around without the necessity of an injunction or any other litigation. This means much, so better attend to it at once." Apparently Untermyer did have some influence on his rebel client, because Dressler never did honor her somewhat cobwebbed contract with Sir Oswald Stoll. Stoll lawyers responded by launching a twelve-thousand-dollar breach of contract suit against the actress. The suit was not resolved until December 1914, when a receiver was appointed to recover a $3,350 judgment against the actress in the Supreme Court.

Peace was eventually declared between Shubert, Fields, and

Dressler when they reached an agreement to sell the *Tillie's Night-mare* production to the actress and Jim Dalton. As Lew Fields wrote to Lee Shubert on October 16, 1911 (probably with a sigh of relief that he would now be less involved with Sunny Jim): "The Fields Producing Company is to sell to the Marie Dressler Company for seventy-five hundred dollars in cash all of its interest in *Tillie's Nightmare* and I turn over to the Marie Dressler Company the contract that I have with her, and this Company assumes the contract with the authors for royalties. I receive one half of the stock of this Company. This one-half I am to divide with you. In other words, as soon as I receive the stock I am to turn over 25 per cent of the total issue to you, and am to retain twenty-five percent of the total issue for myself. The total fifty per cent thus received by you and me is to be transferred by us over to the Fields Producing Company."

Dressler celebrated the deal with a cast party on stage at the Lyric Theatre in Philadelphia, but, despite the new turn of events, there is little doubt that the continual touring, the poor backstage facilities of the provincial theatres, the endless receptions given by small-town hostesses and fawning mayors were all beginning to fray Dressler's nervous system. In December 1911, in an attempt to vary the pace, she single-handedly organized a special performance of *Tillie* for thirty-five hundred children—one hundred fifty of them disabled—at the Manhattan Opera House. The New York Department of Public Schools sent nine hundred youngsters to the event, and others were transported to the show by such institutions as the Hebrew Sheltering Guardian Society Orphan Asylum, the Protestant Episcopal Church, and the Hirsch Home for Working Girls. "I haven't had so much fun as this for ages," Dressler gasped offstage during the performance. "I'm making all the faces at 'em I ever knew I had in my repertoire and acting the fool for all I'm worth." Typically, Dressler also invited another contingent to view proceedings from the Opera House boxes: Mrs. O.H.P. Belmont, Mrs. James Speyer, Mrs. Stuyvesant Fish, and Robert Adamson from the mayor's office, among others. A week later in Cleveland she gave a special Christmas performance for the city's newsboys. But despite Dressler's new status as owner of the production, the *Tillie* road show went on, complete with those hated one-night stands.

During a swing through the Midwest in February 1912, Dressler missed out on one of the most historic events ever staged on Broadway: the Joe Weber-Lew Fields reunion, better known as the *Weberfields Jubilee*. Rumors that the two estranged comedians would not only shake hands and make up but would also appear again together in a theatre had been circulating around the Great White Way for months. Early in the year, the news had became official: the show would be produced at the Broadway Theatre, and it would feature many of Weber and Fields's old crew of favorites. The list included Lillian Russell, William Collier, John T. Kelly, Frankie "Legs" Bailey, Fay Templeton, and Bessie Clayton. Fields biographer Armond Fields says that Dressler was not included in the cast because she was not considered a Weberfields original. Whatever the reason, Dressler was not available, being dutifully on tour with *Tillie* in Chicago on February 8, 1912, the night Jubilee (which also boasted the title *Hokey Pokey*) opened in New York. No doubt the actress read reports of the event with a certain nostalgia, even perhaps envy. Inevitably, there was an auction for opening night seats: nine hundred dollars was not considered too steep for boxes, and there were plenty of offers for thirty-five-dollar orchestra tickets. The Broadway Theatre sold out for $13,700, a tidy sum in 1912.

Felix Isman, a longtime associate of Weber and Fields, described the event in his biography of the two comedians. "The theatre was decorated with American Beauty roses, and Lillian Russell's dressing room was literally carpeted with flowers. The actress herself made a first-act entrance dressed in flesh-colored net embroidered with opal sequins and diamonds. Her scarf was set with turquoises and embroidered with gold, diamonds, and aquamarines as were her shoulder straps. She wore a black velvet hat festooned with pink ostrich plumes and pinned with a diamond and aquamarine brooch. She wore square diamond buckles on her shoes and carried a shepherd's crook of ebony crowned with diamonds." Among those who were clearly stunned by the glittering vision were Diamond Jim Brady, resplendent with jewels of his own, publishers Arthur Brisbane and William Randolph Hearst, producers David Belasco and William Brady, and publishers Charles Dana Gibson and Conde Nast, as well as Alexander Moore, Lillian's fiancé. And, naturally, the leaders of New York's Four Hundred were fully represented.

The show itself was a typical mélange of Weber and Fields nonsense, strung together by songs written by the late Nova Scotia-born composer John "Honey" Stromberg and A. Baldwin Sloane. Stromberg, who suffered terribly from arthritis, had committed suicide in 1891, in his coat pocket a newly completed song, "Come Down, My Evenin' Star," dedicated to Lillian Russell. She sang it to a tearful audience. According to a reviewer for the *New York Clipper,* "the opening performance was more than a performance. It was a general jollification with handshaking all around. . . . Everybody was hungry for one of the old time laughs which used to be handed out at the home of burlesque conducted by these two popular manager-actors. . . . It would be impossible to adequately describe the outbursts of applause with which the playhouse rang as each of the old favorites appeared. Nothing like it has been seen on Broadway."

Dressler had little to say about the Weberfields Jubilee, either in future interviews or in her autobiographies. As a matter of fact, both of her ghostwriters confused the February 1912 Jubilee with her November 1912 appearance in *Roly Poly,* the last of the Weber and Fields collaborations. It is possible, indeed, that her memories of February 8 were not only tinged with envy but a certain discomfort as well. The previous afternoon at the Garrick Theatre in Chicago, several boards on stage collapsed under her 250-pound weight, causing her to fall loudly to the floor. Her February 8 evening performance of *Tillie* was played with a distinct limp.

9

THE HEIGHT OF HER POWER

1912-1913

Dressler constantly insisted that she was not a militant suffragette, though she liked to hold forth on women's need to strive for financial independence. She also never hesitated to speak up in defense of the female underdog, both in and out of show business. "But," she once told a reporter during the days when "Votes for Women" was becoming a rallying cry among New York feminists, "I believe there is something radically wrong with our womanhood when so many are clamoring to take man's place in the management of public affairs. Personally, I am a staunch believer in woman's equality with man, but I believe it is a mental equality, not a physical one and that womankind was never devised to steer the ship of state or to go to the polls and cast the ballot with the men." But Dressler was under extreme pressure to change her mind. New York socialites were beginning to embrace the suffrage cause, and Dressler had no intention of abrogating her enviable position as one theatrical identity who was accepted by so many leading lights of "café" society and the moneyed old guard as well.

The actress was somewhat shaken, in fact, when the influential and formidable Mrs. Oliver H.P. Belmont (the former Mrs. William Kissan Vanderbilt I) led a suffrage parade down Fifth Avenue on May 4, 1912. Many of the most illustrious women on the list of the Four Hundred formed ranks behind Alva Belmont, including the famous Elsie de Wolfe, society's favorite interior decorator. Dressler took comfort in the fact that at least Elsie's good friends, Elisabeth Marbury and Anne Morgan (J. Pierpont Morgan's fiercely independent daughter), believed that the fight for suffrage was nothing more than an "unseemly political display." But she was also aware that the Votes for Women issue had dug some dangerous potholes on the road to social success.

Even so, Dressler continued to appear at the tables of such luminaries as the Stuyvesant Fishes, the Hermann Oelrichs, and the Reginald Vanderbilts. Her frequent visitations to Newport, society's exclusive playground on Rhode Island, invariably assumed the character of a royal procession. As a *New York Telegraph* special correspondent wrote in August 1912, "Marie Dressler wafted into Newport last week from out of the cosmos and was to have furnished the entertainment [at a Stuyvesant Fish dinner dance], but the first breath of ocean air, abetted by a refractory orchestra, put Marie's voice out of business. So the smart circle had to content itself with their favorite actress in the role of honored guest. Miss Dressler attended the big ball in her private character and drew a large crowd around her the minute she entered the Louis XVI ballroom. Later, when she appeared at the opera house, [the crowd] put on their diamonds and splendid dresses and went to see her, carrying bunches and baskets of flowers which they hurled on to the stage." Because of her continuing popularity with the upper crust, Dressler postponed—for almost another four years, as it happened—making any firm commitments to Votes for Women. After all, she liked to argue, her increasingly busy life with Jim Dalton, the responsibility of the Vermont farm, and her packed theatrical schedule made it difficult for her to ally herself with any political group. Later in 1912, in fact, she was preoccupied with two important events: the offer of a leading role in Weber and Fields's next (and final) extravaganza, *Roly Poly,* and an invitation from Toronto to star in a musical festival that would mark the opening of a new seven-thousand-seat facility called the Mutual Arena.

Dressler was pleased and flattered when she received the Canadian invitation. She would be paid fifteen hundred dollars for her single evening performance. Other artists included the well-known lyric soprano Alice Nielsen, violinist Arturo Tibaldi, and coloratura soprano Yvonne de Treville. And, after informing the Toronto festival committee that her husband James Dalton might be persuaded to help the arena's managing director Lawrence

Solman with the planning of the program, the services of Sunny Jim were enthusiastically engaged. No record of Dalton's Toronto fee now exists, but he clearly hoped to profit from the visit. The Mutual Arena opening made headlines throughout Ontario, and Toronto reviewers agreed that Canadian-born Dressler stole the show. "It was reserved for Miss Marie Dressler to raise the enthusiasm of the audience to its highest pitch of intensity," wrote a *Toronto Star* critic on October 12, 1912. "Her appearance on the stage, apparently with all the fidgety nervousness of a novice, created shrieks of laughter, which did not abate one iota during her recitation of her ballad, 'The Glove'—adapted from the German of Schiller by Bulwer Lytton—accompanied by the orchestra. She afterwards gave an imitation of some of the artists who had been taking part during the week, which, while excruciatingly funny, could not disguise the fact that she is no mean vocalist herself. Just at the finish, two ushers in each of the four aisles, each bearing two beautiful bouquets, made a simultaneous rush to the stage and literally covered her with flowers."

Dressler was still basking in the glow of her Toronto triumph when she returned to New York for *Roly Poly* rehearsals. There was still some friction between Dressler and Dalton and the Fields and Shubert interests over Sunny Jim's alleged "theft" of management fees, but the producers were practical businessmen, and there was no doubt that Dressler's unique stage presence was a valuable asset to the kind of freewheeling show planned by Joe Weber and Lew Fields. The Shuberts also apparently believed that the success of the *Jubilee* in February 1912 was worth capitalizing on as soon as possible. *Roly Poly* and its second-act "travesty," called "Without the Law" (a skit on Bayard Veiller's gripping thriller *Within the Law*), would be presented at the new Weber and Fields Music Hall, which had been optimistically built by the Shuberts on Forty-Fourth Street. The opening was set for November 21, 1912.

Dressler, who signed a twenty-week contract for fifteen hundred dollars a week, was assigned the role of Bijou Fitzsimmons, a large lady who pursued Schmaltz (Weber), who is taking the waters at Raatenbad with his friend Tanzman (Fields). Schmaltz is forced to play dead to escape Bijou's attentions, and the act ends with Dressler collapsing on the tall, thin Fields. Besides the three great clowns, the *Roly Poly* cast included Nora Bayes, who sang the hit song "When It's Apple Blossom Time in Normandy," Bessie Clayton, Jack Norworth, and Frank Daniels, all of them familiar vaudeville performers. A Weber and Fields show always promised a stunningly gorgeous chorus line, and *Roly Poly* was no exception. At one point, to the cheers of the audience, the corps de ballet divided with military precision into three groups, one in white, one in green, and one dressed in scarlet. The day after the show opened, a reviewer for the *New York Evening Sun* wrote, "never had a Weberfields show so many pretty girls looking prettier than ever, and never has Miss Bessie Clayton done so elaborate a dance number or numbers as she did last night at the new music hall, destined to take the place of the little old hall down at 29th St. Never have Weber and Fields themselves been so delightfully foolish as in the automobile scene with Miss Dressler and the two comedians of the pied English certainly have never before so lavishly mounted a production as *Roly Poly.*" New York critic Alan Dale wrote later in one of his memoirs, "Dressler appeared in bright green satin, trimmed with a fur rug. She told me she made it herself in the hopes that she would be a laughing stock in it." Dale always believed that Dressler's greatest triumph in *Roly Poly* was a Spanish gypsy dance, in which "her evolutions caused tremendous laughter." The audience also roared ("the Lord forgive it," commented Dale) at her line, "Father you are the one thing in Mother's life I can never forgive." In *Without the Law,* Dressler made her entrance handcuffed to Joe Weber (Inspector Bunk) and, in a gesture of protest against injustice, she raised her arm and lifted Weber clear from the floor.

Despite exceptional first-night reviews (interspersed with caveats concerning the four-hour length of the show), news along the Great White Way was that there was a decided lack of harmony backstage. "The Weberfields are very far from settled into their new 44th St. home," wrote the New York correspondent of the *Boston Transcript* as early as December 5, 1912. "Nora Bayes and Jack Norworth are manifestly ill at ease. They aren't used to the give and take of a place where everybody forgets how really distinguished the 'all-star' cast is. Helen Collier Garrick is sort of restless too, but only because she hasn't anything left to do. When it came to cutting down the four-hour entertainment of the opening night, her scenes suffered so much, she has only three or four minutes left. Arthur Aylsworth is almost as badly off. Marie Dressler, it may be fearlessly stated, is a host in herself. Whether she is contemplating matrimony on little Mr. Weber or involuntarily stopping an automobile, she is always amusing and genuinely, legitimately so. Like no other stout actress of our musical stage, she is a true comedienne. No amount of cutting by the author can spoil Miss Dressler's part." Each of the *Roly Poly* principals did suffer the indignity of cuts to their roles (by December, *Without the Law* was trimmed to a ten-minute skit without scenery and dropped into the last act). Dressler's *Law* part was trimmed to a short speech in which she demands to know how a shopgirl can be expected to steal with any style at five dollars a week. But audience appreciation and applause for Dressler's performance was very much in evidence, much to the discomfort, the actress always claimed, of Lew Fields. "In one part of the show, I wore a fur coat made from a rug with a vicious-looking head hanging over my shoulder and the animal going 'round and 'round my body, the tail hanging loose," Dressler remembered in *Ugly Duckling*. "One night I whispered to Fields to play with the head. When he did, he got a roar of laughter. 'Brute of a thing,' he screamed. 'Let it run around.' I came back with the line: 'It's got all it can do to run around me,' and the laugh I got at my own expense and shape made Lew so angry, the scene was cut out," recalled Dressler. "But the next evening, Weber began playing with the head and Fields told him to drop it. Whereupon I said, kindly: 'Here, darling,' giving it back to Weber who looked so hopeless that it drew another laugh. When Weber and Fields started an argument right on stage, I piped up: 'I'll speak to my lawyer,' and went over and talked to a lamp on a newel post. The laugh drowned out the cutting words of Weber and Fields." Interestingly, however, Fields biographer Armond Fields says he feels Dressler's descriptions of the comedian's behavior were so uncharacteristic that "one must question either her memory or her motives." For years, insists Fields, the comedian had allowed the best lines to go to other principals in his productions.

Dressler had other vivid memories of *Roly Poly.* She recalled that Charles Darnton, dramatic critic of the *Evening World,* called on her during a rehearsal at which one of her funnier scenes was being severely trimmed. "How are you doing?" asked the critic. "All right," Dressler says she answered with a laugh. "I guess I'll be cut out in two weeks." Darnton wrote in his column, though, that the actress would be leaving *Roly Poly* in a fortnight. He also used what he claimed to be a direct Dressler quote: "I feel that I have a mission in life. I believe I was put on earth for a definite purpose. I am the outlet for tired man's brains. He finds relaxation in seeing me make a fool of myself." After reading the Darnton piece, Joe Weber and Lew Fields confronted Dressler with the angry accusation that she was clearly intending to quit *Roly Poly* in two weeks. Later in her life, Dressler insisted that it was all a mistake and that the producers simply told her that she might as well leave the theatre immediately. But on December 24, a reporter for the *New York Telegraph* wrote: "Marie Dressler, so she has informed her friends, is not particularly elated over her abrupt withdrawal from the Weber and Fields company. While Miss Dressler was secretly nursing the idea of leaving the organization, she expected to do so leisurely, after she had consummated other plans and with at least a two weeks' notice of her resignation. Fields, it seems, was exceedingly curt in his conversation with the comedienne on Saturday night, following his discovery that she had her resignation in contemplation. She readily enough admitted the fact when Fields put the question bluntly to her, but was not exactly prepared for his brief reply: 'Then leave at once.'"

Events unfolded swiftly after Dressler's dramatic exit from the show. "That mission in life which Marie Dressler told an evening newspaper critic she felt she had was partially fulfilled yesterday, when the former Weber and Fields star modestly announced her intention of suing Messrs. Weber and Fields for a round twenty-four thousand dollars, said amount being claimed by her as reasonable compensation for her services for one year." Weber and Fields, though, always insisted that Dressler left the company on her own accord and that she had "undermined the efficiency of the company by circulating reports about company members." The suit was eventually dropped. *Roly Poly* itself ran for just seven and a half weeks and was the only time Weber and Fields played together at the theatre named for them. When the last curtain fell on the show, the Shuberts decided to drop the original name in favor of the plainer Forty-Fourth Street Theatre.

The fact that Dressler wasted no time in getting her professional act together after the *Roly Poly* episode enhances the distinct probability that she was planning to depart the Weber and Fields production long before the completion of her contract. Within a scant three weeks, in fact, she and Dalton had put together a company called The Dressler Players, had booked the West End Theatre in Harlem, and had rehearsed a program of Dressler-arranged theatrical "tidbits," which soon became known as *Marie Dressler's All Star Gambol.* Scenery and costumes had also been designed and, in some instances, personally stitched together by the star. The *Gambol's* tidbits were almost eccentrically varied. For one thing, Dressler had signed up a French actress named Mme. Yorska (of the Paris-based Sarah Bernhardt theatre, no less), whom she assured reporters was costing her a fortune to present. Yorska was introduced to New York audiences in the most histrionic scenes from Alexandre Dumas's weeper, *Camille,* with actor Robert Drouet playing her lover, Armand Duval. But just in case audiences were figuring that La Dressler was going legitimate, she and comic opera star Jefferson de Angelis followed up with a burlesque entitled "Clamille," with Dressler as the tubercular heroine and de Angelis as "Almond" Duval. At the conclusion of the skit, the dying Clamille flattens the unhappy Almond under her considerable weight. Then, there was "A Symposium of Terpiscore," or "The Evolution of Dancing" (conceived and arranged by Dressler), which featured comic portrayals of ancient Greek dancing, old-fashioned step dancing, and classic toe dancing. Dressler herself presented some of her best-known acts: "A Great Big Girl Like Me," her now famous and somewhat hoary recitation of "The Glove," and a solo burlesque of "The Prima Donnas of Grand Opera." One of Dressler's most popular operatic burlesques was an impersonation of the famous coloratura soprano, Madame Luisa Tetrazzini. Although the impersonation was quite wicked, Tetrazzini not only told all of her friends that she loved it, the singer became one of Dressler's closest friends.

Both the New York critics and the New York audiences endorsed the *All Star Gambol.* "Miss Dressler, in her own company, is funnier than she ever was or, perhaps, dared to be before," wrote the reviewer for the *New York Journal.* "She teased along for a little while, sympathetically refusing to allow the audience to suffer from an over-dose of mirth and merriment. But the dose kept getting bigger and bigger all the time and just about the time you thought you couldn't laugh any more, she appeared with Jefferson de Angelis as the heroine of 'Clamille.' If you've ever seen Miss Dressler, you can imagine the rest." Dressler was elated over her latest entrepreneurial success. Although she and Dalton realized that as managers they would be assuming considerable financial responsibility, the actress truly believed that her popularity would guarantee good houses wherever the company decided to play. In March 1913, in fact, she cheekily moved the show into the Forty-Fourth Street Theatre after Weber and Fields's *Roly Poly* closed. There was an annoying turn of events that month, however. Dressler received a formal protest from The Lambs' Club (an exclusive actors' group whose unofficial motto was "liquor is the best cushion for the rough highway of life") drawing her attention to the fact that the club always called their charity shows *The Lambs' Gambol*. The protest, signed by Shepherd Joseph R. Grismer, requested Dressler to desist from further use of the 'Gambol' title on the electric sign in front of the Fourty-fourth Street Theatre. Even though the Lambs' remonstrance contained a veiled warning concerning a possible legal injunction, Dressler merely shrugged and tossed off the reply that she had a perfect right to use the words *Marie Dressler's All Star Gambol* at any time she might choose. Weeks later, when Supreme Court Justice Platzek did hear a Lambs' motion for an injunction, he ruled the club had no proprietary right to the Gambol title. Dressler continued to use it, though the infuriated Lambs would try to stop her again in 1914.

Dressler's feisty behavior in 1913 seems to indicate that she was feeling at the height of her personal power. After all, she had sailed through the unpleasant Weberfields break and also seemed to be succeeding as an independent actor-manager. The farm in Vermont was proof that she could work as a comedienne in the theatre and enjoy the dignified life of a chatelaine as well. She had replaced her late maid, Jenny, with a Savannah-born black woman named Mamie Cox, who would give the actress loyal service for the rest of her life. There was no doubt that she was a spectacular social success. That summer, in fact, the new Democratic president, Woodrow Wilson, chose Cornish, New Hampshire, as his summer White House, and Dressler and Dalton found themselves entertaining the Washington visitors and their entourage at their nearby Windsor retreat.

As for Jim Dalton, there was no indication in 1913 that Dressler was anything but smitten by Sunny Jim, despite his short-comings. The actress had taken to calling her companion "Papa," and Dalton himself made it clear to theatrical colleagues and the press that he was indispensable. Spartan dressing rooms were personally transformed by Papa with comfortable chairs and cushions. Dressler was instantly provided with culinary treats, particularly huge helpings of roast duckling and sauerkraut. Later in life, she confessed to her close friend Claire Dubrey that Dalton spent outrageous amounts of money on clothes, made questionable deals without her knowledge, and often disappeared for days without explanation. But in 1913, at least, Dalton received only respectful attention from the always curious members of the Broadway press corps.

Dressler herself was a healthy forty-five years of age. She boasted an awesome reservoir of energy and still displayed enough athletic ability on stage to turn any act into a familiar Dressler tour de force. Offstage, however, Dressler the Gracious Lady invariably replaced Dressler the Vulgar Clown. As one clearly impressed New York columnist wrote in florid language at the time: "An earnest, serious, sensible and most agreeable woman is Marie Dressler, personally attractive, in no way reminding you of the gawky, simpering, bellowing, crushing, bumping Tillie Bloggs, her amusing and really excellent character creation in *Tillie's Nightmare*. She is interesting and entertaining, having the rare and happy facility of putting you at your ease, engaging your thought, telling you many and sundry things about herself, her experiences and opinions without the disagreeable egotism so characteristic of players. Never saying uncomplimentary things as even the Divine Sarah does of her confreres, holding generous views of everybody excepting Roosevelt and fairly burdening her conversation with the praise of those other representatives of the stage who have attained stellar honors or are within near approach to them, she impresses one most agreeably."

Dressler took the *All Star Gambol* on tour during April, May, and June of 1913, but, although audiences were good, it soon became obvious that the momentum had evaporated from the show. In an attempt to give the program a fresh face, Dressler renamed the company the *Marie Dressler and Jefferson de Angelis, All-Star*

Players, and then dropped Madame Yorska (who was then shrilly demanding a higher fee) and the "serious" acts from *Camille.* The "Clamille" burlesque was kept on the menu, as was the "Evolution of Dancing" number and Dressler's solo appearance with "A Great Big Girl," "The Glove," and the "Prima Donna" impersonations. A baritone named Frederick Hastings was engaged to join the road tour and so was Eddie Rowley, billed as "the greatest buck and wing dancer that ever lived."

There were dates in Toledo, Baltimore, and Cleveland (one reviewer called the show "the cleanest and best vaudeville this town has ever seen"), but box-office receipts were disappointing. The story that never did hit the newspapers was that Dressler had decided to hedge her bets with the *All Star Gambol* as far back as May 1913 when she agreed to sign a new personal contract with the Shuberts. There was no agreement concerning a new play, but on the basis of the contract, Dressler managed to talk Lee Shubert into loaning her five thousand dollars—clearly a valuable cushion in the light of the *Gambol's* increasingly shaky bottom line. In July, she wrote to Shubert suggesting the contract be postponed until January 1914 because she intended to shelve the *Gambol* for a time and accept some vaudeville dates on the Keith circuit. She would, she promised, repay the five thousand dollar debt at the rate of five hundred dollars, every week she was employed.

In the last months of 1913, however, Dressler had changed her mind again and was planning a new self-financed revue entitled *The Merry Gambol.* She was so sure that it was a wise decision that she dispatched Dalton to San Francisco to arrange for an opening in the new year.

10

Marie Dressler's Merry Gambol

1914

Faced with the painful reality that their financial resources were dwindling, Dressler and Dalton were optimistic that a new production of *The Merry Gambol* would provide a welcome shot in the pocketbook. After some negotiation in New York, Sunny Jim traveled to San Francisco and signed a forty-week contract with Gilbert M. Anderson, former silent-film cowboy star also known as Bronco Billy, who was owner of the Gaiety Theatre on O'Farrel Street. The contract specified a Monday, January 26, 1914, opening date and stipulated that Anderson would be responsible for production expenses and would pay Dressler twenty-five hundred dollars for signing plus 20 percent of the gross box-office take. It also guaranteed that the Dressler management would retain the right to oversee the show and approve casting. Based on this seemingly favorable contract, Dressler and Dalton assembled a company of eighty principals and chorus members and proceeded to book tryout dates in Sacramento and Stockton, California.

The project was working well until an ominous glitch developed during the last days of the Stockton run. According to an outraged Dressler, the theatre management suddenly seized some costumes featured in an act entitled the "Kewpie Chorus," explaining that Gilbert Anderson and Gaiety manager Jake Rosenthal wanted them for their Los Angeles production of *The Girl at the Gate*. Dressler protested that she had designed and paid for the costumes herself, but the local manager's only response was to confiscate four wigs as well, also on orders from Anderson and Rosenthal. Even worse, when Dressler and Dalton arrived in San Francisco during the week of January 23, they were greeted with the rumor that the January 26 opening of *Gambol* had been postponed. The apparent reason for the rumor? A small *San Francisco Examiner* ad that announced a two-week showing—commencing the very night of the contracted *Merry Gambol* opening—of a steamy movie called *The Traffic in Souls,* based on the currently scandalous Rockefeller White Slave Report. When an irate Dressler confronted Anderson in his downtown office, she was told there had been a prior arrangement with one E. Fleet Bostwick to screen the movie and that a new date for *Merry Gambol* would need to be arranged. As a matter of fact, added Anderson frostily, he had seen Dressler's show in Stockton, and in his opinion it was definitely not up to Gaiety standards. There would need to be extensive revisions, the theatre proprietor plowed on. And when Dressler proceeded to wag an angry finger at him, he hinted that these revisions might also include the signing of a new star for the production.

Dressler and Dalton immediately turned to the always-interested local press in an effort to explain and complain. The real reason for the insulting postponement, insisted the actress, was that she had removed Jake Rosenthal's wife, Kathryn Osterman, whom she sarcastically referred to as Miss Oster*moor,* from the show. This public statement led to an equally infuriated Rosenthal charging Dalton with questionable conduct and claiming that, although Dressler had originally hired his wife, he himself had vetoed her appearance. "Catharine Rowe Palmer, another lady of the company also refused to appear because she felt she was not being treated with proper respect," complained Rosenthal. "I might be tied up with a 40-week contract with Miss Dressler, but thank heaven I have no contract with her husband."

The San Francisco battle of words raged untidily on until the evening of January 26 when, as the *Examiner* reported, "there was a Marie Dressler show at the Gaiety Theatre . . . but the public was not present at it. Instead of *The Merry Gambol,* which had been billed until recently, there was a cordon of special watchmen drawn about the theatre and every precaution taken to repel boarders in case Miss Dressler or the members of her company should forcibly attempt to report for duty. And the famous comedienne, with ire in her eye and determination in all her words, sat in a little electric coupe around the corner on Stockton Street while J.H. Dalton, her husband, and one of her attorneys went through the formality of reporting for duty in her name." And the *Examiner* reported further that "Marie Dressler plans to start proceedings on a complaint of breach of contract, alleging that she was not notified in due manner that *The Merry Gambol* had been postponed. . . . And back of the civil war that now rends the Gaiety is a tale full of hardships related by the *Merry Gambol* people, about eighty in all, who have been making shift on the bounty of Miss Dressler during the past few days while *The Merry Gambol* was playing in Sacramento and Stockton and who held a council of war in Miss Dressler's apartments yesterday and agreed to stick by her in her legal fight." The San Francisco newspapers were awash with the Gaiety drama, printing complaints and countercomplaints as they barreled out of Dressler headquarters and Bronco Billy's office. Readers struggled to untangle the news concerning the comings and goings of the equally confused Merry Gambol personnel. On the evening of January 28, however, there was a surprising turn of events, possibly brought about by Dressler and Dalton's lawyers, who had been commanded to sue. "Late tonight," wrote a correspondent for *Variety,* "Gilbert Anderson announced that all trouble with Miss Dressler had been adjusted and *The Merry Gambol* would open February 3. Miss Dressler will have her own way. The adjustment occurred at the right moment to reap the benefit of the daily newspaper publicity given to the affair. Miss Dressler's husband, Jim Dalton, will clean house and dismiss the attaches. It is said he would like to see Rosenthal go also, but it is doubtful if he will."

The Merry Gambol turned out to be a two-act revue, studded with dances, tunes, and girls, and with lyrics by local writer Arthur A. Penn. Dressler herself offered a highly predictable program: "A Great Big Girl Like Me," her grand opera travesties, and her recitation of "The Glove." She also concluded the first act with a tango with dancer Charles Judels, "whereupon she tore off his collar and ripped his coat-tails up to the neck." It was, decided one reviewer, "a terpsichorean triumph."

Dressler never referred to the *Merry Gambol* row in her two books, although in *My Own Story,* she remembered, "I decided to put on a show of my own. I wrote the piece, directed it, and christened it 'Marie Dressler's Merry Gambol'. With the exception of the merry, it was well-named. I put a mint of money into the production and it turned out to be a first-rate flop in New York. Later, however, I took it to San Francisco, where it enjoyed a nice run." Actually, the run lasted for six weeks at the Gaiety, and after Anderson and Rosenthal digested the first-night reviews, they were probably glad they had made a strategic withdrawal from the battle. "The war is over," wrote Neill Wilson in the *Examiner.* "Appomattox has been reached and all through the Gaiety a deep peace appears to pervade. *The Merry Gambol* had become something of a merry gamble, but last night it was presented to us with Marie Dressler herself as the chief Merry Gamboller. She put her show over, too, did this Joan of Arc of a recent insurgent; she put her show over in a way that was not to be disputed. The curtain danced up and down after the first act as if it were a Bronco Billy being served with another ultimatum. And between ascensions of that red velvet curtain, there was a rocketing of flowers up over the footlights in a way that has not been seen since the floral bombardment of *The Candy Shop,*" the previous attraction at the Gaiety.

A few days later, Gilbert Anderson issued the following statement to the press: "I desire personally and for the Gaiety Theatre company, of which I am president, to repudiate all the statements made by representatives of the Gaiety Theatre company and myself in connection with any misunderstanding and trouble with Marie Dressler and the theatrical enterprise known as *The Merry Gambol* now to be produced. I also desire to state that any misunderstanding which has occurred has been rectified to the entire satisfaction of Miss Dressler, and Miss Dressler will appear at the Gaiety Theatre. I desire to make it clear that the misunderstanding was not in any manner caused by Miss Dressler." Despite the fawning apologies, though, it was obvious that the actress and her husband were still at odds with manager Jake Rosenthal. In late February, pleading "a sudden and alarming attack of illness," Dressler retreated to her apartment at the St. Dominio. There was no evidence that either Rosenthal or Anderson had precipitated the indisposition, but after the Gaiety manager promptly publicized his decision to sign actress Marta Golden for the Dressler role, the comedienne just as suddenly recovered. There was a period of uneasy peace until the second week of March, then Dressler announced firmly that she was quitting the Gaiety forever. "My experience at the Gaiety under the present management has been one long nightmare," the angry actress told reporters. "I will never play under that management again. To deliver the goods to the public, I must have the right kind of support and I had an iron clad clause in my contract that I was to have the hiring of all the members of the company. Saturday night the management discharged twelve chorus girls. I just wouldn't stand for that. I can't be forever rehearsing new chorus girls, as my hands are full as it is with my own work. So I let it be known that I would refuse to go on unless the terms of my contract were adhered to."

But the *Examiner* reported another version of what it called "the ultimate straw that broke the contract." The story included the name of Alan Black, son of Dr. A.J. Black, one of the physicians who had attended Dressler during her February illness. "Together with his juvenile friends, Black enjoyed a party at the Gaiety Saturday afternoon in commemoration of his eleventh birthday as guest of Jim Dalton, manager of Miss Dressler," wrote the *Examiner*. "The party occupied four boxes. Miss Dressler threw Kewpie dolls to the youngsters who in turn, showered the comedienne with flowers. Later, Miss Dressler held a levee with the children on the stage. But still later, a storm broke when thirty-two dollars was deducted from Dalton's share on the day for the four boxes occupied by the children. Dalton said he wouldn't stand for it and the Gaiety management said he would. 'Then I'm through,' Dalton is said to have explained. 'And I don't mind telling you that you are a lot of pikers.'" The pikers then fought back with yet another weapon: they promptly sued Dressler for breach of contract, demanding thirty-five thousand dollars in damages and attaching the Dressler/Dalton account at the Union Trust Company. Steaming with anger, Dressler countersued for fifty thousand dollars, alleging a broken contract and injury to her feelings. She also requested a change of venue from the local to the federal court, a move that in hindsight might have sparked the final act in the Great San Francisco Fiasco. There's no doubt that the warfare between Anderson and Rosenthal on one side of the battlefield and Dressler and Dalton on the other was one of the ugliest ever waged by members of the American theatrical community. Dispatches from San Francisco were eagerly digested in New York and Boston and were even carried by the London newspapers. After the news concerning Dressler's exit from the Gaiety and the conflicting suits, however, theatre-watchers figured there would be the usual lull until one or both of the warring factions backed down.

Instead, the incredible story surfaced that Sunny Jim Dalton had been arrested by federal authorities on a charge that he had violated the Mann White Slave Act—coincidentally, the subject of the highly publicized movie shown at the Gaiety, *The Traffic in Souls.* The charge, preferred by Herbert Choynski, attorney for the Gaiety Theatre Company, alleged that Dalton had a wife in Boston and that, in consequence, Dalton must be either a bigamist or, technically, a white slaver. Marie Dressler was cited as the legal cause of the accusation. In future years and certainly in her two books, Dressler never referred to the Mann Act incident. She does admit that she "suffered a nervous breakdown" after the closing of *The Merry Gambol* in San Francisco but seemed to indicate that it was overwork that caused the malaise. The events of March 1914 must have been devastating for the actress, however, and must also have been a severe test of her relationship with Sunny Jim. Once the arrest was made, Dressler asked if she could appear before U.S. Attorney John Preston—without Dalton being present—to give her version of the case. Preston agreed, after receiving a call from attorney R.I. McWilliams, representing Dalton and Dressler. "I told Dalton," McWilliams apparently informed the U.S. attorney, "that if there was nothing in these charges as he said was the case, he need not waste either your or his time with a visit. On the other hand, if there was something in the charges, he should do his explaining to someone other than a Federal prosecutor." Preston, quite understandably, regarded this attitude as extraordinary and announced that in view of Dalton's failure to make an appearance and give his side of the case, he was strongly disposed to make a further investigation. But he was clearly impressed with Dressler's impassioned solo performance in his office. Not only did she deny all of the charges, she declared that the charges were part of a conspiracy on the part of the Gaiety Theatre personnel to damage her character and to muddy the issues in the two countersuits.

In the meantime, the Gaiety lawyers had managed to secure an affidavit from Lizzie A. Dalton in Boston. "This is to certify that I was married to James H. Dalton in Jersey City, N.J. in 1900 and that I have never secured a divorce from him, and that no papers have ever been served on me to indicate that he had ever applied for a divorce and to the best of my knowledge and belief, I am still his lawfully wedded wife." The document was witnessed by a Nellie R. Rogers and Guy C. Packard, a Pinkerton detective assigned to the case. Responding to this document, Dalton himself told the *San Francisco Examiner* that Lizzie had indeed divorced him nine years before. "As for Miss Dressler," he added, "we have been married for six years. We were married on the Continent."

Preston examined the evidence placed before him and concluded that the Lizzie Dalton affidavit was really the only document that he could consider as significant in the case. The white slavery charge, he concluded, could not be proved, and he said there was no proof that Dalton and Dressler were not man and wife—unaccountably, he did not ask the couple to produce a marriage or a divorce certificate—even if it might be shown that Dalton was a bigamist. "I was urged to lay the case before the Federal Grand Jury," Preston announced to the fascinated press. "But for the present, at least, I have no grounds to proceed under the presumption that this is a case under the Mann Act. Nothing in the evidence presented to me proves there was any intent under the Act. There is no evidence that Dalton brought Miss Dressler here, induced her to come or paid her way here. All that the reports of the detectives show is that so far, no record of a divorce can be found. It seems, at best, a case for the local authorities here or in Massachusetts, rather than a case for the Federal authorities." Preston continued: "It looks to me, off-hand, as if the Gaiety management was trying to get me to pull their chestnuts out of the fire. It seems a bad time to institute such charges when there are lawsuits which may be affected."

Bathed in tears, Dressler told local journalists that she intended to stay in San Francisco until all charges against her and Sunny Jim were disposed of and until she "could show Anderson and his associates in their true light." She also intimated that she was cooking up some new charges of her own against Bronco Billy and his partners but refused to discuss them until there was "a full confirmation" of her statements. Within another day or so, however, Dressler and Dalton had packed their trunks and boarded a train for Los Angeles. As the actress explained in *My Own Story,* "When we stored *The Merry Gambol,* I found myself verging on a nervous breakdown. My doctor ordered me to Los Angeles to rest and bask in the sunshine." In the City of Angels Dressler would turn another fateful corner in her life.

There are two dramatically different versions of how Marie Dressler made her debut in the world of motion pictures. She herself wrote in *My Own Story*—and recounted to dozens of interviewers—that she was literally picked up by filmmaker Mack Sennett in Los Angeles not long after the San Francisco disaster. As she remembered: "One afternoon, in company with my nurse [quite likely Jim Dalton], I dropped into a neighborhood picture house. As we passed through the lobby, I noticed one of a pair of men staring at me oddly. 'Hurry, let's get inside,' I whispered to my companion. 'That's a Broadway exile who's stranded and wants to bum his fare back to New York. He's trying to get up his nerve to speak to me.' When we came out after the performance, we found the two men waiting outside the theatre door. The one I had first noticed approached me with a sort of desperate diffidence. 'Miss Dressler,' he said, jerking his head in the direction of his wild-eyed companion, 'we'd like to talk to you a minute.' I told him I'd see them at my hotel, for I was still weak and trembly and not equal to the ordeal of standing long at a time. When they presented themselves in my sitting room ten minutes later, I discovered that the wild-eyed one was Mack Sennett, and that the spokesman for the pair was Charles Bauman of Keystone Pictures."

The other version of the story was provided by Sennett. According to the producer, he was then trying to persuade Keystone principals Charles Bauman and Adam Kessel to allow him the chance of making the first full-length, six-reel motion picture comedy. "My partners pointed out to me, correctly, that such a picture would not only cost in the neighborhood of $200,000, but demanded a star whose name and face meant something to every possible theatregoer in the United States and the British Empire." Interestingly, Sennett ruled out Mabel Normand, who was then widely known, and even another Keystone player, Charlie Chaplin. His partners also reminded the producer that no one had ever made a six-reel comedy and that the proposed venture was a decided gamble. "Not a gamble with Marie Dressler," countered Sennett.

Kessel said, "Yeah, maybe not with Marie Dressler. But we ain't got Marie Dressler. You might as well think about Weber and Fields or Lillian Russell." (Sennett, who was born Michael Sinnott in Quebec, had actually met Dressler years before when he was just seventeen years of age and working as an ironworker in Northampton, Connecticut. He asked a local lawyer named Calvin Coolidge—who, of course, eventually became president of the United States—to write him a letter of introduction to Dressler, who was playing in *The Lady Slavey* in town. He wanted, he told Coolidge, to become an actor. Dressler met the young man and in turn gave him a letter to theatrical producer David Belasco in New York. "I guess you ought to have a chance, Rivets," Sennett remembers Dressler saying in his notoriously unreliable autobiography, "but God help you.")

After arguing with Kessel and Bauman for days, Sennett received the go-ahead to approach Dressler. He is vague about how this happened, but does say that "when I put Marie Dressler under contract [she] arrived in Hollywood, leased a magnificent house and went on salary from the moment she stepped off the train in Pasadena." Both Dressler and Sennett agree on the amount of this salary: twenty-five hundred dollars a week, an announcement that provoked a near riot on the Keystone lot. Mabel Normand, already known as the Queen of the Movies, was then receiving the less prestigious sum of fifteen hundred dollars a week and, to make matters much stormier, Sennett, who was romantically involved with Normand, ordered her to vacate the star dressing room and allow Dressler to take possession. Sennett did have another luxurious dressing room constructed for his fiancée, but the two actresses never really warmed to each other.

When Dressler took time to explore her new surroundings in April 1914, she discovered a sunlit Garden of Eden, lush with orchards and tropical flowers. Much of Sunset Boulevard was unpaved, and local residents used either horses or horsedrawn streetcars for transport. Dancer Agnes de Mille, who lived in Hollywood in the early years of the century, remembered that there was a sign on the back of streetcars that read, "Don't shoot rabbits from the rear platform." She laughingly believed the authorities worried that someone might hit the policeman. "Hollywood had one policeman and he generally stood at the corner of Hollywood and Vine."

The motion picture industry was very much in its infancy in 1914. The Selig Company was making films in Eastlake Park (old photographs show that walkways were built to prevent cast members and technicians from trampling the cornfield), and Biograph had a studio at Pico and Georgia Streets, Los Angeles, where producer-director D.W. Griffith would winter in the California sunshine. Keystone took over a studio once occupied by the New York Motion Picture Company in Edendale. The studios were often merely a setup of posts strung with canvas-draped wires to shield actors and technical staff from the blazing sun. Later, remembered veteran director Allan Dwan, "enterprising people came from the East and began to put up buildings around these lots—always leaving the roofs open because otherwise we couldn't work. We had no electric light. . . . Sometimes it would be raining on one side of the street and we'd make rain shots and then walk across the street and do sunshine shots."

Dressler never referred to the "magnificent house" mentioned by Mack Sennett in *King of Comedy,* but there's little doubt she could have afforded a substantial rent to keep Sunny Jim and herself in comfort during her Hollywood stay. The big problem at Keystone, she soon discovered, was that no one knew what story they would use for the six-reel feature. In *King of Comedy,* Sennett says the uncertainty lingered for a week until a studio employee with the surname of Hutchison had the bright idea of using the story line of Dressler's celebrated hit *Tillie's Nightmare.* "We outlined that on not more than two sheets of hotel stationery, had it typed in the morning and sent it up to the boys in the gag room with orders to make with the funny business." In *My Own Story,* though, Dressler insists that the choice of Tillie as the basis for a script was strictly her own idea and that she only agreed to come on board the proposed production if she was guaranteed a half interest in the picture and also that it would be leased, not sold to distributors. The actress insists, too, that Bauman and Sennett agreed to send her weekly financial statements after the film was released. Dressler clearly enjoys telling the story that after the contract was signed, she took instant charge of casting the picture. (One story Dressler never publicized was that she refused to consider Keystone actor Roscoe "Fatty" Arbuckle for a role because his huge girth would look inappropriate in a film featuring the equally huge Dressler.)

Wrote Dressler in her autobiography: "Now for actors. Instantly there leaped into my mind the name of a young chap I had seen in London several years before. I knew that boy had genius, that he would some day be acclaimed a star. I had run across him a few days before in Hollywood. Now I started a great hue and cry: 'Where is Charlie Chaplin? I want Charlie Chaplin.' Everybody thought I was crazy. Maybe I was, but I knew what I knew. And I knew that Chaplin could act. He was an enormous success in Tillie. I'm proud to have had a part in giving him his first big chance." Actually, the twenty-five-year-old Chaplin had already made several successful pictures in America (among them, *Twenty Minutes of Love, Dough and Dynamite,* and *Laughing Gas*) and he and Mabel Normand were considered to be the two top stars of the studio—certainly acceptable box office insurance for what the management believed to be an immense gamble. Other actors picked to appear in *Tillie* included Mack Swain as Marie's father, Charlie Bennett as her rich uncle, Chester Conklin, Minta Durfee, Edgar Kennedy, Charlie Murray, Charlie Chase, and a young Milton Berle. Plus the entire corps of zany Keystone Kops.

Despite Sennett's acceptance of the *Tillie's Nightmare* story line, *Tillie's Punctured Romance* is a distinct departure from the stage play. Instead of playing the drudge of Skaneateles, Dressler becomes a farm girl who is persuaded by Chaplin to steal her father's money and run away with him to the big city. There they meet Mabel, Charlie's sweetheart and partner in crime. Dressler becomes intoxicated in a restaurant and, with much falling down, bumping into, and kicking around, executes some wildly comic dances. Charlie absconds with her wallet and escapes with Mabel. In the meantime, Tillie's rich uncle is reported to have perished in a mountaineering accident, and the poor farm girl magically becomes an heiress. Charlie learns the interesting news, returns to woo Tillie once again, then quickly marries her. Together, they move into her uncle's luxurious home and are born again as members of high society. They give a ball, dance together, and, of course, fall down, bump into furniture, kick each other unmercifully, and generally create confusion among their toney guests. In the midst of this mayhem, the rich uncle (not dead at all!) trots into the scene. There is a Keystone Kops chase sequence, collisions, boats upsetting. The Kops' patrolwagon skids into the picture and slams into

Tillie's vast derriere, shoving her off a pier and into the sea. Eventually, both Tillie and Mabel turn against the villainous Chaplin, and the Kops haul him off to the pokey.

Seen today, *Tillie's Punctured Romance* can only be viewed as slapstick of the most rudimentary kind and certainly provides little indication that Dressler had been hailed as one of the finest comediennes on Broadway. But even though it is easy to groan at the actress's flamboyant antics, her ability to throw all caution to the winds and simply play the fool must be seen to be believed. In the years since its release, critics have studied the seemingly endless film and agreed that Dressler's portrayal of Tillie was far too broad for the movies. She clearly needed direction and restraint, but Sennett himself has confirmed that she would not accept this. As he wrote in *King of Comedy:* "No matter that this was her first motion picture, she was a great star and this was her own story. In the midst of a comic scene I had planned carefully beforehand, Miss Dressler would say: 'No Mack, that's wrong. Now this is the way we're going to do it.' I was the head of the studio and I was supervising this particular picture, but neither of these things influenced Marie Dressler. My arguments didn't influence her either. 'Okay, Marie, you do it your way,' I'd say. And I would leave the set. Usually, a sweating messenger would arrive within an hour. Miss Dressler, who didn't know a camera angle from a hypotenuse, always threw the company into a swivel when she took over. 'Mack, there's just a little technicality here you can help me straighten out,' she'd say. 'Sure, sure, Marie, call on me any time.'"

Sennett said that Dressler got along well with Chaplin (the comedian agreed with this in his autobiography, but insisted that he felt *Tillie* itself had little merit), although she clearly overpowered him physically in their love scenes. Once, however, she complained that Chaplin had worn the same, very soiled celluloid collar for sixteen days in succession. If the collar wasn't cleaned up, she told Sennett testily, "I shall enact you the goddamnedest vomiting scene in the annals of the drammer." Chaplin was ordered to change his collar.

When the picture was released later in 1914, Dressler read a news story that sent her into gales of laughter: "One Thomas O'Day, business manager of the Gaiety Theatre in San Francisco and sworn enemy of Marie Dressler, offers an interesting explanation for the booking of *Tillie's Punctured Romance* with Miss Dressler in the leading role. Mr. O'Day, who is frank if not unduly gallant, candidly admits that he is bringing the movie to his house because throughout the comedy scenes, Miss Dressler is kicked by Charlie Chaplin and he enjoys the spectacle. 'It gives me a restful feeling,' he says, 'to see Miss Dressler, even in make-believe, receive a series of salutes from the rear.' Besides, O'Day added, he had heard that *Tillie's Punctured Romance* made a lot of money in Los Angeles. 'It's seldom that a time comes when a man can make money and satisfy an ancient grudge at the same time. I can watch the box-office and enjoy the abuse of a lady who nearly wrecked our theatre.'"

11

MIX-UPS AND MOVIES

1914-1915

Dressler and Dalton headed for the Vermont farm as soon as the train from Los Angeles deposited them in New York. For the actress, it was a welcome surcease from the trauma of San Francisco and the challenging, fourteen-week stint in front of the Keystone movie cameras. It was also a chance for Dressler to be alone with Sunny Jim and to try to rationalize her feelings about the relationship. At some time during the Vermont break, she obviously decided to stick with Dalton, despite his faults. After all, he was an impressive-looking escort, and the actress must have found him useful as a go-between or backup whenever agreements needed to be negotiated with the male establishment. And, despite Dalton's frequent, sometimes fraudulent misdemeanors, Dressler was clearly obsessed with the man.

But if there had been any time when the comedienne believed herself to be the demurely feminine member of the Dressler-Dalton duo, those days were over. In late 1914, for example, Dressler and Sunny Jim were entering the dining room of the Biltmore Hotel in Manhattan one evening, when a male patron loudly commented: "There goes the president of the female boiler makers union." Instead of waiting for Dalton to leap to her defense, Dressler roughly hauled the man out of his seat and demanded—and got—an apology. The report of the affair referred to Dalton as Miss Dressler's husband, which must mean that the New York press had decided to ignore or overlook details of the San Francisco Mann Act scandal.

Once back on the farm, Dressler inspected her reduced colony of livestock (she had sold off most of her cows), consisting of a number of pigs, chickens, and a few horses and dogs that were tended by a small but devoted staff. She renewed her friendship with a laughing parrot named Toby that had accompanied her during her long and boring tours with *Tillie's Nightmare*. She rested gratefully for a couple of weeks, sleeping late and feasting on her favorite foods: roast duckling and peach duff. Then she began making inquiries in New York concerning the progress of *Tillie's Punctured Romance*. To her shock and dismay, she heard from Charles Kessel at Keystone Comedy's head office that distributors were turning thumbs down on the property. The problem, it seemed, was that the exhibition business was wary of a feature-length comedy. Oh, the public had lined up to see such five-reelers as Adolph Zukor's *The Prisoner of Zenda* and the Lasky Company's *The Squaw Man*. But those were dramas with spellbinding plots, not loosely constructed slapstick farces. Kessel admitted that he, Baumann, and Sennett were worried. *Tillie's Punctured Romance* had plunged the company deeply into debt, and creditors were thumping at the door. Dressler sat listening to him in silent concern. Although she had been well paid for the movie job, the Vermont estate was still hungrily consuming a large percentage of her earnings. Sunny Jim also needed money for ongoing personal expenses, and there was the new income tax that had descended on the nation like a plague in 1913. She had hoped, she admitted to Kessel, that there would have been some dividends from the motion picture project by now. After all, she reminded the glum Keystone executive, she did own a half interest in the picture and expected some return in rental fees.

Time dragged on into fall 1914. As it happened, *Tillie's Punctured Romance* did not clinch its first booking for nine weeks, and Dressler became uncomfortably aware that she would need to pin down a new assignment to pay her bills. Broadway, though, was experiencing one of its worst slumps in years and, despite the outbreak of war across the Atlantic, most of the current theatrical hits were European imports. She'd heard that several managers were shutting down their theatres during the upcoming Christmas season. She thought about trying for another movie role and made some inquiries in Philadelphia, where veteran producer Sigmund

"Pop" Lubin owned a studio. But before there were any serious discussions, the actress was contacted by New York play broker Mary Asquith, who insisted on sending Dressler a property she had just acquired. Tentatively entitled *The Sub,* the play had been written by a Maysville, Kentucky, surveyor named Parker A. Hord. Hord had apparently never written anything for the theatre before, but Asquith had decided that *The Sub* was a brilliant comedy and uniquely suited to Dressler's talents. The comedienne agreed to read the Hord script, though she admitted to being cautious about appearing in a nonmusical play. But she also had to admit that a production unencumbered by the budget-breaking expense of a chorus line, lavish costumes, and an orchestra might actually make financial sense at that time. She studied the Hord script, met with Asquith to suggest some changes, then sent a proposal to Lee Shubert: the comedy, now retitled *Angela's Substitute,* was a promising property that the actress believed would do well on tour. If the producer liked the play, she suggested a financial partnership. Because she had been instrumental in bringing the script to Shubert's attention, she wanted 25 percent of the tour profits, but as far as salary was concerned, she would be willing to work for a negotiated percentage of the weekly gross receipts.

Shubert read *Angela's Substitute,* consulted his business associates, then asked the actress to come to his office. He was not unduly surprised when Dalton turned up as well. The producer had always liked and admired Dressler, but he warned both her and Sunny Jim that if the tour eventuated, they must have nothing to do with the management of the play or the bookings. Shubert conceded, however, that Dressler herself could have a free hand in staging the production. There was some friendly conversation and banter, then Shubert nodded his head and agreed to come on board. His company would retain a 75 percent interest in the show, Dressler would own 25 percent but must also contribute 25 percent toward the cost of production, including royalties to Hord. The Shubert Theatrical Company would pay the actress 15 percent of the gross receipts up to five thousand dollars a week and 20 percent of any box-office income beyond that amount. And, yes, his office would arrange and pay for a drawing room and lower berths for Dressler and Dalton plus accommodation for Mamie Cox, their maid, when they were traveling by rail.

Casting calls and rehearsals for the play, again retitled, this time as *A Mix Up*, began almost immediately, and an October opening date was set for Atlantic City with further bookings in Pittsburgh, Cleveland, and Toledo. The cast included such competent performers as Nellie de Grasse, Bert Lytell, and Evelyn Vaughan. It had been agreed that Dressler would flesh out the somewhat skimpy plot by contributing two or three songs.

Naturally, the actress was hoping that her friends in the theatrical press would thump a few drums on behalf of *A Mix Up*, and she readily agreed to interviews at every whistle-stop on the tour. Probably the most creative piece of copy came from the pen of a Pittsburgh reporter who headlined his story "Marie Dressler's Father Survivor of Crimean War." Read the copy: "In these days when war news is read by everyone, it may be interesting to note that Marie Dressler's father, Captain Alexander Koerber, now living in Cobourg, Ont. is said to be the last survivor living in this country of the Crimean war. Miss Dressler, who is to appear at the Alvin Theatre Monday night in her newest success, *A Mix Up*, made this astonishing statement last week in Cleveland and stands ready to prove it. Anyone has only to telegraph the Canadian postmaster at Cobourg Ont. and get an official OK on the statement that Captain Koerber is now living there, that he is 83 years old and that he was a captain in the service of the British army which went to the Crimea in 1856 to aid the Turkish army in fighting the Russians in the siege of Sebastopol." The report continued, "'The amazing thing about my father's service,' said Miss Dressler, 'is that, although of German descent, he had lived in England and was a naturalized British subject when Queen Victoria called for volunteers for the British army. My father . . . fought the Cossacks and the Russian army in a winter that was almost one continuous snow storm, was decorated with the Victoria Cross for bravery and after the war returned to England and immigrated to Canada.'" There is no evidence that Alexander Koerber was still living in 1914 and certainly none that he ever returned to Cobourg. He did not, of course, win the Victoria Cross for bravery.

Reviews of *A Mix Up* once again confirm Dressler's mastery of theatrical comedy. The play with its threadbare story line would have killed the show in the first act without the magic of the Dressler presence. And her decision to include two songs, "Let Them Alone,

They're Married," and "Sister Susie's Sewing Shirts," helped elevate it from banality into a critical and box-office success. There were some reviewers, in fact, who believed that Dressler's role in *A Mix Up* was easily the finest theatrical performance of her career. Decided a *Cleveland Leader* critic: "It's a bigger laughing success than *Tillie's Nightmare,* which must stand as the comparative standard for all time." But, as Dressler instinctively knew, the very sparseness of plot gave her the freedom to invent the kind of stage business that had made her a superb comedienne. The story concerned the character of one Gladys Lorraine (played by Dressler), a prima donna of the burlesque circuit. Gladys decides to visit a friend, Tillie Schartz (played by Nellie de Grasse), and arrives at the right apartment number but at the wrong apartment hotel. Instead of finding friend Tillie's domicile, she wanders into the rooms of a young bridegroom whose wife is away for the weekend. The young man is expecting a visit in a few days from rich and puritanical-minded relatives to whom he has written that his bride is cultured, refined, and deeply religious. But when the uncle and aunt unexpectedly turn up while Dressler is explaining her mistake over a highball and a cigarette, the bridegroom panics and introduces the burlesque queen as his wife. Wrote a reviewer for the *Brooklyn Eagle:* "Nothing reasonable is said, nothing plausible is done. Also nothing unreasonable is left unsaid, or nothing impossible left undone that promises to excite laughter. Miss Dressler is a woman who is not afraid to tumble over sofas, crawl along the floor on her hands and knees, dash around in a manner that would tire a trained athlete, sing, dance, create roars of laughter with her facial expressions and then, now and then, strike a note of pathos that is worthy of a great actress."

Because the Shubert contract gave Dressler carte blanche to use her imagination in the staging of *A Mix Up*, the actress decided to experiment with what she called "scenic innovations." These inventions were actually transparencies that allowed the audience a glimpse of what was going on elsewhere in the play. In one, the wife was seen listening at the other end of a telephone circuit. The transparency was also used to reveal people leaving the apartment house elevator and walking along a corridor before entering the young husband's apartment. As Dressler explained to a reporter during the run of the show, the device gave the audience a chance to anticipate the reactions once new characters came on the scene. These innovations proved to be so successful that Dressler hints in *The Ugly Duckling* that other producers began tinkering with the idea. "Some lighting effects which I had invented [for *A Mix Up*] seemed about to be stolen," she remembered. Apparently the plan had been to keep the play on the road for a while longer, but Shubert decided to capitalize on its success and the interest in its creative production techniques and moved it into the Thirty-Ninth Street Theatre on December 28, 1914. But despite glowing reviews, *A Mix Up* did not do well on Broadway. There was another attempt to tour the play, notably in Philadelphia, Toledo, and Washington, but by the spring of 1915, the show had folded.

Dressler accepted *The Mix Up* closing with philosophical good humor. If she had known that the play would be the last long-running theatrical production in which she would ever star, she might have been less sanguine at the time. But, typically, there seemed to be dozens of other irons in the fire and some problems that needed her attention as well. For one thing, she found herself engaged in a messy row with Keystone. Although *Tillie's Punctured Romance* had opened to excellent reviews and was attracting crowds around the country, the production company had yet to send her an accounting or a check for her share of the earnings. Not only that, she had heard that the picture would be sold to the Alco Film Corporation without consultation with either her or Dalton as joint owners. In December 1914, thoroughly alarmed at Kessel and Sennett's lack of response to her repeated complaints, she applied to the Supreme Court of New York State to appoint a receiver for the picture and to issue an injunction restraining the Keystone Film Company from disposing of the movie. Keystone fought back in court. The company's attorneys, Graham and Stevenson, brandished the original contract and argued that while it gave Dressler rights to the negative of *Tillie,* it clearly gave Keystone freedom to handle the prints and dispose of them as it thought best. To Dressler's horror, the judge, Mr. Justice Newberger, found for the defendants. Held the judge: "The defendant denies that it intends to sell or dispose of the film, but proposes to lease the same for certain territories on what is known as a state rights basis. I can find nothing in the moving papers that would warrant this court in holding that the disposition proposed by the defendant would be a sale, or that the plaintiff would be injured by any such act. The application for a receiver and an injunction pendente litem must be denied."

Dressler and Dalton huddled with their lawyers and instructed them to try again for an injunction. The case was heard later in December, before the Appellate Division of the Supreme Court. And once again, the case was dismissed. But the Keystone quarrel continued to simmer and again came to a boil in the spring of 1915. By then, Dressler had learned, *Tillie's Punctured Romance* had earned the movie company at least $122,000 in leasing fees. Despite the terms of her original agreement, however, the actress had received nothing, and Keystone had stubbornly refused to provide her with an accounting. In May, the dispute again invaded the Supreme Court before Mr. Justice Page, with Dressler demanding that the Keystone Film Corporation and their partners, Alco Film Corporation, be forced to provide her with a financial update and then to pay her one-half of the accrued profits from the movie. True to her theatrical reputation, Dressler provided the court with a show of outraged sensibility and witness-stand entertainment. At one point, she complained tragically to Judge Page that she was "sore on the films," a remark that Keystone's lawyer, Austin G. Fox, successfully had stricken from the record. At another point of the hearing, Dressler was asked by Fox: "Have you ever had any other experience at exploiting yourself in the moving pictures?" Dressler looked back at him haughtily, waggled her jaw, and replied: "I have not, Mr. Fox. It wasn't needed, I assure you." Fox smiled and said: "Would you mind, Miss Dressler, if I ask the court to have your observation stricken from the record as irrelevant and unresponsive?" According to a reporter, "Miss Dressler didn't say so, but looked as if she would."

Apparently, Dressler's pleas for an accounting from Keystone, combined with her riveting court performance, must have charmed Mr. Justice Page. Early in August, she heard that the Keystone Company had been ordered to file a detailed statement of receipts from the leasing of *Tillie*. The actress eventually settled with the producers for fifty thousand dollars and the return of the negative after five years. In the early 1920s, she leased the film to another distribution company and was to receive twenty-five thousand dollars down and a weekly royalty. "But again," she remembered in *The Ugly Duckling*, "the picture has turned out a hoodoo as far as receipts go, as I cannot get any accounting from the second producer, although the film is still being shown. Anyway, the business side of the moving picture business has always been too complicated for me. There are too many middlemen."

Despite her bruising experience with *Tillie's Punctured Romance,* however, Dressler did not turn her back on the young and rapidly growing movie industry. In April 1915, while she was still touring in *A Mix Up,* she signed a contract with "Pop" Lubin's production company in Philadelphia. The original announcement was that she would star in at least three five-reel comedies a year and that, according to reports, Lubin would "select the most expensive list of players that has ever been used in a production." Filming of the first feature (then not named) was set to begin in June, but during her visit to Philadelphia with *A Mix Up,* Dressler proceeded to put an early stamp on the Lubin operation by invading Pop's ranch at Bentwood and poking around the production facilities. As one observer put it: "Miss Dressler is a student of the technical side of the motion picture business and she had the time of her gay young life in the laboratories at the ranch, inspecting the new inventions for improving photoplays and watching the experts there carrying on their experimental work with new printing devices and natural color motion photography."

But the spring of 1915 was a stressful time for Dressler. *A Mix Up* was clearly heading into history, the Keystone quarrel was still simmering, and, despite Pop Lubin's assurances that her association with his company would be an instant success, she was still unsure about her future in the movies. At least Sunny Jim was behaving himself, but there were constant financial pressures, both from Dalton and from the Vermont farm. By June, however, she found herself looking forward to the Lubin shoot. Acton Davies, one of the better-known theatrical journalists in New York, had fashioned a comedy script that had been dubbed *Tillie's Tomato Surprise,* an obvious tip of the hat to the success of *Tillie's Punctured Romance* and a new thorn in the side of an increasingly hostile Keystone group. Explained Dressler when a reporter asked about the plot: "You will not find in it either a policeman, a siphon, a telephone or a revolver and anyone who has ever seen a comic picture will realize that in avoiding these features, we have attained at least some feat and are going to give the public something new in the line of vegetables, if not of photoplays." Actually, the movie, which also featured comedian Tom McNaughton and was directed by Howell Hansel, was just as comically violent as *Tillie's Punctured Romance*. Davies's plot was paper thin, the unlikely story of Tillie losing one million dollars in cash and finding it again, stuffed inside a tomato. This unlikely story was propped up by the usual Dressler mayhem: Tillie is attacked by gunfire and arrows. She falls downstairs. She is pushed through a brick wall and she tumbles out of an automobile. She slips off a bridge onto a freight train. She is half drowned in molasses and almost suffocated by a blizzard of chicken feathers. She even rides a long-suffering horse. "Yesterday I made my way carelessly through a brick wall two feet thick," explained Dressler when asked about the picture by an *Ohio State Journal* reporter. "The day before, I permitted an eight-cylinder to pass over my defenseless body. Last week, a dog and a monkey were honored by being permitted to bite me. I have been thrown out of windows. I have been rescued from cruel waves, have been baked, fried, stewed—not the kind of a stew you think I mean—and all in the cause of art."

Tillie's Tomato Surprise was released at about the same time as Mr. Justice Page ordered the Keystone Company to file a detailed statement of receipts from the rental of *Tillie's Punctured Romance*. This success probably tempered the news that although reviews of the Lubin movie were upbeat, they were scarcely as enthusiastic as those that had accompanied the release of the earlier *Tillie* saga. There were some earnest discussions at Lubin headquarters as to whether the company would make the three Dressler comedies a year that had been announced earlier in 1915, but decisions dragged on until it became obvious that the production company was not interested in going ahead with the plan. Dressler and Dalton, though, celebrated the wrap of the latest movie as well as their triumph over Keystone with a holiday in White Plains, New York, at the Gedney Farms Hotel.

In October 1915 it was clear that Dressler's former lack of interest in Votes for Women had taken a decided turn. The change of heart might have been influenced by her blossoming friendship with social heavyweight Mrs. O.H.P. Belmont, who was still campaigning tirelessly for women's suffrage. While the actress was appearing in *A Mix Up* at the Thirty-Ninth Street Theatre in New

York, she was a frequent volunteer at Mrs. Belmont's free soup kitchen for unemployed working women. Then, at the Gedney Farms Hotel, Dressler made news by "winning over at least fifty men in the hotel to the suffrage cause." Dressler is reported as saying: "At no time has there been such a demand for the vote as now among the women of New York State." According to the story, ten of the men whom Miss Dressler converted were first beaten by her at golf. She exacted from them a promise that they would cast their vote for women's suffrage if they lost.

Alva Belmont was impressed with Dressler's new interest in the Cause. Later that year, she invited the actress to a meeting at her Madison Avenue mansion to discuss a theatrical project that might help bolster the always needy coffers of the Women's Party. The plan was to stage what Mrs. Belmont described as "a suffrage operetta." Music would be composed by a newcomer to the exclusive Belmont circle, a dumpy and unattractive young woman named Elsa Maxwell. And there were hopes that Dressler, actresses Josephine Hull and Marie Doro, and Metropolitan Opera star Frances Alda would star in the show. Other volunteer performers would include some of the most eye-catching young women in the social register: Maud Kahn, daughter of Wall Street banker Otto Kahn; debutante Kitty Bache; Dorothy Gordon Fellowes, niece of the Marquis of Dufferin; and the gorgeous Pauline Disston of Philadelphia. Mrs. Belmont also hinted that she had dragooned Mrs. Rutherford Stuyvesant, Mrs. Harry Oelrichs and architect Addison Mizner (who had carved Palm Beach out of the Florida wilderness) to play supporting roles. The name of the show? *Melinda and Her Sisters.* The production would be staged at the Waldorf, and tickets would cost five and ten dollars.

Mrs. Belmont's suffrage operetta played a single performance on February 18, 1916, and turned out to be an airy trifle that was billed as a "satire of smart society" curiously lacking in the kind of propaganda for the Cause that New York usually identified with the Women's Party. Instead of speeches, declamations, and stirring appeals to rally around the yellow banner, the professional and amateur performers sang, danced, and giggled through Elsa and Alva's somewhat forced sketches. "I'm a little love letter, and I should have known better," warbled socialite Mrs. G.J.S. White, backed by a troupe of the season's debutantes, chanting the woes of the bad little love letter that lost itself. Dressler played the role of society hostess Mrs. John Pepper, dressed in a spangled creation that came slightly above the top of her rather high boots. She had made the dress, she assured reporters, with her own hands. Her stage daughter, Nellie Pepper, was played by debutante Pam Day. Miss Nellie, explained Dressler, had been in Paris studying classical dancing, which explained why she appeared on stage in bare feet and wearing nothing much more substantial than a wisp of gauze draped from her shoulders. Dressler herself brought down the house by impersonating a faun in the Ballet Russe, singing a Maxwell song: "For I will not dally with the Russian leather ballet / and the ballet shall not dally with me."

Although the suffrage operetta cleared some eight thousand dollars for the Women's Party, not all of smart society approved of Alva and Elsa's contribution to the musical theatre. "While it was undoubtedly a great triumph for Mrs. Belmont—and I suppose Mrs. Belmont argues that she can do anything she likes—there is, nevertheless, some question as to just how far it is advisable to mix people up," complained a columnist for *Town Topics.* "Amateur performances are all right so long as they are confined to amateurs and kept, as it were, a close corporation. But when it comes to mixing up young debutantes with seasoned professionals, painting their faces and dressing them up in diaphanous and abbreviated costumes, to kick about for the amusement of a mixed public, it seems to me there should be a limit somewhere." Dressler admitted, however, that she had thoroughly enjoyed the *Melinda* caper. After all, she had always felt completely at home with members of high society, and it had been exhilarating to receive tributes (the press called her "a hard-working suffragist") and flowers from such luminaries as Birdie Vanderbilt, Count Etienne Markoski, and Angelica Brown.

But a few weeks after the show, an unpleasantness developed that almost blacklisted the actress in Alva Belmont's steely eyes. Dressler first received a handsome parasol, with the handle set with semiprecious stones, plus a personal letter from Mrs. Belmont thanking her for her "intelligent and untiring work to make *Melinda and Her Sisters* such a success." This was quickly followed by another letter signed by Theda Baehr, Alva's secretary, insisting that Dressler return the score of the Russian ballet song that the actress had taken home with her. Dressler was aghast. The song, she complained in a return note, had been written by Miss Maxwell expressly for her, and the composer had agreed that it would belong to Dressler once *Melinda*'s curtain came down. The envelope had scarcely been delivered when a second letter from Baehr arrived at the actress's door. This communication explained that all of the scores were needed to be collected by Mrs. Belmont's lawyer so that the final bill for the operetta could be calculated and paid.

Steaming with fury, Dressler took the Ballet Russe score and the valuable parasol and ran around the corner from her current digs at 104 East Fortieth Street to 13-15 East Forty-First Street, the Belmont suffrage headquarters, to hand them over and give Alva a piece of her mind. "I looked up," Dressler said later, "and saw Mrs. Belmont sitting in her private office on the second floor at the front. I sent up my name, but word came down that she was not in. She was blanked glad to see me for six weeks during rehearsals," complained the actress, "so when I was told she wasn't in, I said, I know she's upstairs and tell her that I want to see her." The messenger returned and repeated that Mrs. Belmont was out of town. Almost apoplectic with rage, Dressler flounced home again, carrying both the Ballet Russe score and the parasol. She had scarcely poured herself a calming cup of tea when another letter arrived from Alva Belmont. "Dear Miss Dressler: When Miss Harmon came up a few minutes ago and asked if I would see you, I gave her the same message that I have given to everyone who comes to see me without an appointment. I have made this a rule as otherwise it would be impossible for me to accomplish the work that I have to do. . . . Miss Maxwell and myself copyrighted the whole of *Melinda and Her Sisters* in Washington and Albany and Miss Maxwell has no right to give away any of the music and orchestration of the songs. They belong to the opera *Melinda and Her Sisters* and I think if you will consult your lawyer you will find that I am right. No one in fact, has any right to take any part of *Melinda and Her Sisters* or any score from the operetta without my consent which I shall give to no one, believe me. Yours truly, Alva E. Belmont." Actually, the song had first been performed by Dressler before the Waldorf show on February 8 at a British-American War Relief matinee. At the time, Alva had not objected.

Dressler returned the Ballet Russe score without further comment. She kept the parasol.

12

WAR WORK

1916-1918

Although President Woodrow Wilson had assured the nation that he was a neutral observer of the savage war in Europe, Americans were nevertheless apprehensive about the future. Horror stories brought back to the United States by those who had toured the overcrowded French and Belgian hospitals were casting a pall over the country. Dressler herself attended the Sunday afternoon salons held by her good friends Elisabeth Marbury, Elsie de Wolfe, and Anne Morgan, who had each personally witnessed the devastation as well as the growing problem of the European homeless. In 1915 and 1916, the actress became a highly visible volunteer performer at any war relief rally she was asked to attend.

On Broadway, pickings were slim in the theatrical job market. Few producers seemed prepared to sink large sums into new offerings, so when Charles Dillingham asked Dressler if she would star in a new play by James Forbes called *Sweet Genevieve,* she accepted, though with some reluctance. She worried because the play would have its premiere in Providence, Rhode Island, then travel on to Bridgeport, Hartford, and Atlantic City, an expedition that smacked too exhaustingly of the Road. But work was work, and *Sweet Genevieve* opened on schedule at the Providence Opera House in May 1916.

Although Dillingham insisted that *Sweet Genevieve* would make it to the Great White Way if it succeeded, the play never opened on Broadway, even though Dressler earned solid reviews during its East Coast swing. The actress played the part of a nurse from the psychopathic ward of Bellevue Hospital who takes a rich patent medicine manufacturer to a health farm in the country for treatment. The script descended swiftly into pure farce, and the only music that helped relieve the slapstick was a rendition of "Sweet Genevieve" by Dressler and her costar, Frank Lalor. The show did reasonably well for a few weeks until the actress dug in her heels and refused to continue the trek from small-town theatre to small-town theatre. An annoyed Dillingham had no choice but to terminate the *Sweet Genevieve* run, but with a generous display of good humor, he offered Dressler "one of the starring roles" in an ambitious new show called *The Century Girl*.

The revue, to be staged at the Century Theatre, would be coproduced by Florenz Ziegfeld, and the music would be composed by Victor Herbert and Irving Berlin. Again, Dressler accepted, but it was clear that she was not enthusiastic about appearing as one of a starring *group* of performers. Because of her obvious lack of interest and frequent tantrums over script cuts, Dillingham released her from the show after just three performances. As Dressler herself frankly admits in her autobiography: "Dillingham fired me from the cast of *The Century Girl*—my act was pretty rotten, but then so was the whole show." Broadway pundits disagreed with the actress. *The Century Girl* was voted "a brilliant success," and the "most gorgeous of all the debutantes of the present theatrical season." The "group of stars" included Sam Bernard (who eventually played Dressler's role as well as his own), Leon Errol, Elsie Janis, and Harry Kelly. The consensus was that the sets were breathtaking, including a staircase, which would become Florenz Ziegfeld's trademark, and the songs by Berlin and Herbert included such enduring hits as "The Century Girl" and "You Belong to Me." Interestingly, the show was the last of the Broadway musicals to be named after the theatre in which it was produced.

But other matters were already engaging Dressler's attention that year. The war relief circuit in New York and elsewhere was becoming hungrier for stars who would not only entertain but would coax money out of audiences as well. In June 1916, Dressler appeared with such performers as Anna Held, Nora Bayes, Al Jolson, and Constance Collier at an Allied Bazaar arranged by the Serbian Relief Committee. "This war must be stopped," an emotional Anna Held harangued the audience. "The people of these neutral countries must stop it! If you could see just a little of what I have seen, you would not rest until peace has been declared. If those cruel, old-fashioned rulers have the power to order our husbands and our brothers murdered, then the rulers of the neutral powers should have the power to put an end to it."

Dressler, who had not toured the European battlefront, simply decided to charm cash out of the onlookers instead of making impassioned speeches—a strategy that would change dramatically in the months to come. Observed one New York reporter: "Poised on one foot, with both arms stretched in the air like a plastic Grecian dancer, Miss Dressler exclaimed 'Ladies and gentlemen, loosen up a bit in the financial district. I can't budge an inch until I hear the sweetest music of all—the rat-a-tat of dollars and dimes. I beg of you, ladies—this is a most uncomfortable position. Thank you. On with the dance, my lads and lassies.'" The report continued: "Miss Dressler was doing a one-step with Edgar Selwyn when she deserted her partner and made off after a man. 'Sir, you brushed against one of my actors,' she said as she grabbed the startled person who was making for the exit. 'That will cost you one dime. For ten cents more I shall give you a smile. If you want to push a real actress, just come my way again and bump into me. That will only cost you $5.'"

Apart from her war relief work, Dressler was also nibbling once again at the possibility of succeeding as a movie star. After all, she reasoned, work in films was usually confined to the studio and its environs, and one could go home at night instead of packing up to board a train for yet another bleak theatre dressing room. In August 1916, she signed a contract with producer William A. Brady to appear exclusively in World Film Company productions. A few days later, however, Dressler announced, to the puzzlement of the press, that she and Dalton had taken out papers of incorporation for the Marie Dressler Motion Picture Company and that Brady would be one of the new company's officers. It was reported that the company planned to produce twelve two-reel comedies based on the Tillie theme and that the movies would be distributed through the Mutual Film Corporation.

But despite the birth of the Dressler company, the actress went ahead with a five-reel film for World, originally entitled *Tillie's Night Out* and finally released in early 1917 under the title of *Tillie*

Wakes Up. The script, written by a young former journalist named Frances Marion, who would become a pivotal figure in Dressler's life, was a familiar cocktail of chaos and slapstick, involving marital misunderstandings, a getaway adventure between a henpecked husband and a neglected wife, and a disaster sequence at Coney Island. The taxi carrying the runaways is rammed by another automobile, Dressler and her companion jump into an ice wagon to escape detection, they freeze into the ice and have to be chopped out. After an inevitable chase, they jump into another auto, drive wildly onto the beach and into the sea.

Dressler herself was so impressed with this wild caper that she immortalized it in her first autobiography. "As the car could not, of course, float, it was put on a raft and we were towed out quite a distance and then turned loose. John Hines, who played the neglected husband, was on the front seat and I was on the back. After we had floated out some distance, we felt the car toppling and Hines jumped. This upset the car and I found myself being closed into the hood, which frightened me extremely. I finally managed to extricate myself, however, and dived to the bottom. Fortunately I headed for land without knowing it. Meantime, the five thousand spectators on shore and the camera men were frantic. They were glad indeed when I came up again, but no happier than I. As it was, the experience was such as to knock my nerve so that I could not go on with the scene for two days."

Tillie Wakes Up was an instant hit when it appeared in February 1917. Reviewers told the growing number of American movie fans that "Marie Dressler displays her agility, her keen sense of humor and her skill in making funny falls," and "With the recollection in mind of the reckless abandon and humorous nonchalance exhibited by Miss Dressler in throwing herself headlong into unknown dangers of every description in former releases, it is hardly necessary to record the fact that in *Tillie Wakes Up,* the actress dares every danger in her path." Another wrote, "Sides ache when Marie is pictured. . . . Marie at her funniest." Much of the movie's success must be attributed to the writing of Frances Marion, which injected a badly needed human touch to the story of the runaways.

In early 1917, though, Dressler was preoccupied with matters other than moviemaking. By the end of March it had become obvious that, despite President Wilson's previous assurances that the United States would remain neutral, the war in Europe was about to spill across the Atlantic. With a stunned nation looking on, war on Germany was declared on April 6. Wilson spread the word that he believed the conflict was in its final stages and that American involvement would shorten the agony. Then, he revealed to a group of influential journalists that it would be the responsibility of the United States to organize peace for Europe and the world. Dressler responded immediately to the war news by writing a letter to the White House asking that she be sent to France as an entertainer, but a reply from the war department made it clear that she would be appreciated far more on the home front. Certainly, there was plenty for her to do. The country was awash with bazaars and benefits in aid of everything from the Red Cross to the American Aviation Corps and the Ambulance Francaise de Pierrefonds. In June, she worked as a saleslady at a Garden Party Benefit of the National League for Women's Service in Washington Square. Although Jim Dalton was keeping a sharp eye out for theatrical work, it seemed that Dressler might as well spend her current time and energy in the local trenches. Mobilization through a series of draft lotteries, plus a sudden rise in the cost of living to pay for the war caused the 1917 slump on Broadway to deepen. And motion picture producers were also downsizing their plans.

Aware that money was again becoming scarce in the Dressler-Dalton household, Sunny Jim was keeping a determined toe in the movie business door. The 1916 deal with Mutual Films had quietly evaporated, but Dalton had been negotiating a new agreement with the Goldwyn Distributing Company to handle a series of two-reel comedies produced by the still untried Marie Dressler Motion Picture Company. Not long after the declaration of war, Goldwyn president Samuel Goldfish (who would eventually adopt the name of his company) agreed to release and distribute eight Tillie comedies, beginning with a two-reeler ostensibly written by Dressler, entitled *The Scrub Lady.* Filming would be handled at Goldwyn's studio at Fort Lee, New Jersey. *The Scrub Lady*—which was more notable for its slapstick than its attempt at characterization—had little impact on either the critics or the paying public. But the picture was quickly followed by yet another comedy called *Fired,* this time made at Goldwyn facilities in sunny Los Angeles after motion picture studios in the east were forced to cut back on production because of energy rationing.

But war work was still a Dressler priority—as it also was with other American theatrical celebrities such as Al Jolson, George M. Cohan, Elsie Janis, and Ethel Barrymore. Before leaving for California, Dressler motored to Camp Mills, Mineola, Long Island, to entertain soldiers training for France. "Miss Dressler sang, frolicked and acted blithesome generally and then, just as she was beginning to crack under the strain, a special showing of her latest motion picture, *Tillie the Scrub Lady,* was projected on the screen," it was reported. "Several thousand soldiers stretched themselves on the grass in an improvised open-air theatre and applauded the performance."

Dressler makes it quite clear in her books that her volunteer work during the First World War became far more important to her than any other project that was offered at the time. In 1917, Broadway was still in a state of shock, and Hollywood was busily trying to tackle the touchy question of production content: What kinds of movies would sell to American audiences traumatized by the war? Anti-German scripts or cheer-up themes? Well aware that, despite the deal with Goldwyn, her career was going nowhere, Dressler's sagging self-confidence was visibly boosted by the adulation she was receiving from the boys in khaki and the grateful organizers—many of them old friends from the social register—of the war relief drives.

A story published in late 1917 seems to hint somewhat tartly, in fact, that Dressler believed her tireless work on behalf of the war effort should have been earning more recognition. Apparently Goldwyn star Maxine Elliott had been decorated personally by England, France, and Belgium for her war work, and actress Mary Garden had received the Wreath of Patriotic Devotion and the Red Cross of Serbia. Dressler responded to the news by suggesting that she should be awarded a leather medal. "Of course this medal won't glitter quite as much as those of Miss Garden or of Miss Elliott," Dressler told a fascinated reporter. "But it will take a high polish and about twenty, thirty-point letters in gold." The great trouble with this arrangement, the story went on to say, was that Miss Dressler could not decide what she was to get the medal for. "She is perfectly willing and ready at any time to be decorated for any reasonable service and on demand provided there is a medal in it. She will stop a runaway horse, save two small boys from drowning, either individually or collectively, flag an express before a burning trestle, wear a gas mask or be torpedoed. But she does want to exercise her woman's forethought and prevent embarrassment when people ask her what she got the decoration for. If the medal is just to be worn before the camera, that is a different thing. 'Heaven be praised,' as Miss Dressler says, 'not only that pictures cannot speak but that they cannot answer questions.'"

Dressler buried her touchiness over the medal in an orgy of work—two more energetically tepid comedies, *The Agonies of Agnes* and *Cross Red Nurse,* this time released by World. Receipts reported by Goldwyn's accounting office for *The Scrub Lady* and *Fired* were scarcely encouraging, and Dressler was grimly resigned to the fact that the two new films would probably do no better at the box office. In the meantime, the actress continued with her war relief work, now aware that Washington was concentrating more of its public-contribution appeals on the sale of Liberty Loan bonds. The first loan, organized by Secretary of the Treasury William G. McAdoo in May 1917, had already raked in a massive two billion dollars from the pockets of patriotic Americans. The second loan, launched in October, netted three billion dollars.

In 1917 Woodrow Wilson asked the presidents of several American film companies, including Samuel Goldfish of Goldwyn, to come to the aid of the country. The request resulted in the formation of a National Association of the Motion Picture Industry with a mandate to dream up ways of boosting support for the war effort. The association was asked to help create propaganda that would convince the Allies that the United States was indeed doing its bit in the world conflict. The first ideas reported to Washington involved the production of filmed documentaries that could be sent abroad for viewing in European movie houses: the story of the mobilization of the Red Cross was one possibility, as well as an upbeat look at the munitions industry. Both suggestions were enthusiastically approved by the White House, and the scripts were written and sent before the cameras. It is perhaps an illustration of the motion picture industry's novelty as an entertainment medium in 1917-18 that the scarcely spellbinding films were said to have had a beneficial impact on the troops in the field.

But the most brilliantly innovative and ultimately successful idea was the National Association's plan to recruit a group of top movie stars to tour the country as Liberty Loan bond salespersons. There was no doubt in the minds of the organizers about who they would pick as the dream team: Mary Pickford (who had been born in Toronto, about fifty miles west of Dressler's birthplace in Cobourg), Douglas Fairbanks, and Charles Chaplin. Pickford's films, such as *Rebecca of Sunnybrook Farm, A Romance of the Redwoods,* and *The Little Princess*—some of them scripted by Dressler's old friend, Frances Marion—had already taken both the United States and Europe by storm. Fairbanks was indisputably the swashbuckling heartthrob of the day, and Chaplin's two-reelers had immortalized his Little Tramp persona around the world.

Hollywood's most prominent moviemakers, including Goldfish, Cecil B. DeMille, and Jesse Lasky, backed the Golden Group idea, so it was scarcely surprising that Pickford, Fairbanks, and Chaplin quickly fell into line. So did Mabel Normand and William S. Hart—patriotic Americans all, even though it is tempting to conjecture whether their promised participation was somewhat in personal atonement for the riches and freedom they were enjoying while thousands of their countrymen were in uniform.

In April of 1918, a new loan was announced. At this time Dressler would have had to admit that the superstar status she had experienced in the early years of the century had faded, but, even so, Samuel Goldfish was aware that the fifty-year-old actress still possessed charismatic drawing-power and that she was also currently underemployed. He included her name on a list submitted to Secretary McAdoo, and eventually the treasury department dispatched a letter asking Dressler if she would come to Washington for the kickoff of the new bond campaign. Pickford, Fairbanks, and Chaplin would also be in attendance, the letter confirmed. And as these three actors had already chosen their sales routes (Fairbanks and Pickford, who had yet to marry, would share the northern states; Chaplin would take the South), the suggestion was that after appearing in Washington, Dressler could tour the Midwest and as many major cities east of the Missouri River as possible. Her assignment would end in New York City on May 10. Dressler accepted the Liberty Loan assignment immediately. "I never worked so hard in my life as I did during the Liberty Loan campaign, and

I never got as much joy out of work," she admitted in *My Own Story*. The war effort totally absorbed her time and challenged her creative ability. Effective speechmaking had become an addictive substitute for work in the theatre or on the screen. The name of the game was to coax money out of her fellow Americans as smoothly and as professionally as she had coaxed their laughter and applause. And, of course, the sooner the war was won by the Allies, the sooner the Good Life would return.

The cherry blossoms were at their springtime peak when the Golden Group arrived in Washington to help launch the Third Liberty Loan campaign. Pickford (chaperoned by her mother), Fairbanks, and Chaplin (accompanied by a friend, Rob Wagner) had traveled east together from California. Dressler (shadowed by Dalton) took a train from New York City to the nation's capital. There was an emotional get-together at the hotel before limousines arrived to take the foursome to a football field where they would address a waiting crowd. Pickford and Dressler had already become friends when the Toronto-born actress lived in New York. Dressler knew Fairbanks less well, but she greeted Chaplin with effusive hugs: the diminutive comedian, after all, had been part of her motion picture debut in *Tillie's Punctured Romance*. The limousines carrying the celebrities made a triumphal progress through the streets to a crowded football field, where the foursome was greeted by a group of officials, including Secretary McAdoo and the young assistant secretary of the Navy, Franklin D. Roosevelt. They were escorted to a gaily decorated platform.

Chaplin always remembered that, after making a somewhat panicky speech about the Germans being at everyone's door, he slipped off the stage, taking Dressler with him. Both performers, he added, fell on Roosevelt. Pickford remembered a somewhat different scenario. She always recalled that it was FDR who tripped and fell through the railing of the stand and that Dressler proceeded to fall on top of him. Pickford also remembered that the celebrity team was taken to the White House, where they were greeted by Woodrow Wilson. Dressler, according to Pickford, "told him a story that was not exactly risqué, but definitely off-color. . . . As she moved to the denouement, I kept wishing the parquet floor of the Blue Room would open up and swallow me. I could feel myself blushing all over . . . the president neither smiled nor made a comment." Pickford goes on to say that "we were all overawed by our first visit to the White House, all but Marie, the darling. She remained sublimely unconscious of her faux pas."

Dressler took the opportunity in her own reminiscences to explain why she seemed so cool and calm during the official visit. "One of the perquisites of my Liberty Loan work was the privilege it gave me of going in and out of the White House during war time without a pass. Not that a visit to the Executive Mansion was a novel experience for me. I have been running in and out of the White House for thirty-five years. Unless the Franklin Roosevelts have moved it in the past few months, I know perfectly well where to find the ice box. . . . Beginning with Cleveland, I have met and talked with seven presidents and dined with five."

Both Pickford and Chaplin boasted that they sold an impressive number of Liberty Bonds during the third drive. Pickford wrote in her autobiography, "I raised $5 million in one afternoon and evening in Pittsburgh during the Liberty Bond Drive. The most arduous if not the most productive day of all was in Baltimore. I sold only $450,000 in bonds, but they were almost entirely in small denominations of fifty and one hundred dollars." Chaplin recalled that when he, Pickford, and Fairbanks arrived in New York later in April, "Mary, Douglas and I sold more than two million dollars' worth of bonds." Dressler left the group in Washington to begin her own Midwest leg of the tour and landed in New York May 10. A local press photographer immortalized the occasion with a shot of the actress dancing down Fifth Avenue dressed in a skirted uniform.

There is no doubt that each of the actors who volunteered for the loan campaigns was high on the adrenaline of patriotism and, perhaps, transported by the challenge of racking up impressive bond sales. Their speeches were somewhat overblown, though appropriate for the occasion. During Chaplin's visit to Wall Street, he screamed through a megaphone (public address systems were unknown in 1918): "You people out there—I want you to forget about percentages in this Third Liberty Loan. Human life is at stake, and no one ought to worry about what rate of interest the bonds are going to bring or what he can make by purchasing them. Money is needed—money to support the great army and navy of Uncle Sam. This very minute, the Germans occupy a position of advantage, and we have to got to get the dollars. It ought to go over so we can drive that old devil the Kaiser out of France."

Dressler, who boasted that she made 149 speeches in twenty-nine days during the Third Liberty Loan drive, often spoke somewhat extemporaneously at meetings, dinners, and even on street corners. As the campaign progressed, she began referring to her Teuton lineage. "I am 101 per cent American," she told one interviewer during the tour. "I've added the 1 per cent to drown the last vestige of the strain of Hun blood in my veins. My family name is Koerber, my grandfather was a general in the German army, my father was born in Germany and I am touring the country for the Liberty Loan as a protest against my ancestry." She issued a challenge to those "blithering idiots who still waver because they have German blood in them," stating, "I am talking wherever I can do good and to all kinds of audiences, but you can say that my special task is to get under the callused skins. . . . I want to wake them up and bring home to them the fact that the best means of atonement for them is to get behind Uncle Sam in this war and help wipe out the Kaiser and the bunch of brutes who are supporting him."

One point that emerges from newspaper accounts of Dressler's 1918 war bond travels: Jim Dalton was clearly on hand, "checking baggage, arranging other matters of travel and reminding her of the time," according to one story. There's no doubt, though, that the turn of events must have been a decided shock to Sunny Jim. Income had become nonexistent and savings were already being plowed into tour expenses—particularly when Dressler volunteered to work the Fourth Liberty Loan, which was launched in September. Dressler herself has admitted that she placed herself "and my energy at the disposal of the government and began a strenuous life of going where I was sent, defraying my own expenses and thankful I had anything to defray with." The Vermont farm was sold not long after the November Armistice. Dressler never complained—at least, not publicly—that her demanding war effort contributed to her future professional and financial problems. She boasted, "When the Armistice was declared, I had the satisfaction of having sold more war bonds than any other individual in the United States," but it is obvious that her unstinting patriotic activities in 1917-18 drained her bank account and possibly even eroded her chances of continuing with her movie work or attracting the attention of theatrical producers on the lookout for available talent.

It is more difficult to know if the strain of the war bond tours took its toll on Jim Dalton. It is clear that the man's health had been deteriorating for some time, possibly because of his hard-drinking habits. It is also known that he suffered a stroke sometime between 1919 and 1921 and spent the last months of his life in a wheelchair. Dressler never deserted him. When she returned to vaudeville after the war, then to other minor theatrical roles, Sunny Jim invariably watched her performance from the wings, seated quietly in his special corner.

13

Striking for the Ponies

1919

Business on Broadway picked up considerably during the summer of 1918, though there was a worrying hiatus as the United States battled a savage "Spanish" influenza epidemic. Dressler continued with her war work during the year, professionally alert to the news that theatrical managers were becoming confident enough to cast some new productions. The trend looked promising. But she was also aware that landing a new and important role could prove to be difficult; many of the 1918 offerings were propaganda-tinged war plays—scarcely Dressler-type shows larded with music and mayhem. Movies were just as daunting. Hollywood had just released a film calling for the execution of German militants and one that argued for the hanging of the Kaiser in Times Square. Then, as the lights of the Great White Way flickered on again in 1919, it became obvious that theatrical investors were now seeking young, slim-hipped actresses who could beguile war-jaded audiences. The cult of the flapper and the shimmy (Irving Berlin's antiprohibition hit from the Ziegfeld Follies of 1919 was "You Cannot Make Your Shimmy Shake on Tea") was just around the corner.

In the first months of 1919, Dressler and Dalton realized unhappily that money had become a major concern. Much of the cash realized on the Vermont property had been spent on Liberty Loan tour expenses and personal bills. Dressler did own some bonds of her own, but she prudently kept these in reserve. In April, with no major offers pending, the actress asked Alf Wilton, a Broadway agent, to approach the Keith-Albee vaudeville circuit on her behalf. She recounted the result of the negotiations in her autobiography. "I knew that the quickest way to make some money was to take another whirl in vaudeville, so I sent my agent Alf Wilton to Keith's where I had formerly made $2,500 a week. He returned to me, much embarrassed. 'What's up?' I demanded. 'I don't quite know how to tell you, Miss Dressler,' he stammered. 'Your last salary was $2,500 . . . 'Yes, yes, go on . . .' 'Well, I can't get your old salary,' he apologized. 'They say you have been out [of vaudeville] five years and must have deteriorated.' 'All right,' I retorted. 'Perhaps I have. Go back and ask him how much I have deteriorated.' 'Well, they are willing to give you $1,500 a week,' he said, thinking he was insulting me. Some people would have been incensed to be told they had deteriorated one thousand dollars a week, but I looked the situation in the face. 'There are blamed few folks,' I said, 'who can make $1,500 a week,' and I went at it. To my own surprise and theirs, this come-back proved a tremendous success. It was agreed I had not deteriorated, for I played the Palace three weeks out of five."

Palace audiences endorsed the Keith-Albee decision to stage a Dressler revival. "Marie Dressler's return to vaudeville following a two-year tour of the country devoted to war work can be classed among the greatest triumphs of her 31 years of stage experience," wrote a *Variety* reviewer. "The finesse of the 'old school' has become a lost art with modern comics, male or female, and it is rather a treat to occasionally see a woman who knows the intricate science of turning the most minute twist of a situation into a laugh. Miss Dressler's programming says she is benefiting herself. She is also benefiting vaudeville with this specialty. Miss Dressler carried off the bill's honors without any visible competition Monday evening." Commented the *New York Telegraph:* "This is an occasion to make Broadway sit up and take notice. All of the Forty-Second Street bunch were at the Palace Monday afternoon to welcome Miss Dressler. But they were not disappointed. She was in all her cut-up glory, exactly like the old days of Weber and Fields."

Keith-Albee managers were so pleased with Dressler's unexpected success that they immediately booked her for appearances in Cleveland and Buffalo. And there was yet another upbeat happening during her New York engagement: she was honored with a testimonial dinner at the Commodore Hotel, hosted by the Canadian Club. "For work done for Canadian troops," read the invitations, and many of Dressler's political and society friends, including William H. Taft, William G. McAdoo, Sir Thomas Lipton, Elisabeth Marbury, and Daniel Frohman turned up to wish her well. In a year when Dressler was increasingly beset with fears concerning Sunny Jim's health, a dwindling bank account, and her uncertain career prospects, the dinner was a welcome boost to her confidence. But even so, the summer of 1919 was difficult. Inevitably, the vaudeville engagement melted with the onslaught of seasonal temperatures. Even the Keith-Albee managers could promise nothing definite for fall, and although there were some encouraging sounds from the Shubert organization, Dressler was forced to consider alternatives. But what? Her two most valuable assets, she decided, were her proven theatrical talent and her boundless energy. But then there was her ownership of *Tillie's Nightmare*. It seemed like a long shot and an expensive one at that, but a self-financed revival of the play began to look more promising all the time. In July, she resurrected a moribund corporation called the Dalton Amusement Company and sent a somewhat listless Sunny Jim to beat the bushes for potential backers. Dressler busied herself with some advance casting for possible dates in November, and, despite a stifling month in New York, the sudden renewal of entrepreneurial activity put a new bounce in her step.

Dressler was so optimistic about her plans for *Tillie* that she packed her bags and booked herself and Dalton into an Atlantic City hotel to escape the heat and humidity for a few weeks. Just seven days into the vacation, however, she heard from a New York acquaintance encountered on the boardwalk that an actors' strike was looming on Broadway. Dressler was astonished. The idea was unbelievable. She knew that the seven-year-old Actors' Equity was negotiating with producing managers for a renewal of their two-year standard contract. She also knew that Equity's demands were relatively modest: no hike in current pay schedules in return for a commitment that actors would be compensated for extra matinees played on legal holidays and other special occasions. So why were the managers balking?

Was it possible, Dressler wondered, that the Big Boys on the Great White Way were playing politics? For one thing, it had been rumored for months that Equity was thinking of joining the American Federation of Labor. But if the managers succeeded in weakening the actors by forcing a flawed contract, it was possible that the AFL would refuse membership to a lame duck organization. This, of course, would save the producers the trauma of negotiating with a tougher, strongly backed Equity. Personally, Dressler confided to some of her friends in Atlantic City, she felt it could turn out to be a triumph for the acting profession if it had the courage to walk out of the theatres. She counted the productions that would be devastated if the strike actually materialized: at least ten, she figured, and possibly more than twenty. And she knew there were six scheduled openings that would definitely be affected.

The word spread through the Atlantic City grapevine on August 6 that Equity had voted to go on strike and that within thirty minutes before curtain time, almost one hundred actors closed twelve productions on Broadway. Some shows were spared, notably the Ziegfeld Follies (which soon went dark as well) and *John Ferguson,* a Theatre Guild production not allied with the producing managers. At the Cohan and Harris Theatre, *The Royal Vagabond* was quickly reorganized, with George M. assigning understudies to the starring roles. But then the stagehands and musicians walked out, and the Cohan and Harris had no choice but to close its doors.

Dressler repacked her bags and boarded a train for New York. Ironically, she had never felt the need or the urge to join Equity, but these were her professional colleagues and she loved a good fight. Besides, she was also a good organizer, and perhaps she could be of some use at strike headquarters. By the time she arrived in New York, it had become increasingly obvious that neither side in the dispute would easily throw in the towel. Some prominent actors had already turned their backs on Equity by forming a rival union called the Actors' Fidelity League (Fido for short), and George M. Cohan had pledged one hundred thousand dollars to the new organization and accepted the presidency. The local press was publicizing the names of stars who were thumbing their noses at the Equity rabble by joining Fido: E.H. Sothern and Julia Marlowe, Mrs. Fiske, Otis Skinner, David Warfield, and Margaret Anglin.

Then, with twenty-one theatres closed and the strike spreading to other American cities, a new problem emerged: what to do about the hundreds of chorus "ponies" who had been thrown out of work because of the walkout of principal actors. It is true that the chorus boys and girls (chorus personnel was overwhelmingly female on Broadway and elsewhere throughout the United States) supported Actors' Equity, but they were not members and they had no organization to give them direction. Sensing a propaganda advantage, the producers complained to the press that Equity was clearly abandoning "those little people out there" by giving them no help at all during the fight. And for a while, this seemed to be true until a quick-witted union official organized a huge meeting of chorus personnel in the afternoon of August 13 at the New Amsterdam Opera House. By the time the conclave dispersed, the Chorus Equity Association of America had been born, and Marie Dressler had been elected president.

Dressler relished her experience as a union negotiator as keenly as she had enjoyed selling war bonds. For one thing, it once again propelled her into the public spotlight. For another, the strike handed her a golden chance to change some of the inequities she herself had suffered during her years in the chorus line: no wages during weeks of rehearsal, low wages when a show finally opened (twenty dollars a week was the norm), or none at all if it closed after a couple of performances. Plus the always onerous expense of providing one's own tights, shoes, and stockings. "No, I'm not a member of Actors' Equity," Dressler told a New York reporter after the Chorus Equity was formed. "But I started my theatrical career as a chorus girl at $8 a week. As a matter of fact, I had to go back to the chorus twice. Bad luck sent me, but I worked my way up again. Now I'm in the chorus once more." Interestingly, the new General of the Chorus Amazons, as she quickly dubbed herself, decided to seek a gilt-edged contract for her troops—one that the theatrical press noted was far superior to that being sought by the striking actors. The chorus contract called for a minimum salary of thirty dollars a week when in New York, thirty-five dollars a week when on the road, and a maximum of eight performances a week. Managers would be required to provide tights, stockings and shoes. The chorus people would agree to rehearse without pay for four weeks, but after that, one-half salary for two weeks and full wages if rehearsals continued. The draft contract also called for compensation of two weeks' salary if the show ran for less than two weeks. And managers would be obliged to provide sleeping accommodation on trains when traveling, with only one chorus member to a berth.

Members of Chorus Equity cheered Dressler's reading of the draft contract. In fact, everyone connected with the unprecedented strike (except, of course, Fido and the managers) seemed to be floating on an optimistic cloud. At Chorus Equity's inaugural meeting there was loud cheering as the last chorus holdouts, members of the Hippodrome cast (who were rehearsing for Charles Dillingham's expensive new show, *Happy Days)*, marched symbolically into the New Amsterdam. Ethel Barrymore—who had initially shown up at an Actors' Equity meeting simply because she was curious as to why so many people were crowding the streets—arrived to lend her prestige to the organization of the chorus. And there were other messages of support from stars such as Blanche Ring, Eddie Foy, Lionel Barrymore, Lillian Russell, and Eddie Cantor. After choosing an organizing and constitutional committee consisting of one male and one female from each production represented at the meeting, the initiation fee was set at one dollar. Dressler was enjoying herself. She remembered with obvious relish: "I jumped into the Equity scrap of 1919 on principle, as did many others, but it was more or less a merry war and everybody derived considerable amusement from it. As the reviewers said, it really was entertaining to see participants discussing their wrongs over a table at the Algonquin or the Ritz, and young women with charge accounts at well-known jewelers weeping into grape fruit supreme as they discussed their stage oppressors, K. & E. [Klaw and Erlanger] or Jake and Lee [Shubert]." "Miss Marie Dressler, through her organization of the chorus girls' branch of the Equity, found herself the cynosure of all eyes," Karl K. Kitchin wrote in the *World*. "And while she didn't cause the Hippodrome to close, she got the credit. There is no question that she was a strike heroine and an ample one. In fact, she is of the stuff that two or three heroines could have been made. Her suggestion that both she and David Belasco were old enough to retire caused as much amusement in certain circles as Charles Dillingham's sign at the Hippodrome, following its enforced closing. The name of the attraction, *Happy Days*, was painted over with the words "Nothing Doing," with the result that the sign read, "Nothing Doing, Twice Daily."

The actors' strike of 1919 lasted for precisely a month, but, as Dressler intimated in her reminiscences, it turned out to be a decidedly upbeat event for the theatrical community. They were not performing in the theatres, so they gave performances on the streets to explain their cause to the public. They marched and paraded, carrying American flags and placards inscribed with the strike motto: "No More Pay, Just Fair Play." Dressler and her Amazons marched on Fifth Avenue, singing the official strike song, set cheekily to Fido president George M. Cohan's war classic, "Over There":

> Over fair, over fair
> We have been, over fair
> But now things are humming
> And the time is coming
> When with Labor we'll be chumming
> Everywhere
> So beware, have a care,
> Just be fair, on the square, everywhere,
> For we are striking, yes we are striking
> And we won't come back
> Till the managers are fair.

Strike headquarters at the Longacre Building overflowed with principal actors and chorus personnel jostling to join their prospective Equity associations. More than 1,100 new members signed up on the day of the New Amsterdam meeting, of whom 350 were chorus people. The crush at the Longacre became so great during the following week that there was a special meeting of union brass to decide how to ease the logjam. Luckily, theatre buff Frank Case, proprietor of the Algonquin Hotel, stepped into the picture and offered space in Room 2111 of the hostelry. The Publicity Bureau of Chorus Equity accepted Case's offer and moved in for the duration of the strike. Meals were also provided without charge and Case even contributed one thousand dollars to the general strike fund.

The money was badly needed. When the strike began, there was just $13,500 in the Equity bank account, and early in the battle, members of both the Actors and Chorus Associations met at the Lexington Avenue Opera House to explore ways of raising more funds for the war chest. It was Ethel Barrymore who sparked a rush to reach for the checkbooks: "I know that we are all loyal," she spoke from the stage, "and that we will win the strike. But our ammunition is money. I know a lot of persons here feel impoverished by recent events, but I think that some of us who have a little to spare should give this ammunition. If I can get one hundred and ninety-nine actors and actresses to give five hundred dollars each, I am ready to sign my check for that amount."

Comedian Ed Wynn handed the first five hundred dollar check to Ethel, and her brother Lionel was close behind with a second five hundred dollar contribution. More than twenty thousand dollars was collected before the meeting ended, and Barrymore and Dressler were jointly appointed to increase this sum to one hundred thousand dollars as soon as possible. Young actress Tallulah Bankhead, who was out of work and short of cash because of the strike, was so inspired by it all that she handed over one hundred dollars. That night, she wrote to her grandfather in Alabama asking that he send her the money so that the honor of the South would not suffer.

Later, Dressler convened a meeting of her executives, and the group decided that a practical way of enhancing the strikers' war chest would be to stage a series of benefit performances at the Lexington Avenue Opera House. Co-chair Ethel Barrymore was consulted, and it was then agreed to stage the first of the shows in a week or so. Reported *Variety:* "The Actors Equity's first gala performance of a series of Gala Performances drew a packed house. It was reported that $8,000 was realized from the Monday night show, through the box office, sale of programs and candy by volunteers. Whatever the amount the Lexington got is what a manager would call 'a lot of money for one show.'"

Dressler was prominently front and center at all of the Lexington performances. At the first sold-out night, she created front-page copy by staging a demonstration that she told the audience would show that producers were wrong when they insisted they needed six to eighteen weeks of rehearsal to pull a chorus into shape. "Ladies and gentlemen," she announced from the stage, "I can teach 200 chorus men and women a new set of steps in six to sixteen minutes." And she did, to appreciative laughter and thunderous applause. The rest of the program was greeted with as much noisy enthusiasm: the second act from *Camille,* with Ethel Barrymore in the title role and Conway Tearle as Armond. (Interestingly, Lionel Barrymore played the part of the older Duval, a role he would later make famous on screen in the movie starring Greta Garbo and Robert Taylor). Baritone John Charles Thomas sang several songs at the gala. And then there were appearances by motion picture serial queen Pearl White, Eddie Foy and his theatrical family, Eddie Cantor, Charles Winniger, and W.C. Fields. "One thing about the strike is impressive," editorialized *Variety.* "Nearly every one of the men and women at the head of the movement is above suspicion of being influenced by selfish interests. In fact, those who are waging the fight are not affected by the conditions complained of. They have nothing to gain and everything to lose; for example, players like Ethel Barrymore, Lionel Barrymore, Bruce McRae, John Cope, Marie Dressler, Grant Stewart, Grant Mitchell, Thomas Wise, John Drew and Lillian Russell, to name some of the most active. At this writing, the actors certainly have the whip handle in their hands."

The great actors' strike of 1919 ended on September 6, four weeks after it began. Before that, there were numerous court appearances by such interests as the Shubert Theatrical Company and the Charles Emerson Cook Corporation seeking injunctions against the rebels. The rebels themselves continued cheerfully with their galas, committee meetings, and street demonstrations. At one point, a rumor circulated that the producers would apply for a writ to impound the bank account into which the proceeds from the Lexington shows were being deposited. But then, George Christie, manager of the Lexington Avenue Opera House, suggested the actors title the account Isaiah 59:14, a name he figured would certainly hold up court proceedings. No writ was ever issued, though it is fascinating now to read the Isaiah verse: "And judgement is turned away backward, and justice standeth afar off, for truth is fallen in the street and equity cannot enter." The meeting that would end the standoff was held at the St. Regis Hotel, and actors and chorus were represented by Frank Gillmore of Equity, Francis Wilson, Marie Dressler, Ethel Barrymore, and Lillian Russell. The managers were represented by Arthur Hopkins, Henry W. Savage, John L. Golden, Sam H. Harris, A.H. Woods, William A. Brady, and David Belasco. Playwright-director Augustus (Gus) Thomas was chair, along with Gene Buck of the newly formed Dramatists' Guild.

Surprisingly, there was little argument about the terms demanded by Actors' Equity and the Chorus Association. The producers launched an argument concerning the recognition of the Actors' Fidelity League, but Equity and the chorus group put down their collective foot, refusing to legitimize the company-sponsored union. The producers did score a point by demanding that any new contracts should be in force until June 1, 1924, while Equity had wanted an agreement that would call for renegotiation on December 31, 1921. But apart from this concession, the managers fell somewhat meekly into line, recognizing Equity and the Chorus Association as legal bargaining agents for stage performers.

Dressler was jubilant. Not only had she bargained for and won higher wages and better conditions for the chorus, she had managed to forge an association that would monitor the backstage environment far into the future. "I pulled the minimum up to $35," she told a New York reporter after the strike. "And some of the girls were getting only $20. And just to show you the spirit of those chorus girls—one of them came to me and thanked me for getting the contract, and she said; 'Miss Dressler, I lose by it—I've been doing some extra work that brought my wages up to $42 a week and I'll only get $35, but I'm glad for the others.' And I said, 'Oh no, dearie; you'll get your $42. I made the salaries stand, but got the minimum for the others.' But don't the way she felt make you admire 'em?" Dressler was also pleased that the strike might have brought about better relations between the managers and the people they hired for their productions. "Now the manager hates the actors and the actor hates the manager," she told a reporter. "It wasn't so in the olden times. A manager hadn't much money then and he took a chance and the actors were willing and glad to take a chance with him because if he lost he lost as well as they did. But the commercialism of today has ruined art and that's why I'm hoping the strike will change our relationship," she said. In another interview concerning the fact that the chorus group had signed a better contract than the one accepted by the actors, "They've got an arbitration clause in the actors' contract. They can't strike again within five years. There's no arbitration clause in my contract. I wouldn't stand for it. I can strike whenever I want to and the managers know I will."

The first general meeting of the Chorus Equity Association was held at Amsterdam Hall on October 24. Dressler did not attend because her revival of *Tillie's Nightmare* had completed its schedule of rehearsals, and she was already off on the road with the play. Despite this, she was reelected president but resigned within a month after informing the association that frequent nonappearances because of out-of-town commitments made it difficult for her to continue with the job. Actress Blanche Ring was elected in Dressler's place. Actually, there was more to Dressler's resignation from the Chorus Equity Association than problems with nonappearances. *Tillie's Nightmare* was plowing somewhat laboriously through its bookings on the road; audiences and critics were generally friendly, but the feeling was that the play was dated and that patrons were buying tickets because they were experiencing a certain nostalgia for "the shows of yesteryear." Wrote a reviewer for the *Indianapolis News:* "The most ardent worshippers of the theatrical, or what they believe to be the theatrical past, will have a difficult time to find beauty, charm or good manners in *Tillie's Nightmare.* These qualities it possesses in about the same proportions as a Mack Sennett comedy." Another problem was that the company was so large, the former president of the Chorus Equity Association (now on the other side of the management fence with the Dalton Amusement Company) was finding it difficult to meet the payroll. The trouble began in Terre Haute, Indiana, when Dressler decided to skip an undersold, three-day engagement in Fort Wayne and travel on to Kansas City. Members of the company objected when it was discovered there would be no payment for missed performances and "sleepers" (time spent traveling between engagements). When there was no response, either from Dressler or her company manager, L.J. Rodrigues, complaints were lodged with Actors' Equity and the Chorus Equity Association. It was then that Dressler tendered her resignation from the chorus group presidency.

Unfortunately, the unsavory battle between the actress-manager and her performers waged on. There were loud altercations in New York when the curtain of the Riviera Theatre was held for twenty minutes while Actors' Equity deputies argued that overdue salaries be paid and again in Boston, when there was another row concerning wages that had been only partly settled. When confronted by the Equity deputies, Dressler insisted that she had ordered a holdout of current wages because she felt that $665 paid to the cast during the Riviera argument had been unjustly collected. Why? Because, she haughtily retorted, the dispute had still to come up for arbitration. Okay, agreed Paul Dalzell, deputy for Actors' Equity. There might be an arbitration clause in the Equity contract. But had Miss Dressler forgotten that she herself had expressly opposed this kind of clause in the Chorus Equity agreement? In other words, Dalzell reminded the once-triumphant leader of the Chorus Amazons, that there should be no holdout of pay for the ponies of *Tillie's Nightmare* because of any pending negotiations. Dressler waggled her jaw but did not reply. She ordered that the chorus be paid.

14

MARIE'S NIGHTMARE

1920-1927

The revival of *Tillie's Nightmare* fizzled in the early summer of 1920, and Dressler reluctantly disbanded the company. Early receipts from the tour had adequately covered expenses, but as audiences began to thin out, it was clear that she could not afford to continue meeting a payroll. Besides, Dalton was far from well. Although there is no precise evidence as to when he suffered his stroke, it is more than likely that it happened during the last weeks of the *Tillie* tour or soon after it ended. In any case, Sunny Jim's increasingly serious health problems made it more difficult for the couple to travel. Dressler and Dalton took off on a short vacation after the closing of the play, then settled into a Manhattan apartment to assess possibilities for the future.

Some theatre historians have intimated that social and professional doors closed for the actress because of her militant involvement in the 1919 actors' strike. Although stage assignments were becoming scarcer, it is more probable that managers either believed audiences had forgotten Dressler after her absence from the stage during the First World War or that ticket buyers were now favoring younger performers. As for the actress's acceptance by New York society, there is every indication that she was as popular as ever in the 1920s. She received frequent invitations to the Sutton Place dinner parties hosted by her longtime and influential friends Elsie de Wolfe and Elisabeth Marbury, and she had also become a confidante of J. Pierpont Morgan's daughter Anne. Then there was her continuing friendship with such social leaders as Mrs.

Stuyvesant Fish, Mrs. John King Van Rensselaer and Mrs. O.H.P. Belmont. Lady Alexandra Colebrook, whose acquaintance she made in the early twenties, would prove to be a staunch Dressler friend for the rest of her life.

At fifty-two years old, however, Dressler was developing some new ideas, beliefs, and prejudices that had many of her cronies wondering whether she was becoming an eccentric. She became increasingly critical of the medical profession and had convinced Sunny Jim that he would be better advised by a Christian Science practitioner—a profession becoming more and more popular with Americans at that time—than by a conventional doctor. She loudly ridiculed remedies prescribed by physicians, touting nostrums based on herbs and plants. She became increasingly interested in astrology, seldom making a major decision until she consulted a young former actress named Nella Webb, who was making a name for herself in the field. She also became openly supportive of the new Fascist movement in Italy and its bombastic leader, Benito Mussolini. Although she could scarcely afford the expense, she insisted that she could not do without the services of her own personal maid. She was often heard rationalizing that, after all, everyone who was anyone had one; Elsie de Wolfe had Westy, Anne Morgan had Daisy, and Bessie had her Alice. Dressler's maid was still Mamie Cox, who had remained in her employ since the filming of *Tillie Wakes Up* and, as it happened, would stay—although on a part-time basis at various intervals—for the rest of the actress's life. Even with her bank account at the rattling-empty stage, Dressler luxuriated in the fact that Mamie would arrive at the apartment each morning to manage her personal needs and help her with Dalton. As the actress often told close friends, "It doesn't matter how little cash you've got, as long as you look and feel well-groomed."

Although Sunny Jim was a constant worry in 1920, Dressler continued to be optimistic about the future. In October of that year, it seemed the tide was again turning in her favor. The Shuberts signed her for a leading role in a new show called *Cinderella on Broadway* that would open at the Winter Garden in New York, then play several major centers throughout the Eastern Seaboard. Wrote a reviewer for the *Boston Post* after seeing the show: "On the playbills, Marie Dressler is announced as the star and, prior to witnessing the performance, I formed a picture of the plump co-medienne as a fairy godmother or possibly the pumpkin coach, for Miss Marie loves to burlesque things. But behold! Miss Dressler appears only in acts that have nothing to do with the story, but she is very funny in all of them." The reporter elaborated, "She has a scene in which she straightens out a snarl in the League of Nations; she is also for the moment, Theda Bara. She sings in a quartet from Rigoletto and she impersonates Ethel Barrymore, which is one of the most clever bits I ever saw her accomplish. She imitated Miss Barrymore's peculiar accent and her walk, although in the latter, owing to the difference in avoirdupois of the two la-dies, there was a slight draft on the imagination." After the first night of *Cinderella*, Dressler was confronted by a reporter who wondered if Ethel Barrymore and Theda Bara would be offended by her impersonations. "Well," replied the actress with a familiar shrug, "our audiences are made up of men and women who are serious the whole day long and they revel in being made to realize that the sense of the ludicrous underlies even our most tragic mo-ments. They know when we burlesque the Barrymores or Theda Bara we do it in fun, with no malice aforethought. And they like it."

Cinderella on Broadway, though, survived for only a few weeks and Dressler then quickly accepted a Shubert offer to ap-pear in *The Passing Show of 1921*. She confided to her friends that she was not at all sure that the play would be a success: the producers had established a tradition for presenting an annual *Pass-ing Show*, always in the summer months. But the 1920 warm weather edition had been bypassed and the 1921 offering—ninth in the long series—was scheduled to open in the dead of winter, December 29, 1920. It was clear, in fact, that the Shuberts were economizing, probably because audiences were preferring to spend their dollars at the Ziegfeld Follies' box office rather than Shubert's Winter Garden. Comedians Willie and Eugene Howard, who had appeared in the Shubert's first *Passing Show* in 1912, were brought back for an encore, and earlier ballet spoofs and ideas were re-cycled. Reviewers agreed that the score by Jean Schwartz was "pretty weak."

Dressler was asked to play the fool and provide the pyrotech-nics in a dance sequence entitled "Spanish Love." And, as the *New York Clipper* reported somewhat sarcastically, "she threatened, more than once, to cause the collapse of the runway." The actress proved to be wrong in her predictions concerning the early demise of the show; it ran at the Winter Garden for six months, but Dressler quit the cast after just a few weeks. Actually, cast changes were frequent for *The Passing Show of 1921*, so—although Dressler herself never commented on the reasons for her early defection—it is more than likely that the Winter Garden was not a happy house that year. After taking a short break in early 1921, the actress inquired about more work with the Shubert organization but they could offer her nothing except for occasional vaudeville dates.

Significantly, there are few newspaper references to these 1921 appearances. Much later in her life, Dressler admitted to her Hollywood confidantes that these months were bleak and desperate. She disliked life on the vaudeville stage, the constant shift from theatre to theatre in addition to the trauma of caring for Dalton, who was now trapped in a wheelchair. As often as possible, she would make sure Sunny Jim was brought to the theatre in which she was playing, but as her companion grew weaker from the ravages of Bright's Disease (degeneration of the kidneys), she more often left him alone to rest at their hotel. Late in November, Dressler was on a Shubert circuit swing through the Midwest and had just completed an appearance in Chicago when Dalton announced that he was too ill to accompany her to upcoming performances in St. Louis and Milwaukee. The actress tried to convince her companion that it would be wiser for him to travel with her, but he was adamant. Before leaving their room at the Congress Hotel en route to the railway station, Dressler arranged for a nurse to look in on Dalton and also alerted a local Christian Science practitioner named Henry Davis to the fact that she would be away for a week or so. Dressler never talked publicly about her trip from Chicago to St. Louis or about her valiant attempt to be comical on the vaudeville stage, but her distress and anxiety can be imagined.

Perhaps the news from Chicago that was delivered to her after the second night's performance came as no real shock, but she was nevertheless devastated: Dalton was dead. Choking back tears, she notified the theatre management that she could not continue with the tour, which was scheduled to move into Milwaukee in a few days. Naturally, the management was sympathetically accommodating, and Dressler packed and returned by train to Chicago.

Reporters met her at the Congress Hotel, but all she could tell them was that Jim Dalton had suffered a long illness and that he had apparently died quite peacefully. Yes, she was about to consult an undertaker named James Marshall, based in nearby Austin, who would prepare Mr. Dalton's body for transportation back to New York. And, no, she would not be continuing with the Shubert tour for the time being. Actress Bessie McCoy, she believed, would be taking over her spot in the show.

Later in the day, the undertaker's assistants removed Sunny Jim's body, and Dressler rested briefly in the hotel room before setting about the melancholy job of packing his belongings. She was still in a state of shock, but the practical task of sorting out her companion's shirts and socks seemed to have a calming effect on her nerves. Early next morning, she took a taxi to Marshall's Funeral Home and gritted her teeth in anticipation of seeing Dalton's face once again. She stood quietly by the open coffin, clenching her fists to control her tears and willing herself to speak to the undertaker and complete arrangements for the trip back to Manhattan. Years later, she told her friend Frances Marion about the moment, and the scenarist recounted it in her book, *Off with Their Heads*. "When Jim died—I'm ashamed to admit this," said Dressler, "I wanted to bury him as my husband. I was in the undertaker's standing by his coffin when two men and a police officer entered to claim his body. The order had come from his wife who had waited all these years. There was nothing I could do but let him go. He belonged to her, not to me. I figured that she must have loved him too, or she would have divorced him long ago."

Dalton's body was shipped to Corning, where his wife took possession and arranged for burial in the Dalton family plot. A local reporter wrote that Lizzie Dalton admitted her husband had left her in 1909, that he sent her money each week, and that there had never been any attempt to annul the marriage.

The Christmas of 1921 and the winter of 1922 were a nightmare for Dressler. Friends were almost effusively supportive, but the trauma of Dalton's death combined with the continuing chill at producers' offices had shaken her once unassailable confidence. Nella Webb moved into the New York apartment to keep the actress company and also busied herself with various plans to get Dressler's career on track again. At one point in mid-summer, Nella called an emergency meeting with writers Helena Dayton and Louise Barrett, two staunch Dressler allies, and the group decided to write a movie scenario that would showcase the actress's unique talents. Once they had a script, they bombarded the major motion picture studios with little success, until one studio representative agreed to meet with them. Dressler sadly remembered: "When they told her that they had me in mind for the leading character, the young woman didn't even look at the script. 'Miss Dressler?' she asked pityingly. 'Audiences wouldn't stand for her. All they want nowadays is young love.' 'But we're hoping to get Lionel Barrymore or George Arliss to play opposite her,' persisted my loyal friends. The young woman's eyes brightened with horror. 'Those old fossils!' she said, and turned her assured back on the imbeciles who had dared suggest such folly."

Dressler never forgot the "terrible humiliation" she believed her friends suffered on her account. Eventually, in the fall of 1922, she decided to leave the United States for a trip to Europe. Her longtime friend Lady Alexandra Colebrook was urging her to visit her in Italy. "After all," Lady Colebrook wrote, "Venice in the Fall is an absolute must these days." Another close friend from the social register, Mrs. Robert Morris Phillips, known affectionately as Hallie, was urging the actress to leave New York for a couple of months. As Dressler remarked in *My Own Story*, "Well, I might as well have one more fling before I settled down in the old ladies' home. I sold some of my remaining Liberty bonds and in company with Hallie Phillips, sailed for Europe."

Dressler and Phillips had met during the war, when they were drafted to act as saleswomen in a second-hand clothing store organized for charity by a group of society hostesses. The actress and the social butterfly adored each other on sight. Between 1917 and 1922, they kept in touch, but the friendship became even closer when Hallie literally kidnapped Dressler and bundled her aboard a transatlantic liner. She would prove to be a lifetime Dressler supporter.

"After prowling through most of central Europe, we separated," Dressler recalled. "She to go to friends in England, I to go to France and thence to Italy. Until I discovered the climate of Southern California, I had determined to spend my declining years in Italy. God must have been in a genial mood when he gave Italy her climate." Later, "I landed in Rome just in time to see Mussolini make his triumphal entry on October 30, 1922. He could have had a crown and scepter on a silver platter. But he laid both at his king's feet. 'We are here to save Italy, Sire,' he said. I am not for dictators generally, but I firmly am for Mussolini . . . and I have great respect for the Fascisti movement." It was the beginning of an almost girlish crush on Il Duce, based partly on the actress's opinion that Italy was recovering from the war faster than any other European country. It would also land her in some awkward political controversies, though both Elsie de Wolfe and the actress's future boss, Louis B. Mayer, were both Mussolini admirers.

But for now, the charm of Italy and the flattering attentions of her friends were having a decidedly healing effect on Dressler's fragile nervous system. Venice was packed with dazzling celebrities who greeted the actress with genuine affection: Elsa Maxwell, who by then had become a world famous party organizer. Cole and Linda Porter. Lady Diana Cooper, who held court on the beach at the Lido. Maude "Emerald" Cunard and the former Jane Campbell of New York who was now the widowed Princess Jane di San Faustino. A word from Lady Alexandra brought invitations from U.S. Ambassador Richard Washburn Child and his wife— already longtime fans from the golden Broadway years—publisher Adolph Ochs and his wife, and assorted European dignitaries. Back in Rome, Ambassador Child arranged an audience with Pope Pius XI that had Dressler sitting up half the night cutting up a black evening gown to make a suitable veil. Then, as she relates, "I was winded by the long stairs I had to climb before I reached the audience chamber. I was still panting when I returned from the brief presentation to find a young man from one of the papers waiting in an anteroom, pencil in hand, to record my impression of my first visit to the Vatican. 'Now, Miss Dressler,' he began, 'what in that noble old pile impressed you most?' 'The absence of an elevator,' I gasped. 'I do wish they'd get a lift for fat old women like me.'" Dressler did not realize that the young man would take her literally. "Imagine my chagrin, therefore, when I picked up the morning paper to discover on the front page in bold black type: 'American actress annoyed because she had to climb Vatican stairs!' After this experience, I was always careful to label my attempts at humor as such." But as much as Dressler loved Italy, she knew she could not stay there forever, as what she described as "a pensioner on the hospitality of my friends. When I got home, I found America as youth-mad, as flapper-crazy as ever. At least, that's what the men who had the say-so about the stage and screen told me. Well," she continued, "if they wouldn't let me act on the stage, I'd act off it. I proceeded to give an excellent imitation of a busy woman."

That meant a renewed round of activity on the war-veteran circuit, singing, playing, and swapping yarns with the disabled inmates of local New York hospitals. She approached her old friend Albert Keller, manager of the Ritz Hotel, and asked if she might work as hostess of the Ritz Supper Club on a part-time basis. Keller was so sympathetically accommodating that Dressler decided to press her luck a little further. Friends were becoming so insistent with their invitations to visit or even take up residence that she decided to ask the Ritz manager if he could rent her a small room at the hotel. That way, she could save on apartment rent and avoid the pitying looks of those who knew her from more fortunate days. As Dressler explained in her 1934 book: "No one would be sorry for me if I lived at the Ritz. Keller saw to it that I got the smallest room in the house at a ridiculously low price." It is difficult to know whether Dressler's many friends were impressed or even fooled by her new address at the upscale Ritz. It seems certain that no one who genuinely cared for the actress made a point of cutting her at the many gatherings of the rich and famous she still frequented.

Wealthy feminist Anne Morgan sought out Dressler after her return from Europe to ask a favor: would she help in a fund-raising effort to build a clubhouse for the thousands of New York City's business and professional women who had no common meeting place? Morgan's idea was to launch a club called the American Women's Association (the club actually had roots in a group called the Vacation Association, founded in 1911), that would provide space for lectures, concerts, dances, games of bridge, and, yes, dates. The clubhouse would also offer limited living accommodation at a modest price. Dressler accepted with typical enthusiasm, making speeches, devising radio programs, and producing amateur plays. She already knew most of the women who were working with Morgan: socialites such as Anna Steese Richardson, Mrs. W.K. Vanderbilt (by then, Anne Morgan's inseparable companion), and Ida M. Tarbell. The actress herself became a founding member of the AWA in late 1922, and even when the two million dollars needed to begin building the clubhouse was safely in the bank, she continued to work with Morgan and Vanderbilt as they designed the interior and devised upcoming programs.

There was a ray of hope for her professional prospects in January 1923, when the Shuberts asked her to pad out the bill in a Winter Garden revue called *The Dancing Girl*. The show had a slight plot: a first-class passenger on a liner (played by Bruce Chattfield) falls in love with a steerage-class dancer. But apart from this shred of a story line, *Dancing Girl* was simply a collection of vaudeville acts. Benny Leonard, an authentic boxing champion, was recruited to fight a mock bout on stage and Dressler—who appeared at the very end of the show—was supposed to parody Somerset Maugham's *Rain*, which was making a splash as a play on Broadway. Few members of the audience seemed to understand the point of the sketch, however, and although the show chalked up a respectable run, the Shubert bookers failed to follow up with another assignment after the revue closed. *The Dancing Girl* was obviously so demoralizing for Dressler that she never referred to it in her books or mentioned it when reporters asked for stories about her Broadway career.

In a ghosted article for *Saturday Evening Post* in 1933, the actress does briefly mention a rare five-week tour on the Shubert vaudeville circuit, for which she was booked in 1925. And in many ways, these appearances were probably the most agonizing experiences of Dressler's purgatorial life in the 1920s. "People laughed in gratifying appreciation of my performances," she says bravely. "But when I got back [from the tour], the public was still clamoring for youth. They had no parts to fit my years. They said and said again, 'Miss Dressler has not youth now. She has not beauty.'" Dressler's friend Frances Marion was visiting New York from Hollywood when the vaudeville tour opened at the Winter Garden. Dressler had written that she had landed a "leading" role in a Shubert show, so the scenarist decided to surprise the actress by showing up at the theatre. Her account of that night makes harrowing reading. When Marion took her seat and examined the program, she was puzzled to see that Dressler's name was listed only among a large group of performers and that there was no mention of her being the star attraction. Marion thought this was rather odd: Marie, after all, always demanded top billing and signed no contract without this assurance. "I know that every top artist refused to follow jugglers, trained seals or a song-and-dance team who did phoney imitations," wrote Marion in *Off With Their Heads*. "Marie was sandwiched between a couple of these duds and I worried until I decided that the Shuberts must have decided she would vitalize the show where it was weak and needed the support of her talent." When Dressler finally appeared, Marion applauded loudly, but was unhappy to realize that few in the audience were responding as enthusiastically. Marie, she saw, was dressed in one of her familiarly freakish outfits, and although she greeted onlookers with a wave and a joke, response was slim. Dressler then "rushed blindly into a frenzy of grimaces and gestures and told stories which might have been funny had they been well-timed." Marion's heart sank when she observed that a sullen silence seemed to be falling over the audience, interspersed with an occasional snicker of derision. Dressler then tried to coax the audience into singing along with her, but clumsily backed into the piano with a loud thud. This produced uproarious laughter, and a relieved Dressler kept up the "buffoonery of a battle between the piano and her rear end. Without thought of what damage she might be doing to the base of her spine, Marie kept batting that piano back and forth across the stage until the laughter ceased and she could make her exit. There was no curtain call for her reappearance after her one bow and I heard a man in back of me say: 'Pitiful, isn't it? When will those old-timers learn to quit?'"

Dressler herself often admitted that the first seven years of the 1920s dragged by in a nightmarish haze. "My courage, like my bank account, had run low," she confessed. "I was frightened, and terribly restless." At one point, she made what she frankly called "a terrible mistake" and tried selling Florida real estate—by telephone. "One of my friends got a man she knew on the wire for me," she told an interviewer. "He asked me all sorts of questions I couldn't answer about mortgages and locations. All I knew was that some of our very best people had taken large slices of it. He said—in a dry, laconic manner—that wasn't enough for him and when I learned some of the essential facts with regard to the property I might approach him again." Actually, Dressler admitted, "I sold a good deal of land before I realized that not only was I a sucker, but that I was making suckers of those who bought through me. Almost beside myself with distress, I did what I could to straighten things out. This experience was one of the most humiliating of my life."

At another point, in 1924, she pulled enough money together to make yet another trip to Europe, again to visit her sympathetic friend, Lady Alexandra Colebrook. In their book, *Being Geniuses Together,* writers Robert McAlmon and Kay Boyle remember that autumn in Venice, the sunny city and the galas at Florian's on the Piazza San Marco. They recalled sitting at an outdoor café with Lady Colebrook, Nancy Cunard, and "the better-looking of the Di Robilant boys, Conte Mundano. Next to us was an obviously American woman, certainly an ex-actress. I glanced at her and listened to her, not wisecracking, but being bravely witty, really witty. She didn't look happy, however. She looked to be an aging woman who'd been about a bit and knew it wouldn't get her anywhere to let down. A darn fine type. Suddenly my memory operated. It was Marie Dressler."

Then, in 1925, an old friend, producer Harry Reichenbach, talked Dressler into going to Europe again to make a couple of two-reel movies, which he dubbed "Travelaffs." The idea was that Dressler would be a kind of Mrs. Malaprop on tour in France. One of the films was made in Versailles (which gave Marie the chance to visit with Elsie and Elisabeth at their villa), and the other was made in Fontainebleau. For some reason, however, the actress did not enjoy the shoot, and when the footage was reviewed back in New York, both she and Reichenbach agreed that the experiment had failed. The films were never released. In later years, Dressler spoke of the Reichenbach trip as "a great disappointment." It was probably no coincidence that when she was asked to speak at an October 13, 1925, dinner at the American Women's Association, she told the audience that she was ready to retire from show business. "The sound of those words in my own voice gave me a strange, sickening feeling," she admitted to a reporter. "But it is done and I am glad to be through with the terrible nerve-strain of theatrical work. No one except those who have experienced it knows what it is to go through with a performance, especially in a new part. . . . It is a never-ceasing strain, amounting at times almost to agony."

And the agony continued. For the next year or so, Dressler, as she freely admits in her 1934 book, was "living from hand to mouth," although, despite her vow to quit the theatre, she took a week's engagement here, an evening's work there. In 1926, she appeared on an Old Timers' bill at the Palace Theatre, together with actresses Cissie Loftus, Marie Cahill, May Irwin, and Yvette Rugel. Dressler and Loftus teamed as a sister act, wowing them with such "fast" material as "She never married, did she?" "No, her children wouldn't let her." The show was to have included a rare appearance by Joe Weber and Lew Fields, but when the comedians arrived at the theatre, they found that Dressler's name had been placed above theirs on the billboard. They were so outraged, they declined to appear, pleading illness.

Dressler became an admirer of Dr. John Murray, who was then attracting disciples with his upbeat lectures in Theosophy, through which she had managed to subdue some of her paralyzing fear by the end of 1926. Early in 1927, Dressler decided that inaction had been at the root of her chronic terror and that she would leave the United States and open a hotel in Paris for Americans "who would pass up duck at the Tour d'Argent for Maryland fried chicken and waffles. Above all, a place where coffee is coffee and not ground chicory." Details concerning the financing of such a venture have always remained vague, but there was some mention of "the few securities I had left," presumably the last of her Liberty bonds. In early January, she slipped out of the apartment she was then sharing with Nella Webb and bought her passage to Europe.

15

DOOR TO THE FUTURE

1927-1929

Dressler's friends were frankly horrified at her plan to become a Parisian hotelkeeper. When she returned to the Manhattan apartment with her steamship ticket and broke the news to Nella Webb, the young astrologer wailed, "Marie, you're coming into a new cycle, one of the best periods of your life! The biggest success of all is ahead of you. All your life you've been a clown. Now you're going to be an actress!" Webb was quite specific with her predictions. She had consulted her charts and determined that Dressler was about to enter an extraordinarily productive seven-year period, beginning January 17. And, insisted Webb, wringing her hands, Dressler would make a terrible hotelkeeper, anyway. "Darling," she moaned, "you'd never present a bill!" To reinforce her argument, she telephoned Helena Dayton and Louis Barrett and asked them to bring along another Dressler admirer, playwright Jimmy Forbes, for a solemn conclave. The group sipped coffee and listened quietly while the astrologer explained Dressler's November 9, 1868, astrological chart, in the same breath denouncing the "absurd" Paris plan.

Dressler remembers, "They outdid each other in poking fun at me, in pleading with me. Jimmy, with a dozen brilliant Broadway hits to his credit, had never given up the idea that he would soon write something that would put me back in the big time. I have already told you how Helena and Louise and Nella had struggled to get me a chance in pictures. They believed in me when I no longer believed in myself. . . . But don't think I didn't care that I was a failure. I did, intensely. I still felt the current of life moving strongly within me. I didn't feel finished. But then I thought ruefully, perhaps that's one of the tragedies of age. Everyone knows but you, and your best friends won't tell you!'"

There are at least two stories on record that describe the events of January 17, 1927. Dressler herself remembered: "I got a telephone call from Allan Dwan, one of Hollywood's topnotch directors. He wanted me to play a small part in an Olive Borden picture he planned to screen in Florida. I was not at all keen about it. 'Most important offer of my life!' I scoffed. 'Why, it's just a bit. I'll be lost in the shuffle. The trip will delay me in getting started in Paris and the salary will hardly cover the expense of new clothes.' 'You're going,' said Nella grimly, 'if I have to ship you by freight.' I gave in, but with poor grace."

Dwan came up with a different version, recounted in Peter Bogdanovich's biography, *The Last Pioneer*. The director insisted that he was lunching with his studio manager at the Ritz Hotel when he saw a woman sitting alone at a little table. He asked his companion if the woman could be Marie Dressler and the men eventually called the head waiter to the table. Yes, agreed the waiter, it was certainly Miss Dressler and she was a resident in the hotel. Dwan said he wrote a note, saying, "Dear Miss Dressler, I'm an admirer of your work in the theatre. I'm a director of motion pictures and I'm interested in whether you would care to play in a picture of mine which is to start immediately." The head waiter handed the woman the note just as she was turning to go up some steps that led onto the main floor. She read it, staggered slightly, then grabbed the stair rail. "Well," recounted Dwan, "I thought she's either had a drink too many or she isn't well. Then a bell-boy came to see me and said, 'Miss Dressler would like to know if you'd see her before you go—she's in her room.'" Dwan says that he was directed to a floor that consisted of rooms used only for the servants of guests at the hotel. And in one of these rooms, he met Marie Dressler. According to the director, Dressler told him that he had saved her life by sending her the note. "I've just had my last meal downstairs and I was going to go out that window. I'd reached the end of my strength. The world was through with me and I was through with the world. But this looks like new hope."

The differences between Dwan's story and Dressler's recol-

Right, Dressler as a child, probably photographed in a Lindsay, Ontario, studio, circa
1872. Museum of the City of New York

Below, Marie Dressler at the beginning of her
Broadway career, circa 1890. Courtesy of the
Marie Dressler Foundation

Left, A typical publicity portrait of Dressler in her dressing room during the 1896 production of *The Lady Slavey,* which propelled Dressler into the ranks of Broadway stardom. Museum of the City of New York

Below, Joe Weber, Marie Dressler, and Harry Morris starred in *Higgledy Piggledy,* which was a smash hit on Broadway in 1904. Museum of the City of New York

Above, The full cast of Joe Weber's 1906 Broadway production of *Twiddle Twaddle.* Dressler is in the center wearing white, with Weber on her right. Museum of the City of New York, the Byron Collection. *Below,* The character of Tillie Blobbs in Lew Fields's 1910 production of *Tillie's Nightmare* was one of Dressler's most enduring roles on Broadway. Here the actress yawns her way into the Dream. Photo by Hall, Museum of the City of New York

Right, Dressler in *Roly Poly,* the 1912 show that marked the last time Joe Weber and Lew Fields ever appeared together on stage. Museum of the City of New York

Below, Dressler—in her first motion picture role—and Charlie Chaplin meet in a restaurant in *Tillie's Punctured Romance,* produced by Keystone in 1914. Museum of Modern Art Movie Still Archives

Left, Marie Dressler, Bessie Love, and Polly Moran in a comedy sketch from *The Hollywood Revue of 1929,* produced by Cosmopolitan for MGM. Metro-Goldwyn-Mayer Distribution Corporation, 1929

Below, Dressler back in the chorus for a number in *Chasing Rainbows.* Interestingly, the actress does not seem much heftier than the prevailing chorus-girl size in the year 1930. Metro-Goldwyn-Mayer Distribution Corporation, 1930

Right, Dressler as Old Marthy in *Anna Christie.* Metro-Goldwyn-Mayer Distribution Corporation, 1930

Below, Dressler as Old Marthy and Greta Garbo as Anna Christie in the 1930 MGM adaptation of Eugene O'Neill's waterfront drama. The movie starred Greta Garbo in her first speaking role, but the consensus of both critics and the public was that Dressler stole the show. Metro-Goldwyn-Mayer Distribution Corporation, 1933

Above, Marie Dressler's breakthrough movie, *Min and Bill*, with Wallace Beery. This was the film that won her the Academy Award for Best Actress. Metro-Goldwyn-Mayer Distributing Corporation, 1930. *Below*, Dressler receiving the 1930-31 Academy Award for Best Actress from Norma Shearer, who had won the Oscar the year before. George Arliss (left) and Lionel Barrymore are seated at the head table. Courtesy of the Academy of Motion Picture Arts and Sciences

Above, Dressler and her longtime partner in comedy, Polly Moran, as the "old girls" who were playing the stock market in *Caught Short.* Metro-Goldwyn-Mayer Distribution Corporation, 1931

Right, Dressler and Moran in yet another comedy collaboration: *Reducing,* the story of the dowdy country sister of a metropolitan beauty specialist. Metro-Goldwyn-Mayer Distribution Corporation, 1931

Mamie Cox, Marie Dressler, and Claire Dubrey on Sunset Boulevard, probably taken by a street photographer, circa 1932. Courtesy of John Phillip Law

Above, Dressler and Polly Moran in *Politics*, another hit for the comedy duo. The film also featured romantic leads William Bakewell and Karen Morley. Metro-Goldwyn-Mayer Distributing Corporation, 1931. *Below*, Dressler at home in the house she always liked best: 623 North Bedford Drive in Beverly Hills, which she rented from Adela Rogers St. Johns. Courtesy of the Marie Dressler Foundation

Dressler enjoyed an occasional visit to the Randolph Hearst/Marion Davies estate at San Simeon, and this photograph with Harpo Marx was likely taken there at a party. Notice what Dressler always insisted was her impeccable taste in clothes. Circa 1932. Author's collection

Above, Emma gave young actor Richard Cromwell his first starring role in the movies, and it was Dressler's high-powered lobbying that got him the part of Ronnie. Metro-Goldwyn-Mayer Distributing Corporation, 1932. *Below,* Marie Dressler and friend in a scene from *Prosperity,* her final film with Polly Moran. Metro-Goldwyn-Mayer Distribution Corporation, 1932

The famous final scene from *Dinner at Eight* with Jean Harlow. This is still considered to be one of the classic moments in film history. Metro-Goldwyn-Mayer Corporation, 1932

Above, Dressler as Tugboat Annie with Wallace Beery as her husband and Robert Young as her son. At the time the actress could work only a few hours a day because of her illness. Metro-Goldwyn-Mayer Corporation, 1933. *Below,* The big party for Dressler on her sixty-fifth birthday in November 1933, one of the last times she ever appeared in public. The actress stands between Louis B. Mayer, CEO of Metro-Goldwyn-Mayer, and Governor James Rolph of California. Courtesy of the Marie Dressler Foundation

Scene from *Christopher Bean,* also released as *Her Sweetheart,* with Lionel Barrymore. This was Dressler's last movie before her death in 1934. Author's collection

DRESSLER

Left, Cartoon of Marie Dressler published in New York at the time the actress was trying her managerial luck in London's West End. Courtesy Robinson Locke Dramatic Collection, New York.

Below, Cleveland Leader cartoon of Dressler published in 1914 at the time she was appearing in a tour of "A Mix Up." Courtesy Robinson Locke Dramatic Collection, New York.

MARIE DRESSLER SEEN IN THREE POSES IN "A MIX UP" AT THE COLONIAL

lections of January 17 are wide and dramatic, particularly as the actress noted in her 1934 book that she had already moved out of the Ritz and was sharing an apartment with Nella Webb at the time of her first contact with Dwan. How could she be contemplating suicide if she "felt the current of life moving strongly within" her? There were the witnesses to the Dressler version: Nella Webb, Helena Dayton, Louise Barrett, Jimmy Forbes, and Mamie Cox, who was still working part-time for Dressler. Irrefutable evidence shows that Dwan's claim to Bogdanovitch that he eventually paid Dressler's way to California, furnished her with letters of recommendation to the studios, then "took care of her" is seriously flawed.

Dwan did, however, open the doors to the future for Dressler and certainly on that historic January 17, as Nella had confidently predicted. The movie was *The Joy Girl* for Fox, filmed in Palm Beach, Florida. The society comedy starred Olive Borden as Jewel Courage, Neil Hamilton as John Jeffrey Fleet, and Mary Alden as Mrs. Courage. Dressler played a society dowager named Mrs. Heath. Dwan claims, "I took her out to Palm Beach, and she was a riot with society there—they all knew her—she was very famous with them and every estate opened to our use because she was with us. Really, she was the queen of Palm Beach, and had the time of her life. Everybody entertained her, had dinners and lunches for her." Dressler herself remembered, "In Florida, it was just as I expected. A little mite of a part. I arrived on Tuesday morning. By Wednesday night, my scenes had been shot. I got on the train and came back home to jab at Nella, 'I told you so!' But the truth was, I had got a thrill out of that little role. It had been a long time since I had faced a camera. I liked the feel of it. I always had. . . . Nella was triumphant. 'It's just the beginning,' she crowed. Said I: 'Humph!'"

Dressler gives an unusually detailed description of early 1927 in *My Own Story*, which makes it likely that her version is correct. She says that they sat in the apartment waiting. "Nella refused to step out of reach of the telephone. She went into huddles with her logarithms and Jupiter who, she said, was cutting up didos in my favor." Then Frances Marion reentered the picture. Dressler had not seen her friend since that evening in 1925 when the scenarist met her backstage at the Winter Garden after the disastrous vaudeville appearance. In the meantime, Marion had established herself as one of the most influential writers at Metro-Goldwyn-Mayer, a confidante of producer Irving Thalberg, and a woman who had access to the ear of the powerful Louis B. Mayer. Once in Hollywood, Marion's star ascended rapidly through her friendship with Mary Pickford, Billie Burke, and Samuel Goldwyn. She also kept in touch with her friends in New York, especially Elisabeth Marbury and Elsie de Wolfe. In her memoir Marion does not reveal the identity of the mutual friend who wrote to her about Dressler's struggle to find her way back into the acting profession, saying, "Don't believe Marie's bluff that she's on the up and up. The big part she told you about in the Allan Dwan picture was only a bit, and he gave it to her out of the kindness of his heart. Now she's looking at the want ads. Says she would make a good housekeeper for some family. Can't you do something for her in Hollywood?" The mutual friend is now known to be Marbury.

Marion remembered that she went at once to the MGM story department hoping to find a play or a novel on option by the company that might be a suitable vehicle for Marie's type of acting. She picked out a story called *The Callahans and the Murphys*, the tale of a feuding Irish slum family, written by Kathleen Norris. She read the book in her office, then thought instantly of Dressler and a puckish former vaudevillian named Polly Moran who was already under contract to the studio. MGM producer Irving Thalberg was aware that Marion liked to write comedies and had recently suggested that she do a picture for Moran between scripting a pair of dramas. Although the short Norris novel contained scant material for a five-reel comedy, Marion recalls that, in preparation for a meeting with Thalberg, she "did what all ruthless scenario writers did in those casual days—I let my imagination run wild and wrote an original yarn. As soon as I finished the first draft of the scenario, I gave it to Irving to read." Thalberg liked Marion's work and asked who she had in mind to play the leading roles, Mrs. Murphy and Mrs. Callahan. Marion named Polly Moran for the Murphy part, and the producer enthusiastically agreed. But Ma Callahan? When Marion suggested that Marie Dressler would be perfect and might actually be persuaded to come to Hollywood for a salary of, say, two thousand dollars a week, Thalberg shrugged and insisted that he hadn't heard of the actress in years. Marion found herself arguing emotionally in favor of her old friend. Then she realized that Thalberg was aware of some personal interest behind her words. Marion stopped in mid-sentence. She continued lamely, "Irving, Marie's a friend of mine. She needs a job desperately." She took Marbury's letter out of her handbag and showed it to the producer. When he passed it back, he looked squarely at Marion and said with a smile: "My theory is that anybody who once hits the bull's-eye, it doesn't matter in what profession, has the brains and stamina to stage a comeback." Then he asked Marion to send for Dressler; MGM would start shooting *The Callahans and the Murphys* as soon as the actress arrived. He set Dressler's salary at fifteen hundred dollars a week.

Marion called Dressler in New York with the news. The actress remembered the scenarist's voice coming over the long-distance line: "Pack up your pie box and come to Hollywood. I need you," Marion said. When she heard, "Nella danced a jig in her nightdress. She was triumphant." The two women did not go back to sleep that night. According to Dressler: "While Mamie packed, I put the coffeepot on. Nella and I drank cup after cup of black coffee; we talked and talked. The next morning, I was so excited, I couldn't eat any breakfast. My teeth actually chattered when I went down to the station to pick up the tickets to Hollywood. 'A chance in pictures, after seven years of doing nothing! It can't be true!' I told myself over and over as the giant wheels of the Chief clacked off the miles westward." As they crossed the country, the two women whiled away the time playing two-handed bridge. Frances Marion met Dressler and Webb at the station. "I was shocked when I saw her," she remembered. "She looked old and haggard. What hell she must have gone through to have wrought such a radical change in her." Dressler greeted her friend with her usual show of bravado. She insisted that the summons to Hollywood had come when she was "juggling a big deal" and that she had accepted the offer because she did not want to miss the chance of a visit. Marion later commented: "Same old Marie! Same old bluff!"

Rehearsals for *The Callahans and the Murphys* began almost as soon as Dressler unpacked her bag in Marion's guest bedroom. Moviemaking in Hollywood had changed, though, since the actress had bullied the Keystone crew during the filming of *Tillie's Punctured Romance*. Director George Hill, who was at the time married to Frances Marion, was charming, but he clearly was not bowled over by Dressler's past reputation as a great theatrical clown. The techniques that had succeeded on stage—and that she had used on the Mack Sennett lot—were firmly discouraged by Hill. Overacting and slapstick behavior simply didn't work any more, and Dressler soon discovered that she would need to pay more attention to character development and detail. The camera, she learned, was merciless in exaggerating the broad brush strokes that had made her famous on the stages of large theatrical houses.

Movies had not yet found their voice in mid-1927, but everyone in town was gossiping about Warner Brothers' plan to begin filming *The Jazz Singer* with Al Jolson that June. It was true that D.W. Griffith was predicting disaster for sound and that Mary Pickford had pontificated that "adding sound to movies would be like putting lipstick on the Venus de Milo." But, reasoned Dressler, it was always possible that acting for the films was evolving into a brand new ball game and that it could be in her own interest to keep pace with the changes. She found time during *The Callahans and the Murphys* shoot to catch up with the evolution of Hollywood itself. The dusty little town she remembered from 1914 had become a thriving city, with expensive stores sprawling along Wilshire Boulevard and world-class restaurants such as the Wilshire Brown Derby, Armstrong-Schroeder, and Victor Hugo's attracting the rich and famous. North of Sunset Boulevard, spectacular homes with swimming pools and elaborate gardens had been built to accommodate the elite of the motion picture industry. Hollywood had become fascinated with itself. In June 1927 the wedding of Vilma Banky and Rod La Rocque at the Church of the Good Shepherd made headlines around the world. Six hundred guests were invited and producer Sam Goldwyn—who gave the bride away—had scaffolding built so that news cameras could capture the arrival of such celebrities as Constance Talmadge, Bebe Daniels, Ronald Coleman, Norma Shearer and her husband, Irving Thalberg. Western star Tom Mix arrived in his own open carriage wearing a purple cowboy outfit. The Los Angeles papers gave the event front-page treatment. But then, Hollywood stars were already front-page news, whether they turned up at an Ambassador Hotel party or attended the opening of a new movie at the Pantages Theatre on Hollywood Boulevard.

There were no news cameras or platoons of photographers at the preview of *The Callahans and the Murphys* that steamy July 1927. The film was shown at a suburban theatre to an audience invited from several Hollywood studios. Dressler sat at the rear of the house with Nella Webb, Frances Marion, and Jimmy Forbes, who had traveled from New York for the big occasion. Dressler remembered that evening years later: "My hands were clammy, my heart fearful to suffocation as we waited for the picture to flash on the screen. I had waited nine years for this moment—nine years of marking time, of humiliation, of beating my head against a stone wall of managerial indifference and prejudice. And now the hour had struck on which my future, my very life hung. No audience can be more ruthless than a Hollywood audience of professionals. If they liked Ma Callahan, I was made. If they didn't—well, there was always Paris and my hotel." Dressler remembers, "The theatre went black and the picture came on. Frances had done a good job. The situations were terribly funny. That hard-boiled audience laughed so much that if there had been any sound effects, you couldn't have heard 'em. And such applause at the end! Thrilled and grateful, we tried to sneak out. We wanted to get home, to talk and talk. But they wouldn't let us. They dragged us forth. How kind they were! How generous! Many of them were too young ever to have heard of me, but they were warm in their praise. They outdid each other in rosy predictions for my future. Frances whispered, 'you've done it. You're made. Every producer in Hollywood will be camped on your trail tomorrow. You'll see.'"

But, as Dressler herself often remembered, "There was a joker in the deck." Comedian Harold Lloyd endorsed *The Callahans and the Murphys* as one of the funniest movies ever made. Happily confident that it would be a hit, MGM gave the film top publicity treatment, then opened the show at Loew's, New York, in August 1927. In Hollywood, everyone connected with the project relaxed with the satisfaction of a job well done. Marion was savoring the fact that her good friend would likely become a star once again. George Hill believed he had directed a major success. Irving Thalberg was confident that he had backed a winning moneymaker for the studio. And Dressler herself "was so happy that night I couldn't sleep," she wrote in *My Own Story*, remembering the sensationally successful preview. "I wish I could make you understand how wonderful it all was. Remember, I was fifty-six [actually, she was fifty-nine]. . . . I had never permitted myself to be down, but I knew what it was to be out. And here I was in the game again. A youngster's game. And I was off to a splendid start. I felt the old vitality rising in a strong tide. I could go on and on. I *would* go on and on!"

Initial response to *The Callahans and the Murphys* was decidedly upbeat. "Marie Dressler and Polly Moran teamed in a series of the most comical events ever portrayed on screen," wrote the *Wichita Beacon,* accompanying a full-page photo layout. "They form the screen's first great feminine team." Box-office receipts from New York were excellent. Until the Irish erupted.

The first signs of trouble came from the *Irish World* and *American Industrial Liberator* with front-page coverage of the movie protesting "MGM's deliberate attempt to ridicule the Hibernians." Picketers outside Loew's demanded that the film be withdrawn. The American Irish Vigilance Committee insisted that the movie "vilified Irish home life." Back in Culver City, a worried Thalberg summoned his team and screened *The Callahans and the Murphys* in an attempt to spot the trouble and correct it before the entire MGM investment slid down the drain. The Irish, it appeared, objected to the fact that Dressler and Moran indulged in ugly—albeit comical—quarrels and at one point showered each other with beer. Thalberg made some suggestions for cuts, and the MGM editors went back to the drawing board. The revised print was rushed to New York and the few other theatres across the country that had begun screening the movie, but the demonstrations in and out of the theatres continued. One reviewer for the *Dallas News* wrote: "*The Callahans and the Murphys* was worthwhile to begin with, but the movie has been sliced, carved and grafted in order that state censor boards and tender racial pride be pleased. The result leaves something to be desired by an audience which merely wants entertainment." A scathing editorial in *Irish World* August 20 read: "This so-called revision by MGM consists of the elimination of some of the features to which objection was taken, but it fails. The Simian grimaces of Marie Dressler are vulgar and unseemly and a caricature of Irish women."

Dressler reacted with shock and disbelief when news of the Irish rebellion reached Hollywood. Frances Marion tried to comfort her friend, but it was obvious that the scenarist was just as worried as her star. Marion later wrote that she had been confident the Irish would love the movie but "the Irish translated their affection into picketing the theatres . . . and sent a long scroll to the studio signed by thousands of names, protesting our deliberate attempt to ridicule the Irish." There was bewilderment at the studio, wrote Marion, because just about everyone connected with the movie had some Irish background. The producer, Eddie Mannix, had nothing but Irish blood in his veins. Director George Hill's grandparents were born in Ireland. And Dressler always seemed to be boasting of Irish blood on her mother's side of the family. Larry Gray, the film's leading man, was of Irish descent, and so was Sally O'Neil who played opposite him. No one who had anything to do with the picture meant any offense, wrote Marion, and "we were all heartsick." She revealed that she had suggested changing the title to "The Browns and the Joneses," but because the picture had already attracted considerable attention Thalberg was concerned there would be repercussions if the studio attempted camouflage. The end came when His Eminence Cardinal Dougherty of the diocese of Philadelphia called MGM president Nicholas Schenck and asked that the movie be removed from release. In a somewhat terse statement to the press, Schenck announced that the studio would comply. "It will entail financial loss, but we are happy to meet Cardinal Dougherty's request." *The Callahans and the Murphys* was immediately shelved and was never seen again. It is possible, in fact, that the negative and all existing prints were destroyed.

Dressler consulted with Frances Marion after *The Callahans and the Murphys* disaster, but even her good and loyal friend could give her little immediate hope for another strong movie role. The actress's salary at MGM predictably dried up, so she quickly accepted a minor part in a First National potboiler called *Breakfast at Sunrise*, starring Constance Talmadge. But even as the silent production was being completed, talk in Hollywood was dominated by the incredible success of Warner Brothers' *The Jazz Singer* starring Al Jolson, which had just opened in New York. Had D.W. Griffith been wrong when he predicted that the Hollywood studios would never make talkies for general distribution?

Certainly the top brass at MGM was having second thoughts

about sound. Both Thalberg and his superior at Culver City, Louis B. Mayer had actively pooh-poohed the possibility that talking pictures would ever become important; they pointed to the incredible cost of retooling to accommodate the new technology and predicted major distribution problems. Silent movies could be shipped to any country in the world and, with a few subtitle changes, be understood. If a sound picture was made in English, however, there would be incalculable extra costs for dubbing in perhaps dozens of different languages. Then there was the voice problem. Few well known Hollywood players were trained in speech, and many spoke in thick foreign accents. But MGM bravely bit the bullet, decided to go ahead with the construction of sound stages, and planned to begin introducing sound effects and a few spoken words in some already scheduled productions. Most of this executive soul-searching bypassed Dressler, although Frances Marion filled her in on some of the more sensational scenes being played out in the offices occupied by Louis B. Mayer and Irving Thalberg. By the end of 1927, though, the actress had yet to meet Mayer formally, except for a somewhat cursory introduction on the studio lot. She did know that the CEO of MGM's Culver City operation was awesomely powerful, that he regarded all of his stars and contract players as his "children," and that although he always expected gifts at Christmas and on his birthday, he was notoriously tight with money. A request for a salary raise by one of his children was considered to be a flagrant act of disloyalty. Marion discovered early in her MGM career, in fact, that bonuses promised by Mayer could turn out to be nothing more valuable than a signed photograph and a patronizing pinch on the behind. Dressler herself learned with some amusement that Mayer loved chicken soup, often wept when he wanted his own way, and that he revered motherhood. She was also told that many actors hated "the Boss," whom actress Helen Hayes once called "a courtly but evil villain."

Mayer had little if anything to do with a forgettable assignment in early 1928 that again featured Dressler opposite the irrepressible and good-natured Polly Moran. Based on the then-popular comic strip, "Bringing Up Father," the film featured J. Farrell MacDonald as the henpecked Jiggs, Moran as Maggie, and Dressler as Annie Moore, Maggie's friendly enemy, with a script by Frances Marion. The silent picture was shrugged off by critics and public alike as a prime example of "rolling pin humor." But at least Dressler was working. After the movie was completed, she collected her earnings and took off again for Europe to visit her loyal friends in Italy and France. All of them were delighted that she seemed at last to be making real inroads in Hollywood. In Versailles, Bessie Marbury, who was slowly adjusting to her friend Elsie de Wolfe's marriage to Sir Charles Mendl, predicted that surely dear Frances would come up with the Big One before too long. As usual, the European holiday did wonders for Dressler's morale; the Beautiful People who paid court to Lady Colebrook were aware that she had been working in movies, and she was continually plied with questions about the coming of sound. The Venice high season was over, but there still were some laggards who were taking their time relocating in Rome: Cole and Linda Porter were completing their tenancy at the Palazzo Rezzonico, and Consuelo, Duchess of Marlborough, was visiting with Lady Diana Cooper. Later, in Rome, Dressler spent long afternoons in the smart cafés, acutely aware that Broadway's current funny girl, Fanny Brice, was attracting as much expatriate attention as she was. But then, Marie Dressler would probably be the first of Lady Alexandra's cronies to make a talking picture. The actress indulged herself with large helpings of lobster cooked in cream and happily argued the appropriateness of beach pajamas on Venice's Lido.

Back in Los Angeles, she let MGM know she was available for work and finally landed a strong part in a silent comedy entitled *The Political Flapper* that was eventually renamed *The Patsy.* The star was Marion Davies, already a legend in Hollywood as both an actress and the mistress of millionaire publisher William Randolph Hearst. Directed by King Vidor, *The Patsy* tells the often side-splitting story of a Cinderella (Davies) overpowered by her socially aspiring mother, Ma Harrington (Dressler), who prefers her prettier daughter (Jane Winton). Dressler earned warm reviews for her performance, although the word around MGM was that Vidor needed to work valiantly to keep Dressler's penchant for slapstick from overshadowing Davies in all of the commotion. This movie was followed by *The Divine Lady* for First National in early 1929, the story of the historic affair between Emma, Lady Hamilton, and Captain Horatio Nelson. Basically a silent film, *The Divine Lady* did boast some rudimentary sound effects as well as one of the first songs—"Lady Divine"—presented on screen since the successful release of The *Jazz Singer*. Dressler played the part of Emma's somewhat uninteresting mother, and the two lovers were portrayed by Victor Varconi and the stunningly beautiful Corinne Griffith. First National spent a fortune on the sets, costumes, and photography by John F. Seitz, but even with the sound sequences expensively ballyhooed in its advertising campaign, *The Divine Lady* headed for an early shipwreck.

Dressler fails to mention these early movie performances in *My Own Story*. In fact, she manages to convey the impression that she hung around Hollywood waiting for the telephone to ring between 1927 and 1929. But even with the checks she was receiving for the small parts that came her way, times were lean indeed for the actress. She put her head in her hands and wept with relief on her sixtieth birthday in November 1928 when wealthy friends in New York, Mr. and Mrs. Arthur Neurmberg, sent her a check for ten thousand dollars with a note saying they had intended to leave her a legacy some day but figured she could use the money right away. Perhaps, Dressler thought, Nella's promise of those seven good years was actually beginning to come true. For the first time since *The Callahans and the Murphys* disaster, she felt a strong surge of optimism.

16

Queen Marie

1929-1931

Dressler rented a pleasant white house on Hillside Avenue in Hollywood not long after she decided to stay in Los Angeles. Late in 1929, however, she moved to a three-year-old, Spanish-Mediterranean-style home at 718 Milner Road in Whitley Heights. A year or so later, the actress leased a ten-room house at 623 North Bedford Drive in Beverly Hills from journalist Adela Rogers St. Johns. Both Dressler and her closest friends always agreed that the Bedford Drive residence came close to the kind of home the actress had always wanted. Yet Dressler insisted on moving again toward the end of 1932, this time to a house at 801 North Alpine Drive in Beverly Hills that she bought from the estate of razor tycoon King Camp Gillette.

During her seven years in Hollywood, the actress lived alone, except for her longtime maid, Mamie Cox, and eventually Mamie's husband, Jerry, and Irene Allen, a cook. A chauffeur, simply known as Meadows, was summoned from his own home when necessary to drive one of the two cars (a 1929 Lincoln Berline and a 1931 Ford Tudor Sedan, acquired when she could afford them). There were often house guests, notably Hallie Phillips and Dressler's old friend from Broadway days, Georgie Caine, who had married a prominent San Franciscan. Nella Webb had returned to New York after *The Callahans and the Murphys* calamity to pursue her astrology work. Dressler never mentions Webb in her autobiography after the year 1927, but there's no doubt the two women kept in touch: the astrologer was one of the eventual beneficiaries of Dressler's will.

In 1928, Dressler met Claire Dubrey. Dubrey was an athletic, thirty-five-year-old actress who had trained as a nurse, married and divorced a Los Angeles doctor named Norman Gates, and was then making a decent living playing "vamp" roles in silent movies. Her real name was Clara Violet Dubreyvich, and she liked to tell the story of how she, her mother, and her grandfather traveled west in a covered wagon over the Sierra Nevadas from Idaho in 1897. In 1928, she was almost as alone in the world as was Dressler: she had no brothers or sisters, and her mother had remarried and was living in Santa Monica. Dubrey met Dressler not long after the shelving of *The Callahans and the Murphys.* She had been entertaining friends from San Francisco when one of the men suggested they get in touch with Dressler, whom he had known in New York during her theatrical heyday. No one knew where the actress lived, but the San Franciscan managed to track down an address and telephone number through directory information and promptly made the call. Dressler immediately invited the group to her current home on Hillside Avenue for a drink. Apparently Dressler enjoyed meeting the much younger Dubrey and asked her to visit again. Dubrey was flattered but made no promises until Dressler pinned her down to a date. Remembered Dubrey when she eventually wrote about the incident in her personal memoir: "That was when our friendship began."

The two women did not see much of each other that year: Dubrey worked for a time in San Francisco and Dressler made her trip to Europe. When she returned, she and Dubrey played bridge occasionally and discussed Dressler's chances of getting her big break in motion pictures. From Dubrey's remembrances, it seems that the aging actress did not believe her future was too bright. Over and over again, she would regale her new friend with the now-familiar lament: "I'm getting no younger and the public is demanding new faces, new methods. There's nothing for me at all."

Certainly her movie work through 1928 and early 1929 seemed to offer little prospect of stardom. There was *The Patsy,* of course, *Bringing up Father,* and the hybrid silent/sound feature, *The Divine Lady.* But the Sound Craze was beginning to make important inroads at the big studios. MGM's first all-talkie film, *The Broadway Melody,* opened at Grauman's Chinese Theatre in February 1929, and other studios followed the trend with such movies as O*n With the Show, Gold Diggers of Broadway, The Show of Shows,* and *Sally,* all of them photographed in two-tone Technicolor. Casting departments were searching feverishly for actors who could emote—ideally individuals with theatrical experience. Scouts were dispatched to lobby such prominent New York thespians as Ruth Chatterton, George Arliss, the Marx Brothers, and Walter Huston. Singers were actively wooed. The high-salary contracts drawn up for popular stars such as Sophie Tucker, Jeanette MacDonald, and Rudy Vallee made screamer headlines in the showbusiness press. Then there was the changing character of Hollywood itself. Microphone technicians with their newfangled equipment and wax sound discs were becoming the undisputed studio elite. And actors with heavy accents or squeaky voices were wondering with increasing alarm how long it would be before they lost the respect of producers, directors, and, most important, audiences already mesmerized by the magic of talking pictures.

Dressler was called by MGM casting in mid-1929 to play a small role in a new sound picture starring Bessie Love and Charles King called *The Road Show.* The musical also featured Polly Moran and Jack Benny, but despite a tuneful score, lively script, and the backup of extensive publicity, the movie failed to take off. MGM quickly realized the studio would need to pull out all the stops to equal the success of *The Broadway Melody.*

A few months after the wrap of *The Road Show,* Dressler was called again, this time for a movie produced by William Randolph Hearst's Cosmopolitan Pictures and to be released by MGM, entitled *Hollywood Revue of 1929.* Harry Rapf, whom Hearst had placed in charge of the project, clearly had no plan as far as plot or organization was concerned. Apparently the name of the game was to put together an all-talking, all-singing, all-dancing motion picture, with as many MGM personalities in the cast as possible. This, of course, was difficult because of other studio commitments, so a strategy evolved that required contract performers working on other movies to report for duty at midnight and to work a graveyard shift until 7 A.M. Because of this twenty-five-day hijacking, the cast of *Hollywood Revue of 1929* was understandably impressive: John Gilbert and Norma Shearer, who played a scene from *Romeo and Juliet,* Marion Davies, Joan Crawford (whose attempts at singing and dancing were laughingly amateurish, perhaps because she was half asleep), Buster Keaton, Laurel and Hardy, Jack Benny, Polly Moran, Bessie Love, Ukelele Ike, Charlie King and Gus Edwards. The show was directed by Charles F. Reisner and featured sixteen songs, including Fred Fischer's "Strike Up the Band" and "Singin' in the Rain," a Nacio Herb Brown and Arthur Freed composition that would be destined to become a kind of signature tune for MGM. Dressler made an extraordinary appearance in royal robes, singing/reciting

I'm the Queen.
Once as Lady Godiva I was seen.
The poor horse died of course.
Not of shame or deep remorse.
'Twas my weight that killed the horse.
Still I'm the Queen.

After each queenly pronouncement, she haughtily gestured her disdain for everyone around her, including the audience. She also hammed her way through a lively musical satire in company with Moran and Bessie Love. "Marie, Polly and Bess," as the sequence was dubbed, had the three actresses dressed in kiddie rompers and enormous hair ribbons. And she played a screamingly funny sequence as an elephantine Venus rising from the sea. When the show opened at Grauman's in September 1929, MGM ordered a gallon of perfume pumped through the theatre's ventilators to dramatize the movie's orange blossom finale. At the Astor Theatre opening in New York, traffic in Times Square came to a standstill as a score of chorus girls formed a living billboard, caroling "Singing in the Rain." Mayer always denied he had ordered Jehovah to provide the gentle downpour that obediently materialized. MGM's boss clearly had no influence over the stock market, which laid its famous egg that October. But at least *Hollywood Revue* paid off for its backers: the movie cost $426,000 to produce and made a huge profit of $1,350,000.

"Individually, no one stands out like Dressler," raved *Variety*, but as she confided to Dubrey over bridge one evening, calls from MGM then suddenly dried up and Dressler had decided to renew her connections with other studios. At Paramount, she struck pay dirt by signing for a two-reel talkie short called *Dangerous Females*. The script was written by Florence Ryerson and Colin

Clements, and director William Watson also signed Polly Moran for the film. The plot was unadulterated farce, very much in the Dressler tradition. The ladies mistake an escaped convict for an evangelist but eventually realize their error and capture the criminal. Dressler mugs her way through the entire performance, almost as though she finds it a relief to be let off the leash. There is even a token drunk scene to help her milk the guffaws. It is obvious now when viewing the film that both Dressler and Moran had considerable trouble locating the primitive microphones.

But again, it was work, and so was a part in a movie with Rudy Vallee called *The Vagabond Lover*. The film, released in November 1929, was directed by Marshall Neilan, and Dressler flounced and grimaced her way through the role of Mrs. Whitehall, a nouveau riche social climber. In early 1930, she played the part of a passé actress in *Chasing Rainbows*, "a pleasant little singie" according to the critics, directed by Reisner and starring those perennial all-singing, all-talking, all-dancing sweethearts, Bessie Love and Charles King. Today, *Chasing Rainbows* is chiefly remembered for its hit song, "Happy Days are Here Again." And, out of the blue, actor Edward Everett Horton asked Dressler to play the princess in a stage production of Ferenc Molnár's *The Swan*. She accepted, but after receiving her first week's check for one hundred fifty dollars, she suddenly quit the cast. Horton never forgave her.

And then came *Anna Christie*.

MGM's hugely successful but temperamental Swedish star, Greta Garbo, had been an on-again, off-again resident of the studio since July 1925 and had fascinated audiences with such movies as *Flesh and the Devil* and *Love* opposite the equally successful John Gilbert. She had also made The *Divine Woman*, based on the life of Sarah Bernhardt, in which she had costarred with Swedish superstar Lars Hanson. In 1929, she made her last silent film, *The Kiss*, opposite a young and clearly overwhelmed Lew Ayres, which was directed by Jacques Feyder. The movie did well at the box office but, after its release, Mayer and Thalberg held top-secret meetings that culminated in a top-level decision: Garbo's next appearance on screen would have to feature sound. But what story would be powerful enough to support the equally powerful promise that Garbo would talk?

Eventually, Irving Thalberg settled on Eugene O'Neill's somewhat turgid 1921 stage play of waterfront low life, *Anna Christie*. The story had already been filmed in 1923 as a Blanche Sweet vehicle, but Thalberg believed that the female lead—a young prostitute who returns to the New York docks to visit her father, the captain of a coal barge—could accommodate Garbo's thick Swedish accent. He handed the play to Frances Marion for a new adaptation, then proceeded to cast the other three major roles. The part of Anna's father, Chris Christopherson, was relatively simple to nail down—George F. Marion (no relation to Frances) had played the part in the original stage version and had honed the role to perfection. Charles Bickford, then a popular hunk under contract to the studio, was handed the part of Anna's suitor, Matt Burke. The directorial job was given to the highly respected Clarence Brown. But then there was the challenging role of Old Marthy Owen, Chris's drunken, down-at-heel mistress.

Marion worked diligently on the *Anna Christie* script, quietly strengthening the Old Marthy character. When the scenario was complete, she sent the manuscript to Thalberg and asked for a private meeting. Thalberg was delighted with the treatment and was also pleased that she agreed with his casting choices. But although the role of Old Marthy was still very much in limbo, the slim, dark-eyed producer smiled in disbelief and some astonishment at Marion's suggestion that Marie Dressler would be perfect in the part. For one thing, Thalberg argued, Dressler was a comic, and a good one. True, he agreed, the actress could play a great drunk, but the O'Neill play screamed out for superb acting. Besides, he continued to argue, he wanted established names in support of such a crucial project, and although he admired the aging Dressler, she had scarcely become a household icon since her arrival in Hollywood. Unfortunately, Clarence Brown agreed wholeheartedly with Thalberg and even indicated that he would be very unhappy if Dressler was forced upon him. As Dubrey later wrote: "Marie was in a twitter for weeks while her chance at the role swung in the balance."

Luckily, Marion's reputation at MGM was powerful enough to convince Thalberg and his staff that Dressler at least deserved a screen test. "To everybody's surprise except Frances Marion's," remembered Dressler, "the test came out favorably." Even Brown apparently agreed that Dressler showed considerable promise in the part, but he decided to give the actress meticulous direction during the making of the film. In hindsight, this clearly worked in Dressler's favor: self-direction had too often been her downfall in the past. "He watched Marie like a hawk," remembered Dubrey, "because he wanted to make sure she did not play horse with Old Marthy." She also recalled: "I went to the opening of *Anna Christie* with Marie. We held hands in our nervousness and her ring was imprinted on my finger for days. But we need not have worried. What a characterization she gave!"

Anna Christie was a sensation. It was agreed by all of the major critics and certainly the movie-going public that Garbo had made a successful transition to sound. For months after the March 1930 opening, Garbo fans tried to copy the Swedish star's mysterious, foghorn voice and her first spoken words on film: "Gimme a whisky—ginger ale on the side. And don't be stingy, baby." But it was Dressler who received much of the attention. Wrote *Variety* in March 1930: "Perhaps the greatest surprise is Marie Dressler who steps out of her usual straight slapstick to stamp herself as an actress with an affecting knack of genuine pathos. As a tipsy old street walker, superannuated at her trade but richly human, she accomplished the unusual feat of drawing audience applause at the finish of a scene."

Frances Marion revealed some time later that Garbo hated the O'Neill play and told her that she felt it portrayed Swedes as "low-down characters." She also felt that she had done a bad job of acting in the movie. "Isn't it terrible?" she is reported to have whispered during a showing of the film. "Whoever saw Swedes act like that?" After the opening of the movie, in fact, the actress called on Dressler at her home in Whitley Heights to convey her personal congratulations and deliver a huge bunch of chrysanthemums. Despite the rave reviews flooding in for *Anna Christie*, it is interesting to note there were also front-office caveats concerning Garbo's first all-talking performance. A memo sent to Culver City by W.F. Willis, an MGM executive based in New York, complained: "Garbo does not talk like a Swedish immigrant girl who came to Minnesota at the age of five." And another company bigwig, Col. Jason S. Joy, sent his private rating of the four *Anna Christie* principals to Mayer's office: "Dressler, Marion, Bickford and Garbo in that order."

Dressler herself admitted to her friends that she was delighted with her work in *Anna Christie* and often referred to Old Marthy as her favorite movie role. As she later told a reporter: "I loved doing that part because deep down beneath the sordidness of the character I wanted her fine soul to show through. That's the way I visualized her when I read the script." She also remembered that her experience in vaudeville helped dramatize her various entrances throughout the movie. And stage work had also helped polish her technique for personality development. Even though Old Marthy was indeed a pathetic has-been, Dressler's artistry in depicting a woman who had retained her basic pride and dignity endeared the character to audiences everywhere.

Clarence Brown's professionalism as a director—and, increasingly through the shoot, his respect for Dressler—also contributed significantly to her success in *Anna Christie*. Typically for those days, the movie was photographed as though it was a stage production with the cameras placed on one side of the set. But Brown decided to use two pieces of equipment so that he could order close-ups as well as medium shots of the action. Looking at the film today, Dressler's sixty-one-year-old face, with its craggy lines, jutting jaw, and expressive eyes, seems to dominate the screen. And Brown's meticulous direction shows he must have been aware that he had a major talent on his hands. The director gave Dressler some unusual elbow room during a scene at Coney Island when Old Marthy stumbles onto a rendezvous between Garbo and Bickford. Garbo quite clearly does not want her handsome new friend to know that she had already met the dreadful old wharf rat, and Dressler senses the young woman's unease. She tactfully begins her retreat but not before she delivers a parting line that, according to Dressler, she couldn't bear to cut—"Well, kid, it's a hell of a life at best." "Hell" was not permitted in the movies at that time. As Dressler recounted years later: "Lots of grand lines had to go from *Anna Christie,*" but "I came to that line and I couldn't bear to let it go. So I timed a hiccup so it would break just where the hell was to be and saved the line." Dressler never did explain why the word was included in the script in the first place. But if the story is indeed true, Clarence Brown must have approved Dressler's change. The MGM top office basked happily in the warm glow of the upbeat reviews and the long box-office lines that greeted the opening of *Anna Christie.*

The film had cost the studio $376,000 to produce, but eventually the profit would total $576,000. Not only were the figures highly respectable, the studio's expensive Swedish star seemed to be heading for even greater prominence in talkies. And they had inadvertently stumbled on an incredible new moneymaker—a fat, homely woman of sixty plus who was already outdrawing MGM's carefully promoted blondes and leggy young heroines.

Thalberg summoned Dressler to the studio and offered her a contract at fifteen hundred dollars a week. This was considerably less than big star salaries, which were already reaching the twelve thousand dollars a week mark, but Dressler celebrated her change of fortune by leasing the larger house on North Bedford Drive owned by Rogers St. Johns. She and Dubrey, assisted by Mamie and her husband Jerry, began furnishing the extra rooms, mainly from the bargain basement of Barker Brothers furniture store in downtown Los Angeles. The explanation for her thrift seemed to express her continuing mood of caution: "I don't want to buy a lot of stuff I'd hate to leave behind if they ever catch on to me in pictures."

In spite of this, though, she waited eagerly, even confidently, for the next MGM assignment. When it came, she fought to hide her disappointment: the studio had decided to feature her in a William Haines comedy entitled *The Girl Said No*. This forgettable movie, released in April 1930, was directed by Sam Wood. The cast also included the perennial Polly Moran, Francis X. Bushman, and Leila Hyams. "The movie has a few genuine laughs, a title that has possibilities it doesn't live up to and a cast of players, all out of their element except Polly Moran and Marie Dressler," complained *Variety*. Other reviewers agreed with *Variety* that the movie "sadly overstayed its time and left the spectator bored."

It seemed fairly obvious, in fact, that although MGM was impressed with Dressler's potential and excited by the box-office response to *Anna Christie,* the top office did not know how to handle their unique new contract player. Louis B. Mayer, who had already informed his minions that he wanted Dressler to be marketed as a mother figure who was also a battered veteran of life's wars, asked her to lunch in his private bungalow on the Culver City lot. Not only did Dressler appear to be a substantial mother figure in real life, MGM's boss was also aware that the actress exuded an easy air of upper-class panache. She was, he decided, a far classier individual than the Hollywood glamour girls he often professed to disdain.

Irving Thalberg also invited the actress to lunch but could promise her nothing more important than a loan-out to United Artists to play the princess in *One Romantic Night*, billed as Lillian Gish's first talking picture. The assignment was highly ironic: the script was based on *The Swan*, the Molnár play that—to Edward Everett Horton's annoyance—she had abandoned just a few months before. Gish eventually wrote that Dressler was given some gorgeous costumes to wear in the film but was asked to act as though she was cavorting in *Tillie's Punctured Romance*. Dressler tried to be cheerful during the shoot, but as she confided to a sympathetic Dubrey, *One Romantic Night* and *The Girl Said No* had been disappointing after the euphoric experience of *Anna Christie*.

The United Artists loan-out was quickly followed by yet another Dressler-Moran team-up that MGM believed would profitably mark time while they figured out what to do with their interesting new property. *Caught Short*, with a script by Willard Mack and Robert Hopkins, involved a couple of feuding boardinghouse landladies, each with a son and a daughter who happened to be in love with each other. The gimmick in this particular movie was that the "old girls," as Dressler and Moran were beginning to be dubbed, were playing the stock market. And winning. With the trauma of the 1929 crash rapidly fading—and despite the fact that the Depression was beginning to hurt—the film was a surprising success at the box office. Not only were Dressler and Moran incredibly funny, they were proving themselves to be great performers as well. Movie fans were beguiled by the fact that their clowning was always believably human. *Variety* even enthusiastically endorsed *Caught Short* as "the apex of the career of this pair of sublimated funmakers." The two stars were supported by Charles Morton, Anita Page, and Greta Granstedt, and the picture was handsomely directed by Charles Reisner. The show opened at the Capitol in New York on June 20, 1930.

Possibly designed as a corporate pat on the back for the somewhat unexpected *Caught Short* hit, MGM then announced a project for Dressler that it believed would have considerable clout: a Thalberg production of Rachel Crothers' 1929 stage comedy, *Let*

Us Be Gay, that would costar Dressler with Thalberg's wife, Norma Shearer. The script was by Frances Marion and the movie would be directed by Robert Z. Leonard. Dressler played a society matron (a role that was dangerously close to becoming a Dressler cliché) who wanted to save her granddaughter (played by Sally Eilers) from the clutches of Norma's former husband (Rod La Rocque). The story revolves around how Dressler persuades Shearer to lure La Rocque back into the marriage. Others in the cast included Hedda Hopper, Gilbert Emery, and Raymond Hackett. *Let Us Be Gay* was shot in a respectably modest twenty-three days, cost the studio $257,000 and made a nice profit of $527,000. The critics agreed that MGM had produced an expensively entertaining, though overly talkative movie and that Dressler and Shearer (both Canadian-born, the feature-writers duly noted), lived up to expectations. Dressler, in fact, was again singled out as a performer who could not only draw gasps of delighted recognition from audiences but loud applause as well. Decided *Variety*: "This tells louder than fan mail or anything else how the character comedienne rates in New York and probably all over."

In the meantime, Marion had been thinking hard about her friend's future—and, no doubt about the studio's investment in Dressler as well. Old Marthy had made such an incredible impact on movie audiences, Marion wondered if she could come up with another screenplay that would incorporate the endearing qualities of the waterfront derelict, while endowing the character with the trappings of a screen heroine. Foraging among MGM's optioned literary properties, she found a novel called *Dark Star* by a friend and former screenwriter named Lorna Moon. *Dark Star* was essentially a tragicomedy involving the San Pedro tuna fleet, but the plot included a strong female character, and Marion decided this aspect of the story could be exploited to Dressler's advantage. She also decided that the male character could be strengthened so that Dressler could at last have her "romantic" leading man.

Negotiations with Moon—who was then in a sanitarium suffering from tuberculosis—were completed when producer Harry Rapf agreed to pay the writer seventy-five hundred dollars for the movie rights, provided Marion promised she would handle the scenario. During one of these preproduction meetings it was agreed that the title *Dark Star* was too gloomy and that the picture needed something more upbeat. Marion was asked about the names chosen for the two leading characters, and her answer clinched the new title for the movie: *Min and Bill*. It was a foregone conclusion that the part of Min was the exclusive property of Marie Dressler, and the role of Bill was offered to Wallace Beery, a rough-edged, middle-aged actor who had made a favorable impact in *The Big House,* a dramatic prison picture scripted by Marion. The scenarist's husband, George Hill, was assigned to direct *Min and Bill,* and Thalberg decreed that the project would be budgeted for a forty-day shoot at a cost of $350,000. As it turned out, Hill brought in the movie in thirty-eight days for $327,000, and the film was the studio's top earner for 1930, chalking up a clear profit of $731,000. Lorna Moon died of a hemorrhage two weeks before the release of the movie in late 1930. She was cremated and her ashes buried in "her wee home on the Scottish cliffs above the sea."

Thalberg and Mayer looked on with undisguised delight as box-office figures for *Min and Bill* rolled in from across the country. The Depression-scarred public, clearly responding to a movie hero and heroine who looked as though they were more at home handling life's problems than sipping champagne in a speakeasy, lined up to see the show. Critics, though, were divided as to whether MGM's latest offering had any merit at all. "Marie Dressler and Wallace Beery are teamed in an unedifying film version of Lorna Moon's novel *Dark Star*," pontificated the *New York Times* in November 1930, "which emerges from the MGM studio as *Min and Bill*. That these two undeniably talented players do good work when the opportunity arises is admitted, but their efforts are wasted on this unsavory production." Wrote the Motion Picture News: "Any picture featuring Marie Dressler and Wallace Beery will be box office. But why MGM or anyone else would dare to take a tragic story like *Dark Star* for this combination of funmakers as their first teaming picture is beyond comprehension. That they did dare to do it and that it is a fine picture, is a tribute to somebody's courage." And later in the review: "It is Miss Dressler's picture."

Dressler was more than happy with her work in *Min and Bill*. At last, she had been handed another chance to act rather than to clown her way through a scenario. As she later remembered: "The characters were so rich, so meaty, that we constantly had to guard against the danger of overacting. Hitherto, in working up a role, I had first to get my teeth into it, so to speak, and then sort of roll it over and put gravy on it before it was really mine. This time, the part had everything when it was handed to me. I had only to translate Frances Marion's dream into flesh and blood. Wally played Bill superbly."

Wallace Beery and Dressler seemed like a perfect match in *Min and Bill,* and they were destined to appear together in two more movies, but it has never been made clear as to whether they were actually compatible. Irene Powell, Dressler's cousin, recalled that the actress's sister Bonita was sure that Dressler "hated that fellow she played with—Wallace Beery—they didn't get along at all well." Yet George Hill told an interviewer: "When they gave me two such unconscious scene-stealers as Marie and Wally to work with, I had visions of having to tear them apart when they were before the camera . . . but each wanted the other to have all the business. It must be love!" And director Mervyn LeRoy revealed that Beery became quite testy when an ailing Dressler was late during the making of *Tugboat Annie* and loudly complained that he was tired of waiting for "that old bag." Personally, Dressler had little to say about her relationship with Beery, and her friend Claire Dubrey made no comment on the topic in her memoir. All we now have are the three Dressler-Beery movies (*Min and Bill, Tugboat Annie, Dinner at Eight*) to examine for clues and the fact to ponder that Dressler's superstardom began with the first of them, *Min and Bill.*

Decades later, it is easy to smile at the somewhat overblown, highly sentimental story of Min, the owner of a hotel in a dock slum and her tough, rough-talking man, Bill. Here we have the tale of the big, tired-looking woman with the black hat, nondescript blouse, and plaid skirt who is bringing up Nancy (played by Dorothy Jordan), daughter of a broken down alcoholic (Marjorie Rambeau). The daughter knows nothing of her origins and finally meets the wealthy man of her dreams who asks her to marry him. The drunken mother decides to gate-crash the wedding so she can claim some of her daughter's money, but Dressler shoots and kills her during a quarrel. A distraught Bill does his best to help his lady-love escape, but she is apprehended by the police and taken into custody. Certainly this dour tale seems to live up to the original spirit of *Dark Star,* but in the adroit hands of Dressler, Beery,

Hill, and, of course, Frances Marion, *Min and Bill* turns out to be a sometimes hilarious comedy, touched with true drama and pathos. Dressler's performance is a classic for its day. She immediately establishes herself as a Character, a woman who has seen it all and has accepted her hard lot with strength and dignity. She again shows herself to be the master of the shrug and gesture. Her mobile jaw, her shoulders, and, as always, her expressive eyes tell the story just as eloquently as do her lines. And her scenes with Bill are human, affectionate, and very funny. For any Dressler fan, the final scene of *Min and Bill* will surely be remembered as one of the finest of her movie career. After Bill discovers the murder and tries to rush Min to his boat, the need to see Nancy depart for her wedding overcomes the older woman's fear of capture. She stops and watches the happy young couple from a distance; her weather-beaten face, with a fresh bruise on one cheek from the scuffle with Nancy's mother, breaks into a radiant smile. Her eyes reflect her profound joy. And even as she is arrested and the police lead her away, the smile and the joy are sustained. When the movie was shown in 1930 and 1931, the final fade-out was enough to leave entire audiences sobbing in paroxysms of heartbreak and happiness.

No wonder moviegoers throughout the country nodded in approval when Dressler and Beery were asked to leave their footprints in the cement forecourt of Grauman's Chinese Theatre. On January 31, 1931, Sid Grauman inscribed over the two pairs of prints: "America's New Sweethearts, Min and Bill."

17

THE LITTLE DOCTOR

1931-1932

Life for Dressler had begun to change even after the release of *Anna Christie* in 1930. But by the time *Min and Bill* was dominating the national box office, followed in January 1931 by the release of the less-successful Dressler-Moran comedy, *Reducing,* MGM was delivering fan mail to the Bedford Drive house in sacks. Social invitations from such Hollywood luminaries as Mary Pickford and Douglas Fairbanks, Marion Davies and William Randolph Hearst, and Norma Shearer and her powerful husband, Irving Thalberg, began to roll in. Dressler dutifully turned up at some of the parties, but as Claire Dubrey made clear in her memoir, the actress was essentially a homebody who preferred to arrange her own small dinner parties at Bedford Drive, always followed by a game of bridge or backgammon. Few Hollywood performers ever received invitations to these soirees. Polly Moran, who had become something of a fixture in Dressler's professional life, never visited Bedford Drive, essentially because she hated to play games. In 1930 and 1931, those who were invited to cross Dressler's threshold were almost always visiting socialites from New York or high society expatriates from the East who had settled in Santa Barbara to the north of Los Angeles. Dressler remained conspicuously aloof from the local nightclub and first-night scene. She did take some weekend trips to Hearst's extravagant estate at San Simeon, mainly because the publisher liked to include interesting statesmen and power brokers as well as actors in his mix of guests. Otherwise, the actress's visits out of town were almost always at the invitation of non–showbusiness friends who had homes nestled among the eucalyptus trees and jacarandas in the Santa Barbara suburb of Montecito.

Dubrey continued to see Dressler in 1930, then as the volume of fan mail threatened to become an avalanche, she suggested to the actress that she might occasionally help out as a secretary. According to her memoir, she believed this would be a good way of repaying Dressler for all of the hospitality she showered on her. The actress herself quickly denied that Dubrey needed to repay anything, but agreed to the arrangement when the younger woman pointed out that she always seemed to be at Bedford Drive for dinner and bridge, anyway.

"As a matter of fact," related Dubrey, "we spent much time alone. I was expected every night, regardless of what was going on and great were the loving reproaches that greeted me if I stayed away. It was sweet, but more than a trifle binding, though I never stopped in without being asked. I always hoped they would forget, just once. But every day, Mamie would phone and say, 'are you coming tonight, Miss Clara? Miss Dressler expects you.' Or Marie would ring in the morning. 'I'm going to shop for my linens today, dear. Do go with me and we'll lunch downtown.' If I skipped a single evening, the whole household acted as if I'd been in hiding for weeks!" Dubrey wrote. "It was sweet, it was dear, it was flattering. My other friends teased me about giving them the air for Marie Dressler. I did, in a way. Certainly I had little time to see them. Before I realized it, I found myself adopted, almost absorbed. Only a quarrel could have broken the ties, but I loved her too much for that."

Dubrey admits in her memoir that she still received a respectable amount of mail from fans who had enjoyed her silent films, but never had she experienced the incredible volume and variety of letters that arrived at the house, addressed to Marie Dressler. A small, but sizable number of letters were "truly beautiful" notes from appreciative fans who wrote simply to thank the actress for the pleasure she gave them, hastening to add that they expected no acknowledgment. Other letters were unapologetic pleas for old clothing, demands for money ("you'll never miss just one week's salary"), and original stories or movie scripts, often followed in ten days by a threatening letter from an attorney demanding either payment or a hand-delivered return of the manuscript. "Others, and dozens of them, would like a full, detailed account of her life and in her own handwriting. One modest youth sent her a blank autograph book, brand new, fully three hundred pages. He asked her to take it around to the studios and fill it with all the other stars' signatures. Prisoners forwarded small silver bracelets and bangles, value two dollars. They all had been unjustly sentenced and were trying to earn money enough for a lawyer. Chain letters were a source of annoyance, and cranks wrote and warned her to repent, the end of the world was at hand. Others told her of girls they were saving from sin, reveling in writing lurid, erotic details. Many requests were pitiful and some must have been genuine. But there was no easy way of determining the truth, so I answered the ones that seemed honest and explained that it was impossible for Miss Dressler to help them all." Dressler received one proposal at the time. The gentleman was a house painter, and he enclosed a photograph. Dubrey returned the picture with no comment. The suitor must have concluded that his extreme youth was against him because he promptly sent it back, with a mustache penciled in.

Dubrey carried a briefcase of the fan mail everywhere. If she called into Bedford Drive in the morning to go shopping with Dressler, she left a batch of letters and her typewriter at the house. "Well I knew I wouldn't get back to my own home before bedtime, so after our return to Bedford Drive, I'd knock out a dozen answers before Marie had the heart to tear me away." The mail also accompanied them on weekend and overnight visits to Santa Barbara and certainly to any hotels in which they stayed. Bellboys brought autograph albums from strangers downstairs. Oil paintings and all kinds of gadgets were sent up to be purchased. "I worked at the mail while taking a sun bath in my back garden and in her automobile, tearing up the dead wood and scattering it along our trail as if we were playing fox and hounds," wrote Dubrey. "I even used to slit envelopes while I was a dummy at bridge! It was my only chance to keep up with the load."

Dubrey often wondered why she took on the exacting task. After all, she reasoned, Dressler could well afford to hire a secretary, so why didn't she ever suggest it? Dubrey had her own answer to this question. The aging actress, she believed, was lonely. Although she had literally thousands of acquaintances and friends, she was not truly gregarious. "She liked people, but she preferred certain *persons*," wrote Dubrey. "Some of those whom she loved didn't play games. It bored her to sit and converse and she rarely asked those to her home who merely sat and chatted. She knew that other friends were in love and Marie played second fiddle to no one. Still others made her nervous, much as she liked them. I daresay there were plenty she would have been content to have in my place, but she clung to me because I was handy. And the fan letters were an additional tie."

It is likely, too, that Dubrey suspected that Dressler clung to her because there were no obvious competitors for the attention and loyalty she was now showering on the actress. Dressler admitted to her friend that she was still tormented by the painful memories of Jim Dalton's infidelities, treacheries, and frequent disappearances, and these memories must surely have reinforced the actress's longing for the kind of close and exclusive relationship she hoped she had been forging in 1908. Despite her well known alliance with Sunny Jim, in fact, there have been frequent rumors and conjectures as to whether Dressler was a lesbian, perhaps allowing this long-suppressed characteristic to surface after the humiliating experience with Dalton. Biographer Antoni Gronowicz has intimated that Dressler had a sexual liaison with Greta Garbo. But the writer loses credibility by ignoring Garbo's better-documented affair with social dilettante Mercedes de Acosta as well as those she is known to have had with writer Salka Viertel and Swedish aristocrat Countess Ingrid Wachtmeister. Besides, Garbo herself insisted she had never met or talked to Gronowicz. Certainly Dressler enjoyed, even preferred, the company of women—particularly after Dalton's death—and many of them were openly lesbian.

She was a confidante of New York's famous "bachelors," Elisabeth Marbury and Elsie de Wolfe as well as Anne Morgan and her lover, Anne Vanderbilt, the second wife of the late William K. Vanderbilt. Mercedes d'Acosta was also a friend and so was openly lesbian social arbiter Elsa Maxwell. During the actress's years as a Hollywood celebrity, she was constantly in the company of gay men (including actors Ramon Novarro and William Haines), all of them eager for her friendship and approval. The actress's intimate association with astrologer Nella Webb could easily be interpreted as a lovers' alliance. So could her close-knit relationship with Claire Dubrey. Not surprisingly, there is no hint of lesbian-ism in Dubrey's disarmingly frank memoir, though she never hides the fact that the friends always shared a room whenever they traveled together. Other astute observers of the Hollywood scene, such as biographers Donald Spoto and Charles Higham, say there has never been any evidence that Dressler was known in the movie community as a lesbian, though they also admit that this kind of sexual behavior was seldom the subject of gossip at the time. However, composer David Diamond, who spent many years in the Hollywood of the 1930s, insists that Dressler was known as an active lesbian and was friendly with other well known lesbian actresses such as Thelma Todd and Patsy Kelly. In any case, it is easy to believe that the bulky, sixty-year-old Dressler and the slimly attractive, thirty-five-year-old Dubrey must have appeared as something of an Odd Couple, even to the sophisticates of Santa Barbara.

After the release of *Reducing* in January ("the film is only saved by the genius of Marie Dressler," complained *Variety*), Dressler and Moran were shoehorned into yet another comedy, this time a homely story about gangsters and corrupt politicians called *Politics*. The script was adapted from an original story by Zelda Sears and Stuart Boylan, and direction was handled by reliable MGM standby Chuck Reisner. Because of Dressler and Moran's enduring appeal, audiences lined up to see the movie when it was released in July 1931. But many critics, including those at *Variety*, were already warning MGM that, while the picture was okay, "the very evidence of lack of real action by the two principal characters in the cast, Dressler and Moran, is a weakness Metro may not be able to afford if another movie is planned for the pair. It's taking a long chance with the earned drawing power of these two." In the meantime, fan mail poured in as Dressler continued to enjoy the miraculous turnaround of her fortunes. She talked to Dubrey about joining her for a trip to Europe later in 1931 and certainly a holiday in New York, which would be her first real visit to the city since her 1927 arrival in Hollywood. She drove to Santa Barbara in July, just before the release of *Politics*, and it was there that Dubrey first detected signs that Dressler was not well.

Not that Dressler was one to complain about illness. If she was indisposed in any way, she consulted her "little doctor," a chiropractor-natureopath who had lived opposite her house in Whitley Heights. Problems were always satisfactorily corrected by spinal adjustment, a massage or a herbal remedy. "If you told Marie that snake root and jimson weed possessed healing qualities, she'd lay in a ton of them," remembered Dubrey. She had even been known to shrug off a stomach disorder by insisting that the planets were in an unfavorable position that day. Dubrey, who had trained as a nurse and had lived with a doctor, periodically begged Dressler to have a medical checkup, even as a second opinion, but the actress always refused. That July in Santa Barbara, Dubrey was surprised that her friend actually admitted she was suffering from a headache that could not be explained by the vagaries of Saturn. She knew Dressler well enough to refrain from suggesting a painkiller or a physician, though it was obvious that the actress was relieved to be heading home to Los Angeles that evening. The next day, Dubrey called her friend, and Dressler confessed that she was still plagued by the headache and that she had sent for her little doctor. "Marie had a fever," remembered Dubrey. "But the little doctor astonished and pleased me by ordering a blood test. Mamie phoned me the next afternoon and I hurried over. Marie was calm and determined. 'I have a swelling in my right side,' she said, 'and my little doctor thinks I should have it out. I'm going to the hospital tomorrow and I hope you'll go with me. I want you to watch the operation.'" Dubrey assured Dressler that she would be glad to do this and expressed some surprise that a chiropractor was connected with an institution that performed surgery. Dressler replied testily that her little doctor believed in surgery if it was absolutely necessary, and Dubrey decided to drop the subject.

Because she was a qualified nurse, Dubrey sought permission to stay in the room throughout the operation and, at Dressler's insistence, was granted the privilege. As she later remembered, "after the cyst was removed, it was thrown into a basin along with some soiled dressings. I remember so well how I debated with myself. Training had taught me that it was absolutely imperative to have any diseased specimen examined. But the habit of saving Marie's money urged that this was a needless extravagance. I could just see the report coming back negative with a bill for fifteen dollars. Training won. After all, they don't cut things out of you every day and one never has a better opportunity to have them analyzed. 'I think you should have that specimen examined,' I spoke up. The surgeon gave me an astonished look over his mask and murmured an order. The cyst was retrieved. Perhaps he fully intended to have it examined and that was the reason for the look."

A few days later, Dubrey met Dressler's little doctor in the hospital lobby. He seemed flustered, but he swallowed hard, then told Dubrey that the cyst had turned out to be malignant. The young actress couldn't believe her ears. Except for an abscessed tooth and an infected toe during the filming of *Min and Bill,* she knew that Dressler had been in the best of health. She started to ask the chiropractor some questions when he interrupted her. "I told Mr. Mayer's doctor," he said. "We play golf together and I decided to tell him." Dubrey was stunned. "You told Miss Dressler's employer's doctor?" I gasped. "What for, in God's name? How dared you? Why on earth should you? I never heard of anything so unethical in my whole life!" She realized she had become almost hysterical with anger and shock.

Dubrey confided the terrible news to Mamie, but decided to say nothing to Dressler for the moment. After all, the actress was recovering comfortably from the operation, and there was every possibility that the surgery had removed all of the cancer. As it turned out, the little doctor phoned Dubrey in a week and reported that the cyst had been reexamined at a New York lab and found to be benign after all. He also reported that he had called Louis B. Mayer's doctor to reverse the previous diagnosis. Dubrey was mollified, but still angry about the man's behavior. She had still to discuss the incident with Dressler, but the actress was then recuperating at home and beginning to regain her strength. Nothing was ever said about the incident, although the actress fired her little doctor after the surgeon he had recommended sent her his bill for a wildly exorbitant four thousand dollars.

In September, a restless Dressler decided it was time for a real adventure. She was scheduled to begin work in October on a new Frances Marion script entitled *Emma,* so she figured there would be ample time for that promised trip to New York. Typically, the plan was hatched over a game of backgammon. Wrote Dubrey: "'Double,' said Marie, 'let's go to New York.' 'All right,' said I, accepting double. 'When?' 'Tomorrow,' answered my girl friend, shaking a six-one and covering her bar point. 'Tomorrow?' I gasped feebly. 'Well, make it the day after,' conceded Marie generously.

'Do you want to re-double?' I can't say I wasn't warned when I first began going places with her. 'Always keep your hat handy,' she had said." When Dubrey asked Dressler why she wanted to go to New York, her answer was an echo from the extravagant days when she was the toast of Broadway: "Oysters, clams and white-fish. Also ducks and squab. I intend to see if I can't have them shipped to Beverly Hills by plane. Those are the only things they don't raise bigger and better in the west." The actress conceded, though, that it would be fun to see her New York friends as well. Theatre? Dressler grimaced and shook her head. She seldom, if ever, expressed a wish to revisit the scenes of her previous professional career. She avoided movie theatres as well. She was not interested in viewing her own films, and when Mayer once ordered a projec-tor and reels of new movies sent to her home, she returned the Boss's gift with only perfunctory thanks. But why a New York visit? Oh, there was the lure of oysters and duck, but there's little doubt Dressler was already savoring the possibility that her trip east could actually develop into a triumphal procession.

And it did. By the time the transcontinental train pulled into Chicago, the local press had received word of Dressler's trek back to the city that had turned its back on her in the twenties. The flashbulbs at the railway station were blinding, but it was obvious that Dressler was enjoying every minute of the ordeal by media. She smiled indulgently as the questions were fired at her: "Do you have any children?" "Did you get married in Hollywood?" "Does one have to be young and pretty to succeed in pictures?" The smile faded a little when she was asked to pose astride a policeman's horse. It was then, remembered Dubrey, that the two friends de-cided to escape. "Imagine!" laughed Dressler as they hurried down the platform. "Imagine having so little consideration for a horse!" Dressler became hostage to the redcaps and a surprising number of fans who had heard about the stopover. "Hello Miss Dressler!" grinned one porter. "Sure glad to see you back again." Dressler greeted the redcaps as old friends, as indeed they were. Through the gate and into the crowd of fans, Dressler autographed scraps of paper and crumpled envelopes and patted children fondly on the head. Dubrey hustled her into a taxi, and they enjoyed touring the city for the hour they had to spare. The driver, Bill, had a wife and children, and the entire family loved Dressler's pictures. More autographs for both Bill and his wife, of course, then they were back on the transcontinental and ready for the next stop in New York.

Although Dressler had almost recovered from her operation, she had already warned Claire that she might not be "doing the town" during her visit. As it happened, she need not have taken a step outside of her suite at the Savoy-Plaza to greet her friends and admirers. The procession of visitors and well-wishers seldom slowed from the moment she arrived until the moment she and Claire taxied back to Grand Central Station for the return trip to Los Angeles. Polly Moran, currently on a personal appearance tour to publicize *Politics,* dropped by to deliver flowers and jokes. Longtime friend Hallie Phillips came for tea, and so did Lady Irene Ravensdale, novelist Faith Baldwin, and the Princess Nina of Greece. Dressler even received a visit from Bertha Maser, who had been housekeeper at the Ritz when Dressler was living in the servants' quarters. And Anne Morgan came with her friend Anne Vanderbilt.

Dubrey remembered that during Morgan and Vanderbilt's visit Dressler had originally wanted a room service lunch of oysters and caviar served to the high society women, but when this menu was greeted with lukewarm interest, Claire playfully suggested they might all enjoy a simple meal of ham and eggs. To her surprise and delight, both Morgan and Vanderbilt were enthusiastic, though Dressler was obviously disappointed that her attempt at entertaining with the best in the house had fallen flat. This obvious need to impress, in fact, was apparently Dubrey's first real experience with the "grand dame" aspect of Dressler's otherwise down-to-earth personality. Dubrey knew, of course, that her friend enjoyed the company of socialites, but until that first trip to New York, she had managed to escape a serious exhibition of Dressler's grander than grand behavior, almost always enhanced with an exaggerated British accent. As Dubrey eventually discovered, to her discomfort, the proximity of social status and/or titles seemed to trigger an attack. The evening spent with Lady Ravensdale, daughter of the late Lord George Curzon, viceroy of India, barely escaped disaster as Dressler's posturing spiraled closer and closer to the laughable. In her memoir Dubrey muses about her friend's "worship of society with a capital S": "This particular quirk puzzled her friends and all of them deplored it, none more than those so-cial registerites themselves who loved her for her warm personal-ity and accomplishments, not for her name and fame. She knew plenty of aristocrats, all right, and many of them are charming—charming enough to be likable regardless of whether their grand-fathers made a fortune in tallow or their great-great-grandmoth-ers knew Charles II." Dubrey pondered Dressler's behavior in an attempt to understand her friend. "I do not say Marie did not have friends in humbler walks of life. I was one of them. But she did love names, background, dignity. Dignity was the key to the mys-tery. For many years, Marie appeared before the world as a clown. There on the stage, in the full glare of pitiless lights, she took funny falls, wore funny clothes and made funny faces. The more ridicu-lous the position she got herself into, the more they shrieked with laughter—those stiff white dress shirts out front, those elegantly gowned ladies. The harder she sat down when someone jerked a chair from under her, the harder they laughed. They snickered at her moth-eaten boa, the absurd feather in her hat. . . . That undig-nified clowning, the roars at her gawkishness rolling over the foot-lights, her large size which did not make for tender solicitude on the stage, in her rough and tumble work with male partners, did something to her. It gave her a growing hatred of the theatre and she sought to balance accounts between her public capering and her private life by breaking into society."

Dressler clearly enjoyed her successful visit to New York, and cradling a one-pound jar of caviar, she also enjoyed the adulation of redcaps and members of the local press as she boarded the trans-continental for California. She admitted to Dubrey on the train that she was looking forward to making *Emma*. Actually, Dressler and Dubrey had known the story of *Emma* months before Marion finished the screenplay; much of the plot was developed, revised, and redeveloped over dinners at North Bedford Drive. The char-acter of Emma, the down-to-earth Smith family housekeeper, was, of course, tailored to measure for Dressler. And the actress herself was consulted on the other main casting decision: the signing of Jean Hersholt, an accomplished screen veteran, as Mr. Smith. But there was another pivotal role yet to be cast, the part of young Ronnie Smith who was, as the publicity blurbs put it, "the apple of Emma's eye."

Over cigarettes and candy on the transcontinental, Dubrey and Dressler talked about how they had plotted to make an idea of Claire's reality: to have the part of Ronnie handed to a boyish-looking, twenty-two-year-old actor named Richard Cromwell. Cromwell had appeared in *Tol'able David* for Columbia Pictures in 1930, but although he had earned good reviews, his career now seemed to be at a standstill. Dubrey had met Richard through acting colleagues such as Anna Q. Nielson, who admired his talent as a painter and sculptor as well as a motion picture performer and had befriended the young man. Neilson's interest in Cromwell, to whom she always referred as "one of my children," so intrigued Dressler that the actress eventually asked to meet him. She made a visit to his studio and was so impressed with Cromwell and his work that she bought one of his paintings and hung it over the bed in the main guest room at North Bedford Drive. But how to maneuver Cromwell into the plum part of Ronnie? The project had already been galvanizing Dressler and Dubrey before they left for New York that September. Unfortunately, Frances Marion was on an extended trip to Europe, so Dressler, with the typically out-of-control enthusiasm that had brought her both grief and triumph in the past, decided to approach *Emma's* director, Clarence Brown. Brown was courteous, but, no, he hadn't seen Richard Cromwell in *Tol'able David,* and, besides, the boy was working for Columbia, wasn't he? Dressler sailed on to an equally unresponsive casting office and then to Mayer with the idea. The Boss was also courteous, but unshakably unimpressed. Remembered Dubrey: "Marie set her jaw. By this time it was *her* fight. She'd forgotten I had suggested Dick in the first place. She had only seen him once and wouldn't have known him if she'd met him in the street, but he was going to play Ronnie if she had to take it up with MGM's Supremo himself, Nick Schenck."

Dressler called the Loew's-MGM president in New York a few days before returning to Los Angeles. Schenck immediately invited the actress to lunch and the two met in the company's private dining room. Dressler wasted no time in telling the powerful movie tycoon what she wanted: the Ronnie role for a young actor named Richard Cromwell. Schenck listened sympathetically as his studio's top moneymaker aggressively made her point. Well, he wondered, had she ever seen this fellow on the screen? Dressler shook her head. No, but she knew he was good. Well, Schenck went on with an imperceptible sigh, did she have any ideas for the rest of the cast? After all, they must look like a family, Marie must realize that. Dressler waggled her jaw. She didn't give a damn about the balance of the company. She suggested they be chosen to resemble Richard Cromwell. Dubrey was obviously impressed, even taken aback with Dressler's passionate interest in her young protégé. As she later wrote: "It was really funny. Marie was the biggest seller in pictures. She topped them all, as exhibitors' polls were already showing. Yet here she was, fighting her way from an assistant casting director to the president of the company, all for a boy who she didn't even know. Mr. Schenck was nice. He loved Marie and wished to make her happy. If she wanted Cromwell, Cromwell she should have. I drew a long breath when Marie told me about the meeting. My child would play Ronnie."

Back in Los Angeles, the studio received and meekly accepted Schenck's orders. Cromwell had drawn fifty dollars a week at Columbia, but MGM paid five hundred dollars to borrow him for *Emma*. The relatively unknown actor was also given second billing, right under Dressler's name and ahead of the studio's own featured players, including Myrna Loy in her first important role. Unfortunately, there were serious problems during the first day's shoot, but a clearly nervous Cromwell gritted his teeth and set about mastering the role. Dubrey was on the set when he made an early entrance that even had the stagehands grinning with delight: A young, vibrant Ronnie flings open the door of his father's laboratory, seizes Emma, and kisses her. "Hello, beautiful!" he cries. "My God," exulted Dubrey, "the kid is actually trouping!"

Cromwell received warm reviews for *Emma*, but the picture itself was greeted with less than enthusiastic plaudits from the critics. Most, including *Variety* and the *New York Times*, felt that Frances Marion had delivered seventy minutes of overly sentimental screen entertainment—the story of an elderly housekeeper who marries her equally elderly employer, watches him die of a heart attack on their honeymoon, inherits his entire fortune, and is accused of murder by his outraged family. All, that is, except Ronnie, the apple of Emma's eye, who races to her trial in his private plane and crashes in a violent storm. As usual, though, Dressler emerged, smelling sweetly of roses: "There are probably twenty picture actresses who would have fitted the role of the old servant who spent a lifetime with the Smith family, watching the children grow up and then who turn against her in her old age. But there is only one Marie Dressler, a character woman of unique distinction, a trouper with a genius for characters of comic surface but profound pathos. The hoke sympathy here is the jolt and it has been laid on very thick," complained *Variety* when the movie was released in February 1932. Seen today, *Emma* is a distinct disappointment for even loyal Dressler fans. Although there are some highly comical moments in the movie, the characterization seems forced, and Frances Marion's attempts at pathos and riveting drama fall well short of the mark. It is possible, in fact, that director Clarence Brown believed that a Dressler picture had become such a shoo-in, he need merely coast through the entire exercise.

If so, maybe Brown was right. Despite the indifferent reviews, *Emma* proved to be a hefty box-office hit, a fact that at least assured Dressler that the extreme discomfort she had suffered during the making of the movie had not been in vain. Some of the pivotal action involved Emma's honeymoon trip to Niagara Falls with her new husband, so the company relocated at Arrowhead Lake, a mountain resort about one hundred miles from Los Angeles. It was cold at Arrowhead, with October breezes gusting over the water, but Dressler was required to wear a thin cotton dress for almost all of the outdoor work. At one point, she takes Jean Hersholt, her ailing bridegroom, on a ride in a rowboat. The little craft was attached to a wire so it could not move out of camera range, but this made it difficult for Dressler to pull the small craft. Besides, she was chilled to the bone during the entire shoot, even though Mamie had brought her some long woolen underwear to wear beneath her flimsy costume. At another point in the movie, Dressler humors a persuasive young Ronnie and tries out a flight simulator. In the finished film, the sequence is hilarious as a frightened Emma hangs on grimly through the twists, turns, and dives. But, as the exhausted actress had to admit as she motored home to Beverly Hills each night, *Emma*'s location work was scarcely hilarious for her.

Neither was *Emma* too hilarious for Dubrey. Just before the Lake Arrowhead shoot, the young actress landed a bit part in *Mata Hari,* a new MGM film starring Greta Garbo and Ramon Novarro.

Dressed as a nurse but playing the role of a spy, Dubrey was supposed to slip behind a screen in Novarro's hospital room and listen to his conversation with Garbo; later, at a court-martial, she would repeat what she had overheard. Unfortunately for Dubrey's faltering movie career, she never faced the cameras: Dressler buttonholed George Fitzmaurice, the director of *Mata Hari*, and convinced him that the studio would be far better served if her loyal friend went on the *Emma* location with her. Dubrey spent the frigid days at Lake Arrowhead wrapped in a heavy camel's hair coat, answering Dressler's fan mail.

18

THE TREATMENT

1931-1932

By the end of 1931, the deepening Depression was beginning to devastate the seemingly inviolate dream factories of Hollywood. Most of the studios had been able to ride out the first years of the financial holocaust with profits from the novelty of sound, but now it was becoming more difficult to attract the cash-strapped public into the theatres. In an attempt to turn the tide, RKO Radio spent money it could ill afford on an expensive adaptation of Edna Ferber's western novel *Cimarron*. The movie made major stars out of newcomers Richard Dix and Irene Dunne, and the picture racked up a profit. Even so, RKO unhappily reported a huge corporate loss of five and a half million dollars for 1931. MGM and Paramount reported healthier bottom lines, and Universal Studios made money with its horror megahits, *Frankenstein* and *Dracula*. But by the time the Fox Film Corporation admitted it was deeply in the red, there was talk throughout the industry of draconian salary cuts.

Dressler was so busy in the fall of that year, she was scarcely aware of the fiscal crisis. She had been delighted to hear that British movie fans had voted her their most popular female star in the annual John Bull poll of movie favorites and that she had been included for the first time in the *Motion Picture Herald's* prestigious list of top money-making stars. The shooting of *Emma* had yet to be completed, and the exhausting schedule of location and studio work was eroding her strength. In fact, it was with mixed emotions that she heard in early November that she was one of five nominees for best actress at the Academy of Motion Picture

Arts and Science's fourth annual awards night. The ceremony would be held on November 10, the day after her sixty-third birthday, and all nominees were asked to attend the presentation banquet. But could she manage to handle the tiring pace of the *Emma* shoot and spend a long evening at the Awards party as well? She worried aloud to Dubrey as they motored home after another day before the cameras. Besides, she argued, it could all turn out to be a fruitless, certainly wearying exercise. Look at her competition: that new German sensation Marlene Dietrich for *Morocco;* Irene Dunne for *Cimarron;* Ann Harding for *Holiday;* and Norma Shearer for *A Free Soul.* A fat, sixty-three-year-old Marie Dressler winning for *Min and Bill?* Not likely.

Dubrey disagreed with her friend. There were the polls, she pointed out. None of the other nominees were hitting the polls except Norma Shearer. And Shearer had won the Academy Award last year for *The Divorcee,* a good bet that there would not be a repeat. Another thing: everyone in Hollywood knew that Dressler was a formidable moneymaker for MGM and probably for the industry as a whole. "Don't take it for granted," she replied, as a tired Dressler continued to insist that the award would certainly go to a younger, more glamorous actress.

Dressler spent the day of the Academy Awards banquet at an airport near Los Angeles, shooting some retakes of a big scene with Dick Cromwell. The actress was driven back to North Bedford Drive almost fainting from fatigue. Mamie helped her into bed for a rest, and Dubrey checked the simple black evening dress her friend had chosen to wear to the event. By the time they were scheduled to leave for the Biltmore Hotel, Dressler was feeling better. She smiled and shook her head as Mamie and Jerry assured her that a special place had been set aside in the living room for the statuette they were sure she would be bringing home.

Dressler groaned a little as police cleared access for her automobile through the cheering crowd gathered outside of the Biltmore. She had been told that Mayer, who was in charge of the guest list, had invited two thousand to the banquet, but this looked as though the entire population of Hollywood had converged on the hotel. Once inside the lavishly decorated Sala D'Oro, she realized that the Boss of MGM must have combed his impressive address book to make sure everyone in the movie capital knew that he knew just about everyone of importance in the world. Dressler was formally introduced to as many of the two hundred invited members of the American Newspaper Publishers Association (who were having their convention in Hollywood) as could fight their way to her side. She shook hands with Governor James Rolph of California; a former assistant U.S. attorney general; Will Hays, custodian of the Motion Picture Code; and an assortment of generals and admirals. President Herbert Hoover's vice-president Charles Curtis kissed Dressler's hand and swore she was his favorite movie star, and his sister, the regal Mrs. Dolly Gann (who was at that time actively challenging Mrs. Alice Roosevelt Longworth over the seating order at national capital social functions) smilingly told her she had seen *Min and Bill* three times.

After she finally made her way to her table, Dressler looked around the room. It was obvious the Boss had forgotten no one who had any clout in the motion picture industry. All of the major directors were there, from Norman Taurog to Clarence Brown. Plus every working actor and actress in town: Clark Gable, Joan Crawford, Wally Beery, Edward G. Robinson, James Cagney, and Ronald Coleman sat at nearby tables. So did the nominees for best actress as well as those for best actor: Richard Dix, Fredric March, Adolphe Menjou, Lionel Barrymore, and ten-year-old Jackie Cooper, who was a sentimental favorite to win for his tearful performance in Paramount's *Skippy.*

After dinner the best actor and actress nominees were asked to proceed to the speakers' head table. Dressler was seated beside young Jackie, who promptly leaned on her ample arm and went to sleep. The actress herself wished desperately she could do the same thing, especially as the speeches droned on and on until midnight: J.N. Heiskell, the editor of Little Rock's *Arkansas Gazette,* lambasted Vice-President Curtis on the stupidity of Prohibition. Conrad Nagel, a founder of the Academy and nominee Ann Harding's costar in *East Lynne,* asked those present to pay tribute to Thomas Edison, who had just passed away. An admiral stood to praise the spirit of democracy. Will Hays read a self-serving eulogy of the Hays Office. The governor of California saluted the vice-president, and the vice-president himself took over the podium and rambled on about the picture industry's "glorious opportunity to render a great and steadying influence on your fellow Americans."

Once the awards ceremony finally began, a now-fading Dressler sat uncomfortably through the presentation of the Scientific and Technical Awards, the Cinematography Award, the Interior Decoration Award, and the Sound Recording Award. There were the Writing and Adaptation awards and the Direction Award (to Norman Taurog for *Skippy*), then George Arliss dominated the spotlight with his announcement of the coveted award for "best performance of the year by a male actor." Jackie Cooper scarcely stirred on Dressler's arm as the distinguished British star handed the gold statuette to Lionel Barrymore for his riveting performance in *A Free Soul*.

Dressler felt the familiar tension of stage fright as Norma Shearer, the winner for 1929-30, stepped to the podium to announce the best actress prize. She glanced down into the sea of white tablecloths and caught Dubrey's encouraging eye, then the smiling face of Frances Marion. Shearer was telling the audience that the winner she was about to announce had been ill quite recently "but," she went on, "when she comes on the set and hears the call 'ready on the set,' she charges across that lot like an old firehorse that hears the gong. The award goes to the grandest old trouper of them all, Marie Dressler."

Even before she spoke Dressler's name, as Dubrey remembered, "the banquet hall was in pandemonium. The waiters made most of the uproar, throwing their service napkins into the air with delight when Miss Shearer's preamble reached the point where she gave a hint of the winner with the words, 'an old firehorse that hears the gong.'" Dressler herself recalled: "Halfway down on my right, I caught Will Rogers grinning encouragement at me. Nearby, Lionel Barrymore was blowing his nose with unnecessary vigor, while Billie Burke was frankly crying." In a later interview, she admitted that it took her a few moments to get to her feet after the announcement. "Like an old Model T Ford," she explained, "I had to be cranked up." Dressler scarcely remembered the moment when Shearer handed her the statuette, but she did tell Dubrey later that she knew she was then On Stage and that she was expected to give a performance. She stood, smiling and nodding her thanks as the audience continued with its thunderous ovation. Then she squared her shoulders and launched into her thank-you's. After those, she paused, looked down at the vice-president's table, and said with a disarming grin, "I have always believed that our lives should be governed by simplicity. But tonight, I feel very important. In fact, I think Mrs. Gann should get up and give me her seat." Smiling at this cheeky reference to her Washington protocol battle, the vice-president's sister rose and offered her chair to the best actress. The entire audience exploded in a roar of laughter and applause.

By the time Paramount's boss, B.P. Schulberg, named RKO's *Cimarron* as the Best Picture and the Academy's new president, M.C. Levee, announced the conclusion of the festivities, it was almost 2:30 A.M. Dressler was feeling light-headed with excitement and fatigue, but she dutifully shook hands and accepted congratulations on her way to the Biltmore lobby. Dubrey was close behind, holding her wrap and apologizing to well-wishers who were begging for a chance to meet the new award winner. It was obvious that her friend was close to collapse, and she sighed with relief when the Lincoln drew up at the door with Meadows at the wheel. Once inside the car, Dressler gave Dubrey the statuette, rested her head against the cushions, and closed her eyes. It had been an unforgettable night, but she knew she had to be on the *Emma* set the next morning.

After that night, Dressler seldom, if ever, referred to her Academy Award in interviews and mentioned it only once in *My Own Story*. The day after the banquet, she read an obituary of a former colleague from the Road. "Dark, pretty little Jane and big, homely Marie" had been friends "dancing together in the pony ballet of a third-rate musical comedy" many years before at the start of Dressler's career, and now Jane had committed suicide at the age of sixty. Dressler was so upset at the death of "a self-confessed failure," that she slipped the golden symbol of her own success into a bureau drawer.

The national media responded to Dressler's burgeoning celebrity by bombarding her with interview requests. Readers wanted to know how the actress felt about achieving such spectacular success at a mature age, and Dressler responded with outpourings of personal philosophy: "It is never too late to begin living, but it's a pity so many people waste half their time on earth before they learn that living is supposed to be fun, and that it is a stale, flat and unprofitable business unless you can manage to put a little zest into it. . . . Personally, I believe that the years after fifty should be the richest, the most fruitful and satisfying in one's life, particularly in a woman's life. By the time we hit fifty, we should have learned our hardest lessons. We should have found out that only a few things are really important. We should have learned to take life seriously, but never ourselves. That's the trouble with us females—it's always hard for us to learn to take ourselves with a grain of salt."

Dressler quickly regained her strength after the *Emma* wrap. She spent New Year's at La Quinta, the luxurious desert resort near Palm Springs that was managed by her friends Allen and Kitty Walker. Then in mid-January, she joined a group of Hollywood notables—including Louis B. Mayer and his wife Margaret, Hattie Carnegie and her husband John Zanft, and director Raoul Walsh—on a getaway across the Mexican border to Tijuana. The big attraction was the Agua Caliente Resort where well-heeled Los Angelenos could gamble at the casino, play the horses at the racetrack, and leave Prohibition behind by drinking legally purchased liquor. Dubrey, who accompanied Dressler in her limousine together with Dressler's friend Georgie Caine, remembered that when Dressler entered the resort restaurant a huge party of naval officers and their wives rose to their feet and toasted the actress. The ranking officer asked if she would shake hands with members of his group, and Dressler agreed. "When she returned to Georgie and me she was smiling with pleasure but trembling with nervousness. We decided it would do her good to order a bottle of sparkling burgundy. And leave it on top of the table."

It was during this seemingly carefree excursion, however, that Dressler's life took a dramatic turn. After a multicourse dinner on the hotel patio with the Mayers and a few of his business acquaintances, the Boss leaned over the table and commented on a slight rash on Dressler's arms. The actress laughed. "Oh, I'm perfectly all right," she insisted. "I've never felt better in my life." Mayer persisted. "Marie, do you want to do something to please me?" Dressler nodded. "I'd give you my right arm, Mr. Mayer. You know that!" Replied Mayer: "Keep your arms, my dear. But let my doctor look at them, that's all I ask. I'll make an appointment for you when we get back."

Dressler loudly protested when the call came to North Bedford that the Boss's physician would see her the following day. It was all quite ridiculous, she told everyone who would listen, and, besides, she hated going to see doctors. But she supposed that the Boss was the Boss, so she asked Mamie to make sure Meadows would have the car ready on time. Dubrey would have liked to have accompanied Dressler, but her mother was having her tonsils removed that day. Mamie kept Dressler company instead.

Actually, Dubrey was not unduly worried about the appointment. The rash, she believed, was merely symptomatic of an acid condition, and she had no reason to think that Marie had not fully recovered from her July operation. She was astonished, in fact, when Ida Koverman, Mayer's personal assistant, called her at home to ask whether she would meet the Boss at his Culver City office the next day. No, Miss Dressler would not be there. Naturally, Dubrey agreed to the meeting, then sat for a moment, wondering what on earth was going on. Mayer had never spoken to her privately about Dressler, although he knew they were close friends. She wondered for a fleeting moment if the Boss was about to sign her to a contract, but quickly dismissed the thought.

When she was ushered into Mayer's spacious bungalow-office, she knew from the look on his round, bespectacled face that something was very wrong. He motioned Dubrey to a chair. "Marie has cancer," he said quietly. There was a brief silence, then Dubrey spoke up. "But they examined that cyst last July," she protested. "The report came back negative." Mayer shook his head. "It came back positive," he said. "They lied to you, but they told my doctor the truth!" Wrote Dubrey in her memoir: "Too late for recriminations. Useless to regret that she hadn't been forced to see the greatest of specialists. Too late for anything, except a forlorn hope. No use to operate again, Mr. Mayer told me. Too far gone for radium. Why hadn't his doctor alerted him before this?" But Mayer was saying something about there being a chance, "provided we will take it." Dubrey leaned forward in her chair to listen. Mayer was reminding her about Marie's friendship with millionaire-philanthropist John J. Murdock, the former president of RKO Pictures Corporation and general manager of the Keith vaudeville circuit before the war. Because of J.J.'s deep regard for Marie, Mayer continued, he had decided to ask for his advice. Everyone who knew J.J. well, knew that he had been cured of cancer of the rectum by a Canadian pathologist named Thomas J. Glover. As a matter of fact,

J.J. was so convinced that Glover had unlocked the secret of a cancer cure, he had plowed a million dollars into the doctor's research facility in New York. "J.J. feels," Mayer told Dubrey, "that a course of treatment could control or even eliminate Marie's problem."

Dubrey's eyes sparkled with excitement. Treatment? What kind of treatment? Would Marie have to go to New York? Mayer shook his head. No, she could be treated right there in Hollywood. Glover would send a member of his staff with the serum, and Marie would need to rest at home for six weeks. Claire had trained as a nurse, so he'd like her to move in with Marie and make sure that she behaved herself. The serum? Mayer grimaced, then smiled. "J.J. tells me that Glover makes it from the blood of live horses." Dubrey remembered in her memoir: "Mr. Mayer argued that there was no harm in Marie trying the Glover serum. 'After all, it can't possibly hurt her, and if we see it is not helping at the end of six weeks, when they say she should show some improvements, we'll stop it. My doctor holds out no hope. He gives her a year to live. This serum is our only salvation. Will you help?'" Dubrey continued, "Of course, I agreed. There was a discussion as to whether Marie should be told about the cancer, but I pointed out that she did not feel ill and the unpleasant treatment we were suggesting was going to be difficult enough to explain, anyway. Perhaps it would be wiser to protect her from having to face the trauma of a cancer diagnosis as well. She was expecting to begin shooting *Prosperity* the following week and knew Polly Moran and the rest of the cast had been engaged so we painstakingly concocted a story. 'I'll tell her we have to revise the dialogue,' decided Mr. Mayer. 'I'll ask her to rest until it is finished, as a favor to me.' I suggested that Mr. Mayer's doctor tell her he had found a slight trace of anemia, to account for the serum. She could believe she was taking injections of iron. Mr. Mayer nodded that would be fine, but then he added: 'Of course, we will have to take her off salary while the production is held up. We'll extend the time on the end of her contract.'"

Dubrey remembered clenching her fists for courage then blurting out: "You can't do that! If you do, she won't believe you are revising the dialogue. She'll know it's because of her that the picture is being delayed and she'll suspect something serious." Mayer thought about this for a moment, then nodded his agreement. MGM continued to pay Dressler's salary every Saturday for the rest of her life. Dubrey insisted in her memoir that the amount that Dressler was paid, even then, at the height of her popularity and at a time when other MGM personalities were commanding ten thousand dollars or more, was relatively modest—no more than two thousand dollars a week. It seems that Dressler's salary remained low for two reasons: She never asked for a raise, and Mayer—and apparently Thalberg as well—never offered her one. "It was Dubrey's view," according to writer Norman Zierold, "that the comedienne was simply a commodity to Mayer and that his only concern was to learn if he could get another picture out of her." Dubrey also told Zierold that Dressler had once bought herself an antique diamond ring for five thousand dollars and "waggled it around proudly before her friends, saying that MGM had given it to her as a Christmas gift." During the last interview ever granted by Dubrey, in fact, she claimed that, although her friend often told outsiders that she earned five thousand dollars a week, "she lied. She only made $1,500." This figure was somewhat less than the one Dubrey had reported almost sixty years before, but Dubrey was a frail one hundred years of age at the time of the interview. But it is significant that after Dressler's death, Mayer publicly admitted that he "didn't give her all the money she earned. She would have given it all away."

Whatever the studio's most effective moneymaker had been drawing from MGM in January 1932, the Boss must have been devastated by the news of her terminal illness. Why he waited from July 1931, when Dressler's condition first came to the attention of his personal physician, until January of the following year to act upon the information, raises interesting conjectures. If he did, indeed, regard Dressler as a mere commodity, he might have accepted his doctor's grim prognosis and simply hoped the actress could complete at least one more picture before her demise—without upsetting the actress or her fans with gloomy details about her failing health. But as the enormity of Dressler's popularity became more and more evident through polls, awards, and booming box-office receipts, he decided to seek J.J. Murdock's help in keeping her alive for as long as possible. Dressler's "little doctor," of course, was either told to keep quiet about the laboratory results or was spoon-fed the wrong report. And Mayer's personal physician was naturally not obliged to tell Dressler she had cancer because the actress was not his patient.

That day in January, however, Dubrey left Mayer's office with high hopes that her friend would be cured and also with Mayer's permission—because of her special status as Dressler's gatekeeper—to ask Murdock about the serum. Her memoir provides only sketchy information about the nature of Dr. Glover's work—probably because Mayer insisted that the treatment be kept secret, she calls Murdock "Mr. Jayse" and Glover "Dr. Gant"—but she scatters enough clues through the manuscript to help future researchers flesh out the story. Dr. Thomas Glover began his experiments at St. Michael's Hospital in Toronto some time after the First World War. Basically, he believed that cancer was a specific infectious disease caused by a pleomorphic microorganism and that it could be controlled or even cured by a therapeutic antitoxin. The pathologist-serologist claimed considerable clinical success with a serum produced after injecting a cultured medium into young horses. After six to nine months, reported Dr. Glover, antibodies were produced in the bloodstream of the animals, and the blood was then refined and injected into cancer patients. When Toronto newspapers gave Dr. Glover's work front-page coverage in 1920, his clinic at St. Michael's grew so large that he had to close its doors because of a dwindling supply of serum. As was reported at the time, Glover believed he needed to conduct more research into the correct potency and dosage of the serum, and early in the 1920s, he quit the Toronto hospital and relocated in the United States. He was desperately short of funds, however, and after he successfully treated J.J. Murdock's illness, he accepted the philanthropist's offer to set up the Murdock Foundation in upper Manhattan.

Dubrey contacted Murdock, who confirmed to her that Dr. Glover's serum had cured his cancer but cautioned that "even Dr. Glover will tell you that some advanced cases must be considered as hopeless. Yet these patients have often shown a marked improvement in physical and mental health and some are still living." He agreed that it was kinder to keep the truth from Dressler for the moment. One of Dr. Glover's assistants would soon arrive in Los Angeles to begin the serum injections.

Mayer called Dressler the next day and told her she needed building up with iron injections and that, in any case, the *Prosperity* dialogue changes would take some time to complete. He employed all of his charm and fabled powers of persuasion (because of his informal acting ability, colleagues often dubbed L.B. "Lionel Barrymore" Mayer) to coax his star into accepting a six-week rest cure. The performance was so successful, Dressler smilingly put down the telephone and announced she was "going to bed to please Mr. Mayer. All nonsense, my dear, but you know how he is. He had a *fit* when he learned I have a touch of anemia, and he begged me, as a personal favor, to stay in bed and build myself up until the picture is ready. I'm only taking these darned shots to satisfy him."

Because Dubrey also needed to satisfy Mayer as well as blunt any suspicion on Marie's part, she suggested that it might be a good idea if she moved in to look after her—particularly, she explained to her friend, since she "wasn't really ill and simply needed some help when the doctor came to give her the injections." Dressler was delighted with the idea. "For two years she had urged me to live with her and I always refused," Dubrey remembered in her memoir. "Up to this time I never had stayed overnight at her house, having learned how quickly an occasional dinner had become a hard and fast rule."

Dressler's course of experimental treatment with the Glover serum began on February 2, 1932, and ended on March 7. Dubrey performed as duty nurse for the entire period, taking and reporting pulse rates and temperature for the doctor's information, making one of two daily urinalyses, and detailing the actress's diet, which had to be kept mostly alkaline. She also sterilized the physician's instruments and rubber gloves and set up everything the practitioner would need on a temporary table by Dressler's bedside. The actress took a calm, almost sanguine attitude toward this activity during the first week or so but became restless and rebellious after the doctor insisted that no visitors be allowed into the house. Well, declared Dressler defiantly, fun was fun, but she had had enough of it. The actress was so rebellious, in fact, that Dubrey begged the physician to allow at least one trusted friend of Dressler's to stay at North Bedford Drive so that Dubrey could take an occasional break and also report to Mayer as ordered. When she received the somewhat grudging permission, she sent an S.O.S. to Hallie Phillips in New York. Hallie immediately wired Marie: "Bored to distraction. Longing for a sight of you. Hear you are taking a rest cure. How would you like me to join you?" Dubrey remembered: "Marie was delighted. Hallie took the first train and her impending visit kept Marie quiet—for another few days."

Once Hallie Phillips came on board, Dubrey was free to leave the house every now and then—ostensibly to help with a show planned by her women's club but also to visit with Mayer, who expected full reports of Dressler's condition. She admitted in her memoir, however, that it was a distinct relief to get away from North Bedford Drive, even for a few hours. Dressler quickly became "exceedingly difficult. She still retained her good nature but she became highly autocratic and egotistical. Perhaps her intuition warned her of danger and her new attitude was one of defiance." Dubrey and Phillips were summoned to the actress's room every morning for a mandatory reading of the morning paper, then Dressler presided over an examination of selected fan letters and clippings that Claire felt would amuse her. Her reaction to this material was unlike anything her friends had seen before. "All during Marie's years of stardom on Broadway, taking her own shows on the road, heading in vaudeville, she had garnered no clippings, saved no programs, had less than a dozen old photographs," wrote Dubrey. "Whatever the view, she seldom cared to look backward and the only mementos she had kept from the past were the two statuettes of herself as 'Tillie' and a gilt laurel wreath in the card room. She had saved not a line of her notices in *Anna Christie,* but from the time of the injections, she began to hoard all kinds of things."

In February 1932, Dressler received a clipping in the mail that affected her profoundly. It was a copy of a poem with an unsigned letter attached: "Here is a verse written by a man named Keith. I clipped it from a newspaper because it exactly expresses how I feel about you." The clipping read:

> Her face is like a god's come back to life—
> A face that shows the pain of mortal man,
> And happiness that centuries have known—
> A god who speaks as only idols can.
> Perhaps she learned the truth when Time was young,
> And comes again with Heaven-songs of mirth;
> And leaves her god and goddesses alone,
> To live with us a little while on earth.

"Never, thereafter, was this poem out of hand's reach," remembered Dubrey. "Poor Marie! Exulting like a beginner over praises that promised eventual success. She who had been and was a success. But she *was* a beginner—in a struggle with physical oblivion. Everything shows that subconsciously she knew it, for all her outward denial. Did the written and printed assurances of her hold on the world give her a seemingly firmer hold on life? Time has made me believe so." Dressler had the poem etched on a small silver plate which she carried around in her handbag wherever she went.

A burned-out Hallie Phillips finally had to bow out of the North Bedford Drive drama in mid-February, and an equally burned-out Dubrey then persuaded Georgie Caine to visit from San Francisco. Dressler continued with her autocratic demands, her fits of self-aggrandizement, and her loud threats to fire the doctor and discontinue the treatments. Dubrey reported this to Mayer, who worriedly discussed the advisability of telling Dressler the truth in the hope she would become more amenable to proper care. Dubrey remembered that Georgie, Mamie, and herself were "violently against it. We felt we understood Marie better than anyone else did and we were well aware of her deliberate self-deception in matters unpleasant. We felt and agreed that even though she sometimes asked questions that showed she was suspicious, she relied on us to give her misleading replies." The six-week ordeal finally ended for everyone concerned, with Georgie returning to San Francisco, Dubrey checking into Good Samaritan Hospital under her doctor's orders to rest, and Dressler being told by Mayer that she could begin working with the *Prosperity* cast and crew on March 22. The Boss added, however, that the actress's schedule would be restricted to a few hours a day and that he had been advised the "iron injections" should continue for a while longer. Dressler was so delighted to be allowed into the outside world again, she decided not to complain. She also decided not to tell the Boss that she wanted to go to New York after *Prosperity* was finished. At least, she wouldn't tell him for now.

19

Prosperity

1932

Prosperity, the eighth movie to star the Marie Dressler–Polly Moran comedy team, turned out to be the last. When the picture went into production in March 1932, breadlines were longer than lines at the theatre box offices, and MGM's bosses were well aware that the therapeutic laughter generated by talented screen comics was worth its weight in stock options. The glossy, big name pictures being manufactured at the Culver City studio were still contributing handsomely to MGM's profit; Mayer banked on the sex appeal of Crawford, Harlow, Garbo, and Gable, and the competition battled back with popular comedians such as Eddie Cantor, Joe E. Brown, Will Rogers, and Laurel and Hardy. But only MGM could exploit the awesome drawing power of moviedom's reigning queen of homespun humor, Marie Dressler.

On the *Prosperity* set that spring, she was treated like genuine royalty. Mayer and Thalberg—and certainly Nick Schenck at MGM-Loew's headquarters in New York—were clearly hoping their company's run of good fortune during the Depression would spin on forever. Not that the picture itself was budgeted as a studio blockbuster. The script, written by Sylvia Thalberg and Frank Butler, was a lightweight story about a hilarious, intermittently dramatic run on a family's banking business. Possibly because MGM rationalized that the two female stars would carry the show, others in the cast were considerably less well known: a young Anita Page, Norman Foster, and Henry Armetta. Even before the cameras began turning in March, there had been arguments in the top office about the wisdom of making a picture called *Prosperity* when the country was still staggering under the most severe financial downturn in decades. But those in the studio who supported the idea won over the opposition, mainly because of the Dressler involvement and the fact that ace director Sam Wood had accepted the *Prosperity* assignment.

Claire Dubrey visited Dressler on the *Prosperity* set in early April not long after being released from her hospital rest cure. She felt that the actress looked tired, even though she worked only a few hours a day and spent long periods of time in her portable dressing room (given to her as a birthday gift by Marion Davies) while a stand-in rehearsed and set up her shots. But the fact that Dubrey was safely back on board seemed to galvanize the actress into an orgy of extravagant planning. To begin with, she insisted, they would both go to New York as soon as the picture was finished. A few days before, Anne Morgan had phoned to ask if she would make a speech at the tenth anniversary banquet of the American Women's Association. She and Anne were both founders, she reminded Dubrey, and she simply had to be there for the occasion. Then there was that trip to Europe she wanted to make; Claire had never been to Rome and Paris, and she wanted to see her favorite haunts through her friend's eyes. No, she hadn't mentioned any of this to Mr. Mayer as yet, but she intended to march over to the bungalow and tackle him in the next day or so.

Dressler did tackle the Boss, who told her firmly that he wanted her to stay in Los Angeles and continue with her treatment, even when *Prosperity* was finished. That evening, over a game of backgammon, the actress was sulky and rebellious. "Look," she told Dubrey, "if I'm too ill to go to New York, I'm too ill to work. I feel like going on strike." But instead, she turned her rebellion in an alarmingly different direction: she decided to buy a new house and move out of the comfort and convenience of North Bedford Drive.

Dubrey shivered with apprehension when Dressler described the property she wanted, which she had seen on one of her recent days off. The three-story brick home on North Alpine Drive in Beverly Hills had twelve rooms and a half-acre of grounds, and the executors of the King Gillette estate would accept her offer of just fifty thousand dollars. Dubrey tried to argue against the idea.

After all, Marie didn't need so much room—she seldom had house guests and then never more than one at a time. And Dressler would need to care for the grounds herself, whereas Adela, her current landlord, was responsible for the lawn and gardens at North Bedford. Then there was the cost of upkeep and taxes, the expense of furnishing all of the extra rooms, and the continuing worry of fixing the roof and the plumbing and Lord knows what else. And was this really the ideal time to take on so much, with the movie, the treatments, and various trips in the offing? Dressler could not be moved. "The house was purchased on impulse," Dubrey wrote. "Seething inside because the studio did not want her to go to New York, she needed an outlet. It gave her restless energy something to work on when she had to buy furniture. The house was brick, strong and tangible. Did so concrete an object, indisputably hers, help to quiet intuitive dread? Did the solid foundations whisper that, since she owned them, she was as firm and imperishable as they were?"

Echoing the extravagantly optimistic days of *Tillie* and the Vermont farm, Dressler bought and bought: silk couches, satin chairs, marble-topped tables, oil paintings. She asked her friend actor Bill Haines to design and furnish the new card room, and she built a conservatory to extend the drawing room space. The comfortable, secondhand furniture she had acquired after the *Anna Christie* success was given away or sold. "But," wrote Dubrey, "while the North Bedford place was a home, North Alpine was merely a house. The card room was small and no amount of ruffled white curtains could make it seem more than a box. In Adela's house, we played our games in a sun parlor which was a direct continuation of the living room. At night, when the curtains were drawn, one still had a sense of space and cheer. The new card room had windows only on one side and at night we were completely walled in. The unpleasant effect must have bothered Marie more than any of us, but she said nothing, so naturally neither did we. The silken drawing room remained uninviting. The conservatory was cold, the furnace wouldn't work and the plumbing was temperamental. The bedroom, the dining room and the card room was all she used."

But the move from North Bedford to North Alpine had at least helped siphon off some of Dressler's simmering rebellion. *Pros-*

perity was finally finished in late April; the actress promptly announced she had never felt better in her life and that it was time to quit subjecting herself to the pesky iron injections and pack for New York. Yes, she told Dubrey, she would be talking to Mr. Mayer the next morning, and she saw absolutely no reason why they shouldn't leave in a few days. Claire had better start packing. Dubrey obediently shopped for new clothes and had her own bags packed on May 2 when Georgie Caine, who was keeping Dressler company for a few days, phoned to say the New York trip was off. Mayer had apparently told Dressler that her health depended on her staying in Los Angeles and continuing with her injections. Dressler was so angry, she threw her handbag across the office. An annoyed Mayer ordered her out of the room. She left, holding her head high, slamming the door behind her. Outside the bungalow, she related the incident to Georgie, and her friend persuaded Dressler to go back and apologize. Somewhat reluctantly, the actress accepted the advice, and Mayer—quite possibly with his typical overtones of deep and tragic hurt—graciously forgave her. A chastened Dressler told the Boss she would stay at home.

The next day, Dubrey joined Dressler and Caine for dinner at North Alpine Drive to hear about the Mayer confrontation firsthand. "Marie thinks Mayer simply wants her to stay home to get his own way," she wrote. "She kept muttering about showing the Boss next time he wants her to work." Dressler said she wouldn't make another picture if the Boss considered her unable to travel. She insisted that she felt better than she had in years. Dubrey and Caine "tried to pacify her and reminded her of how good the Boss had been when she first started taking the iron injections. All of those flowers and the use of a talking motion picture machine just to keep her amused." By the time Dubrey left that evening, Dressler, who was willing to admit that Mayer had been kind, was "still simmering" and announced that they would leave for Santa Barbara the next day. Dressler's injections with the Glover serum had been reduced to two a week by May 1932, so she argued that even if Mayer heard she was leaving Los Angeles for a few days there should be no objection. She hadn't been out of town for so long, she complained, and she wanted to see her friends. Dubrey agreed. Marie was badly in need of a morale booster, and there was no doubt that the relaxed, almost aristocratic atmosphere of Santa

Barbara always gave Dressler the sense of being on holiday. Dubrey made reservations for the three of them at El Mirasol, a hotel being managed by their friend Allen Walker for the summer. Walker settled the women into a luxurious three-bedroom cottage and filled the place with flowers and huge boxes of Marie's favorite candy. When word of the actress's visit got around, prospective visitors began to phone: Doris and Stanhope Nixon, Salisbury Field, the fabulously wealthy Van Rensselaers. Dressler enjoyed bridge, dinner, cocktails, and adulation. Mayer telephoned to see how she was feeling, and she told him fine "as usual" and even joked about the blow-up in his office. "I could see that Marie was in high spirits," Dubrey wrote. "She was still annoyed about New York, but feels she has gained partial victory by coming to Santa Barbara. She was 'showing Mr. Mayer.' After all, this is the first trip she has taken since January, an all-time record since I've known her."

The friends managed to make other trips to Santa Barbara that May. They had teas at Lillian Child's, cocktails with Countess Dorothy Di Frasso, dinner at the Gerard Hales'. But back in Hollywood, Dressler had another confrontation with the Boss. She complained that she wanted to go to New York because she had promised Anne Morgan to make a speech at the American Women's Association banquet. Mayer was impressed that his star was so close to the Morgan family but quickly suggested a compromise. MGM would make a film of Dressler reading her speech and provide the equipment necessary to project it in New York. That way, Marie could stay in Los Angeles and continue her treatment. Dressler sulked and fumed, but she could not discount Mayer's generosity.

She had no way of knowing that the Boss had other reasons for wanting to keep his star healthy and handy: Advance screenings of *Prosperity* had been disastrous, and Mayer and Thalberg had agreed that a major portion of the footage needed to be rewritten and refilmed. Though the rescue operation would be expensive, it would cost more to allow a Dressler vehicle to flop at the box office. The script department was ordered to come up with a new version of the story, revamped to reflect rather than ignore current economic conditions. Mayer ordered them to make it sound optimistic and hopeful. The title of the picture would not be changed, mainly because it had been widely publicized. The new shoot was tentatively scheduled for August.

In the meantime, Mayer pondered Dressler's condition and wondered if she might become more cooperative if he told her the truth about the injections. Whether he consulted his doctor, J.J. Murdock, or even Irving Thalberg is not known, and he certainly did not discuss the matter with Dubrey, but one morning in June, his assistant called North Alpine Drive and asked Dressler to come to the Boss's office the next morning. The actress agreed. Perhaps she could argue again about New York; in any case, she would give Mayer a piece of her mind about those silly iron shots. Meadows drove her to Culver City. Dubrey remembered that evening in her memoir: "Mr. Mayer called Marie to his office and told her the truth. I knew nothing of his intentions, after all our careful plots and discussions and lies until I joined her that evening, June 27, for dinner. She was playing solitaire in the card room. She stood up and embraced me. 'Claire,' she said, entirely composed. 'L.B. told me today I have cancer!' The surprise almost staggered me. 'He also told you that you are practically cured, didn't he?' I asked quickly to cover the blow. 'Oh yes! I know now why I have been taking all those injections.'" Dubrey apologized for her part in the ruse. "'I'm sorry we didn't tell you before, dear, but you know how you feel about medicine and we were afraid you would not believe in this wonderful new treatment.' If we only had known she would take it like this! I felt like a traitor for having helped deceive her. 'I'll tell you what,' she was saying. 'I don't believe for a minute that I've got it!' I stared at her. Were we never to face the truth, even now? Face it and do something about it? I quickly agreed it was likely that she didn't have cancer, and then suggested that she visit a specialist to confirm this for sure. She smiled again and said: 'No dear, I don't need any doctor to tell me how I feel. I feel fine. I never felt better in my life.'"

If Mayer believed that telling Dressler the truth would keep her at home, his hopes were in vain. The actress simply used her new knowledge—even though she privately refused to accept it—as a lever to force his permission for a trip to New York. If she was really so ill, she insisted, the Boss must surely indulge an old woman in some special requests. Only by informing his star that the new script for *Prosperity* was ready for production could he postpone the inevitable. So, from week to week, all kinds of excuses were made for the delay. Finally, consumed by a new storm of anger and resentment, Dressler decided to drive to Lake Tahoe. The doctor from Dr. Glover's laboratory loudly disapproved of her traveling long distances in an automobile, but he had little authority. Waggling her famous jaw, Dressler insisted that she was submitting to the silly injections only to please her employer. If she missed a few of the shots by going away until *Prosperity* was ready, let the doctor console himself with the thought of how many she already had taken—and remain conscious of the favor she was doing him in continuing to take them at all. The physician most likely complained to J.J. Murdock and the MGM top office. Mayer hatched a plan. He had often been told by Dressler that she could "never go away without Claire because she protects me from people," so before the Lake Tahoe excursion could get under way, a job for Dubrey suddenly materialized at the studio. Ethel Barrymore had sprained her ankle the day they began shooting *Rasputin and the Empress,* and Claire was called to rehearse her part while Barrymore rested at home.

Dressler was outraged when Claire told her that Lake Tahoe was impossible for the moment. She immediately sailed into Irving Thalberg's office and demanded that her friend be released from the stupid assignment. Thalberg patiently informed the actress that this was impossible because Claire had already been fitted for the extravagant costumes she would need to wear as Barrymore's stand-in for lighting and blocking; it was simply too late to replace her. Dressler was grudgingly mollified until she visited the studio one day and found Ethel Barrymore waltzing healthily around the soundstage while Dubrey sat reading a book in a corner. "It's ridiculous!" she complained to a startled Ida Koverman in Mayer's office. "There's Claire, doing nothing at all and I have to give up my trips because I can't go without her. Tell Mr. Mayer that if I'm too ill to travel, I'm too ill to work." Two days later, Dressler and Dubrey were on their way to Santa Barbara.

Luckily for everyone's nerves, the new version of *Prosperity* was finally whipped into shape and work began on August 23. Claire was not only relieved that Marie would now be busy at the studio, she excitedly told Dressler that she was in line for a small part in *Rasputin:* the role of a screaming, ragged Bolshevik peasant. But there were angry words between Dressler and Claire after Johnny Waters, the assistant director of *Prosperity,* called Dubrey and suggested that because of Dressler's shortened work hours and frequent breaks he would like Dubrey to rehearse for her friend just as she had done for Barrymore. Dubrey protested. She was hoping for a part in *Rasputin*, and she did not want to rehearse all day for Dressler because she spent almost every evening with her. And then she complained to Dressler. "Guess what they asked me to do?" she exploded over the card table as the actress looked up in amazement. "They asked me how I would like to rehearse for you, after I've just finished sitting around for six weeks for Barrymore. I told them I wouldn't do it! Can you imagine them wishing it on me? Just because I'm anxious to work. Why won't they hand me a broom and be done with it?" Dressler looked down at her cards. "Why darling, I think it would be nice." "Nice!" fumed Dubrey, "Sarah Bernhardt couldn't rehearse for you. At least Barrymore and I are sufficiently alike so I could give some kind of a performance! If I rehearse for you, every time I leave the set and you step in and do your stuff, I'll look like a rank amateur." Dressler tried to sound reasonable. "Now, dear, you're a very good actress." "Then why don't you tell them so? What will rehearsing get me? I'll fool around for ten weeks at it and then we'll go to New York and I'll achieve nothing. My only chance to work is when you're making a picture. Otherwise we're flying up and down the coast like a couple of seagulls. I have to do something on the screen before I'm forgotten." Dressler put down her cards and confessed that she had been actively lobbying the casting office to use her friend in odd jobs around the studio. "It's my fault you haven't been getting acting jobs. I'm scared to death they'll find out what you can do and that they'll keep you so busy you won't want to go to Europe with me in the spring. Forgive me, Claire, for being a selfish old woman." The actress seemed so genuinely contrite that Dubrey surrendered. "All right, I'll sit on your blasted set," she smiled. "And now I think I can beat you at backgammon."

Dressler and Dubrey worked on the *Prosperity* set through September and October. Mayer visited frequently to see how Marie was feeling, and director Sam Wood tried to make the work day as easy as possible for the actress. The company was rehearsed every morning and evening with Dubrey "playing" Marie's part, so when the star arrived on the set at ten or eleven, she only needed to run through the lines once or twice to check positions. She was urged to stay at home whenever she felt like it, but Dressler's instincts as a trouper overcame any discomfort or weakness she might have been experiencing. "'How was Marie feeling last night?' was the first question that greeted me at nine each morning," Dubrey wrote. "It was difficult for everyone. I didn't displace as much room as Marie, which sometimes affected crossing and positions on the small set, unless someone remembered and made proper allowances. The sound man could not adjust his delicate equipment for my voice, along with those of the rest of the cast, since Marie eventually was going to speak 'my' lines. Of course, I couldn't do the scenes at all as she did them, so the other actors were in danger of becoming set in rehearsal only to be confused when Marie did the takes in her own inimitable way. The camera man and electricians fared somewhat better because Iris Lee, a young woman whose coloring was like Marie's, wore padded duplicates of her costumes and stood in for the lighting. . . . A flurry would run over the stage as the heavy doors opened and Marie rustled in, followed by Mamie and Meadows, bearing a thermos of hot broth or cold juice. 'Hi everybody, here I am! Were you waiting for me, Sam?' 'No, darling, we're just finished lining up the lights. Take your time changing your clothes, dear. We're having a little microphone trouble this morning.' 'How is she, Mamie?' I asked while Marie was busy scribbling her lines and the hairdresser curled her hair. 'She says she's just fine, Miss Clara, I don't think her color is so good today and I tried to get her to stay in bed, but you know how she is. She's worried about holding them up and keeping Mr. Wood behind in his schedule. You see how you think she looks. I'm kind of anxious about her.'"

The remake of *Prosperity* was well larded with laughs to keep the movie patrons happy as well as dramatic moments to illustrate Dressler's qualifications as an Academy Award winner. The scriptwriters were aware that a modicum of propaganda was needed to keep a 1932 movie about the banking business on track, so the star was provided with some lines that helped explain the movie's title and theme: that *prosperity* was really a state of mind and that the Depression had shown that one didn't need sixteen rooms and four baths to be happy when two rooms would do just as well. MGM hoped that upcoming events would work in the revamped picture's favor. The presidential election would be held in November; although Democratic candidate FDR was not universally favored over Hoover by the studio's top brass, they all hoped that prosperity would return to the nation in 1933.

When the picture was eventually released just after Roosevelt won the election, Mayer, Schenck, and Thalberg had to agree their timing was incredibly fortuitous. Drawn by the promise of yet another Dressler laugh-fest and attracted by the aggressively optimistic title, lines began forming outside the Capitol and Loew's Metropolitan theatres in New York so early that both managements decided to open the doors at 9:30 A.M. *Prosperity*, even the critics had to agree, was a "money picture," though the same critics had their usual caveats. *Photoplay* magazine wrote that "*Prosperity* isn't bad, but not good enough for the Dressler-Moran team." *Variety*, while praising Dressler extravagantly, complained that the movie needed trimming. Despite that, box-office receipts showed that movie fans across the country loved the story of Maggie Warren (played by Dressler) and her small-town bank. And how a comically stupid depositor named Lizzie Praskins (played by Moran) causes a run on Maggie's institution. The critic of the *New York Times* was so tickled by the movie that he spent a paragraph of his review on one of the movie's jokes: "Mrs. Warren has a white dog that answers to the name of Mutt. She has only to glare at this animal and he understands that he had better get off Mrs. Praskins's sofa. In one episode, Mrs. Warren and her son John are searching for a railroad ticket to be used on his honeymoon and it is finally found on the floor near Mutt. Mrs. Warren looks at the ticket and then declares 'He has swallowed Niagara Falls.' It wasn't the line that was so hilarious, of course, it was the way Dressler delivered it: deadpan dignity with the perfect lift of an eyebrow that always reduced the audience to howls of appreciative laughter."

After the *Prosperity* wrap, Dressler told Dubrey that there was absolutely no reason they shouldn't take off for New York. Dubrey was dispatched to buy rail tickets for October 31, the day after the picture was hastily cut and previewed, and luggage was taken to the station that morning. At four o'clock in the afternoon, however, Mayer tried again to keep his star in Los Angeles by telling her that some retakes might be necessary. And, he added as persuasively as possible, Marie had been nominated for yet another Academy Award (for *Emma*), and he was sure she would want to be at the banquet, either to accept the statuette or to present it to the new best actress. Dressler was grimly determined to stick to her guns, and apparently another shouting match took place in Mayer's office. Later, at home, the actress told Dubrey they would be leaving the next day, November 1. Although somewhat anxious about Dressler's health, Dubrey heaved a sigh of relief. Two of Dressler's attractive young male admirers had been invited to join them on the four-day rail trip, so Dubrey would have help if she needed it. Jack Winslow, who had long been an available escort and extra man at dinner, had already been appointed as Dressler's new secretary. And Jack's close friend, John, had also been included in the party because he could serve as a fourth at bridge.

The trip through the station resembled a Roman triumph. Four redcaps formed the vanguard, carrying luggage and other belongings. Then came "Augusta Maria," as Dubrey often called her friend, surrounded by cohorts, sprouting great bunches of orchids in place of traditional laurel but treading the way as firmly as Caesar himself. Flashbulbs popped as the travelers headed for their railway car. Porters and station attendants tipped their hats and shouted greetings. Officials dispatched from the top offices of the railway company appeared to make sure that Miss Dressler was entirely satisfied. The crowd swelled with messenger and telegram boys, reporters, and autograph hunters.

All of "the family," as Dressler liked to call her loyal standbys, came to the station for the sendoff, and gifts were showered on the actress by her courtiers: air mail envelopes as a delicate hint, perfumed water softener, playing cards, candy, and a vivid artificial parrot to brighten the railway environment. Frances Marion turned up to present Dressler with a soft camel hair blanket. As a joke, the "boys" to be left behind gave a backgammon set to Dubrey, who was not enamored of backgammon and had been overjoyed to hear that Dressler had decided to leave her folding board at home in favor of playing bridge during the getaway.

Dubrey settled back to enjoy herself. She already knew that the railroad company had given the group a "through" car so there would be no need to juggle baggage in Chicago like lesser mortals, and it seemed they would also have the entire car to themselves. Unfortunately, the travelers were subjected to hours of switching and loud bumping, but Dressler enjoyed the special courtesy being paid to her. "After all," remembered Dubrey, "the one-night stands were never like this and she had not forgotten the long cold hours of waiting to make connections. She openly reveled in the change in her fortune and one of her most endearing charms was that she never grew blasé." News had circulated that Marie Dressler was on her way east again, and crowds lined the railway platforms at every stop. At one stopover in the Midwest, the train was delayed by a storm, and people stood for three hours in the snow for a brief glimpse of their favorite star. Reporters tapped timidly on the drawing room door, pleading that editors had told them not to come back without a story. Veteran conductors came to chat about trips Dressler had taken with them years earlier, and eager dining room stewards begged for the privilege of having special dishes prepared for her. Enjoying herself enormously, Dressler announced: "Ain't we got fun?" Wrote Dubrey: "Yes, but when she emerged from her throne room to stretch her regal limbs and breathe a draught of fresh air on a station platform, she had to be rescued from her too demonstrative subjects. Once, when she ventured outside, she was almost carried away bodily. When I succeeded in getting her back on the train, I saw that her eyes were sparkling, her cheeks were pink and she looked at least ten years younger. She laughed up at me as she settled into her chair: 'Ain't we got fun, Claire?'"

20

GOD'S EXHIBIT A TO THE WORLD

1932

The fun continued as the party detrained at Grand Central Station. J.J. Murdock and MGM publicity staffer Milton Beecher were on hand to greet the star and to help clear a path through the fans, reporters, and fawning redcaps to a waiting limousine. A platoon of mounted police had to escort the automobile through the crush outside of the station and, after a slow drive, into the foyer of the Savoy-Plaza Hotel. Friends were waiting in the suite with flowers, gifts, and adoring hugs and kisses: Hallie Phillips, Jimmy Forbes, wealthy bachelor Herman Sartorius, and violinist Fritz Kreisler and his wife Harriet. There were the inevitable questions about Marie's health and Marie's new picture and Marie's plans during the visit.

Some of the schedule had already been set by the studio, and Beecher was somewhat grudgingly granted a half hour to explain what Dressler was expected to do while she was in the city. The publicity department had arranged for her to broadcast a short address to tell her fans about *Prosperity* on November 17 at the National Broadcasting Company's studio on Fifth Avenue. NBC would pay Dressler twenty-five hundred dollars for the privilege of featuring the talk on its national network. The following night, NBC would beam a special radio message to the assembled guests at the fifth Academy Award banquet in Los Angeles. Dressler had been nominated once again for a best actress award, along with Lynn Fontanne (for *The Guardsman*) and Helen Hayes (*The Sin of Madelon Claudet),* and she would need to either accept the honor for the second year in a row or congratulate the new winner. Mayer asked that she attend at least two theatrical performances in New York: Sidney Howard's play, *The Late Christopher Bean,* and George S. Kaufman and Edna Ferber's hit, *Dinner at Eight.* MGM was thinking of buying the rights to both plays as future Dressler movies. Dressler sighed, nodded her head, and assured Beecher she would do anything that Mayer wanted her to do, but at the moment her friends were waiting. She dismissed the publicity man with a disarming smile.

Dressler had her own itinerary for the stay in New York. She planned to have lunch with Adolph Ochs, owner and publisher of the *New York Times,* to pay a visit to Bessie Marbury at Sutton Place, and to make a trip to the home of Anne Morgan and Anne Vanderbilt, just out of town at Mt. Kisco. She would dine at the Algonquin, Sherry's, the Pierre, and the hotel, with the meals followed by bridge. She would also attend the gala tenth anniversary banquet of the American Women's Association and personally read the speech she had filmed during those tense days in Los Angeles. At J.J. Murdock's request, she would visit Dr. Thomas Glover for injections, an assessment, and a firsthand look at his work. The Glover visit would be something of a waste of time, Dressler complained to Dubrey that first night in New York; she didn't really believe she had cancer, and she hated being around anything that reminded her of doctors and hospitals. But J.J. wanted her to do it, and she had promised. She planned other interesting distractions. She would celebrate her birthday in a few days' time with a dinner with her favorite friends and perhaps some bridge as well.

The presidential election to be held in a few days should be fascinating—would it be Roosevelt or Hoover this time? Dressler hoped FDR would win; she had often rejected her old friend from the Liberty Bond days, but she had come to believe he would make a fine new president. During the recent campaign, she had received a telegram from him asking that she sit in his box when he made a speech in Los Angeles. Not long after that, Dressler and Dubrey lunched with Mayer—who was a strong Hoover supporter—and the actress showed the Boss Roosevelt's wire. Mayer wrinkled his nose. "I don't consider it good policy for our stars to take sides," he said. Dressler gave in immediately. "Very well," she nodded. "I won't answer the telegram." Later, Dubrey remonstrated with her friend about the decision. "You can't ignore Roosevelt's invitation," she argued. "It's a compliment to be asked to attend his meeting, but if you don't wish to go, let me wire an excuse." Dressler shrugged. "All right. Do whatever you think best."

In those weeks in New York at the close of 1932, Dressler played several off-stage roles, all of them superbly. She appeared in turn as the celebrity actress, the nervous wreck, the crusading Jeanne d'Arc, the grande dame, the thoughtful friend, the big spender, and the penny-pincher. The extraordinary sequence of real-life playlets began its run on November 7, not long after her arrival in the city, when J.J. Murdock escorted them both to Dr. Glover's laboratory in upper Manhattan. Dressler was obviously disenchanted with the whole idea, but she graciously greeted the dark-eyed, forty-five-year-old Canadian pathologist and answered his questions while he reviewed the reports dispatched by the physician who had administered the serum injections in Los Angeles. Afterward, she sat quietly in the laboratory, staring out of the window or powdering her nose while J.J. Murdock and Dr. Glover showed an excited Dubrey over the premises.

"Dr. Glover's laboratory takes up the whole of an old-fashioned, three-story house," Dubrey wrote. "A colored, leaded glass fanlight over the door throws rich reds and blues over the waxed oak floor of the entrance hall. To the left is a reception room and beyond it are small white cubicles where examinations are made and dressings and treatments given. Or at least, Dr. Glover did give treatments there in the past. He had accepted Marie as a patient, not because she was the great Dressler but because J.J. Murdock interested himself in her case as a favor to his friend, Mr. Mayer. In the rear of the building, were incubators and ice boxes. Toxins brewed in an isolated cabinet. Cultures were grown for the serum and a special cell, sterilized before he used it, had been built by Dr. Glover so that when he mixed and bottled the serum, no contamination was possible. On the third floor were large storage rooms where extra-fine filters and supplies were kept. Some of the equipment had to be made to order, according to Dr. Glover's own specifications since none were manufactured by supply houses that exactly answered his purpose. Dr. Glover said this was one reason why other scientists had difficulty in working on his experiments, even though he gave them his notes, carefully setting out his formulae, step by step."

A fascinated Dubrey was shown Dr. Glover's dead animal specimens—rats, guinea pigs, and monkeys, carefully tagged and indexed. She also saw living experimental animals dragging tumors larger than their emaciated bodies and "examined the most repulsive cultures, smelled toxins, looked at vials of serum and racks of test tubes with blood sent for diagnosis." Finally, Dr. Glover showed Dubrey what he claimed were cancer germs. "I saw them under the microscope," she wrote. "They looked like little black dots at first and then grew to be transparent circles, resembling spores. They were very active indeed." She was so impressed with what she saw, she ran to fetch Dressler, who was still sitting alone, obviously bored, near the window. "I got her to look through the microscope and see the germs for herself," Dubrey remembered. "Before that, she had not believed they existed." Dressler became interested and began questioning the pathologist about his experiments and other patients he had treated. How much did he charge? What success had he had? Did other members of the medical profession agree with his findings? J.J. Murdock interjected at times but generally allowed Dressler and Glover to talk. At the moment, the pathologist told the actress, a vial of serum holding five injections cost one hundred twenty-five dollars. He had treated thousands of cancer patients in the decade or more that he had been working, many of them successfully. And thanks to one of his most successful patients, J.J. Murdock, he had needed to make no charges for consultation or treatment. Even when—or if—the serum was placed on the market, in fact, neither he nor Mr. Murdock would ever benefit financially. No, there was currently little consensus among members of the medical profession about the usefulness of the Glover serum either as a treatment for or an inoculation against cancer.

The sudden change in Dressler's mood clearly startled both Dubrey and Murdock. The actress began chatting animatedly with Dr. Glover about "her" cancer, and the pathologist responded by warning her that although her condition was favorable she would need to rest as much as possible. He explained that the Bartholin gland was affected by the disease, and walking and even sitting was a constant irritation. At one point, the pathologist cautioned Dressler to avoid making more movies for "a long time." He recommended a continuation of the twice-weekly serum injections, and Dubrey promised to deliver her friend to the laboratory for treatments.

Back in J.J. Murdock's limousine, Dressler began waving her arms and fantasizing about her cancer. "This is why I was born," she announced dramatically. "This is why I made a success in the theatre. I know now why I was laid on the shelf and forgotten. The whole world was thrilled at the comeback of a middle-aged woman. I was guided by God to give them hope for their own work when the years seemed to be a drawback. But there's a bigger purpose back of it all. I was raised up until all the peoples of the earth knew and loved me, then I was given cancer that I might go up and down the length and breadth of the land where I am known and trusted to show humanity that this disease can be cured." She turned to Dubrey and Murdock. "My dears, I am God's Exhibit A to the world! J.J., I want to raise money so that Dr. Glover can continue with his work."

Murdock was visibly shaken. He quickly told Dressler that he couldn't permit anyone but himself to contribute to Dr. Glover's discovery. "There never has been any question of money, Marie. Dr. Glover will persevere for another twelve years if necessary, but not on the public's donations." He went on to remind Dressler that when they both had begun life in the theatre, they and their colleagues were still regarded as mountebanks. Now, he wanted to spend his fortune making sure that the poor mountebanks would remove a terrible scourge from the world. "That is my job," the worried Murdock told the actress, "and I cannot accept help from anyone."

"Marie listened but her determination was unshaken," Dubrey recalled. "A higher goal beckoned than the pinnacle she had reached as a motion picture star. In the days ahead, Mr. Murdock and Dr. Glover were given a glimpse of it that terrified them. They impressed on her the fatality of premature publicity. Neither wished to have their work exploited until it was accepted by the medical world as an established fact. Dr. Glover honestly admitted that he might be mistaken. It was entirely possible the scientists working on his discovery might prove to him that he was wrong. 'What will you do if that happens?' I asked him one day at the lab. 'I'll be disappointed, of course,' he admitted. 'I'm very tired and I want to rest. But I'm a pathologist and all I'm searching for is the truth. If my work is a fallacy, I'll scrap it and start all over again from the beginning.'" Despite the protestations from Murdock and Dr. Glover, though, Dressler refused to abandon her crusade.

At a private luncheon hosted by Adolph Ochs at the *New York Times* she held forth about her illness and talked excitedly about Dr. Glover's important work. Could dear Adolph do anything to have the serum accepted? Ochs listened patiently, then responded with gentle skepticism. His own physician had looked into the Murdock Foundation lab several years ago, he told Dressler, and the doctor had not been impressed. "Quite frankly," the publisher said, "I don't think you have cancer, Marie. Why not go to a hospital for a week and check up?"

Dressler was known to value Adolph Ochs's advice, but this time it fell on deaf ears. "Will you send someone up to the laboratory?" she asked. "The *New York Times* is a great newspaper. You ought to know the facts in this matter. You could do a lot of good towards furthering the cause if you did." Dubrey leaned across the suddenly tense luncheon table: "Marie, Dr. Glover doesn't want any publicity. Mr. Murdock could arrange that if they were ready. Please don't ask Mr. Ochs to send a reporter up there." Dressler's eyes blazed. "Well then, Adolph, will you ask your doctor to go again, with me? I'll open up his eyes! You'll see!" Ochs sighed and promised that he would ask his physician to revisit the Glover laboratory but cautioned that he could not promise that he would actually go. "That," said the publisher firmly, "will rest entirely with him." The next day, Ochs called the hotel and told Dressler that his doctor refused to have anything to do with Dr. Glover and that from what Ochs had told him about Marie, he agreed that she possibly did not have cancer. Remembered Dubrey: "I had seen Marie annoyed because Mr. Mayer forbade her to come to New York. I had seen her furious with 'the boys' when they once begged off from their habitual Sunday night supper. But I never before saw her in a rage like this one. She hung up the receiver and paced the floor. 'I'll show that doctor! When Roosevelt's in office I'm going to Washington and tell him all about this cure. So Adolph's doctor doesn't think I have cancer? How does he know? He's never laid eyes on me! I have got it, I have, I have! I guess I know what I've got! I'll tell the president! I'll have him pass the word to the government laboratories. And I'll give up making pictures and travel all over the country and hold big meetings. Just like I did for the Liberty Loan drive. I'll be Exhibit A to the universe! That's what I was born for!'"

Franklin D. Roosevelt was elected president on November 8, and Dressler celebrated her sixty-fourth birthday the following day with a dinner at the Colony with Dubrey, Hallie and her husband, and Jimmy Forbes. Later, the group played bridge in the Savoy-Plaza suite and were joined by Jack Winslow and his friend John, and stockbroker Starr Anderson. Dressler was still talking incessantly about the wonders of the Glover laboratory, but she was beginning to feel nervously anxious about the upcoming broadcasts at NBC. She wondered what on earth she could say about *Prosperity*, and she was furious that she had not been told there would be a small audience in the studio. Didn't Mr. Mayer know that she always had stage fright in front of audiences? How could he forget that? Dubrey tried to calm her by promising to make some notes that might spark ideas for a speech, but Dressler fidgeted unhappily for days.

Howard Dietz, who was then chief of publicity at MGM's New York offices, dropped by the Savoy-Plaza and left a speech for Dressler that he had written himself. The actress read it, agreed that it was well done but felt it was too blatant an advertisement for the picture. Dubrey played around with some themes, but her friend rejected them all. Dressler was still thinking of the Big Plan and the black spots she had seen under Dr. Glover's microscope. "Prosperity is a germ," she suddenly announced during a quiet lunch with Dubrey. "What?" asked Dubrey, putting down her fork. "I said, prosperity is a germ," repeated Dressler. "It can infect people." Dubrey ran for paper and pencil, then wrote a somewhat rambling discourse. The prosperity germ first causes society to sink into violent delirium, then sparks depression "which reduces swelling of the head and is really the beginning of the cure." The infectious germ then allows "sanity and true optimism based on sound sense to return. Real American grit courses through the national veins, which have been clogged with ticker tape." The speech ended with the inevitable plug for the picture: "You listen to old Doc Dressler. She's been around and seen a lot and she's been through two or three panics. In fact her whole life has been a panic and they say her new picture which, by the way, is called *Prosperity* is a panic too. . . . When the next prosperity germ bites us we'll have a good laugh and buckle down to work with a saw or a hammer in one hand and a glass of beer in the other. Happy days!"

Dietz made little comment when the new speech was handed to him. Instead, he told Dressler that he would escort her to the NBC building in a few days for the evening broadcast. A small audience would be present in the studio, but he would tell Rudy Vallee, who was hosting the show, to make sure people were not intrusive. Dressler was still nervous. The afternoon before the broadcast, she refused to see anyone at the hotel. She and Dubrey played double solitaire to keep her mind off the ordeal.

When she got to the studio, "Marie read the speech perfectly but not with her customary vigor," recalled Dubrey. "She seemed utterly calm but when she came off the stage she was ice cold and trembling. She had to sit down for fifteen minutes to recover and I had a hard time keeping people away from her." The *Prosperity* speech was the first for which Dressler was ever paid, and she admitted to Dubrey that "she would have paid more than the $2,500 that NBC gave her to get out of it."

Luckily, Dressler was in a far better mood for the Academy Awards broadcast the following night. Dubrey had written two short speeches, "taking care of whichever way the cat jumps." A special studio had been provided by NBC for the event, and the room was comfortably furnished with sofas, a grand piano, and a fake fireplace filled with glowing electric coals. Dressler was accompanied by Dubrey, Hallie Phillips, Jack Winslow, and John. She seemed pleased to see that L.B. Mayer's daughter Irene and her husband David O. Selznick were in the studio as well as director King Vidor, who had been nominated for MGM's *The Champ*. Radio technicians were working behind a plateglass window, and a businesslike desk with a microphone was set up in one corner. The party was settled and provided with refreshments, and the proceedings in Los Angeles were piped in through a loud speaker.

There were the usual tributes and speeches, then the award winners were announced: Walt Disney received a special award for the creation of Mickey Mouse, and Norma Shearer presented the Best Actor award to Fredric March for *Dr. Jekyll and Mr. Hyde*. The listeners in the studio held their collective breath as Lionel Barrymore announced the Best Actress award: Helen Hayes for *The*

Sin of Madelon Claudet. Dressler led the other studio listeners in applause. Louis B. Mayer accepted the Best Picture Award for MGM's *Grand Hotel,* and following his acceptance speech, Academy president Conrad Nagel stepped forward to announce a tie for the Best Actor award. Wallace Beery had polled just one vote less than Fredric March (which, according to Academy rules, constituted a tie), and he was presented with a statuette for his work in *The Champ.* When the audience settled down after this surprise, Nagel stepped up to the podium to introduce a special broadcast from New York.

David Selznick first sat down at the NBC microphone and introduced "last year's Best Actress, who would like to congratulate this year's winner." Next, Dressler read her short speech: "It is an honor enough for me to be mentioned for an award in company with Helen Hayes and Lynne Fontanne. Dear Helen, you will know that my hand clasps yours under the hand that hands you the gold prize which you have won so brilliantly." There was applause in Hollywood, then audible gasps as Dressler continued. "I am under strict doctor's orders to remain in New York for several weeks." For most people in the movie community, it was the first indication there was anything amiss with MGM's important moneymaker. Looking back on Dressler's message now, though, it is interesting to conjecture why she broadcast this sensitive information across the country. Although she was certainly visiting Dr. Glover's lab for serum treatments, there is no evidence that she was under strict orders to receive them in New York. The pathologist, in fact, had already discussed with Dubrey the possibility that she might take over the administration of the injections in Los Angeles. And as for being seriously ill, the record shows that Dressler's program from November 18 to her departure for California on December 12 was packed with sometimes demanding social activity. After the broadcast, Dressler, Dubrey, and "the boys" saw the other guests into taxis, then walked up Fifth Avenue to the Savoy-Plaza in the quiet, early hours of the New York morning. In hindsight, it seems possible that the message was intended for Mayer, to gain Dressler more time away from the studio.

The day after the Academy Awards broadcast, Anne Morgan sent her car to the hotel, and Dressler and Dubrey were driven to Mt. Kisco to spend the day with Morgan and her friend Anne

Vanderbilt. The two wealthy women owned townhouses at Sutton Place but liked to spend as much time as possible at their country estate, a ninety-minute drive from Manhattan. The Mt. Kisco retreat turned out to be a low, rambling white house built on a knoll in the midst of rolling green acres of lawns and trees. Dubrey remembered with amusement the first time she had met the tall, gray-haired Morgan and the gentle, white-haired Vanderbilt during Dressler's previous visit to New York, when the women shrugged off the grande dame's lavish luncheon menu and opted for ham and eggs instead.

This time, Dubrey settled back with her prelunch cocktail and listened appreciatively to the conversation. The women discussed Bessie Marbury, who was reported to be delighted with FDR's presidential win but who remained in poor health; Morgan was happy that Dressler and Dubrey would be visiting Marbury at Sutton Place during their New York visit. They talked about plans for the future and the American Women's Association anniversary banquet. The visit was pleasant, even though Dubrey thought that Dressler held forth too dramatically about Dr. Glover and even persuaded Morgan and Vanderbilt to visit the lab next time they were in Manhattan. Then as the women moved toward the luncheon table Dressler's grande dame persona suddenly emerged. "'That grandfathah's clock reminds me of one of my fathah's, deah,' began Marie, in her horrifying 'elegant' accent. Ye Gods!" recalled Dubrey, "were we in for another of those Ravensdale interludes, in front of these unpretentious women?" Dressler continued: "My fathah's clock had a crest on it, though, I took the design for granted as a child, being so used to seeing it, but I've always regretted not awakening him about his family. A veddy aristocratic one, I'm shuah. The lawst time I was in Europe I ran across the statue of an old German emperor. The veddy image of my fathah, my deahs. I wish I had taken a photograph of it. Even the ears were identical. It really was quite startling to see. I'm certain the emperor was one of my ancestors. You know my fathah was a Prussian officah, my deahs. None but the nobility are officahs in Germany. Von Koerber, you know."

That, apparently was the birth of the "von." Later, in her autobiography, Dressler would state unequivocally that her family name was *von Koerber,* and many theatrical biographies say the same. Dubrey claimed that the idea had been germinating since two years before the visit to Morgan and Vanderbilt. She recalled giving Dressler a letter about that time from an American academic who expressed his high regard for her work and closed with the suggestion that perhaps their families had similar roots. He signed himself *von Koerber*. Dressler was fascinated with the letter. "Von Koerber, von Koerber," she had mulled over the note at the time. "It's very pretty, isn't it? I shouldn't be at all surprised if our name was originally Von Koerber as well."

At Mt. Kisco that day, Morgan and Vanderbilt were impeccably gracious. They nodded a polite "how very interesting" whenever it seemed to be needed. "Mere Morgans and Vanderbilts," remembered Dubrey, "they sounded more bewildered than crushed by being put in the shade of royalty, nobility and vons. I stared at the fire, trying to hypnotize myself with the flames. Maybe if I concentrated hard, I wouldn't hear the 'little English mothah—a real lady, my deahs,' part of the monologue. Fortunately, just as Grandfathah Henderson's fleet of ships burned at the dock—why didn't he carry insurance?—and 'my poor little mothah had to give up her governess, deahs,' luncheon was served and Marie's cloak of grandeur disappeared. It was like a feat of legerdemain. Now you see it, now you don't. Her attacks were always like that. Out of a clear sky, then gone again, not leaving a trace."

The November days in New York spun on. They had Thanksgiving dinner with Adolph Ochs and his wife at their immense, fifty-six-acre estate in White Plains. They paid a visit to Elisabeth Marbury at her Sutton Place house and spent an afternoon conversing with the three-hundred-pound former literary agent and influential member of the National Democratic Committee. Marbury, as Dressler knew, was the friend who had alerted Frances Marion to the fact that the actress needed help in her failing career. The two women greeted each other with genuine affection and respect. Those days, Marbury could not walk without the aid of metal braces on her legs, but she had still managed to drive to Chicago that year to speak at the National Democratic Convention. "America needed Roosevelt," she told Dubrey and Dressler. "And I was going to tell them so, even if I died in the attempt!"

They had lunches at the Pierre and dinners at the hotel, followed by piquet or bridge. "Marie never seemed to be behind in her sleep," Dubrey noted. "I was well. She was ill and had been warned over and over to rest. Even 'the boys' who came east with us complained of the pace. We took turns at the bridge table, for usually extra guests filled at least one place. 'Working' in relays, as we did, Marie out-sat, out-did, out-paced all three of us, who were twenty years younger than she was. I am convinced that if she had conserved her remarkable vitality, had hoarded her strength, given nature and her magnificent constitution half a chance, she would have added length to her life. But no truce was possible. Even to parley with the enemy was a confession of weakness, of doubt. Charge on! Ignore them! Marie Dressler was invulnerable!"

Dressler had already confided to Dubrey that part of her Grand Plan was to introduce as many of her influential friends to Dr. Glover as she could. The pathologist was cool to the idea but had finally conceded that because he was seeking medical endorsement rather than funds he would cooperate provided visitors brought along their own physicians to any meeting. Dressler shrugged this off. Pooh! If Dr. Glover was besieged by hordes of sufferers from all over the world, the American Medical Association would have to sit up and take notice then, wouldn't it? After all, the Glover serum couldn't be a fake. Wasn't he treating her, and wasn't she predestined to get well?

Dressler and Dubrey met Morgan, Vanderbilt, and Herman Sartorius at Glover's lab on the morning of December 1, and although Claire was concerned that they had not brought medical observers with them, Marie cheerfully ignored the omission. Dr. Glover greeted the visitors politely. He had invited several out-of-town physicians for the occasion as well as a dozen patients he claimed to have cured. One was a doctor who had suffered from a skin malignancy after being burned by X-rays. "He told us he went to Europe for help and was advised to return home to die," Dubrey wrote. "He took the serum instead and, except for marks on his hands from the old burns, he was as well as ever. Another told us he was a specialist from Philadelphia who had lost his practice when his associates learned he was using the serum and stopped referring cases. All of the doctors were intelligent, professional-looking men who had graduated from good medical schools." Dr. Glover introduced some of his successful patients: a Catholic nun from Albany who assured the guests she had been cured of breast cancer, a rosy-faced Irish woman of fifty who had lost her entire nose to cancer before taking the Glover serum, a middle-aged woman who had been cured of rectal cancer, a skin case, a bone case, another rectal case. Morgan and Vanderbilt listened with obvious interest, then followed Dr. Glover through the lab while he talked about diagnosis and his work with blood samples sent for his examination from across the country. "I stayed close to Mrs. Vanderbilt in the specimen room," remembered Dubrey. "Older than Marie, of fragile build and with an extremely sensitive face, I feared she might faint at the sight of the dead monkeys. They looked a good deal like infants done to death in some ghastly way. We remained in the chamber of horrors a long time while she and Miss Morgan questioned the doctor. The room had no windows and the tanks of formaldehyde were quite overpowering. I was relieved when they finished and walked briskly into the fresh air. It was an incredible exhibition of intestinal stamina on both their parts."

Dressler sat quietly on her usual stool at the window and shrugged when Dubrey wondered aloud whether the visit was proving too difficult for Vanderbilt and Morgan. Shouldn't she restrain Dr. Glover just a little? "They want to see everything," replied the actress. And that was that.

21

MAYER'S MARATHON

1932-1933

The New York visit ended with an orgy of social activity, despite the fact that Dressler suffered a slight hemorrhage—an incident that sent the actress and Dubrey hurrying to Dr. Glover for advice and reassurance. The pathologist agreed that such events were worrying but explained that, because there were no arteries involved, the bleeding itself was not dangerous. But he repeated his previous warnings: Dressler should rest and keep off her feet as much as possible.

But there was so much to do before leaving for California! Dressler hosted a lavish dinner for ten at the American Women's Association, then on December 6, she attended the AWA's tenth anniversary banquet to present Anne Morgan with the Anna Warner Porter medal for "constructive service" and to deliver her long-awaited speech. Dr. Glover attended the dinner and afterward escorted Dressler and Dubrey back to the Savoy-Plaza for a drink. It was obvious that the pathologist enjoyed the actress's company, but when he began talking excitedly about his work, Dressler openly stifled her yawns. "My God," she complained after the doctor apologized and left, "he tells me to rest and he keeps me up till morning. That's a man for you."

The next day, she told Dubrey that she wanted to buy Dr. Glover a gift. A few days previously, she had asked her friend to sound out the pathologist on the subject of a check. He had refused unconditionally, even when Dubrey explained that it was being offered by Dressler in lieu of a personal gift and not in payment for his treatments. "Thank Miss Dressler," the pathologist said, shaking his head. "But there's nothing I want." Despite this rejection, Dressler plowed on with her idea. "She asked me to shop around and find something suitable," Dubrey recalled. "Feeling that the best was none too good for the man who, presumably, was saving her life, I recklessly invaded a fine jewelry store. They were having an unusual sale and I selected a platinum wrist watch with distinct numerals and minute hand. It wasn't an inspired choice, but the watch case was plain and handsome and the works were good for a hundred years. It was something a doctor could use and rely on and it would serve as a constant reminder of Marie's gratitude and affection." But when Dubrey showed Dressler the gift she had chosen, it "left her cold. 'I'll go out myself and find something,' she said. As we sallied forth, I reminded her that Dr. Glover already had an automobile. Naturally, I thought she intended to do something really big. 'Well, never mind,' she told me. 'Let's stop in here.' I was surprised when she finally made her purchase: a picture frame, very pretty, made of composition metal and set with white jade. It was a good bargain at $27 and back at the hotel, she signed and inserted a photograph."

Dubrey had little faith in Dressler's longtime reputation as a consistently generous person. Many years after Dressler's death, Dubrey would say that "Marie was mean." This may have been a harsh assessment, but according to Dubrey's memoir, Dressler dispensed her largesse somewhat quixotically. Early in their friendship the actress gave Dubrey a handsome gold chain and pendant brooch set with jewels for her birthday. But on another festive occasion, Dubrey received a dyed gray fox scarf that Dressler had long ago discarded from her own wardrobe. When a manufacturer sent Marie some complimentary tin first-aid kits, she passed them out as gifts for "the boys" one Christmas season, and another year she gave members of her extended family cheap cigarette boxes, each with a five-dollar tip tucked inside. Her presents were often wildly inappropriate. She sent loads of flowers and sometimes potted plants to friends who had elaborate gardens. Children who owned far too many toys received even more. But then she seldom contributed money to actors' charities except for the 1 percent of her salary that was deducted as company policy for the Motion Picture Relief Fund. She always gave MGM employees small gifts at Christmas, even remembering the studio gatemen and police. The Dressler household budget was generous, and bills were meticulously paid on time, but inconsistencies could apparently emerge there as well. "Meadows," a frail Dubrey revealed during her deathbed interview, "only got two dollars a week to live on. Marie was stingy."

During the last few days of the New York visit, Dubrey learned that her mother was quite ill and under observation in a Santa Monica hospital. According to the telegram she received, the doctors might decide to operate. When Dressler and Dubrey made a farewell visit to the laboratory, Dr. Glover administered a serum injection and told the two women that Dressler's cancer was in remission and a three-week cessation of the shots would be beneficial. He asked Dubrey if she was willing to assume nursing duties in early January, and she agreed that she was except for the fact that her mother was unwell and consequently she might not always be available. Dressler shrugged and laughed and told Dr. Glover that of course Claire would give her the shots without interruption.

The departure from New York was as frenetic as the arrival had been seven weeks before. They were surrounded by the smiling redcaps and the fans and the mounted police and the flashbulbs. Dressler sailed calmly through the chaos, carrying her jar of caviar and smiling at the cameras. Once on the train, she relaxed over a cup of tea and admitted she was glad to be going home. She was planning a special Christmas party at La Quinta, and she expected to entertain Claire, Jack and John, and another "boy" who had been left out of the New York excursion. Later in the day, Jack Winslow encountered Dubrey in the carriage corridor and wondered aloud whether the condition of her mother could prevent her from making the trip to the desert. When Dubrey told him it certainly could, Winslow replied, "Well, you'd better tell Marie, hadn't you?" Dubrey grimaced. "And have her work on me until we get home? What's the use? It will only wear me out and make her unhappy. I'll tell her in plenty of time." Later, Winslow brought up the subject at dinner. "Marie looked at me sharply," Dubrey wrote. "'Nonsense! Your mother will be all right, my dear. She won't mind lending you to me for the holiday.' 'Don't count on me, pet,' I replied. 'You'll have plenty of company. We've been away seven weeks and I spent Thanksgiving with you. I've got to rally round the home fires a little. Besides, Mamma's ill. I won't know just how ill until I see her.'"

Back at the North Alpine Drive house, Dressler grew more insistent about La Quinta. The actress watched her friend fussing with the test tubes for a new kind of urinalysis Dr. Glover had ordered. "Who's going to do those for me in La Quinta?" she asked. "What did your mother say about sparing you over Christmas?" Dubrey replied that she wanted to stay near her mother because her condition was uncertain. Dressler snorted. "My dear girl! Put her in the hospital and if she has the operation it will be all over by the time we get back. You can't do any good staying at home. You might as well be enjoying yourself with me as hanging over an operating table." Dubrey turned to Dressler angrily. "You wanted me to hang over yours, didn't you? Well, I certainly intend to do as much for my mother!" She wanted to say more, but she bit back her words and hurried home before the incident could deteriorate into an ugly quarrel.

On December 21, doctors had still not given Dubrey a definite diagnosis concerning her mother, and an annoyed Dressler and her three escorts prepared to leave for La Quinta. Dubrey drove that morning to North Alpine Drive to wish them all a merry Christmas, but Dressler glowered at her and replied that it would be anything but merry for her. She accused Claire of trying to ruin the entire excursion. Two days later, Jack Winslow telephoned from La Quinta and told Dubrey that Dressler was still expecting her to arrive in time for the big day, but Dubrey had to tell him that there was no way she could manage the trip. Dressler called the day after Christmas to tell her how much she missed her. She said that she would not stay over New Year's unless Dubrey turned up soon. Claire sighed and promised to join the party just as soon as she knew the results of the X-rays and felt that her mother would be okay. After a short silence, Dressler said in a tight voice: "If you don't come, I'll have to come home. Claire, I can't live without you." These were the last words Dressler ever spoke to Dubrey.

On December 29, Dubrey received optimistic reports from her mother's doctors and wired La Quinta that she would be there for New Year's. The next morning she received a telegram from Dressler that read: "Under the circumstances don't think you'd better come down. Marie Dressler." Dubrey thought the communication was odd, and she wired back immediately that she was packed and intended to leave on the noon train "unless she didn't want me." Dubrey went to North Alpine and asked Meadows to drive her to the station. "Irene came out of the house and said Jack Winslow had called my home and found me gone, so he telephoned North Alpine to say Marie was perfectly well and didn't need me. Jerry had already asked Meadows to garage my car and drive me to the train in Marie's limousine. But then Irene had to tell us that Jack said Miss Dressler's instructions were that neither Jerry nor Meadows were to take me under any circumstances." The servants were bewildered, and so was Dubrey. On the way back home, she alternated between fury and hurt, indignation and profound distress. A few days later, she went to the MGM studio and sought out a man who was known for keeping himself well informed concerning the contract players, on and off the lot. She forced herself to ask whether he had any idea as to why, as she said, "Marie had tossed me out of her life." "Did it ever occur to you that you might be too thick with Marie to suit others?" asked her contact. Dubrey replied that she was unwilling to consider that possibility. After all, her position as "constant companion" was not enviable. "Well then," continued her contact, "did it ever occur to you that she's a sick woman and if anything happens to her you'd probably get all of her money?" Dubrey protested; surely no one believed that she was after Marie's money! The studio employee then suggested that "the boys" were trying to make quite sure that Dubrey would never get a cent of Dressler's cash. In fact, he said, Marie had been told that Dubrey's mother was not sick at all and that she had been seeing one of her old boyfriends instead. Dubrey left the studio saddened but enlightened.

New tests eventually revealed that her mother was suffering from cancer, and the news plunged Claire into an orgy of grief and bitterness. Friends who had once included her in invitations suddenly shunned her, and she had difficulty finding employment in the studios. Still, Dubrey kept closely in touch with a sympathetic Mamie Cox and with Dressler's friends Allen and Kitty Walker, who were pleased to keep her informed about the actress. Dressler herself revealed her feelings to no one and proceeded to dive almost headlong into a year that would prove to be one of the most productive of her career.

In January 1933, the *Motion Picture Herald* revealed its influential yearly poll of twelve thousand American exhibitors who had been asked to name the "ten players whose pictures drew the greatest number of patrons to your theatre from September 1, 1931 to September 1, 1932." Marie Dressler headed the list, followed by Janet Gaynor, Joan Crawford, Charles Farrell, Greta Garbo, Norma Shearer, Wallace Beery, Clark Gable, Will Rogers, and Joe E. Brown. A greatly pleased Mayer sent Dressler a large bouquet of flowers and a request that she attend a private "welcome home" luncheon at the studio. No known record exists of this meeting, but the Boss must have discussed Dressler's visit to New York, her health, and the fact that her latest triumph at the polls surely necessitated a major response from MGM. Nick Schenck had purchased the rights to *Dinner at Eight,* and the studio had also acquired rights to *The Late Christopher Bean* and Norman Reilly Raine's *Saturday Evening Post* series, "Tugboat Annie." The actress already knew that at least two of these properties had been earmarked as starring Dressler vehicles, and sometime in January she learned that the Boss wanted to complete all three of the movies in as little time as possible—between April and September 1933, he suggested. Because Dressler was an MGM exclusive contract player, Mayer could, of course, decree whatever he wished. But Mayer knew Dressler as a major star who was known to balk when things did not go her way, and he realized that her health problems might also prevent her full cooperation. Once again, it was a tribute to Mayer's incredible powers of persuasion that the ailing actress agreed to the punishing schedule. Nowhere in her personal recollections does she comment on those months of work as anything more than a regular, though exacting, tour of duty. And no record of the period even hints at one distinct possibility: that MGM's Boss might well have accelerated events in order to get the three movies in the can before Dressler's active career came to an end.

Other imperatives also must have crystallized Mayer's decision. Unlike other Hollywood studios, Loew's Inc. was still solvent in early 1933; even so, MGM badly needed major hits to keep the Depression wolf from the door. The studio's top producer, Irving Thalberg, had suffered a heart attack, and an alarmed Mayer had enticed his son-in-law, David O. Selznick, to resign from RKO and take responsibility for at least six motion pictures at MGM.

The first would be *Dinner at Eight,* which Selznick wanted directed by George Cukor, who had recently handled *A Bill of Divorcement,* the picture that RKO successfully marketed as Katharine Hepburn's film debut. Mayer, who admired Cukor's work as a director, personally disliked him because of his homosexuality. (At that time, the Boss was continually at odds with MGM players such as Greta Garbo and Ramon Novarro, whom he felt disgraced the studio with their openly gay liaisons.) But MGM wanted *Dinner at Eight* to be another multistar blockbuster in the mode of *Grand Hotel* or even *Hollywood Revue of 1929,* and Cukor was obviously talented. Some of the studio's brightest stars—Dressler, the Barrymore brothers, and blonde bombshell Jean Harlow—were available, but schedules were so tight that *Dinner at Eight* would need to be completed in no more than thirty days. Could Cukor do it?

While MGM's top brass was negotiating the start of her new movie in February, Dressler—with Mayer's approval, even insistence—traveled again to New York for a consultation with Dr. Glover. This time, she took Jack Winslow and Mamie Cox with her and avoided the flamboyant fanfare that had characterized her previous expeditions across the country. Within a few days of checking in at the Savoy-Plaza, the pathologist advised her that there was a recurrence of her cancer and that he wanted her to undergo another operation. Dressler resisted at first, because of her fear and repugnance of hospitals, but finally gave in after a telephone conference with Mayer. She remained in the hospital for one week, then demanded that she be transferred by ambulance to her suite at the Savoy-Plaza, where Mamie and a nurse would care for her.

She returned to Los Angeles in late March. At the station, the local press, alerted by the MGM publicity office that Dressler was arriving back in town "after a successful minor operation in New York," turned out en masse. Facing the reporters and the inevitable cameras, the weary, still-recuperating actress said, "I never felt better in my life." The day after she unpacked at North Alpine, she reported to the studio for fittings of the elaborate costumes she would wear in *Dinner at Eight.*

The MGM brass was excited and optimistic about the Selznick picture. Frances Marion and Herman Mankiewicz had been assigned to adapt the Kaufman-Ferber play, and negotiations in

March had nailed down much of the blue ribbon cast. Early talks had revolved around the possibility of using Joan Crawford for the ingenue role of Paula, but this part was finally handed to Madge Evans. Alice Brady was briefly considered for the role of Mrs. Jordan, the character eventually played by Billie Burke. And Clark Gable was summoned to talk about the role of Dr. Wayne Talbot, but this was finally assigned to Edmund Lowe. Other casting decisions went smoothly: Wallace Beery, Lionel and John Barrymore, Lee Tracy, Jean Harlow, Jean Hersholt, May Robson, and many of the second-echelon players on contract to the studio were signed.

Although George Cukor approved most of Selznick's decisions, he worried about the inclusion of the woman who would receive top billing in *Dinner at Eight*. As he later remembered: "When I learned that Marie Dressler was to play Carlotta Vance, I said to myself: she is not quite my idea for the part, not the way it was played on the stage by Constance Collier. Constance was enormously distinguished, she had been leading lady to Herbert Tree. But, very shrewdly, Louis B. Mayer contended that Dressler was the biggest thing in pictures, although she looked like a cook and had never played this type of part." Though Cukor couldn't really picture her as a former beauty with scores of lovers, "she acquired a peculiar distinction, a magnificence. She was a law unto herself. She'd mug and carry on—which she did in this picture—but she knew how to make an entrance with great aplomb, great effect." As the shooting of *Dinner at Eight* progressed, Cukor learned to adore Dressler as "a woman who's a fabulous personality."

Later, Cukor would admit that *Dinner at Eight* was not one of his favorite movies, though the film stands today as one of the director's most famous, most revived pictures. Perhaps it was the uncompromisingly caustic tone of the story that distressed a technician who preferred to weave tales of sweetness and light. In *Dinner at Eight,* he was directing characters who were frauds, drunks, suicidal egotists, and airheads. Yet, Marion and Mankiewicz churned out a script that subtly—even hilariously—contrasted the superficiality of America's elite against the very real tragedy of the continuing Depression. We meet Oliver Jordan (Lionel Barrymore) and his scatterbrained wife (Burke), who invites to her home for a formal dinner a disparate group of individuals—a matinee idol (John Barrymore) whose career has been tarnished by the talkie craze; the Jordans' vapid daughter who is having a messy affair with him; the greedy businessman (Beery) who wants to ruin Jordan; Beery's wisecracking wife, Kitty (Harlow), who happens to loathe the lout; the couple's philandering doctor (Lowe), who is sleeping with Kitty behind her husband's back; and the now-penniless former star (Dressler), who is desperately trying to borrow money. Mrs. Jordan, who wants very badly to be a brilliant social success, does not realize that her husband's finances are in a shambles and that he is dying as well.

Despite Cukor's opinion that Dressler was not suitable for the Carlotta role, the actress clearly enjoyed the chance to play a lady of distinction. Though the role was not large, she dominated the screen whenever she was before the camera, dripping fox furs and fondling a Pekingese dog named Tarzan. (Dressler wanted to name the dog Mussolini but MGM felt the Italian government might be offended). Her lines are among the funniest in the film, and she occasionally sounds veddy British: When a secretary mentions that she remembers as a girl she saw the actress perform, Dressler coolly and devastatingly replies: "We must talk about the Civil War sometime—just the two of us." And, of course, the final scene in *Dinner at Eight* has long been immortalized as a movie classic: Dressler and Harlow are walking in to dinner, and the stunning blonde says that she was reading a book the other day. Dressler does a perfect double take. "Reading a book?" she asks in astonishment. Harlow continues to chatter. "Yes, it's all about civilization or something, a *nutty* kind of book. Do you know that the guy said that machinery is going to take the place of every profession?" Dressler's reaction, as she eyes Harlow from head to satin slippers, employs every trick she has ever learned as a performer. "Oh, my dear," she murmurs, "that's something you need never worry about!"

As usual, the Dressler magic worked with the audiences. She was hilarious but believable, with that unmistakable touch of pathos. Of course, she was a glamorous actress at home in the Manhattan salons, but she was also highly vulnerable like those sitting in the movie theatre. As in her own private life, the celluloid grande dame alternated effortlessly with the down-to-earth persona. Dressler looks hale and hearty in the *Dinner at Eight* footage, but it was a different story off-camera. A stand-in helped with the blocking and lighting chores, and a sofa was nearby out of camera range so that she could rest between takes without having to walk the few feet to her portable dressing room. She was allowed in the studio only three hours a day, and the Boss made sure that his star left on time. Mamie was a constant presence on the Culver City lot, serving juice and small snacks, massaging Dressler's feet, and keeping unwanted visitors at bay.

Luckily, the *Dinner at Eight* shoot was brief. Cukor completed the picture in twenty-five days for a bargain $387,000, and it eventually earned a profit of three million dollars for MGM. Dressler made few public comments concerning the film, but she did praise Jean Harlow's performance, much to the young actress's gratitude. "Being in the same cast with Marie was a break for me," she told reporters. "She's one trouper I'd never try to steal a scene from. It'd be like trying to carry Italy against Mussolini." Dressler was so impressed with Harlow that she included a paragraph about her in her autobiography. "It was whispered behind more than one hand that Jean Harlow, Metro's much-advertised platinum menace, was picked for parts that called for more allure than art. And in *Dinner at Eight,* she had to throw a bomb in the works by proving that she is a first-rate actress! Her performance as the wife of the hard-boiled, self-made politician played by Wally Beery belongs in that limited category of things which may with reason be called rare. The plain truth is, she all but ran off with the show!" (Perhaps Dressler and Harlow shared some mystical rapport. Harlow, who died tragically at the height of her career in 1937, is buried in a crypt almost exactly opposite Dressler's tomb in Forest Lawn Cemetery, Los Angeles.)

Dinner at Eight opened at the Astor Theatre in New York on August 23, 1933, and was an immediate box-office hit for MGM. Critics were almost unanimously generous. "The story grips from beginning to end with never relaxing tension," wrote *Variety's* reviewer, "its sombre moments relieved by lighter touches into a fascinating mosaic for nearly two hours. . . . Acting honors probably will go to Miss Dressler and Miss Harlow, the latter taking hold of her fat role and making it stand out, even in this distinguished company." Added the critic: "The role of Carlotta doesn't find Miss Dressler in her popular vein. It's a dressed-up part for one thing, while the fans have been accustomed to her in more rowdy character. But she handles this politer assignment with poise and aplomb that would be hard to match. This veteran trouper probably would do a trapeze specialty with the same finish if they called for it."

After the April wrap of *Dinner at Eight,* Dressler was unlikely to have been speculating on future reviews. Even those who had been shielded from the truth about her roller-coaster condition were beginning to speculate as to whether her career might be finished. Wrote movie columnist Elinor Hughes in the *Los Angeles Times*: "Giving her strength as generously as ever, Marie Dressler insisted that she was well enough to appear in *Dinner at Eight* and did so. She was over optimistic, not having recovered from the operation that she underwent in New York a few weeks ago and, as a result of working on the big special film, she is so ill that she will be unable to work for many weeks. This means that in all probability, *Tugboat Annie* and *The Late Christopher Bean,* both of which were intended for her especial use, will be indefinitely postponed, perhaps canceled altogether. Marie isn't very young any more and she's anything but strong. Too bad the studio was in such a hurry to complete the production that she couldn't have been allowed a longer rest." But gossip columnists did not have access to the top-office strategists at Culver City. When *Dinner at Eight* was safely stashed in the can, Mayer contacted Dressler and asked if she was ready to start work on *Tugboat Annie.* The telephone call must have been received in private, because no one—not even Mamie Cox—knew precisely how the actress responded. Mamie did tell a still-concerned Dubrey that Dressler was exhausted after the *Dinner at Eight* assignment and that she was spending much of her time in bed. A physician briefed by Dr. Glover was continuing to give her injections twice weekly. But not only was Dressler a trouper who could not resist a challenge, Mayer most likely used this opportunity to offer her a cash incentive. Months later, Dressler told Allen and Kitty Walker that the Boss had promised to pay her a one-hundred-thousand-dollar bonus in return for her almost superhuman participation in the three-movie marathon. Whatever Mayer told her that day, however, it obviously set the legendary fire bells ringing. A *Tugboat Annie* script arrived at North Alpine almost immediately. Dressler began work on the picture just a week later.

22

And to All, Goodnight

1933

Norman Reilly Raine, the Canadian veteran of the First World War who created "Tugboat Annie," always insisted that he had written the successful *Saturday Evening Post* series with Marie Dressler in mind. The seven original stories revolved around the tough female captain of the tugboat *Narcissus* working out of the Puget Sound docks in Washington State. Captain Annie Brennan was a widow in the *Post* tales, but after MGM acquired the property, Annie's spouse, Terry, was resurrected so that Wallace Beery could rejoin Dressler in a quasi–*Min and Bill* reprise.

The studio was clearly betting that the venture would result in fat profits at the box office. Fans of the series had long been drawing MGM's attention to the fact that Dressler would be perfect as *Annie,* and production brass had been quietly tinkering with the idea since 1931. When Mayer and Thalberg began talking seriously about the picture in late 1932, though, Dressler was still in New York, and the Boss had yet to approach her with the ambitious triple-production plan. Nevertheless, other *Annie* details were moved to the front burner. Producer Harry Rapf was assigned to handle the project. Scenarists Zelda Sears and Eve Greene began working on an adaptation of the Raine stories. Director Chuck Reisner was sounded out as to his mid-1933 availability. And MGM contract newcomer Robert Young was told that he would be wanted for the role of the Brennan son, Alec. Madge Evans, who had played Paula in *Dinner at Eight,* was tapped for the part of Pat, Alec's love interest, but by the time *Dinner* was completed, studio consensus was that the young actress was not top-of-the-line MGM material. Early in 1933, the role of Pat was handed to another Hollywood newcomer, Maureen O'Sullivan. And at about the same time, the studio borrowed Harry Warner's son-in-law, Mervyn LeRoy, to take over the direction of the picture from Reisner.

Once she had committed herself to the project, Dressler found she was uncomfortably intimidated by the scope of the *Tugboat Annie* script. The story called for her to negotiate the tricky anatomy of a boat, withstand bruising storms, and perform as nimbly as she had done in *Tillie's Nightmare* two decades before. Mayer was smoothly reassuring. Although the docks at Lake Union in Seattle and many of the local tugboats and their captains would be used for atmosphere, much of the picture would be filmed under controlled conditions right there in California. Parts of the Seattle waterfront were already being reconstructed on the MGM lot and on a lake not far from the studio. And Stage 22 was being transformed into the *Glacier Queen*, a liner that would figure prominently in the story. Crews of the Foss Tugboat Company's fleet were used in the movie, as well as scores of Seattle residents from Smith Cove and Lake Union. A sixty-three-year-old local housewife, Maria Fisk, who lived in a wharfside boathouse, was recruited as Dressler's double for the Seattle long shots. Luckily, Dressler did not need to worry about tiring wardrobe fittings before the *Tugboat Annie* shoot. Her costumes were highly reminiscent of *Min and Bill:* a rough shirt, cardigan, and skirt, a man's fedora, and a peaked cap. As he had previous arranged for *Dinner at Eight,* Mayer ordered that the star's working day be confined to three hours, that stand-ins be used for rehearsals, and that a sofa be available for Dressler's use when the cameras were not turning. Mamie Cox was given the run of the lot so that she could fetch whatever the star required.

Then, when the cast and crew were needed to work at the lakeside location, Dressler had the use of a small cottage as her dressing room and for overnight stopovers when necessary. Mayer could not have picked a more successful way of convincing the star that, despite the punishing schedule, he truly cared about her. "Oh yes, they spoil me handsomely out here in Hollywood," Dressler gushed in her autobiography. "I just sit back and lap it up

like a cat with her nose in a saucer of cream. When we were filming *Tugboat Annie,* we had to be on location for several weeks on
end. Mr. Mayer sent me snapshots of half a dozen nearby houses
from which to choose living quarters. I said that any one of them
would be fine and added purely in fun that what I really should
like would be a little vine-covered cottage we had passed on our
way to location. The next thing I knew, there was the cottage with
a blue bow of ribbon tied to the handle of the front door and a
card which said, 'Welcome Home, Marie!' Mr., Mayer had bought
it, vines and all, and had it moved for me." (A story made the
rounds that the Boss later had the cottage transported to Santa
Barbara for Dressler to live in, but there is no evidence that this
happened.)

Nevertheless, as Mamie Cox reported to Claire Dubrey that
summer of 1933, "*Tugboat Annie* was a hard picture." Even
Dressler the inveterate trouper permitted herself a rare complaint
in the pages of *My Own Story:* "The most grueling piece of physical labor I ever put in was during the filming of the storm scenes
in *Tugboat Annie.* One coastwise sailor in the cast told me that in
twenty years' experience aboard tramp steamers he had never encountered rougher seas than those manufactured in our studios.
They should have been good. Mr. Mayer spent $30,000 on the
dock alone! Able-bodied men were slapped down by waves the
script described as mild. There was more than one arm in a sling,
and at least one leg in a plaster cast before we got through."

Mervyn LeRoy managed to spin an entertaining photoplay
out of script material that now seems a hackneyed, often overwrought version of Raine's colorful series. We meet the formidable
Annie, her shiftless but lovable husband, Terry, and their son, Alec,
who—unbelievably for his tender years—has landed a berth as captain of an ocean liner. The lovable Terry is an unrepentant drunk,
and Captain Annie shoulders the frustrating task of trying to keep
him sober. Toward the end of the movie, Terry redeems himself by
risking his life in the *Narcissus*'s boiler room so the tug can help
save his son's ship. But before we get to this point, the Dressler/
Beery team serves up its expected smorgasbord of slapstick brawl-
ing interspersed with drama and irresistible doses of sentiment. And
the scriptwriters took care to give Dressler some of the lines and
situations that the fans obviously expected. In a hilarious drunk scene,

Annie keeps Terry sober by consuming his drink whenever she sees him holding a glass. And there is a poignant sequence that illustrates Dressler's unparalleled command of the heart-tugging episode, when her son urges her to leave the tugboat and his irresponsible father. The actress registers shock and sadness, then softly replies: "Why, Son, I married him." Finally, after a further argument, the dismayed Annie strikes Alec, and he angrily leaves while the unhappy Annie calls after him, then stands staring at the door with tears in her eyes. The entire movie is a classic example of what MGM believed the moviegoing public wanted to see in 1933.

Despite the difficult shooting conditions and the fact that she became quickly exhausted, Dressler apparently enjoyed making *Tugboat Annie*. Mayer's elaborate ministrations clearly helped make the job possible, but she also found personal satisfaction in revisiting the type of character that had enhanced her screen reputation in the past. "I love any role," she told a magazine writer, "which shows that if you aren't afraid of life, life can't hurt you. That's what *Tugboat Annie* does. She licks fate because she can look it in the eye and not be afraid. I always love a role in which I can get that idea over to audiences, because I think that's the kind of stimulant that we need in American life right now." American audiences obviously agreed with her. *Tugboat Annie* had its world premiere in Seattle at the Fifth Avenue Theatre in late July, then opened in Los Angeles and New York on August 11, 1933. The fans stood in line for hours to buy their tickets. Prices were hiked from forty to fifty cents at some theatres, but the crowds still clamored for a chance to see the weather-beaten Dressler and Beery in their latest sentimental slugfest. The Ohio Theatre in Columbus reported: "We're creating all-time attendance records for any Columbus theatre. The Sold Out sign has been outside since the opening of *Tugboat Annie,* and that includes early matinee shows." Attendance at Loew's State in Los Angeles in August broke records, and the movie was held over a second week after playing to 67,000 patrons in the first seven days. "It's the draw of the century," the theatre's manager told the press. In San Francisco, the Paramount began opening its doors at 9 A.M. every morning and screening two after-midnight shows as well. Reviews were almost uniformly favorable. A few complained about the flimsy story but, as *Variety* wrote, "Those who will be irritated or annoyed by the story's hokey, sobby, stale baloney nature are likely to be a very small minority. The average Dressler-Beery fan, of whom there are many, will eat it up." After the movie opened in Britain, the *London Daily Telegraph* reported: "Especially remarkable is the vitality shown by Miss Dressler. The 62-year-old star, sick though she is reported to be, climbs ladders, fights her way through waves and generally reveals the spirit of a girl of 20."

Back at Culver City, the MGM top office basked in the profitable glow of success. On August 7, *Time* magazine made history by honoring Marie Dressler with its first-ever cover story featuring a movie actress. The piece was scarcely a journalistic *tour de force*—its most interesting revelation was that Dressler maintained a correspondence with General John J. Pershing—but it did give enormous weight to MGM's highly publicized claim that Dressler was now the most popular screen performer in the world. Certainly the box-office results were vindicating the studio's earlier decision to spend an unprecedented $614,000 on *Tugboat Annie*. The movie had already outstripped *Prosperity* in ticket sales and was eclipsing such heavyweight competitors as *Morning Glory,* starring Katharine Hepburn; *Voltaire,* headlining George Arliss; and the surefire screen confection *Gold Diggers of 1933*. And now Mayer was congratulating himself that he had decided to release the already completed *Dinner at Eight* on August 29, more than two weeks after *Tugboat Annie's* opening in New York. With *Annie* breaking attendance records everywhere, fans besieged the box office to enjoy yet another Dressler performance.

Dressler completed *Tugboat Annie* with a distinct sense of relief, then took off in July with Mamie Cox in attendance for a two-week holiday in Santa Barbara. Mayer had given her the script of *The Late Christopher Bean* to read while she was away, and she had promised to be back in Los Angeles for the start of the movie two weeks later. In the meantime, though, she settled into her suite at the Biltmore and held court until she felt strong enough to leave the hotel for a few social occasions. All of her Santa Barbara friends vied with each other in welcoming her back "home" among the jacarandas. With the La Quinta desert resort closed for the summer, Allen and Kitty Walker appointed themselves unofficial gatekeeper and secretary, fielding telephone calls and shuttling adoring visitors in and out of the suite. Eventually, the actress accepted some invitations, one of them from developer and construction millionaire C.K.G. Billings, who owned an extensive estate in nearby Montecito. Dressler had met the wealthy businessman and his wife several years before at La Quinta and had once stayed in one of his luxurious guest cottages, but this time the couple made an effort to consolidate the friendship. After hearing that Dressler was considering a trip to New York in September when *Christopher Bean* was in the can, they invited her to take a trip up the coast on their yacht, which was docked at Long Island. Actually, Dressler—who was still trying to recover from the rigors of the *Tugboat Annie* nautical experience—was a poor sailor, but she told Billings that if she did travel east she would enjoy visiting them on their yacht. She then confided to the developer that she had asked Allen Walker to negotiate the purchase of a small lot in Montecito on which she was hoping to build her retirement home and suggested that she might want to rent one of Billings' guest cottages in 1934 while her own house was being built.

In the meantime, Dressler had the third movie in Mayer's cinematic marathon to tackle. Sidney Howard's successful play (which had starred Pauline Lord on Broadway) had been adapted by Sylvia Thalberg and Larry Johnson, and MGM had retained Harry Rapf as producer and the highly professional Sam Wood as director. The cast was first class, though not extravagant in MGM terms: Dressler, Lionel Barrymore, Beulah Bondi, Helen Shipman, Helen Mack, and Jean Hersholt. Once again, Dressler was cast as a loyal family housekeeper, an echo of her successful role in *Emma*. This time, however, she plays Abbie, employed by a small-town physician (Barrymore) who is short of money because of his habit of extending credit to patients who constantly disregard their bills, and Abbie is being let go after nineteen years of service. One of the defaulting patients, an artist named Christopher Bean, has died before settling a one-hundred-dollar medical debt. Three men claiming to be art fanciers offer to settle Bean's outstanding bill in return for a look at any paintings the artist might have left with the doctor as partial payment. It turns out, somewhat predictably, that Christopher Bean paintings are now fetching astronomical prices, and the movie tracks the physician's feverish search for canvases and chronicles the distress of his wife (Bondi), who has burned a bundle of Bean paintings in the backyard. Finally, it is revealed that the loyal Abbie not only rescued the canvases before they were destroyed, she had secretly married the penniless Christopher Bean as well. *Alors,* we now have a widow and former housekeeper who is also an instant millionaire.

Generally, critics were not smitten with Dressler's latest movie, retitled simply *Christopher Bean* (and *Her Sweetheart* for some releases). *Variety* called it "so-so" and predicted that the picture would not attract the kind of boffo business that had rewarded *Dinner at Eight* and *Tugboat Annie.* "Marie Dressler, of course," wrote the reviewer, "is tremendously popular, but this is not one of her outstanding performances. If it went all the way and was frank hokum it would be a more satisfactory picture. As it is, *Christopher Bean* is most of the time a faintly ironical study of human greed." Most likely, the screenwriters found it a tough task to stretch the Howard play to ninety minutes, hence an overlong sequence that has Dressler coping with a runaway automobile and some silly moments involving the actress as a caring housekeeper. A final, unnecessary scene with an old gentleman in a railway carriage seems obviously tacked on, as though the writers had been told to elasticize the action. But *Christopher Bean* must be considered in context: Dressler's final movie in many ways turned out to be her most charming. Even in slapstick, she exudes a sweetness of character that was not truly evident in her earlier MGM films, which makes it easy to understand why a penniless artistic genius fell in love with her. She is, of course, no beauty, but she is warm, disarmingly practical, and bubbling with the kind of homespun humor that the rest of the doctor's household plainly lacks.

Dressler looks radiantly healthy in *Christopher Bean.* She was known to avoid heavy makeup for her screen appearances, and there is no reason to believe that Abbie's firm, unlined cheeks and sparkling eyes are anything other than Dressler's own. MGM did, as usual, pamper their star during the making of the film, and director Sam Wood was ordered to suspend the action, if possible, whenever he felt Dressler needed a break. Even so, the ailing, sixty-four-year-old trouper dominates the picture with an awesome energy that belies the fact that her life would soon come to a close.

Dressler had told Mamie Cox in August that she should prepare for another visit to New York as soon as she was released from the *Christopher Bean* shoot. She wanted to see her friends in the East, and she also wanted to consult with Dr. Glover. Another incentive to take the trip: She had been invited to the White House for dinner and an overnight stay in honor of her sixty-fifth birthday. After delays in early September for sound-track retakes, the actress, accompanied by Mamie and Allen and Kitty Walker, boarded the transcontinental train. Dressler was unusually irritable during the long journey, and Mamie reported later to Dubrey that the actress appeared to be "rather grim" in New York. But the prospect of speaking privately to Roosevelt excited her. After all, wrote Dubrey, "the president had been in office for almost a year and she had not yet been able to take the first step toward her Plan for Dr. Glover."

A few days after her arrival in Manhattan, Dressler and Mamie traveled to Washington. "At the White House, they were shown into a suite of bedrooms on the second floor," Dubrey recorded. "Mamie's room was an alcove through which she could see the mantle in the adjoining chamber occupied by Marie. Carved in the marble were words commemorating the fact that in this room, Abraham Lincoln had signed the Act of Emancipation and a card on the mantle stated that Marie's bed had been used by President Andrew Jackson." Dressler never divulged what she and the president discussed, but she had told Dubrey months earlier that she planned to tell FDR about Dr. Glover, and, as Claire remembered, "she wasn't one to give up an objective." Mamie later reported that the next morning "Marie was in exceptionally high spirits."

Back in New York, Dressler tried to enjoy herself as she always had done in the glamorous city, but she had only a limited reserve of energy. She accepted some invitations to dinner, because she wanted "to give the Walkers a good time," she explained to a concerned Mamie. She even gritted her teeth and boarded the Billings's yacht for a short cruise. At the request of *Vanity Fair,* she consented to a sitting with the magazine's celebrated staff photographer Edward Steichen. The portrait, published in January 1934, is startling. The actress is portrayed by Steichen as hunched and brooding, eyes staring desperately, hands flopping over her knees. Her hair is a curly mop combed unbecomingly to each side of her sagging face. She reveals a Marie Dressler unknown by either friends or fans, giving no hint of Tillie Blobbs, Old Marthy,

Min, Emma, or Carlotta. The portrait does not show the Marie Dressler of the Great White Way or even the grande dame of Santa Barbara. So had Steichen peered into her very soul?

Dressler paid a visit to Dr. Glover's laboratory for a checkup and, no doubt, an enthusiastic report of the White House visit. When Dressler left for the return trip to California, according to Mamie, she believed she was free of any malignancy. Even so, Dressler was aware that she was not well. MGM announced that she would make an appearance in a film called *The Hollywood Party,* but the assignment was canceled. Then, when Mayer told the actress he would be staging an enormous birthday party for her on November 9, she tried to dissuade him, just in case she might not be able to attend. The Boss responded by switching on the old charm. He planned the birthday bash of the century, and everyone in Hollywood would be there to honor Marie as she deserved. Marie sighed. How could she refuse?

The morning of the big show, W.R. Wilkerson, *Hollywood Reporter* columnist, gave his readers a taste of things to come: "Tonight between 8:30 and 9:30 o'clock, every station on the big National Broadcasting Company chain will tune in on the dinner-dance that L.B. Mayer is giving Marie Dressler. This broadcast was not sought by the publicity department of MGM, but was solicited by NBC due to public demand." He noted that a message of congratulation had been sent by President and Mrs. Roosevelt and that 9 governors and 318 mayors had issued proclamations for Dressler's birthday. Loew theatres had provided special boxes in their lobbies to collect over nine hundred thousand birthday messages for the actress, and Western Union had installed extra wires in anticipation of the number of telegrams. Wilkerson continued, "Through the MGM publicity department's offer of two hundred fifty dollars for the best poem written around Marie for this, her 65th birthday, more than 28,000 poems have been checked so far with the count still growing." Numerous birthday cakes had already been received, their senders dutifully recorded before they were donated to poor families. "Every ward in every hospital in this town will be loaded with flowers sent to Miss Dressler through the American Florists Association by her admirers," Wilkerson predicted. Cobourg, Ontario, was staging a special celebration in honor of its most famous native.

The party exhausted Dressler. After viewing the giant cake that had been donated by General Foods, she returned to the head table to thank Mayer and the guests. Then, with her eyes glistening with tears, she whispered huskily: "Good-bye, au revoir, auf weidersehen, and to all, goodnight." The next day, the MGM publicity department would distribute one of the many news releases that were apparently designed to boost Dressler's morale as well as divert the public's attention from the actress's declining health. "Marie Dressler, who yesterday celebrated her sixty-second [*sic*] birthday, will start work within the month on *Mrs. Van Kleek*, a south seas story selected as her next film for MGM," wrote Ralph Wilk in *Film Daily*. In the coming months, without bothering to explain why other projects had been jettisoned, the studio would announce such Dressler projects as Louis Bromfield's *Living in a Big Way* with Jean Harlow and *Ferike the Great* with Wallace Beery.

Mamie Cox always said that Dressler changed dramatically, both physically and mentally, after the night of her sixty-fifth birthday. Claiming that she couldn't bear to think about food after all she had been expected to consume at the MGM party, the actress suddenly subjected herself to a liquid diet of orange and tomato juice that lasted for almost a week. By the time she agreed to try eating again, she found it impossible to retain solid food. Her alarmed servants saw that she was growing noticeably weaker. Jack Winslow and a few of "the boys" would suggest backgammon or bridge, but Dressler most often waved them out of the house, pleading fatigue. She sat alone in the little card room, playing solitaire and listening to her radio.

Dressler was unhappy with the house on North Alpine Drive. The building itself was disintegrating, and even though the actress would not admit it, the accommodation had proved to be disappointingly uncomfortable. By December, she began taking daily drives with Mamie just to escape from the place. "We used to drive for three or four hours," Mamie told Dubrey. "We just went around and around, usually to the beach. Miss Dressler didn't seem to care, so long as we were moving." Most alarming, Mamie told Dubrey, was that Dressler "didn't sit up like she used to and I thought maybe her coat was too heavy. She straightened up quick and said 'no' when I asked her, but pretty soon she began to sag down again.

You know how straight she always sat up, Miss Clara. I got scared when I saw she was beginning to slump. She didn't talk much, either. She just sat and stared out of the window while Meadows drove along easy. Sometimes she spoke of the plans she was making for the cancer cure and I told her she ought to have a good rest first because one-night stands weren't easy. We'd played a lot of them and we knew. She was counting on the $100,000 she said the studio had talked about after those three pictures all in a row. At night, she'd go to bed early and just dream, sort of, and listen to the radio. That wasn't like her. It worried me, although I was glad she was resting at last."

In January, a new flurry of telephone calls from friends, visits from the studio brass, and frantic requests for press interviews began. The *Motion Picture Herald's* poll of exhibitors would soon crown the new king or queen of American screen performers—or perhaps the reigning monarch again? Hollywood had been speculating for weeks that Dressler would repeat her 1932 triumph because of the trio of smash successes in 1933, but even the pundits were astonished at the *Herald's* published results. Hollywood columnist Elinor Hughes wrote, "It is indicative of something or other that Joe E. Brown nearly crowded Joan Crawford out of 10th place and was himself closely pressed by Lionel Barrymore, the Marx Brothers and Bing Crosby. Dietrich and Garbo are rather far down on the list." Hughes then listed the somewhat formidable names of movie performers not mentioned in any position on the *Herald* questionnaire. Among them: Charles Laughton, Mickey Mouse, Charles Chaplin, Cary Grant, Jeanette MacDonald, and W.C. Fields. But then came the winning scores: Joan Crawford, 27.8 percent; Norma Shearer, 33.3 percent; Mae West, 36.3 percent; Clark Gable, 36.5 percent; Jean Harlow, 40.6 percent; Wallace Beery, 44.8 percent; Eddie Cantor, 60.1 percent; Janet Gaynor, 61.4 percent; Will Rogers, 65.6 percent. Marie Dressler topped the latest Motion Picture Herald poll with a stunning 74.4 percent of the vote.

23

Flutter of Doubt

1934

Dressler had been picking away at a project since September 1933 that at first she regarded as a necessary duty but had come to feel was a decided bore. She had agreed to cooperate with literary agent Edith Burrows and her client author Mildred Harrington on a series of four autobiographical articles, to be published in *Redbook* magazine. The articles would then be expanded into a book "as told to" Harrington. Little, Brown and Company of New York had expressed an interest, and during her visit to New York in October Dressler had signed a contract with Harrington and Burrows giving her a 50 percent cut of any book royalties. After her return to California, Dressler amused herself with periodic dispatches to Harrington, spending several hours a day recalling details of the past few years in Hollywood and dictating anecdotes and long-winded flights of personal philosophy to Jack Winslow, who had taken over the actress's secretarial work. She also directed Winslow to copy and mail large chunks of her 1924 autobiography, rationalizing that although *Ugly Duckling* had been ghost-written by Helena Dayton and Louise Barrett, it was jointly owned by the three former friends. Her orders were to have far-reaching legal consequences. No one will ever know whether Dressler recalled at that time that Claire Dubrey had been keeping a diary that both she and Dubrey had openly assumed would one day be published. In any case, Dressler's interest in Mildred Harrington and the *Redbook* articles—to be entitled "Life Begins at 60"—deteriorated rapidly in early 1934.

By February of that year Dressler found herself in need of a medical consultant who was more accessible than was Dr. Glover in New York. Friends suggested she make an appointment with Dr. Herbert Moffitt, a highly celebrated but retired specialist who was then living in San Francisco. Getting away from the North Alpine house appealed to Dressler, and she asked Winslow to set up an appointment. No record now exists of Dr. Moffitt's medical findings, but Mamie Cox told Dubrey that he indicated that Dressler's cancer was in remission but recommended that she place herself in the care of a physician in Los Angeles who could keep her under close observation. "But I don't believe in doctors!" she apparently told the specialist. Still, Dressler wanted a plausible excuse to leave her Beverly Hills house, so when Moffitt recommended a physician in Santa Barbara, she happily accepted his suggestion.

Dressler and Mamie returned from San Francisco and prepared for the exodus. Jack Winslow told the actress he wanted to leave her employ and, although their once-cordial friendship had cooled during the previous months, Dressler was angry when she received his notice. He did, however, agree to stay on at the house with Irene Allen and Jerry Cox to finish work still on hand, and when she and Mamie stepped into the limousine for the drive to Santa Barbara, he ran out to wish her good-bye. "Drive on, Meadows!" Dressler ordered, staring coldly ahead. As Dubrey observed in her memoir, "Another page was turned in the family album."

Dressler and Mamie checked into the Biltmore hotel in Santa Barbara, and although the actress was comfortable enough in her suite, she quickly developed headaches and a fever. Dr. Franklin Nuzum, the new physician, was summoned, but all he could do was prescribe a sedative and forbid any visitors from worrying his patient. He also recommended that she engage a nurse, and eventually a young woman named Alice Ferris arrived at the Biltmore to join Mamie in caring for the actress. Dressler obeyed orders for more than a month, but tired of the enforced isolation she hatched a plan to move into one of the cottages owned by C.K.G. Billings and for Allen and Kitty Walker to move in with her. After all, La Quinta, which the Walkers managed, would soon close for the summer, and surely Dr. Nuzum could not object to her having resident guests around, whatever he might feel about casual visitors. Dressler immediately began the task of organizing what she considered to be an interesting, even entertaining, recuperation. Dr. Nuzum agreed that regular companions could be beneficial, provided they did not overtire his patient.

In early May the move from the Biltmore to 820 Cima Linda Lane was accomplished, and although there was much laughing and hugging and promises of good times when Dressler met the Walkers at the cottage, she soon excused herself and retired to bed. The next day, Dr. Nuzum sent along a night nurse to relieve Mamie when Ferris was off duty. Dressler's spirits began to improve during the next few weeks. She played bridge with Allen, Kitty, and Martha Gray, a Montecito resident she had known for years and who was at the cottage so constantly that she was considered a fixture. Dressler became interested again in her Grand Plan for Dr. Glover as well as in the house she wanted to build on her nearby lot. There was talk about architects and blueprints and decorators and conversation about the trip to Europe she wanted to take with Allen and Kitty when her strength improved. Perhaps they might pick up furnishings for the new house in Italy and France, and while they were away, Mamie and Jerry would be able to vacation in Savannah and visit the family they had not seen for so long.

But between moments of optimism, Dressler admitted to the Walkers that she was apprehensive and not only because of her maddeningly quixotic health. She owned a conservative stock portfolio (which included respectable holdings in American Water Works and Electric Company, Arkansas Power and Light, and Ohio Edison), much of it bought on the advice of Marion Davies and William Randolph Hearst. But prices fluctuated wildly and dividends had dwindled during the Depression. Although her contracted MGM salary was to be paid every Saturday, income tax, at the then 25 percent top rate, took an enormous bite out of the check. And expenses were growing more onerous all the time: doctors, nurses, the rent and other household bills in Montecito. And that horrible white elephant was eating its head off in Beverly Hills. If only, she complained over and over again, the studio would hurry up with that $100,000 bonus!

Actually, someone from MGM—once Mayer himself but more often publicity chief Howard Strickling, Frances Marion, or one of the many bright young men who paid court to the Boss—visited Cima Linda Lane quite regularly during the early summer of

1934. They brought flowers and candy, fond wishes from the Front Office, and news of yet another picture the studio was considering for its celebrated star. The "Tish" stories, written by Mary Roberts Rinehart, were being discussed as a Dressler vehicle, she was told, and the Boss wanted to make sure she had read the books and approved of the idea. And did she know that Polly Moran's MGM contract had expired but that the studio wanted to bring the comedienne back to Los Angeles for yet another Dressler–Moran team-up? The actress smiled politely. She knew the fans loved to laugh but, as she had often confided to Dubrey, drama was her real forte and she was damned good at it. Surely her successes in *Emma* and *Christopher Bean* had elevated her from the more superficial ranks of the movie comics!

The MGM visitors dutifully drank tea, admired the view of the Pacific that Dressler could glimpse from her living room, and delivered the latest Hollywood gossip—which, again, the actress politely endured. Where, she unfailingly complained to Allen and Kitty after the studio representatives departed, was that bonus check? Instead, she was rewarded with the news that after Walt Disney had dubbed the Academy Award statuette "the Oscar" at the March banquet the silly name was beginning to stick. Dressler nodded somewhat listlessly when she was told that the Boss was still furious that *Dinner at Eight* had been shut out of the March awards and that the studio had received only one Best Picture nomination, the Norma Shearer/Leslie Howard tear-jerker, *Smilin' Through*. And that Clark Gable was back in Mayer's good books after he had starred in that smash hit *It Happened One Night* for Columbia. No doubt, the columnists were buzzing, the king of Culver City was regretting that he let Gable escape the studio net in the first place.

The check came in late May, pressed into her hand by one of the always cheerful studio executives. Mamie remembered that Dressler crushed the envelope in her lap during the remainder of the visit, responding to the jokes and the gossip but obviously anxious to examine her prize. Once she was alone with her friends, she tore open the envelope and waved the check triumphantly. "I've got it! I've got it!" she shouted. "What did I tell you? They gave it to me! Now I'm all set for the rest of my life. With what I have already, this will be plenty. A check for a hundred thousand dollars!" She kissed it, laughing and crying with relief and joy. "That's what I get for not fussing over my salary! I always know what I am doing!" She handed the slip of paper to Allen Walker. "Put it in the bank, dear. Isn't that a nice nest egg?"

Walker studied the check. It was for $10,000, not $100,000 as Dressler had so passionately hoped it would be. Clearly, Dressler's determination to believe what she wished to believe had clouded her eyesight. Walker consulted with Mamie and they addressed the question to Dr. Nuzum and the nurses. What to do? The reply was unanimous. Let Dressler be happy and ignore the issue as long as possible. Dr. Nuzum revealed to Allen Walker that Dressler's heart was showing distinct signs of weakness and that an extreme disappointment might prove to be very serious.

Unfortunately, the moment of truth arrived sooner than anyone expected. For a few days, Dressler was highly exhilarated. She talked endlessly about putting her Big Plan into action at last and getting her career moving again. Walker flinched when she suddenly asked him to bring her a copy of her bank balance. "And I want a list of everything I own," she added. "I'm about ready to get up. I'm wasting good time, you know." When he obeyed her orders, she happily adjusted her glasses and studied the figures. "Why, this can't be right!" she protested. "You've made a mistake, dear. Where's my hundred thousand dollars?"

Walker had to tell her. Later, Allen, Kitty, and Mamie reported the scene to Dubrey, who dutifully recorded it in her memoir: "Marie raged for three days. So this was gratitude! This was what she got for working when she should have been resting! For stringing along with a measly two thousand, twenty-two hundred, twenty-five hundred dollars a week when another star on the lot was reported to be getting nine thousand! She was the biggest seller in pictures; everyone admitted it! She could have demanded her share of the profits! But no! 'They' were going to take 'care' of her! She'd show them! She'd go to another studio just as soon as she got her strength back! The other company had offered her *twelve* thousand a week, but like a fool she had stuck to her bargain—and got stuck for her pains! Well, this wasn't going to whip her. She'd take that twelve thousand dollar salary and in a couple of pictures she would have her nest egg again. Her Plan might be delayed, but it would never be abandoned!"

Dressler announced that she would start with a fresh slate. "Sell the house!" she commanded. "It's holding me back. It stands between me and God!" She relaxed somewhat when a highly alarmed Walker assured her that the house was sold; he was just about to tell her so. Soon, another nurse was engaged, and yet another, for a total of five. The increase in staff had become necessary because four strong individuals were now needed to lift the actress. While she was conscious, Dressler firmly insisted that she must always leave her bed to attend to natural functions.

"Sublime, pitiful, foolish," wrote Dubrey. "Getting up and down was a tax on the already overtaxed heart. She was now unbelievably swollen [because of kidney failure], her skin stretched to the bursting point. It was kept oiled to prevent cracking. Now, it took a long time to help her from bed. Slowly, slowly the torso was raised to an upright position. Slowly the edematous limbs were eased over the side. Two nurses, Mamie, and Allen Walker supported her while she took a step to the waiting commode. After the effort of regaining her bed, scarcely would the last pillow be tucked under her neck before the whole procedure must be gone through again."

Gently, Walker talked to Dressler about making a will. The actress resisted at first. After all, she told those in the room, she was still getting in and out of bed wasn't she? And because she could still take care of herself, she wasn't too ill, merely resting. A will? Well, perhaps. But it would be only tentative. She'd make another at the end of the year, by which time she'd have a great deal more money. But, very well, it might be a good idea to ask Mr. Billings's attorneys, Bradner and Weil, to attend to the job. After all, if they became familiar with her affairs by drawing up a will, they could take care of things when she went out campaigning for Dr. Glover.

Once the lawyers arrived at her bedside on May 29, Dressler took little time pondering the contents of her last will and testament. As a matter of fact, Walker remembered, she rattled off her bequests and wishes as though she had already given considerable thought to the subject. An important item was the sum of $35,000 and all of her wearing apparel—except that otherwise bequeathed—to Mamie Cox. She left $15,000 to Mamie's husband, Jerry, together with her two automobiles, and she also decided to leave the couple all of her flat and hollow silverware "as a remembrance from me to them for their silver wedding anniversary." She matter-of-factly recited other bequests: the sum of $5,000 to her friend and astrologer, Nella Webb. A pin of pearls to Frances Marion. The sum of $5,000 to her long-time theatrical colleague May Duryea. The sum of $10,000 to the American Women's Association. All of her shares of stock and her mink coat to Kitty Walker. A large diamond bracelet to Hallie Phillips and a diamond necklace to her other theatrical friend, Georgie Caine. Two etched crystal urns, one to Mrs. Blanche Billings and the other to Mrs. Martha Gray. The sum of $2,000 to her cook, Irene Allen, and the sum of $5,000 to Ida Sutcliff, a cousin who lived in Winnipeg. She forgave two debts, one for $5,406 owed by her broker, Starr Anderson, and another for $8,928 owed by Newell Van Derhooef. After all of these bequests were noted, she instructed that the residue of her estate be paid to her sister, Bonita Ganthony.

Before completion of the will, however, she consulted with her lawyer, then directed the document be made very clear that she was intentionally omitting and disinheriting all persons "claiming to be her heirs" who were not specifically included in the document. If anyone did come forward with this type of claim, she would allow them the sum of one dollar. She also directed that all inheritance taxes levied on her bequests be paid from the estate residue. Allen Walker was appointed executor of the will, and she granted him full power to sell all her property, both real and personal, without applying to any court for permission to do so. Then, once the will was completed and typed, she was helped up in bed to sign her name. The document was witnessed by two Santa Barbara neighbors: Earle E. Johnstone and Marion B. Sanders. "Well," sighed the actress, "that's done."

Dressler's condition deteriorated rapidly in the next few weeks. Old friends called the guest cottage from Santa Barbara and Los Angeles, but Allen and Kitty Walker were asked to check first before handing her the telephone. The Walkers' position was difficult: many of the callers had known the actress for years, but in most cases she responded with comments such as "I don't want to see him," or "Say I can't be disturbed," or, occasionally, "No, I won't talk to her. I hear she's going back to her husband." The callers always protested. "But we've known each other for twenty-five years." Or "Have you told her that I want to drive up today?" Or "Don't you realize you are keeping us from seeing her?" Little did they know that Dressler was listening to the Walkers' telephone excuses and nodding her approval. When some friends actually made their way to the cottage door, they had to be shown to her room, but most of the time Dressler pretended to be sleeping until they tiptoed out again.

"Perhaps it reminded her too much of a death-watch. Perhaps anxious visitors caused a flutter of doubt," Dubrey wrote. Dressler's mind began to wander, and because of uremia she now weighed three hundred pounds. Her bloated tissues made it necessary for the nurses to slit her nightgowns to her waist. But her doctors were amazed at her tenacity; as far back as mid-June, they had been ready to pronounce her dead. Her heart had failed, her respiration ceased, and her pulse was undetectable. Her eyes rolled back, and her face was blue. Those who attended her remembered some of her feverish ramblings, which have since been quoted as Dressler's last words: "I don't believe in doctors!" "Have we got enough money?" "It will make a fine story!" "I'm putting up a good fight, aren't I?" "I'm sorry to be so much trouble." The actress slipped into her last coma on Friday, June 29. Like the grande dame she often pretended to be, the last coherent sentence she was heard to breathe was, "Thank you, dear." Dr. Moffitt, the great specialist Dressler had consulted the previous February, stood by her unconscious form with somewhat unprofessional tears in his eyes. Mamie heard him say softly before he hurried out of the room, "Good-bye, Miss Dressler. Have a nice, long rest."

Marie Dressler finally relinquished her grip on life at 3:35 P.M. on Saturday, July 28, 1934. Her death was attributed to congestive heart failure contributed by uremia and recurrent carcinoma. Some aspects of her death certificate are interesting. It showed her date of birth as November 9, 1871, a three year difference from the correct date of 1868. It showed her father to be Alexander Rudolph Koerber, "birthplace unknown," and her mother's name and birthplace are also shown as "unknown." Under the section designed to indicate marital status, "single, married, widowed or divorced," there is the word "single."

The world reacted to Dressler's death with shock and genuine sadness. Members of the motion picture community, including

Harold Lloyd, Mae West, Norma Shearer, Wallace Beery, Joan Crawford, Clark Gable, Jean Harlow, and Polly Moran, were quoted in pages of tributes published in newspapers everywhere. Editorialists, columnists, and obituary writers vied with each other in their attempts to celebrate Dressler's life and achievements. "She is now hailed as one of the foremost American actresses by a generation that has never seen a road show and has scarcely been inside a legitimate theatre," wrote the *New York Tribune.* "It was a wonderful triumph for the great trouper tradition to which Miss Dressler was an authentic heir. Long years of a kind of experience which Hollywood scarcely dreamed of went into that sudden conquest of its citadels. . . . She was one of the not too numerous group who have been bringing a new content into the films—a member of the old school, she helped, in Hollywood's eternal war between art and economics, to revivify the new. It was a singular achievement, but a magnificent one."

There were, of course, extravagant tributes from the front office of MGM. "Marie Dressler leaves behind a monument of success that will ever stand as an inspiration to those whose lives seem paved with obstacles," said Irving Thalberg. Louis B. Mayer was in London when he was informed of Dressler's death and quickly issued a statement to the local press: "Surely there never breathed a woman more beloved than our own Queen Marie. . . . The screen has lost one of its greatest characters. Personally, I have lost a very dear friend." There was a general outpouring of sorrow from the fans themselves. Letters from everywhere in the United States, Canada, and Europe poured into the MGM offices with suggestions for memorials, many of them containing verses in memory of the actress. The Stage Relief Fund announced it would create a special Marie Dressler memorial fund for the benefit of unemployed actors. And in her birthplace of Cobourg, Ontario, flags flew at half staff from municipal and county buildings on July 30.

Dressler had never admitted the possibility that she might one day need a funeral, so she never expressed a preference for any kind of ritual or burying ground. Mamie Cox remembered that once as they had returned from a drive, the actress had casually remarked on the beauty of Forest Lawn, so funeral arrangements were based on that chance observation. Dubrey, however, wondered whether it really was a chance remark. "Marie talked as freely as the average woman but her thoughts ran even faster than her speech. She usually had sufficient reason for every word she said. Jim Dalton is buried in his family plot in Corning, N.Y. Marie's parents lie in Flushing, two graves empty beside them. Her sister has long lived in England. Marie said, 'Forest Lawn is a beautiful cemetery,' and those who knew her remembered and buried her there. She had a reason for everything."

The funeral service was held on the sunny Tuesday morning of July 31, at the Wee Kirk o' the Heather Chapel in Forest Lawn Memorial Park in Brentwood. Allen Walker had told reporters that Dressler would not want crowds of mourners to be present and that he was limiting the invited guests to one hundred, most of them the actress's close friends or those who had worked with her during the few years she had lived in Hollywood. Those who filed into the church included Lionel Barrymore, Polly Moran and her husband, May Robson, Norma Shearer, Jean Hersholt, Frances Marion, and Jeanette MacDonald, who would sing "Abide with Me" and "Face to Face" during the service. Mamie and Jerry Cox sat together in a front pew, where they were joined by Claire Dubrey, who had received a hand-delivered invitation from Allen and Kitty Walker.

The brownstone chapel was filled with wreaths and flowers, and floral tributes overflowed onto the outside lawn. A tall cross of gardenias stood before the small altar, with two similar crosses at the chancel rail. MGM had sent a blanket of orchids that hung like a tapestry against the left wall of the building, and flower arrangements sent by friends and motion picture celebrities lined the aisles. Afterward, reporters noted those who had sent their tributes: Charles Chaplin, Greta Garbo, Alice Brady, William Randolph Hearst, Marion Davies, Adolph S. Ochs, Clarence Brown, Mildred and Harold Lloyd, Constance Bennett, Irving Thalberg. When the sealed bronze casket was finally placed before the altar by the six honorary pallbearers—directors W.S. Van Dyke, Clarence Brown, Jack Conway, Mervyn LeRoy, Charles Reisner, and William K. Howard—just two floral offerings were arranged on the lid. One was a simple spray of red roses from Hallie Phillips, and the other was a single calla lily from Dressler's friends Salisbury and Serena Field of Montecito.

As Dressler would probably have wanted, the funeral service

was Episcopalian, conducted by the Rev. Neal Dodd, pastor of the Little Church Around the Corner in Hollywood. But, also as Dressler would probably have wanted, the service was short: some prayers, two songs, the twenty-third Psalm, then the Keith poem that the actress loved so much, read by the Rev. Dodd. Eventually the little silver plate that Dressler had had engraved with the poem so that she could carry it with her for comfort would be cemented to the wall of her tomb.

The mourners then joined a procession across the park grounds to the mausoleum, where Dressler was interred behind a huge slab of marble in the Sanctuary of the Benediction. Dubrey walked to the crypt with Polly Moran and her husband, Martin Malone, and the three stood for some time grieving as workmen sealed the tomb. Later, they drove back to Hollywood in Polly's limousine and, as Dubrey wrote in her memoir: "I sat silently, though Polly wept softly. She was dressed in black, a color she never wears, purchased to do full honor to her old teammate and as a mark of her own sorrow. 'Marie was a great woman!' she said as she wiped her eyes. I nodded. 'Did I do anything wrong at the funeral?' she asked, like the child at heart she is. 'Why no, Polly! What makes you ask?' 'Well, Marie always told me to be more dignified,' she replied. 'I guess she was right. Anyway, I wanted her to approve of me. Maybe for once in their lives, people can't say Polly Moran was vulgar. I hope Marie knows.'"

Back at the North Alpine Drive house—which Allen and Kitty would occupy until Dressler's furnishings were sold and the property was turned over to its new owner, Roger L. Mandel of Chicago—Mamie told Dubrey that she planned to go home to Savannah as soon as possible. She confided that she had bought Dressler's bed so no one else would ever sleep in it. She said that she and Jerry had arranged for flowers be placed regularly on Dressler's tomb and that the couple would make a yearly pilgrimage to Forest Lawn. "Nobody was ever like Miss Dressler," Mamie told Dubrey. "I'll always remember that she went through an awful lot, but she never gave up."

Marie Dressler's films have seldom been seen by the moviegoing public since her death. None have been reissued for general release since 1936, although *Tillie's Punctured Romance, Min and Bill,* and *Dinner at Eight* are available on videocassette. Specialty movie channels and public broadcasting services occasionally air a film, but dedicated Dressler buffs must rely on film archives to view such movies as *Caught Short, Reducing,* or *Let Us Be Gay.* Even the later, more prominent Dressler successes, including *Emma* and *Christopher Bean,* are rarely screened, even on television networks devoted to cinema classics. Naturally, the only visual record of her triumphs on the Broadway stage consists of grainy photographs, most of them printed in pre-1919 editions of newspapers. In the past few years, however, the Marie Dressler Foundation—based in her birthplace of Cobourg, Ontario—has unearthed and presented many of the actress's early movies at its annual celebration of her November 9 birthday and at its popular summer festival of films.

Those who regularly attend these events can see for themselves why Dressler was a true member of showbusiness royalty: a unique, seriocomic actress whose timing and technique were honed and perfected through decades of hard work in the theatre and on the screen. In fact, it is easy to spot well-informed Dressler fans by asking for a rundown of their most unforgettable memories of Queen Marie. The list can vary, of course, but it invariably includes some scenes that have actually become woven into the broad tapestry of film legend. There was the outrageous spectacle of Dressler in high cavort with Charlie Chaplin in *Tillie's Punctured Romance.* Her unbelievably funny "For I Am the Queen" sketch in *The Hollywood Revue of 1929.* Her inspired antics with Polly Moran in *Caught Short* as the two comediennes sit uncomfortably side by side, beaming with motherly pride tinged with extreme hostility. Her effortless domination of the entire *Anna Christie* cast and her beer-drinking scene with a clearly outclassed Greta Garbo in a waterfront bar. Her smile of unquenchable happiness in *Min and Bill* as she watches her adopted daughter leave for her honeymoon while she, herself, is arrested for murder. Her obvious joy and contentment in the closing scenes of *Emma* as she turns her back on a fortune and her late husband's angry offspring and takes her place as a housekeeper and nanny in a modest new household. Her scenes in *Tugboat Annie* when she stands up loyally for her lovable but drunken husband because "I married him." Her brief exchange with Jean Harlow at the end of *Dinner At Eight.*

Nothing will ever tarnish such images for those who recognize the best when it is honestly and lovingly offered by those who want nothing more than to give it. As Marie Dressler told her admirers in the last pages of her autobiography: "If I have done anything worthwhile, your laughter and your tears, your encouragement and devotion are responsible. . . . What a horde of memories enrich me. The thousands upon thousands of lines I have memorized—comedy, tragedy, vaudeville skits, the classics, opera scores, all were grist to my mill. The countless pieces of business I have worked out. The costumes I have loved; the costumes I have hated. The men and women who have walked with me from time to time. Ah, a lot of water has run under the bridge since fourteen-year-old Leila Koerber defied her father and went away to act on the stage."

MARIE DRESSLER FILMOGRAPHY

Tillie's Punctured Romance. 1914. Also released as *For the Love of Tillie* and *Tillie's Millions.* Based on play, *Tillie's Nightmare.* Keystone Production. Directed by Mack Sennett. Cast: Marie Dressler, Charles Chaplin, Mabel Normand, Phyllis Allen, Billie Bennett, Charles Bennett, Joe Bordeaux, Charles Chase, Chester Conklin, Alice Davenport, Minta Durfee, Alice Howell, Gordon Griffith, Edgar Kennedy, G.G. Ligon, Harry McCoy, Wallace MacDonald, Charles Murray, Mack Swain, Al St. John, Slim Summerville, Eddie Sutherland, Hank Mann, Milton Berle. Six reels. Remade by Paramount in 1928 with Louise Fazenda as Tillie.

Tillie's Tomato Surprise. 1915. Lubin/Christie production. Directed by Howell Hansel. Scenario, Acton Davies. Marie Dressler, Tom McNaughton. Six reels.

Tillie Wakes Up. Also released as *Tillie's Night Out.* 1917. William Brady for Peerless/World. Marie Dressler, John Hines, Harry Davenport, Frank Beamish, Rubye de Remer, Ruth Barrett, Jack Brown. Scenario by Frances Marion. Five reels.

The Scrub Lady. 1917. Marie Dressler Motion Picture Company, released by Goldwyn. Marie Dressler. Two reels.

Fired. 1917. Marie Dressler Motion Picture Company, released by Goldwyn. Marie Dressler. Two reels.

The Cross Red Nurse. 1918. Marie Dressler Motion Picture Company, released by World. Marie Dressler. Two reels.

The Agonies of Alice. 1918. Marie Dressler Motion Picture Company, released by World. Marie Dressler. Two reels.

The Joy Girl. 1927. Fox. Directed by Allan Dwan. Scenario, Frances Agnew, adapted by Adele Comandini from a magazine serial by May Edington. Olive Borden, Neil Hamilton, Mary Alden, William Norris, Helen Chandler, Jerry Miley, Frank Walsh, Marie Dressler, Clarence J. Elmer, Peggy Kelly, Jimmy Grainger Jr.

The Callahans and the Murphys. 1927. MGM. Directed by George Hill. Scenario, Frances Marion from a novel by Kathleen Norris. Marie Dressler, Polly Moran, Sally O'Neil, Lawrence Gray, Eddie Gribbon, Frank Currier, Gertrude Olmsted, Turner Savage, Jackie Coombs, Dawn O'Day, Monty O'Grady, Tom Lewis.

Breakfast at Sunrise. 1927. First National. Directed by Mal St. Clair. Scenario, Gladys Unger from screen story by Fred De Gresac, adapted from the French play *Le Dejeuner au Soleil* by André Birabeau. Constance Talmadge, Alice White, Bryant Washburn, Paulette Duval, Albert Gran, Marie Dressler, Burr McIntosh, David Mir, Don Alvarado, Nelly Bly Baker.

Bringing Up Father. 1928. MGM. Directed by Jack Conway. Scenario, Frances Marion from a story by George McManus, based on his syndicated comic strip. Marie Dressler, Polly Moran, J. Farrell MacDonald, Jules Cowles, Gertrude Olmsted, Grant Withers, Andres de Segurola, Rose Dione, David Mir, Tenen Holtz, Toto the dog.

The Patsy. Released as *The Political Flapper* in Great Britain. 1928. MGM. Directed by King Vidor. Scenario Agnes Christine Johnston from a play by Barry Connors. Marion Davies, Orville Caldwell, Marie Dressler, Dell Henderson, Lawrence Gray, Jane Winton.

The Divine Lady. 1929. First National. Singing sequences by Vitaphone. Directed by Frank Lloyd. Scenario by Agnes Christine Johnston with titles by Harry Carr and Edwin Justus Mayer, adapted by Forrest Halsey from the novel by E. Barrington. Corinne Griffith, Victor Varconi, H.B. Warner, Ian Keith, Marie Dressler, William Conklin, Michael Vavitch, Evelyn Hall, Montague Love, Helen Jerome Eddy, Dorothy Cumming.

Dangerous Females. 1929. Paramount. Directed by William Watson. Scenario by Florence Ryerson and Colin Clements. Marie Dressler and Polly Moran. Two reels.

The Vagabond Lover. 1929. RKO. Sound by Photophone. Directed by Marshall Neilan. Scenario by James Ashmore Creelman. Rudy Vallee, Sally Blane, Charles Sellon, Marie Dressler, Norman Peck, Danny O'Shea, Eddie Hugent, Nella Walker, Malcolm Waite, Alan Roscoe, the Connecticut Yankees.

The Hollywood Revue of 1929. 1929. Produced by Cosmopolitan for MGM. All talking, all singing. Movietone. Technicolor sequences. Directed by Charles Reisner. Production numbers staged by Sammy Lee. Music by Nacio Herb Brown and Arthur Freed. Settings by Cedric Gibbons. Conrad Nagel, Jack Benny, John Gilbert, Norma Shearer, Joan Crawford, Marie Dressler, Polly Moran, Bessie Love, Lionel Barrymore, Cliff Edwards, Natacha Natova & Co., Marion Davies, William Haines, Buster Keaton, Charles King, Gus Edwards, Karl Dane, George K. Arthur, Ann Dvorak, Gwen Lee, Albertina Rasch Ballet, The Rounders, The Biltmore Quartet.

Chasing Rainbows. Also released as *The Road Show.* 1930. MGM. Movietone. Technicolor. Directed by Charles Reisner. Scenario, Bess Meredyth, adapted by Wells Root; dialogue by Charles Reisner. Robert E. Hopkins, Kenyon Nicholson, Al Bossberg, Bessie Love, Charles King, Marie Dressler, Jack Benny, George K. Arthur, Polly Moran, Gwen Lee, Nita Martan, Eddie Phillips, Youcca Troubetzkoy.

Anna Christie. 1930. MGM. Directed by Clarence Brown. Scenario, Frances Marion from the play by Eugene O'Neill. Greta Garbo, Marie Dressler, Charles Bickford, George F. Marion, James T. Mack, Lee Phelps.

The Girl Said No. 1930. MGM. Movietone. Directed by Sam Wood. Scenario, Sarah Y. Mason from a story by A.P. Younger; dialogue by Charles MacArthur. William Haines, Leila Hyams, Polly Moran, Marie Dressler, Francis X. Bushman, Clara Blandick, William Janney, William V. Mong, Junior Coghlan, Phyllis Crane.

One Romantic Night. 1930. United Artists. Directed by Paul L. Stein. Scenario, Melville Baker from the play *The Swan* by Ferenc Molnár. Lillian Gish, Rod La Rocque, Conrad Nagel, Marie Dressler, O.P. Heggie, Albert Conti, Edgar Norton, Billie Bennett, Philippe De Lacy, Byron Sage, Barbara Leonard.

Caught Short. 1930. MGM/Cosmopolitan. Directed by Charles Reisner. Scenario by Willard Mack and Robert E. Hopkins from a story by Willard Mack. Marie Dressler, Polly Moran, Anita Page, Charles Morton, Thomas Conlin, Douglas Haig, Nanci Price, Greta Mann, Herbert Prior, T. Roy Barnes, Edward Dillon, Alice Moe, Gwen Lee, Lee Kohlmar, Greta Granstedt.

Let Us Be Gay. 1930. MGM. Directed by Robert Z. Leonard. Scenario by Frances Marion from the play by Rachel Crothers, with additional dialogue by Lucille Newmark. Norma Shearer, Rod La Rocque, Marie Dressler, Gilbert Emery, Hedda Hopper, Raymond Hackett, Sally Eilers, Tyrrell Davis, Wilfred Noy, William O'Brien, Sybil Groves.

Min and Bill. 1930. MGM. Directed by George Hill. Scenario by Frances Marion, loosely adapted from the novel *Dark Star* by Lorna Moon. Marie Dressler, Wallace Beery, Dorothy Jordan, Marjorie Rambeau, Donald Dillaway, DeWitt Jennings, Russell Hopton, Frank McGlynn, Gretta Gould.

Reducing. 1931. MGM. Directed by Charles Reisner. Scenario by Willard Mack and Beatrice Banyard with additional dialogue by Robert E. Hopkins and Zelda Sears. Marie Dressler, Polly Moran, Anita Page, William Collier Jr., Lucien Littlefield, Sally Eilers, William Bakewell, Billy Naylor, Jay Ward.

Politics. 1931. MGM. Directed by Charles Reisner. Scenario by Wells Root from a story by Robert E. Hopkins with additional dialogue by Zelda Sears and Malcolm Stuart Bylan. Marie Dressler, Polly Moran, Roscoe Ates, Karen Morley, William Bakewell, John Miljan, Joan Marsh, Tom McGuire, Kane Richmond, Mary Alden, Bob Perry.

Emma. 1932. MGM. Directed by Clarence Brown. Scenario by Leonard Praskins, Zelda Sears from a story by Frances

Marion. Marie Dressler, Jean Hersholt, Richard Cromwell, Myrna Loy, John Miljan, Purnell E. Pratt, Leila Bennett, Barbara Kent, Kathryn Crawford, George Meeker, Dale Fuller, Wilfred Noy, Andre Cheron.

Prosperity 1932. MGM. Directed by Sam Wood. Scenario by Zelda Sears and Eve Green from a story by Frank Butler and Sylvia Thalberg. Marie Dressler, Polly Moran, Anita Page, Norman Foster, Jacquie Lyn, Jerry Tucker, Charles Giblyn, Frank Darien, Henry Armetta, John Roche. The version of *Prosperity* eventually released was a reworking of an earlier film that MGM decided was unsuitable for distribution.

Tugboat Annie. 1933. MGM. Directed by Mervyn LeRoy. Scenario by Zelda Sears and Eve Greene from stories by Norman Reilly Raine. Marie Dressler, Wallace Beery, Robert Young, Maureen O'Sullivan, Willard Robertson, Tammany Young, Frankie Darro, Jack Pennick, Paul Hurst.

Dinner at Eight. 1933. Produced by David O. Selznick for MGM. Directed by George Cukor. Scenario by Frances Marion and Herman J. Mankiewicz from the play by George S. Kaufman and Edna Ferber. Marie Dressler, John Barrymore, Lionel Barrymore, Wallace Beery, Jean Harlow, Lee Tracy, Edmund Lowe, Billie Burke, Madge Evans, Jean Hersholt, Karen Morley, Louise Closser Hale, Phillips Holmes, May Robson, Grant Mitchell, Phoebe Foster, Elizabeth Patterson, Harry Beresford, Hilda Vaughn, Edwin Maxwell, John Davidson, Edward Woods, George Baxter.

Christopher Bean, also released as *Her Sweetheart*. 1933. MGM. Directed by Sam Wood. Scenario by Sylvia Thalberg and Laurence E. Johnson from the play *The Late Christopher Bean* by Sidney Howard, itself adapted from the French play *Prenez garde a la peinture* by René Fauchois. Marie Dressler, Lionel Barrymore, Helen Mack, Beulah Bondi, Russell Hardie, Jean Hersholt, H.B. Warner, Helen Shipman, George Coulouris, Ellen Lowe.

Notes

Note: See Bibliography for complete publication information for the sources listed below.

Information concerning the life of Marie Dressler was drawn from three major sources: the Robinson Locke Dramatic Collection in the Billy Rose Room of the New York Library of the Performing Arts; an unpublished memoir written between 1927 and 1934 by Dressler's close friend Claire Dubrey; and Dressler's two autobiographies.

Scrapbooks from the Robinson Locke Dramatic Collection contain newspaper clippings painstakingly assembled by Locke, *Toledo Blade* editor and drama critic, between 1860 and 1920; the scrapbooks devoted exclusively to Marie Dressler are numbered 163 and 164. All clippings are clearly dated and conveniently clustered in chronological order as to month, year, even subject, but, unfortunately, many lack identification of origin.

I have drawn extensively on an unpublished memoir written by Claire Dubrey, who was Dressler's close friend between 1927 and 1932. My acquisition of the rare and—until then—forgotten manuscript occurred only by chance. After writing to film historian Tony Thomas in 1993 about research difficulties with the Dressler project, Thomas advised me to ask Sonja Bolle, editor of the *Los Angeles Times Book Review*, to publish a request for help. I asked if anyone reading the newspaper could forward information concerning individuals who had been Dressler associates during her years in Hollywood. I included a short list of names, one of which was that of Claire Dubrey, who had frequently been mentioned as a Dressler intimate in the news reports and articles I had managed to locate. To my delight, I soon received a note—written on prescription notepaper—from a Los Angeles pediatrician who told me that Dubrey was still living in West Hollywood and that she was one hundred years old and extremely frail. He recommended that I get in touch with actor John Phillip Law, a longtime Dubrey friend and also her conservator. I followed the advice, and Law eventually confirmed that Dubrey was indeed still living but probably incapable of responding to an interview. The actor also confirmed that the woman had been close to Dressler for at least five years but that he had never seen or heard of any diary or letters that might tell me more about the friendship. I had almost written off the Dubrey lead when Law called to tell me he had asked the woman's housekeeper to search her house for any surviving papers involving the Canadian-born superstar. A parcel had been found that contained a typed manuscript with the name "Marie Dressler" clearly marked on the paper wrapping. The parcel had apparently remained untouched for sixty years. In the months ahead, I visited Los Angeles, met, and even talked to an extremely weak Claire Dubrey and obtained Law's permission to use the manuscript. The document turned out to be a memoir rather than a biography, a highly revealing account of Dressler's personal life, soaring success, and eventual illness and death. But why did the memoir disappear, and why did no one attempt to edit and publish the manuscript while Dressler was still affectionately remembered in the 1930s?

After corresponding with Little, Brown, the Boston firm that had published Dressler's 1934 ghost-written autobiography *My Own Story*, I was eventually granted access to a file that helped solve the mystery. Letters and memos supplied by the publisher showed that when Dressler agreed in 1933 to cooperate with New York journalist Mildred Harrington in writing a series of articles for Redbook magazine there was a further consensus that the pieces could be expanded into an as told to autobiography. Dressler worked at the job of dictating relevant material to her secretary, but she soon became bored with the project and directed that large sections of her 1924 ghosted book, *The Life Story of an Ugly Duckling*, be dispatched—without any appropriate explanation—to the unsuspecting Harrington. By that time Dressler had severed relations with Claire Dubrey and had either forgotten or chose to ignore the fact that her former friend had been working on a memoir for some time. The Redbook pieces were published between August and November 1934, but Little, Brown had already begun making plans for *My Own Story* (originally entitled *You Made Me What I Am Today*) before Dressler's death in July of that year. The publisher's files show that the company wanted to publish the autobiography in October, believing it would be a wise move to release the book while the Dressler legend was still fresh in the public mind.

By August 1934, however, it became clear that the Harrington book was heading into stormy waters. The first hint of trouble came when Richard Butler Glaenzer, an editor with Robert M. McBride, complained that if Little, Brown's book incorporated material similar to articles then being published in Redbook, his firm would give notice of intention to protect its rights under copyright. "Be advised," read Glaenzer's letter, "that the major part of Redbook's material appears to be quoted verbatim from *The Life Story of an Ugly Duckling*, published by us." The next and even more serious sign of trouble came from Los Angeles. Marie Dressler's executor, Allen Breed Walker, wrote to Mildred Harrington's agent warning that because the actress had died before approving the final manuscript of an autobiography—or even before approving the appearance of any book at all—he could not allow such publication by Little, Brown to go ahead. Interestingly, several newspaper stories appeared at this time concerning a Dressler book written by Claire Dubrey, apparently headed for publication some time later in 1934. So was the Walker objection somehow linked to Dubrey's belief that her manuscript would not only sink the Mildred Harrington–Little, Brown property, but also take advantage of the still-current interest in Dressler's roller-coaster life? It is tempting to believe so. Allen Walker and his wife Kitty were not only close Dressler friends but Dubrey intimates as well. There is strong evidence that the executor was unhappy that the two women were estranged, and a personal letter accompanying the Dubrey memoir shows that Walker not only knew of the ongoing work but approved highly of the result.

A memo contained in the Little, Brown file, in fact, reports that a company staffer encountered Walker in Los Angeles sometime that August and learned that he was actively pursuing a publisher for the Dubrey manuscript. Walker gave the staffer Dubrey's address, and there was even a telephone conversation during which Dressler's former friend was invited to send her manuscript to New York for an appraisal. This never happened. Sixty-year-old notes accompanying the memoir show that the writer submitted the work to a string of leading publishers, none of them Little, Brown. The number of rejections could have meant that no publishing house was interested in pulling the fascinating though disorganized material into shape, but it is more likely that the publishers themselves were wary of any Dressler book because of the widely publicized legal headaches being endured at Little, Brown. Nothing more was heard of the Dubrey memoir until it was discovered in 1993.

The first of Dressler's autobiographies, *Life Story of an Ugly Duckling* (1924), was ghostwritten by two of Dressler's friends, Helena Drayton and Louise Barrett; the second, *My Own Story* (1934), was, as mentioned above, "as told to" journalist Mildred Harrington. Unfortunately, both books frequently contradict each other, even though Dressler supplied an unknowing Harrington with large sections of the first autobiography.

I drew also on newspaper and periodical clippings maintained by the Margaret Herrick Library in Los Angeles; the Museum of Modern Art film library, New York; the Toronto Public Library; the Free Library of Philadelphia; the Ohio State University Library in Columbus; Little, Brown in Boston; and the Shubert Archives, New York.

A potentially important source of information, the MGM Archives then managed by the Turner Entertainment Company, Culver City, remained consistently unavailable, even after numerous requests for access; the archives, currently housed in Atlanta, Georgia, are apparently still closed to researchers.

1. BIRTHDAY WISHES

On Friday, November 10, 1933, newspapers throughout the United States and Canada were crammed with stories concerning Marie Dressler's lavish birthday party the previous evening at the MGM studios in Culver City. Extensive reports were published in the *Los Angeles Times*, the *Santa Barbara Daily News*, and the *San Francisco Examiner*. Most assumed that the actress was sixty-two years of age, but W.R. Wilkerson of the *Hollywood Reporter* got it right by informing his readers that Dressler was sixty-five. The *Toronto Star* of November 10 and the weekly *Cobourg Sentinel Star* ran special stories and features honoring the Ontario-born motion picture celebrity. I have relied on these reports as well as miscellaneous news stories published before the party and features published during the week of November 13 in *Film Daily and Variety*.

2. FIRST TASTE OF DRAMA

Because of the inconsistencies in Dressler's two autobiographies, I had difficulty substantiating many of Dressler's childhood memories, particularly those concerning her family. Some stories that appear in *My Own Story*, for example, are not included in the earlier *Ugly Duckling*, and most stories from both are lacking in dates, locations, and proper names. The reminiscences of veteran Cobourg residents and those of Irene Marsh Powell, a Dressler second cousin, have helped flesh out the frustratingly sparse information provided by the actress's two autobiographies. Even in Dressler's lifetime the record was muddy. "When my name was blazing in lights on Times Square, Saginaw put in a lusty claim to me as a native daughter. This claim was disputed by Toronto (Canada), Bay City (Michigan), Findlay (Ohio) and other places too numerous to catalogue. I was so thrilled to find myself fought over that I tacitly decided to allow myself to be adopted by each community in turn. But I was actually born in Cobourg, Ontario, Canada," she wrote.

Some hard facts are available, though. The microfilm records of St. Peter's Episcopalian Church in Cobourg are preserved in the archives of the Anglican Church of Canada (Diocese of Toronto) and clearly show the actress was born in the small southern Ontario city on November 9, 1868. (The registrar mistakenly recorded her first name as "Lalia.") Details of her father's background are simply not available, though we do know from the church record and from Guillet's

Cobourg that he worked as an organist and piano teacher and enjoyed staging "tableaux." The history of Dressler's maternal grandparents is so suspiciously theatrical in *My Own Story* that I was grateful for the down-to-earth research supplied by Bruce C. Stinson of Allison, Ontario, who has been tracing the story of the Marsh family—close relatives of Dressler's mother, Anna Henderson. The story of Dressler's grandfather George Henderson Jr. and his murdered brother Thomas was published in W. Arnot Craick's *Historical Sketches of Port Hope* (Port Hope: n.p., 1901). Craick's book contains the quotes from former Cobourg residents Mrs. Floyd Smith and Murray B. Smith. Dressler's great uncle was murdered by a George Brogdin, who claimed that Henderson had eloped with his wife. During his trial, the jury was so understanding of Brogdin's husbandly anguish that they acquitted him of the crime.

Another source of information concerning Dressler's childhood is the national press: The actress loved giving interviews and many of these contained anecdotes about her father, mother, and sundry aunts and uncles who were never satisfactorily identified. *San Francisco Chronicle* reporter Frances Joliffe, in the spring of 1913, wrote the story of Dressler's uncles sitting as Canadian members of parliament. The information that Dressler never penned anything more substantial than brief messages and thank-you notes is contained in Dubrey's memoir. The story about the actress giving a recital at the age of four was written by an unnamed *Philadelphia Telegraph* reporter in 1915.

I am indebted to Dr. Roberta Raider Sloan, now with the University of Central Oklahoma, whose perceptive 1970 thesis, "A Descriptive Study of the Acting of Marie Dressler," contained excerpts from letters and interviews with Dressler's cousin Mrs. Roy S. (Irene Marsh) Powell. Mrs. Powell—who was chosen to unveil a provincial historical plaque at Dressler's birthplace in August 1970—died not long after these contacts with Dr. Sloan, and, despite extensive research and advertising, I could find no survivors of her family. All letters and photographs known to be owned by Mrs. Powell seem to have vanished. Dr. Sloan also corresponded with another Dressler cousin, Moss McWhirter of Winnipeg, Manitoba. MacWhirter died in 1981. Yet another Winnipeg cousin, Ida Sutcliff, died in 1953, although a niece now living in Montreal wrote to tell me that Mrs. Sutcliff took "a long trip" after receiving a five-thousand-dollar bequest from Dressler's will in 1934. Further research and advertising throughout the United States and Canada have not revealed the existence of any other individuals who are aware they are related to the actress or who know any significant details about her life.

The extravagant town hall that was opened in Cobourg in 1860 by Edward, Prince of Wales, still stands and is now known as Victoria Hall.

3. On the Road

There is evidence that Dressler was hurt that no relatives bothered to photograph her as a child. Her cousin, Irene Powell, remembered daguerrographs of the the actress's sister Bonita and an unnamed cousin holding the rope of what was presumably a sled; Dressler made a joke out of the daguerrograph story in her autobiographies. She recalled that when visitors asked "And where were you dear?" she invariably replied, "I was sitting on the sled." Dressler has also told us about her height and hair coloring. The comment concerning her hands comes from a *Boston Herald* report of July 1904. The Findlay resident who remembered an early performance of *Under Two Flags* was a Mrs. Hurin, speaking to a reporter of an unidentified local newspaper.

I am grateful to theatrical historians Cecil Smith, David Ewen, Brooks Atkinson, and Gerald Bordman for invaluable information on the American theatre scene in the late nineteenth and early twentieth centuries. Philip Lewis has written eloquently of the early road shows, and manager Robert Grau allowed me a glimpse of the touring theatrical life.

4. Champion of the Underdog

The Panic of 1893 has been well documented by American political historians, particularly by Golman. Bordman (*American Musical Theatre*), Atkinson, and Churchill provided me with insights into theatrical activity during the close of the nineteenth century as well as details concerning Abraham Lincoln Erlanger and the syndicate. My sources also include Bronner; Lyman, who describes the theatres attracting large audiences on Broadway and the Madison Square district; and Collins Brown's journal, *Valentine's Manual*, which provides information about life on the Great White Way.

Dubrey recalled an incident that could provide a real clue as to whether Dressler really married the shadowy George Hoeppert in 1899. While Dressler was filming *Prosperity*, a table had been set up outside of the studio commissary to allow the thousands of MGM workers a chance to register for the upcoming election. Dubrey suggested to her friend, who was always interested in politics, that it might be a good idea to register at that time, but Dressler replied: "Not now. I'm busy." Dubrey stopped to attend to her own registration, then caught up with Dressler on her way to the set. "Why didn't you get it over with?" she asked the actress. "Oh, you know," replied Dressler. "I'd have to go into all that business about being born in Canada." "But," responded Dubrey, "you married a U.S. citizen. That makes you one, doesn't it?" Dressler waggled her jaw. "It makes me a good enough one to go out and pay my own expenses for a year while I sold Liberty Bonds. But there still seems to be some red tape about it and I don't feel like standing in front of the commissary answering questions!"

Later, in 1934, when the House Committee on Immigration and Naturalization in Washington was exploring a new measure that would legislate tough new rules for foreign actors wanting to work in the U.S., Dressler again invoked the name of Hoeppert. But it is perhaps significant that Montreal-born Norma Shearer found that a 1928 amendment to an Act of Congress not only deprived her of Canadian citizenship when she married Irving Thalberg, it forced her to apply for U.S. papers as well; perhaps Dressler feared the same. Even if she had married Hoeppert, she might have believed the 1928 law also applied to individuals who had previously taken their vows. Interestingly, Claire Dubrey admitted during the last interview before her death that "Marie claimed she never married anyone."

Morell was an invaluable source of information concerning Lillian Russell. Russell deserted Signor Perugini not long after the marriage that so worried her friend Dressler. Four years later, Russell married publisher Alexander P. Moore of Pittsburgh and eventually retired from the stage. In 1921, after a European trip, she fell on the deck of a ship and was injured. She died from complications resulting from the accident in 1922.

For many details of Dressler's life before 1920 I relied on the Locke collection. The story of Dressler's joust with actress Beula Coolidge is dated April 6, 1899, but the name of the newspaper publishing the report is not given. The clipping informing readers about Dressler's controversial outing at the New York Aerial Grove with a "negro servant" was published in November 1899, but its origin was also unidentified. The servant involved was not named, but I assume it was Jenny, because, according to *My Own Story*, she was working for Dressler at that time. The story of Dressler's complaint that she was unfairly considered to be an alien and attributed to the Associated Press was published in the *New York World Telegram* February 24, 1934, and was included in a file of miscellaneous Dressler clippings in the Locke collection.

Because Dressler failed to adequately document her theatrical appearances, her autobiographical reminiscences had to be checked against the more reliably dated Locke clippings and against general information gleaned from theatrical histories by Bordman and Cecil Smith as well as other informal readings. I am also grateful to have been able to examine the Marie Dressler clipping files from the Free Library of Philadelphia and the Harvard University Library Theatre Collection, which were invaluable in helping me arrive at a consensus concerning the nature and scope of Dressler's career as a Broadway actress and star.

Maurice Barrymore's career took a tragic downturn a few years after his work on *Waldemar, The Robber of the Rhine*. He was committed to the Long Island Home for the Insane in 1901 with syphilitic paresis of the brain. The talented actor died on March 25, 1905, at the age of fifty-five.

Dan Daly was no relation to the equally great actor-manager Augustin Daly.

May Irwin, a Canadian born in Whitby, Ontario, just a few miles from Dressler's birthplace, enjoyed a long and successful career in vaudeville. But she will always be best known for her participation in the Edison Company's 1895 film, *The Kiss*. The short movie has become one of the most famous early films in the history of the cinema.

"Coon songs" were ballads that were supposed to treat audiences to a "warm and affectionate look at the Negro lifestyle" (popular tunes: "If the Man in the Moon Was a Coon" and "Hot Tamale Alley" [by George M. Cohan]). They fast became a theatrical fad in the 1890s and were accepted without public protest until at least 1906 and were not really discouraged by theatrical producers until the formation of the NAACP in 1909.

Dressler's cousin Moss MacWhirter wrote from Winnipeg to Ph.D. candidate Roberta Raider Sloan in 1970.

5. Entrepreneurial Spirit

Press reports of Dressler's foray into theatre management with *Miss Prinnt* appeared in Boston, Albany, and Philadelphia. Most of the coverage of her bankruptcy in March 1901 was originally published in New York. The report of the Sire brothers' offer of the lead role in *The King's Carnival* was published in a May 1901 edition of *Billboard*, and Dressler herself remembered the comic falls with Louis Harrison and Dan McAvoy in *Ugly Duckling*. *Billboard* also reported the story of Dressler's brief interest in "Kid" McCoy's hotel in its October 26, 1901, issue.

It is interesting to note how many feature writers beat a path to Dressler's dressing room door in search of article material in 1901-2. Sunday supplement pieces under bylines such as Mlle. Manhattan, Lady Holyrood, the Meddler, and John Mars could run for more than two thousand words and most included several photographs ("a typical Dressleresque pose—an effect produced on the farm with a ragged curtain, faded flowers and other old things") and scores of sometimes outrageous Dressler pronouncements. Occasionally, the features even included a ghost-written piece ("Miss Dressler's Advice to Young Stage Aspirants") with a Dressler byline. Outrageous or controversial pronouncements literally cram Dressler's turn-of-the-century press clippings, and she had no trouble bringing her complaints about the "fondling and cuddling" of chorus girls by stage managers into sharp public focus. Her high profile with Manhattan journalists became so well established that when she fell ill with typhoid in the fall of 1902, New York newspapers rushed to report every aspect of her condition. One November 19 dispatch in the *Telegraph* informed readers that Dressler was "near death," and pages of the Locke scrapbooks are packed with pieces concerning her mother's coincidental demise, Dressler's delirium, her loss of hair and weight, and the efforts of her fellow thespians to stage a benefit on her behalf. Dressler herself contributed various but somewhat scrambled reminiscences about this period of her life in the pages of her autobiographies. Other writers, such as Adela Rogers St. Johns and Leonard S. Smith, profiled her in several long episodes for the *New York Post* in 1934 and tried to capture some of the life-and-death drama and irrepressible high jinks of the period, but her friends in the Manhattan press did the best job of all: lavish picture features showing Dressler with her army of young peanut vendors on the Coney Island boardwalk and other layouts showering her with publicity for the Dreamland concession ("Miss Dressler shown drinking tea at her Chinese eating emporium; Miss Dressler with her sixteen-ounce incubator baby") survive in the Locke scrapbooks.

6. Theatrical Aristocrat

The theatrical press and even news journalists obviously found Dressler's debut at Weber's Music Hall in 1904 worthy of enthusiastic attention, and scores of clippings give detailed background to the story and its eventual aftermath. Armond and L. Marc Fields trace the career of Weber and Fields and their unique contribution to the American theatrical scene, and I am personally indebted to Marc Fields, who generously shared his opinions of the Dressler-Fields-Weber relationship and its influence on the individuals concerned. Dressler herself reminisced in her autobiographies about the years between 1904 and 1907, but she typically ignores the most unflattering aspects of the way she turned her back on Joe Weber in 1906.

Bordman, Atkinson, and Ewen were important sources for this chapter; Cleveland Amory's two books and Jane S. Smith's provided important information on the subject of New York's society celebrities—especially Mrs. Mamie Stuyvesant Fish, Dressler's influential patron. There's no doubt that Mrs. Stuyvesant Fish endeared herself to Dressler and, in fact, the actress may have, knowingly or unknowingly, modeled herself on the wealthy but unconventional hostess. One story recounted by Amory is particularly illustrative: Once, at the beginning of the friendship, Dressler asked if she could come to dinner rather than arrive afterward to entertain the guests "because," she explained, "I want to tell my mother I have had dinner with Mrs. Stuyvesant Fish." The hostess smilingly replied: "I will be proud to tell my children that Marie Dressler has dined with me."

Twiddle Twaddle opened the same night as the biggest hit of the 1906 season, George M. Cohan's *Forty-five Minutes from Broadway*, starring former Weber and Fields superstar, Fay Templeton. Songs from the show, "So Long Mary," "Mary's a Grand Old Name," and "Forty-five Minutes from Broadway" became classics of the American musical theatre.

7. SUNNY JIM

A clear picture of James H. Dalton is not possible from available sources. Dressler's friends, Adela Rogers St. Johns, Frances Marion, and Claire Dubrey have mentioned him in their reminiscences but never actually described the man, even though they were generally unenthusiastic about his personal qualities. Dressler herself ignored Dalton in her autobiographies—except one enigmatic statement that she had loved only one man, who "has been dead for many years"—despite the fact that the record clearly shows their lives were intimately intertwined. Clippings from the Locke collection yield only three fuzzy pictures of Dalton; he was tall, corpulent, and he wore a bowler hat with flair. Feature stories published in the national press between 1910 and 1920 occasionally drop hints concerning Dalton's appearance—an unidentified San Francisco piece published in 1911 mentions his "gold chains and gewgaws"—but there were frequent between-the-lines hints of Dalton's unpredictable persona. In her memoir, Frances Marion revealed that Dressler had told her in the late 1920s that Dalton had persuaded the actress to sell her property in Elmhurst to help sweeten the London pot.

Frohman was drowned when the *Lusitania* was torpedoed by a German U-boat in May 1915. Coincidentally, his West End rival, George Edwardes died in October of that same year.

I am indebted to W. Macqueen Pope, Daphne du Maurier, and J.A. Hammerton for their colorful portraits of the people and places that made—and still make—London's West End a target for theatre professionals. Because Dressler was a favorite newsmaker in the New York press, Locke found it possible to collect enough clippings in 1907 and 1908 to fill several pages of his scrapbooks on the subject of the actress's appearances at the Palace. London reviews were published in New York, and the *Herald* even assigned a special correspondent to keep an eye on her activities and published the story of her lack of interest in Alfred Butt's three-year contract. The *Telegraph* scooped its New York rivals in January 1908 with the report that Dressler was thinking of staging a musical comedy under her own management in London. Although Broadway reporters seemed sympathetic to Dressler's adventures in the West End, their editors were just as happy to allow their columnists and critics to dissect her failure with *Philopoena*.

Dressler's own recollections of the fiasco in her autobiographies are sketchy and clearly unreliable.

8. The Working Girl

I am grateful to Maryann Chach, archivist of the Shubert Archive in New York, who sent me photocopies of memos, letters, and contracts relating to *Tillie's Nightmare*, Lee Shubert's violent disagreement with Jim Dalton, and the decision in 1911 to sell the production to Dressler and her companion. Judging from the number of angry communications flying between Shubert, his lawyers, and members of his staff, it is clear that the manager had little respect for Dalton or even for Dressler when she began making noises about abandoning the show for a stint with Sir Oswald Stoll. A letter from Lee Shubert's office to lawyer William Klein on July 19, 1911, indicates, in fact, that both Dressler and Dalton were thought to be preparing a clandestine escape to London in order to avoid the service of papers on Sunny Jim.

Little of this backstage drama seems to have come to the attention of the Broadway press. The *New York Telegraph* did report somewhat precipitously in July that Dressler had actually quit the Shuberts and was heading for London, and a story about her on-stage party at the Lyric Theatre in Philadelphia also appeared. Typically, Dressler had nothing to say about this controversial matter in either of her autobiographies. There was ample coverage of *Tillie*, of course, not only in New York, but also in other venues in which the play was performed. Long and detailed stories out of Skaneateles also carried generous layouts of photographs.

Again, I am indebted to Atkinson, Morell, L. Marc and Armond Fields, Cecil Smith, Bordman, and Ewen for their insights into this period of theatrical history.

Sam, the third Shubert brother, died in 1905 after a mysterious explosion wrecked a train on which he was traveling from New York to Pittsburgh.

9. The Height of Her Power

Extensive news reports and features appeared in the *Toronto Star and Globe* on the Toronto visit in 1912; the *Star* also reported that managing director Lawrence Solman was delighted to accept the help of James Dalton in planning and staging the big music festival. Preliminary coverage as well as reports of the event itself even surpassed that lavished on a six-day bicycle race to be held at the new Mutual Arena the week following the gala. The Mutual Arena eventually became known as the Terrace and was popular with Torontonians as a roller-skating rink. Despite protests from the Toronto Historical Board, the seventy-seven year old building was demolished in 1989.

Churchill's book contains a discussion of the Lambs Club. The author noted that actor Henry E. Dixey, a prominent Lamb, was once asked why he consumed so much alcohol. Dixey replied, "When I drink, I think, and when I think, I drink." Apparently, this was rated as cold, clear logic at the Lambs Club. Churchill also reported that the Lambs thought very little of their rival actors' club, the Players. The Players boasted members such as Edwin Booth and John Drew as well as some prominent writers and artists, a mix of membership that drew scorn from the exclusively theatrical Lambs.

Numerous news stories published in the summer of 1913 show that Dressler and Dalton were flattered by their chance to entertain the Woodrow Wilsons at their Vermont farm, even though it was well known on Broadway that the actress had backed the defeated Republican presidential candidate William Taft in the 1912 presidential election. Dressler and Dalton were so flattered, in fact, that they also spent a considerable amount of money feeding and watering the armies of newspaper correspondents and secret service agents who accompanied the presidential party to Cornish. One story had Dalton "dropping in" on the entourage and remarking that he had a "little" place up the road with a pool table or two, a swimming pool, tennis courts, a few cows, and a well provided cellar. Later, according to the report, "Miss Dressler met the cavalcade on the veranda." Interestingly, this happened at a time when the *All Star Gambol* was becoming something of a financial drain. I am indebted to Maryann Chach and the Shubert Archives for copies of Dressler's 1913 personal contract and a letter written to Lee Shubert concerning her five-thousand-dollar loan and contract postponement.

In May 1917, Dalton and Dressler were sued by soprano Nielsen for fraud. The complaint was that the singer was "inveigled" into investing in the stock of Ulida Consolidated Copper Company of California with Dalton listed as president. The shares were eventually proved to be worthless. This investment was made in 1914—Nielsen became friends with Dressler and Dalton in Toronto and became one of the regulars at Loafhaven—but the "fraud" was not discovered until 1916. Dressler made no public comments concerning the suit and Nielsen herself never did receive compensation from the actress. However, the singer claimed the forty-five hundred dollars against Dressler's will in 1934, and the probate court upheld the petition.

10. MARIE DRESSLER'S MERRY GAMBOL

The New York press was relatively noncommittal concerning Dressler's proposed entrepreneurial activity in San Francisco. Stories in the *Dramatic Mirror*, the *Telegraph*, and the *New York Review* in January and February 1914 reported progress—and lack of progress—

with the *Merry Gambol* show at the Gaiety. But the richest source of information was the San Francisco press, particularly the *Examiner*, which ran detailed stories in early February 1914 (now on microfilm at the San Francisco Public Library) of the Gaiety row, the Mann Act scandal, and its aftermath. Most stories were front-page news and were accompanied by large photographs of Dressler—clutching her bosom in outrage and distress—and "Bronco Billy" complete with six-guns. Pieces published in the eastern newspapers were incomplete and confusing by comparison.

Pioneer Hollywood producer Mack Sennett wrote his version of the *Tillie's Punctured Romance* filming in his autobiography, but these reminiscences must be balanced against Dressler's version of her movie debut in *My Own Story*. Certainly Sennett never hinted at the contractural agreements or subsequent problems that eventuated after the Los Angeles shoot. The Roscoe "Fatty" Arbuckle anecdote is from Edmonds, and Chaplin's reaction to his work in *Tillie* is described in his autobiography and in Robinson. I am indebted to Finch and Rosenkrantz and Brownlow for their descriptions of early Hollywood and Bogdanovich and Berg for their biographies of Dwan and Goldwyn, respectively. The story of Thomas O'Day, business manager of the Gaiety and why he would be showing *Tillie* at his theatre was published in the New York *Telegraph* on January 19, 1915.

11. Mix-ups and Movies

Dressler was so busy professionally and socially during the years 1914 and 1915 that there is no paucity of press clippings to help track her activities. Court proceedings involving the contract altercations with Keystone were covered in detail by the *New York Evening World*, the *Telegram*, and the *Review* and picked up by newspapers across the country. Once again, I am indebted to Maryann Chach and the Shubert Archives for making available copies of the company's October 1914 contract with Dressler for *Angela's Substitute*, the play that was eventually renamed *A Mix Up*. Chach also supplied copies of memos and letters relating to this agreement.

Dressler's exploits as a drum-thumper for Mrs. O.H.P. Belmont received considerable coverage in New York. Elsa Maxwell, who wrote the music for *Melinda and Her Sisters*, remembered in her memoir that Mrs. Belmont liked her because she had "get up and go," which is perhaps the reason that the formidable Alva warmed to the equally formidable Dressler.

The actress also made friends with a young Louella Parsons at this time. No doubt the fledgling columnist was intrigued to hear from the actress why she decided to try the movies as a career in 1914 and 1915. According to a September 15, 1915, column in the *Chicago Her-

ald, Dressler told Parsons: "I went into movies for the same reason that took me into vaudeville. I needed the money." Another footnote on the theme of newspaper columnists involves Mary Pickford, whose byline appeared on a *Daily Talks* column for the McClure Newspaper Syndicate in 1915 and 1916; even though Pickford was already a busy movie star in Hollywood, the column often followed Dressler's bewilderingly diverse adventures. This is not surprising in the light of the fact that Pickford was a fellow-Canadian and that the column was actually written by another close friend of Dressler, scenarist Frances Marion.

12. WAR WORK

Once again, the scrapbooks of the Locke collection are the most reliable sources for details of Dressler's theatrical and motion picture activities in 1916 and 1917. Clippings from the *New York Telegraph*, the *World*, the *Mail*, the *Toledo Blade* and *Moving Picture World*, checked against Cecil Smith's *Musical Comedy in America* and Dressler's autobiographies, provide strong material on which to base the actress's story during this period. Ferrell's book provided insights into the events of April 1917 and the declaration of war between the United States and Germany. Berg's book was invaluable for information on the beginnings of the National Association of the Motion Picture Industry, and Ferrell's history was helpful in tracing the birth and progress of the Liberty Bond campaigns. An interesting footnote gleaned from Ferrell's research: in 1917 the United States Treasury enrolled children in a penny and nickel-saving campaign to buy 25-cent thrift stamps that would hopefully accumulate into interest-bearing certificates by the end of the war. The campaign was accompanied by a slogan that read "Hush little thrift stamp, don't you cry: you'll be a war bond, by and by." Ferrell also believes that the bond sales of 1917 and 1918 accustomed Americans to purchasing paper instruments of value. Charlie Chaplin and Mary Pickford both wrote about their experiences during the Liberty Loan campaign in their memoirs; their reminiscences are roughly identical, except for one or two differences concerning the Dream Team's visit to Washington. I gained further insights into the Liberty Loan tour from Robinson, Walker, Eyman, Herndon, and Brownlow. Dressler herself spent fewer words than Chaplin and Pickford on her Liberty Loan travels in her autobiographies, but she never failed to mention her contribution whenever an interviewer asked about her whereabouts during the war years. "When the Armistice was declared, I had the satisfaction of having sold more bonds than any other individual in the United States," she boasted.

I have not found an appropriate quote by Dressler, but there is no doubt that the actress must have been delighted in August 1920 when the nineteenth amendment gave American women the vote. It was well known that President Woodrow Wilson opposed women's suffrage, but he changed his views during the First World War. Wilson felt that women had earned the vote because of the way they took the place of many men in industry and agriculture as well as in the Navy and Marine Corps. It is possible that the president might also have had Marie Dressler and other dedicated actress-salespersons in mind.

13. Striking for the Ponies

"I never could keep out of a good fight," Dressler says in *Ugly Duckling*, "and in the year following the close of the war, I jumped into the Equity scrap of 1919." The scrapbooks of the Locke collection show how the actress kept herself solidly center stage during the unprecedented actors' strike of that year. Her position as president of the chorus girls' union earned her more publicity than of the other Equity dissidents, and photographs of her striding militantly down Broadway or flashing the "No More Pay, Just Fair Play" banner became an integral part of strike coverage in the national press. Her activities during the brouhaha made so much of an impact that when she addressed a group of striking garment workers to "cheer them up" after she had won her chorus contract, the New York press rushed to cover the normally low-key event. A story published in the *New York Sun* on September 9, 1919, three days after the actors' strike ended, shows she happily accepted an invitation to address members of the Women's Trade Union League. Dressed in a lace gown and wearing a pink hat with feathers, she admitted that the proudest day of her life was when she found that she and the other chorus girls "had shoved the President of the United States" off the front page of the newspapers. I have also drawn on Harding, Kotsilibas-Davis, Peters, and Atkinson. The story of Dressler's embarrassing altercation with Paul Dalzell, deputy for Actors' Equity, backstage at the New York Riviera appeared in *Variety* April 21, 1920. It was not until 1933 that minimum pay for actors was written into Equity agreements and then just forty dollars for performers who had been Equity members for two years and twenty-five dollars for all others. It was also not until the mid-1930s that rehearsal pay was written into the Equity contract. One reason for the delay seems to have been that actors liked to think of themselves as artists, not laborers, and that negotiating for cash was not considered to be dignified.

14. Marie's Nightmare

In *My Own Story* Dressler makes it quite clear that she believed Benito Mussolini to be a great man and certainly the savior of Italy after the First World War. She rationalized that Italy recovered from the war much faster than other countries and that Il Duce was responsible for the comeback. Confirmation of Dressler's mistrust of the medical profession comes from Dubrey and from December 1921 newspaper reports of Jim Dalton's death that indicate he was being treated by a Christian Scientist practitioner. Dubrey quotes Dressler's maid, Mamie Cox, who remembered that Dressler was always more interested in natural remedies than in prescription drugs.

Dressler's fascination with astrology is well documented by Dubrey and by the actress herself in *My Own Story*. Dressler described her friend astrologer Nella Webb in her 1934 autobiography as "small, dark, animated, with the grace of a hummingbird and the persistence of a bull pup. She and I have known each other since the days of my early Broadway success, *Lady Slavey*." Webb died December l, 1954, at the age of seventy-eight. Her obituary in *Variety* describes her as a former musical comedy actress who appeared in the original production of *Babes in Toyland*. She toured England and Australia with the show, then worked as an astrologer after her retirement from the theatre.

The account of Dressler's work with filmmaker Herry Reichenbach was provided by the actress herself in *Ugly Duckling*. I am grateful to Spitzer's book for information concerning the actress's appearance at the theatre in fall 1925.

15. Door to the Future

Dressler was quite specific about the events of early 1927 and spends several pages of *My Own Story* describing them. These pages are the only record of Nella Webb's predictions and of Dressler's fateful meeting with director Allan Dwan except for Dwan's own recollections in Peter Bogdanovich's book. I have drawn from both sources, taking particular note of Dwan's conflicting claim that he paid Dressler's way to Hollywood and "took care of her." I have drawn on Marion's recollections as well as Dressler's *My Own Story* to tell the story of her April 1927 trip to Hollywood; it is unclear whether the first message from Hollywood about *The Callahans and the Murphys* role was in the form of a telephone call or a telegram. The Dressler and Marion books both confirm the story of Irving Thalberg's acceptance of his scenarist's recommendation of Dressler in the Ma Callahan role and the eventual disaster when the movie was released. News stories concerning the disapproval of Irish groups when the film was publicly screened appeared in *Variety* and the major New York dailies in July and August 1927. The most critical coverage was concentrated in the *Irish World* and the *American Industrial Liberator*. These files are available in the Billy Rose Room of the New York Public Library of the Performing Arts.

I am indebted to Higham, Kreuger, Marx, Eames, and Maltin for insights into the end of the silent era and the advent of the talkies in Hollywood. Movies of the period were reviewed, complete with full cast and technical information in the *New York Times* and *Variety*. The story of Marion's "bonuses" from Louis B. Mayer was recounted by Harry and Brown. Dressler's happy memory of Mr. and Mrs. Arthur Neurmberg's birthday check in 1928 is recorded in *My Own Story*.

Marion was an individual who—like Dressler—valued old and new friendships. She first met the actress in San Francisco during the 1912 tour of *Tillie's Nightmare*. At the time, Marion was a reporter with the Hearst newspapers and Dressler was currently boycotting the group because of a questionable quote. The young journalist was so distraught when the famous comedienne refused to grant her an interview, she tearfully threw herself on Dressler's mercy. Dressler, in turn, graciously gave in. Marion never forgot the gesture. The two women met several times during the next few years and at one time, Dressler even helped nurse the young writer back to health after an illness. Then, of course, there was the close professional association during the filming of *Tillie Wakes Up*.

George Hill and Frances Marion were separated in 1931 after the couple admitted that their short marriage had been a failure. Hill committed suicide on August 10, 1934. Marion herself died in 1973 at the age of eight-six.

16. QUEEN MARIE

For this and succeeding chapters I drew heavily on Dubrey's unpublished memoir. The *Saturday Evening Post* published a ghost-written article by Marie Dressler in September 1933, entitled *Down and Up Again*, that was helpful in tracing some of the actress's personal activities before and after her arrival in Hollywood. Much of the information is also available in *My Own Story*. I have drawn on Guiles, Davies, and Lambert for insights into the early MGM all-talking musicals. Background on the *Anna Christie* shoot came from Dubrey, *My Own Story*, Marion, Paris, Maltin, and Bainbridge. I was also fortunate in gaining access to a Special Collections file at the Margaret Herrick Library of the Academy of Motion Picture Arts and Sciences in Los Angeles that yielded memos from MGM executives after the *Anna Christie* release. The story of Dressler's acting assignment in *The Swan* was recounted by Lillian Gish in her autobiography. Dubrey, and Dressler herself in her autobiography, remembered much of the studio and personal activities behind the production of *Min and Bill*, and this information is backed by Marion in her memoir. I drew from director LeRoy's biography for his opinion of the Dressler-Beery relationship, though his comments concern his involvement with a later movie, *Tugboat Annie*, a film that LeRoy erroneously identifies as Dressler's last before her death. Sources also include Eames and Crowther.

17. THE LITTLE DOCTOR

Reading of movie magazines and entertainment publications between 1930 and 1933—the years when Marie Dressler became a genuine celebrity in Hollywood—confirm that she seldom appeared at the high-profile gatherings that attracted most movie stars at the time; she accepted some invitations from Marion Davies and William Randolph Hearst to visit San Simeon, and today's tourists can catch a glimpse of her—wearing what seems to be an extremely ratty fur coat—on one of the Chief's home movies. According to Swanberg, though, Dressler thought Hearst was an ogre and was afraid of him. Certainly, the media tycoon's zoo animals were occasionally intimidating. Glynn tells us about a Hearst chimpanzee named Jerry who would defecate when visitors came by and fling the results at the offending humans. Dressler was once the object of Jerry's unwelcome attentions. But the actress was openly friendly with Hearst's mistress, Marion Davies. Claire Dubrey describes a visit to Davies's luxurious beach house in Santa Monica that Dressler clearly enjoyed. These occasions were rare, however. Dubrey's memoir documents few social occasions that did not involve Dressler's preferred friends in Santa Barbara or New York.

Sources of information concerning Dressler's growing amount of fan mail after the release of *Min and Bill* include *My Own Story* and the Dubrey memoir. In July 1932 *Modern Screen* ran a feature by Jack Jamison entitled "Hollywood's Cruellest Story." The subhead read "It seems unbelievable that Marie Dressler—generous, open-hearted Marie—should be forced to suffer so from the very fact that she is so generous and fine. It is her very good nature which has created for her an incredible group of enemies." The story dealt mainly with the "bushel-baskets" of pleading, even threatening, letters but went too far with its statement that MGM "is forced to send Marie out of town between pictures against her wish, to keep her from wearing herself out calling on persons who are ill and interviewing those who need comfort, advice or money. Except under orders, she will not stop and you can imagine what a drain it is on her strength." The Dubrey memoir makes it clear that although some fan letters were shown to Dressler, most were answered by Dubrey.

The search for any confirmation of Dressler's possible lesbianism proved to be difficult and frustrating. I hasten to admit the possibility that the actress's close friendships with Nella Webb and Claire Dubrey were what was known as platonic "Boston marriages," but a reading of Dubrey's manuscript shows that her liaison with Dressler was highly emotional. During an interview with John Phillip Law, Dubrey's conservator in her later years, the actor told me he had often asked the woman about a love affair with Dressler and that Dubrey had always given him noncommittal answers. He added that the aging Dubrey had admitted to her longtime housekeeper that she and Dressler had been lovers.

Dubrey does not indicate the name of the hospital that handled Dressler's 1931 operation, but an archivist at the Los Angeles College of Chiropractic believes it was the Beverly Hospital, which, at that time, was associated with many chiropractors. Neither Dubrey nor Dressler ever revealed the name of the actress's "little doctor."

Dubrey indicated there were other witnesses to Dressler's "lah-de-dah" posturing, but no one except Dubrey—not even the actress's close friend Frances Marion—ever wrote about it. A gentleman named Alan Brock, who now lives in Hastings on the Hudson in New York, told me that in 1931 he visited some movie-industry friends in Los Angeles; his hosts took him to a restaurant in the Spanish Village, where the group joined Mrs. Wallace Reid, wife of the well-known actor, and some guests. One of the guests was Dressler, apparently enjoying a rare summer outing. Mr. Brock did not recall whether Dubrey was present, but he did remember that the actress "played the grand lady, playing it up like Constance Collier, and talking on and on about her friendship with Elsie de Wolfe. I had the feeling that she wanted to appear more glamorous than she really was."

Richard Cromwell's career took off after *Emma*; he eventually played leading roles in *Lives of a Bengal Lancer*, *Jezebel*, *Young Mr. Lincoln*, and *Parachute Battalion*. He was briefly married to Angela Lansbury. Dressler became a close friend and recommended him to stars such as Tallulah Bankhead and Joan Crawford, who both commissioned portrait masks from the actor and artist. Some of his ceramic tiles were acquired by the Pantages Theatre. Dubrey bought several sculptures from Cromwell, and she regarded them as among her favorite possessions. I saw two stone heads by the actor in Dubrey's West Hollywood garden. Cromwell died of cancer in 1960 at the age of 50.

18. THE TREATMENT

Sources concerning the economic health of the motion picture industry in the Depression years of 1931 and 1932 included the files of *Variety*, the *Hollywood Reporter*, the December 1933 issue of *Fortune*, and Eames, Higham, and Baxter. Stories of Dressler's awards in Britain's John Bull poll and her inclusion in the *Motion Picture Herald*'s list of top money-making stars appeared widely in the motion picture press in September 1931.

Insights into the night of the 1930-31 Academy Awards come

from Wiley and Bona, Brown and Pinkston, reports in the *Los Angeles Times* for November 11, and stories published in *Variety* and the *Hollywood Reporter*. Dubrey's memoir provided more intimate details. Interestingly, the Oscar (as it eventually became known) was not listed as a bequest in Dressler's will. Recently, it was discovered that the statuette is now in the possession of Marilyn Read, a niece of Howard Strickling, the late publicity chief of MGM. Mrs. Read told me that she does not remember details of how or when her uncle acquired the Oscar except that Dressler gave it to him "because they were good friends." The Marie Dressler Foundation continues to ask Mrs. Read to exhibit the award at one of its festivals, without affirmative response.

Detailed obituaries of John Murdock's life appeared in the national press on December 9, 1948, the day after his death in Los Angeles. He was said to be eighty-five years of age, but other reports claim that he was actually ninety-one. Sources for the Thomas Glover story include the Dubrey memoir, the Murdock obituaries, clippings from the *Toronto Globe* dated through June 19, 1920, and the *Globe and Mail* for September 4 and October 10, 1963, and December 11, 1964.

Because of the public ban imposed by Murdock, Dr. Glover, and possibly Louis B. Mayer, Dressler's treatment with the Glover serum was never widely revealed. The question is whether the injections begun in early 1932 resulted in her intermittent remissions or whether they influenced her remarkable periods of energetic productivity in that year and especially in 1933. Dr. Glover stated in the November 1925 edition of the *Canadian Journal of Medicine and Surgery* that patients in the final stages of the disease who were given the serum "showed marked diminution of pain, lessening of discharge and improvement in mentality." He was optimistic about the possibility of a lengthened life span for these individuals. Many other distinguished doctors and pathologists—including Dr. Harrison Leffler of the National Institute of Health in Washington and Dr. Julian Loudon, chief physician of St. Michael's Hospital in Toronto—endorsed his findings. Today, Dr. Loudon's son, Dr. James Loudon of Belleville, Ontario, points out that, apart from those who concurred with Dr. Glover's work in North America and Europe, other well-known scientists, such as Dr. James Young of Edinburgh, arrived independently at the same conclusion. A clipping from the *Toronto Globe and Mail* dated October 31, 1996, reads, "Medical researchers hypothesize that some event, perhaps the trauma of an operation or an infection, stimulates the production of antibodies that destroy a cancer. Around 1900, Dr. William Coley of New York experimentally induced bacterial infections in cancer patients. The use of vaccines, called 'Coley's toxins,' made up of killed bacteria, has caused some tumors to shrink or disappear. In the 1970s, researchers were able to isolate the 'tumor necrosis factor,' a powerful tumor-killing molecule." Discouraged by the lack of response in the United States to his serum, Dr. Glover returned to Toronto in 1938 and established his own private practice as a physician and cancer specialist. For the next thirty years he continued to accept patients and claimed he had considerable success. He died in 1969 at the age of eight-two, not long after a coroner's court investigated the death of a sixty-six-year-old Glover patient and ordered him to cease using his serum.

19. PROSPERITY

Claire Dubrey's memoir is undoubtedly the most reliable—and possibly the only—source of information concerning Marie Dressler's personal and professional activities in 1932. The memoir was checked against books and clippings already examined for insights into MGM productions as well as reviews published in the *New York Times*, *Variety*, and the *Los Angeles Times* in November 1932. The story of Dressler's portable dressing room was supplied by the actress in *My Own Story* and was reported in *Architectural Digest* for April 1992. The magazine also published a photograph.

20. GOD'S EXHIBIT A TO THE WORLD

Once again, I have drawn extensively on Dubrey's unpublished notes for details of Dressler's visit to New York in late 1932. The story of the NBC broadcast to the Academy Award ceremonies in Los Angeles on November 17 is confirmed in Behlmer, Irene Mayer Selznick, and Wiley and Bona. Elisabeth Marbury died less than two months after Dressler's visit to her home in New York. She was seventy-six years of age.

21. MAYER'S MARATHON

I am grateful to Jane Lowenthal, archivist of Barnard College at Columbia University in New York, who sent me details of the American Women's Association papers now filed at Barnard. The papers show that after 1922 the AWA increasingly became an international center and a pioneer in student exchange programs throughout the forties, fifties, and sixties. Its well known Committee on Friendship dinners featured addresses by such influential women as Amelia Earhart, Frances Perkins, Margaret Sanger, and Dorothy Thompson. Marie Dressler bequeathed ten thousand dollars to the AWA, and her name remained on the honor roll of founders. Both she and Anne Morgan would have been happy to hear that, in 1949, the AWA became one of the National Non-Governmental Organizations to be accredited as a representative at the United Nations. The association was disbanded in 1974 when the Internal Revenue Service challenged its tax-free status.

For insights into the production of *Dinner at Eight* I drew on Lambert, McGilligan, Behlmer, Shipman, Stenn, and the Marie Dressler file in Special Collections at the Academy of Motion Picture Arts and Sciences, Los Angeles. One MGM document in the Academy library files shows that Dressler wanted the Pekingese dog featured in the movie to be called Mussolini but the studio felt the Italian government might be offended. The dog was eventually named Tarzan. Another MGM file in the same location shows that when the studio planned to reissue *Dinner at Eight* in 1936, Mayer applied for a certificate of approval under the prevailing production code. A May 15, 1936, memo to Mayer from Joseph Breen of the Motion Picture Producers and Distributors of America indicated that approval would be granted after changes to the original film were made: Dressler's line containing "son of a bitch" was to be cut; the embrace of Kitty and Dr. Talbot was to be cut from the moment she puts her hands on his shoulders to eliminate the rest of the kiss when they sink down on the bed; Dressler's line to the dog about wetting the carpet was to be cut; as was the close-up of Barrymore turning on gas to commit suicide. Another memo to Irving Thalberg from James Wingate of the Association of Motion Picture Producers recommended the trimming of twenty profanities from the movie including "God," "damn," "hell," and "damn fool."

Cukor had an unusual rapport with the difficult John Barrymore and also with Jean Harlow, even though she worked just ten days on the picture. He admitted that the blonde actress was "so bad, she was comic," in early movies such as *Hell's Angels*, but that she was marvelous in *Red-Headed Woman* and *Red Dust*. While making *Dinner at Eight*, Cukor realized that Harlow knew exactly what she was doing and allowed her to do it. "I don't think," he said later, "that you can teach people how to be funny."

22. AND TO ALL, GOODNIGHT

I am grateful to Edwin Haynes, archivist of the Marie Dressler Foundation in Cobourg, Ontario, for his generosity in allowing me access to a scrapbook donated to the foundation by a nephew of Norman Reilly Raine. The scrapbook was assembled by Raine before and during the filming of *Tugboat Annie* and contains news clippings and articles from various newspapers, chiefly those published in Los Angeles and Seattle but also in Britain. Because little documentation exists in library clipping files or in biographies or autobiographies (except a few pages in LeRoy, *My Own Story*, and Dubrey), to help recreate the *Tugboat Annie* project, I have drawn extensively from the Raine scrapbook. It is a pity, however, that the writer did not find it necessary to add his own comments concerning the 1933 shoot. Nowhere does he personally assess the filming of his famous stories, and nowhere does he tell us whether he met any of the movie's principals. The clippings, however, serve as a compact guide to the activities of the motion picture industry in the summer of 1933 as well as a mine of information about Annie itself. *Tugboat Annie* outdrew such films as *Morning Glory*, starring Katharine Hepburn, *Midnight Club*, starring George Raft, Marlene Dietrich in *Song of Songs*, and *The Gold Diggers of 1933*. MGM ran enormous advertisements in major national newspapers proclaiming its "Tenth Championship Year" and the fact that *Annie*'s box-office figures had already outstripped those for *Smilin' Thru'*, winner of *Photoplay* magazine's gold medal for best picture of 1932, and *Prosperity*. The movie made such an impression on the citizens of Washington state that a Tugboat Annie towboat race was reportedly staged in Tacoma Harbor on August 21, 1933. The prize was a Marie Dressler silver loving cup said to have been donated by Dressler herself, but, even with the help of the Seattle Public Library, I was not successful in confirming this.

The story of Dressler's visit to the White House with Mamie Cox is told in the Dubrey memoir, apparently related to the young actress by Mamie herself.

The dramatic statistics accompanying the announcement of the *Motion Picture Herald* poll were published in the *Los Angeles Times* on January 4, 1934. Writer Elinor Hughes concluded her report: "There will probably be plenty of editorials written on this poll, since every day the motion picture business assumes more and more importance in the news of the day. But the most important thing about it is the continuing public fondness for Marie Dressler."

23. Flutter of Doubt

Sources for the move to Santa Barbara were supplied by the Dubrey memoir, courtesy of Mamie Cox and Allen Breed Walker, who kept in close touch with Dressler's former confidante. This is confirmed by a covering letter from Walker that accompanied the Dubrey manuscript. The text of the letter reads as follows: "Thank you for permitting me to read in manuscript your book on that wonderful woman, the late Marie Dressler. I found it not only interesting and amusing, but truthful and understanding in every detail. No one had greater opportunity to understand her unique and fascinating personality than you. There was no living person she loved better. Mrs. Walker and I know that well. Hallie and Mamie have always said so. Marie once laughingly told me, 'I have to be nice to Claire. She knows more about me than anyone else. I've told things to Claire no one else knows, some day she will use it all in our book.' That was the first inkling that you and she were planning this book. It explains the times Marie used to say, 'put that in the book, dear,' when she finished telling some funny or touching experience. Later, of course, I knew all about it. How often I have seen you get up from the dinner table to make notes on the pad in the telephone booth. I am happy your book is being printed. I feel the public who loved her as a motion picture star will know her and love her better as a woman after reading it. That's how we knew her and loved her—as a dear, altogether human friend with all a human being's little inconsistencies, with all her womanly impulses, her extraordinary courage and her genius for living. That is how we shall always remember her, and that is how she would wish to be remembered by the world."

I am indebted to the Marie Dressler Foundation for allowing me access to copies of the actress's will and probate documents filed with the Superior Court, county of Los Angeles, and Dressler's death certificate, filed in the Santa Barbara Hall of Records. I also had access to the Inheritance Tax Appraiser's report filed with the Superior Court of the State of California.

Many newspapers carried stories concerning the actress's funeral, including the *New York Times*, the *Los Angeles Times*, and the *Toronto Star* of August 1, 1934. Tributes and editorials began to appear in the Canadian and American press on July 30 and accelerated in number during the following week. Dubrey's memoir provided the most intimate and graphic reports of Dressler's death and the funeral rites at Forest Lawn.

Originally, Marie Dressler's estate was estimated to be worth three hundred thousand dollars, but after real and personal property was sold and funeral expenses, federal taxes, and executor and attorney fees paid, the value had shrunk to $194,945. Some of this value was in cash, some in bequeathed property, but then there were more inheritance taxes to be paid and these reduced the estate still further. This incredible disappearing act clearly alarmed Dressler's sister, Bonita, who had enjoyed a brief moment of fame and fortune in Richmond, England, when the U.S. lawyers informed her that she had inherited the "residue" of the Dressler estate. Ganthony, in fact, appointed her own legal representatives, the firm of S.T. Hankey in Los Angeles, to keep an eye on probate proceedings, and she instructed her attorneys to object when the $9,906 bill for her sister's funeral and burial in Forest Lawn was made public. "You can bury a peer of the realm for less than that!" Ganthony complained as residuary legatee. Her objections were turned down by the Probate Court in March 1935. By then, however, it had been established that Bonita Ganthony's residue would total $17,881.59, out of which she received just $13,529.47 after taxes—which, of course, Dressler could not instruct to be included in this open-ended bequest. She also received a gold toilet set engraved with Dressler's initials which did not sell at a reasonable price during the personal effects auction. The set was appraised at three hundred twenty-five dollars. And there was also her sister's share of *My Own Story*, a book that was already embroiled in legal problems because of Dressler's death before publication and its obvious resemblance to the 1924 autobiography. Unfortunately, it took time for any substantial royalties to materialize and because Bonita Ganthony died in 1939 at the age of seventy-six, the income was inherited by her adopted son, Peter.

The Probate Court did deal with two other claims before the Dressler estate was finally settled. There was soprano Alice Neilson's successful claim for $4,500, and Claire Dubrey asked for twenty-five thousand dollars to cover "secretarial and personal nursing services". The court ruled that this sum was exorbitant and allowed Dubrey a payment of three thousand dollars.

Allen Breed Walker died on September 27, 1970, at the age of eighty-three at his home in Cuernavaca, Mexico. His wife, Kitty, had died in 1951. Polly Moran died in Hollywood on January 24, 1952, after a long siege of heart trouble, at the age of sixty-eight. Wallace Beery died at his home in Beverly Hills following a heart attack on April 20, 1949; he was sixty years old. Louis B. Mayer was relieved of his command of MGM in 1951 and died on October 29, 1957, at the age of seventy-two. Irving Thalberg died in Los Angeles on September l4, 1936, at the age of thirty-seven. It can only be assumed that Mamie and Jerry Cox returned to Savannah, though a search by staff members of the Savannah Public Library produced no news reports of their return and no obituaries. Claire Dubrey died on August 1, 1993, in West Hollywood, at the age of one hundred.

BIBLIOGRAPHY

Amory, Cleveland. *Who Killed Society?* New York: Harper, 1960.
Anger, Kenneth. *Hollywood Babylon*. New York: Straight Arrow, 1975.
Atkinson, Brooks. *Broadway*. New York: MacMillan, 1970.
Bainbridge, John. *Garbo*. Garden City: Doubleday, 1955.
Baxter, John. *Hollywood in the Thirties*. New York: Barnes, 1968.
Beer, Thomas. *The Mauve Decade: American Life at the End of the Nineteenth Century*. New York: Octagon, 1980.
Berg, A. Scott. *Goldwyn, A Biography*. New York: Ballantine, 1989.
Bloom, Ken. *Broadway: A Guide to the History, People, and Places of Times Square*. New York: Facts on File, 1991.
Blum, Daniel. *A Pictorial History of the American Theatre: 100 Years*. New York: Bonanza, 1960.
Bogdanovich, Peter. *Allan Dwan: The Last Pioneer*. New York: Praeger, 1971.
Bordman, Gerald. *American Operetta*. New York: Oxford Univ. Press.,1981.
——. *American Musical Theatre*. New York: Oxford Univ. Press, 1978.
Bronner, Edwin. *Encyclopaedia of the American Theatre*. San Diego: Barnes, 1980
Brown, Peter Harry, and Pamela Ann Brown. *The MGM Girls: Behind the Velvet Curtain*. New York: St. Martin's, 1983.
Brown, Peter H., and Jim Pinkston. *Oscar Dearest*. New York: Perennial, 1987.
Brownlow, Kevin. *The Parade's Gone By*. London: Secker and Warburg, 1968.
——. *Hollywood: The Pioneers*. London: Collins, 1979.
Carey, Gary. *All the Stars in Heaven*. New York: Dutton, 1981.
Chaplin, Charles. *My Autobiography*. New York: Simon and Schuster, 1964.
Churchill, A. *The Great White Way*. New York: Dutton, 1962.
Crowther, Bosley. *Hollywood Rajah: The Life and Times of Louis B. Mayer*. New York: Holt, Rinehart, and Winston, 1960.
——. *The Lion's Share: The Story of an Entertainment Empire*. New York: Dutton, 1957.

Csida, J., and J.B. Csida. *American Entertainment.* New York: Watson-Guptill, 1978.

Davies, Marion. *The Times We Had: Life with William Randolph Hearst.* Indianapolis: Bobbs-Merrill, 1975.

de Acosta, Mercedes. *Here Lies the Heart.* New York: Arno, 1975.

Dressler, Marie. *Life Story of an Ugly Duckling.* New York: McBride, 1924.

——. *My Own Story. As told to Mildred Harrington.* Boston: Little, Brown, 1934.

Eames, John Douglas. *The MGM Story.* New York: Crown, 1975.

Edmonds, Andy. *Frame-up: The Untold Story of Roscoe "Fatty" Arbuckle.* New York: Morrow, 1991.

Ewen, David. *New Complete Book of American Musical Theatre.* New York: Holt, Rinehart, and Winston, 1970.

Eyman, Scott. *Mary Pickford, America's Sweetheart.* New York: Donald I. Fine, 1990.

Ferrell, Robert H. *Woodrow Wilson and World War I: 1917-1921.* New York: Harper and Row, 1985.

Fields, Armond, and L. Marc Fields. *From the Bowery to Broadway: Lew Fields and the Roots of American Popular Theatre.* New York: Oxford Univ. Press, 1993.

Flamini, Roland. *Thalberg: The Last Tycoon.* New York: Crown, 1994.

Gilbert, D. *American Vaudeville: Its Life and Times.* New York: Whittlesey, 1940.

Gish, Lillian. *Lillian Gish: The Movies, Mr. Griffith, and Me.* Englewood Cliffs: Prentice Hall, 1969.

Golman, Eric F. *Rendezvous with Destiny.* New York: Knopf, 1965.

Grau, Robert. *Business Man.* New York: Broadway, 1910.

Green, Stanley. *The World of Musical Comedy.* New York: Ziff-Davis, 1960.

Gronowicz, Antoni. *Garbo: Her Story.* New York: Simon and Schuster, 1990.

Guillet, Edwin Clarence. *Cobourg, 1798-1948.* Oshawa: Goodfellow, 1948.

Harding, Alfred. *The Revolt of the Actors.* New York: William Morrow, 1929.

Higham, Charles. *Merchant of Dreams: Louis B. Mayer, MGM, and the Secret Hollywood.* New York: Donald I. Fine, 1993.

Isman, F. *Weber and Fields.* New York: Boni and Liveright, 1924.

Kotsilibas-Davis. *The Barrymores: The Royal Family in Hollywood.* New York: Crown, 1981.

Kreuger, Miles. *The Movie Musical: From Vitaphone to 42nd Street.* New York: Dover, 1975.

Lambert, Gavin. *On Cukor.* New York: Putnam's Sons, 1972.

———. *Norma Shearer: A Life*. New York: Knopf, 1990.

Laruie, Joseph Jr. *Vaudeville: From the Honkey-Tonk to the Palace*. New York: Henry Holt, 1953.

LeRoy, Mervyn. *Take One*. New York: Hawthorn, 1974.

Lewis, Philip. *Trouping: How the Show Came to Town*. New York: Harper and Row, 1973.

Loos, Anita. *Kiss Hollywood Goodbye*. New York: Viking, 1974.

Lyman, Susan E. *Story of New York*. New York: Crown, 1964.

Maltin, Leonard. *The Great Movie Comedians*. New York: Crown, 1978.

Marbury, Elisabeth. *My Crystal Ball*. New York: Boni and Liveright, 1923.

Margetson, Stella. *The Long Party: High Society in the Twenties and Thirties*. Farnborough: Saxon, 1974.

Marion, Frances. *Off With Their Heads*. New York: MacMillan, 1972.

Marx, Samuel. *Mayer and Thalberg: The Make-Believe Saints*. New York: Random, 1975.

Maxwell, Elsa. *RSVP*. Boston: Little, Brown, 1954.

McAlmon, Robert, and Kay Boyle. *Being Geniuses Together*. London: Hogarth, 1984.

McGilligan, Patrick. *Cukor: A Double Life*. New York: St. Martin's, 1991.

Mordden, Ethan. *Movie Star: A Look at the Women Who Made Hollywood*. New York: St. Martin's, 1983.

Morell, Parker. *Lillian Russell: The Era of Plush*. New York: Random, 1940.

Morgan, Anne. *The American Girl: Her Education, Her Responsibility, Her Recreation, Her Future*. New York: Harper and Brothers, 1925.

Paris, Barry. *Garbo, A Biography*. New York: Knopf, 1995.

Peters, Margot. *The House of Barrymore*. New York: Knopf, 1990.

Pickford, Mary. *Sunshine and Shadow*. Garden City: Doubleday, 1955.

Pope, W. Macqueen. *Carriages at Eleven*. London: Hale, 1947.

Robinson, David. *Chaplin: His Life and Art*. New York: McGraw Hill, 1985.

Robinson Locke Dramatic Collection. Scrapbooks 163 and 164. Billy Rose Room, New York Library of the Performing Arts, New York.

Schickel, Richard. *The Stars*. New York: Dial, 1962.

Selznick, David O. *Memo from David O. Selznick*. Ed. Rudy Behlmer. New York: Viking, 1972.

Sennett, Mack. *King of Comedy*. Garden City: Doubleday, 1954.

Shipman, David. *The Story of Cinema*. New York: St. Martin's, 1982.

Slide, Anthony. *The Vaudevillians*. Westport: Arlington, 1981.

Smith, Cecil. *Musical Comedy in America.* New York: Theatre Arts, 1950.

Smith Jane S. *Elsie de Wolfe: Life in the High Style.* New York: Atheneum, 1982.

Spitzer, Marian. *The Palace.* New York: Atheneum, 1969.

Sloan, Roberta Ann Raider. "A Descriptive Study of the Acting of Marie Dressler." Ph.D. Diss., University of Michigan, 1970.

St. Johns, Adela Rogers. *Love, Laughter, and Tears: My Hollywood Story.* New York: Doubleday, 1978.

Stenn, David. *Bombshell: The Life and Death of Jean Harlow.* New York: Doubleday, 1993.

Swanberg, W.A. *Citizen Hearst.* New York: Scribner, 1961.

Toll, Robert C. *On With the Show: The First Century of Show Business in America.* New York: Oxford Univ. Press, 1976.

Variety Movie Guide. New York: Prentice Hall, 1992.

Vermilye, Jerry. *The Films of the Thirties.* Secaucus: Citadel, 1978.

Wiley, Mason, and Damien Bona. *Inside Oscar: The Unofficial History of the Academy Awards.* New York: Ballantine, 1993.

Wuerthele-Caspé, Virginia Livingstone. *Cancer: A New Breakthrough.* Los Angeles: Nash, 1972.

Zierold, Norman. *The Moguls.* New York: Coward-McCann, 1969.

ACKNOWLEDGMENTS

This biography could not have been written without the generous cooperation of John Phillip Law and his assistant, Sierra Pecheur. I also owe a special debt of gratitude to Edwin Haynes, archivist of the Marie Dressler Foundation in Cobourg, Ontario, and to the custodians of the Robinson Locke Dramatic Collection at the New York Library of the Performing Arts. Without their invaluable help, this project would have foundered. Because a biography is essentially a mosaic of often unrelated facts, I also extend my sincere thanks to institutions and individuals throughout Canada and the United States who gave me their help when I needed it most: Maryann Chach, archivist of the Shubert Archives, New York; Sam Gill of the Margaret Herrick Library, Los Angeles; staff members of the Museum of Modern Art film library, New York; Jane Lowenthal, archivist of Barnard College at Columbia University, New York; staff librarians at the Toronto Public Library; staff librarians at the Free Library of Philadelphia; staff librarians at the Ohio State University Library, Columbus; Brenda Taylor at Little, Brown and Company, Boston; Dr. Roberta Raider Sloan, University of Central Oklahoma; Marty Jacobs, Museum of the City of New York Theatre Collection; Sonja Bolle, editor of the *Los Angeles Times Book Review*; Tom Williams, Mike Mamakos, and Associates, Los Angeles; Robert Osborne, the *Hollywood Reporter*; biographers Margot Peters, Donald Spoto, Charles Higham, Eve Golden, Eileen Whitfield, Armond Fields; and, also, Robert Andrew Bonnard, Bill Bowers, Bruce Stinson, John S. Thatcher, Jean Macwhirter Cranston, Delphine Patchett, Selia Karsten, Cari Beauchamp, Marilyn Strickling Read, Chris Calnan, Holland Taylor, Liz Smith, Elwy Yost, Tony Thomas, Weimer Gard, Dr. Scott Schubach, Dolores Bryan, Dr. James Loudon, Dr. Seema Rathee. And, continuing gratitude to my friend Dorothy Knight for her support, encouragement, and patience.

Index